Hadrian's Wall Bridges

Frontispiece:A Watercolour by David Mossman showing the early stages of excavation at Chesters in 1860; the uppermost surviving course of the main abutment face of bridge 2 has been exposed.   (Reproduced by permission of Tyne and Wear Museums Service)

B Watercolour by David Mossman showing trench across the north wing-wall of bridge 2 at Chesters (the seated figure is out of scale, exaggerating the size of the masonry). (Reproduced by permission of Tyne and Wear Museums Service)

English ⌗ Heritage

Archaeological Report no 9

Hadrian's Wall Bridges

P T Bidwell and N Holbrook

with contributions by A D H Bartlett, L Bown, J C Coulston, J N Dore, K Hartley, N Shiel, P Wilthew, and N Hammo Yassi

Historic Buildings & Monuments Commission for England
1989

Copyright © Historic Buildings and Monuments Commission for England 1989

First published 1989 by
Historic Buildings and Monuments Commission for England
Fortress House, 23 Savile Row, London, W1X 2HE

Printed by Page Bros (Norwich) Ltd, Mile Cross Lane, Norwich

British Library Cataloguing in Publication Data
Bidwell, Paul T.
   Hadrian's Wall bridges. - (Historic Buildings and Monuments Commission for England. Archaeological report; 9).
   1. Northern England. Roman Empire fortification : Hadrian's Wall
   I. Title II. Holbrook, N. III English Heritage IV. Series
   939.2'88104

ISBN 1 85074 166 2

Contents

Preface and acknowledgements

'Those who have seen the magnificent remains of the Pont du Gard (justly the pride of *Gallia Narbonensis*), lighted by the glorious sun of Languedoc, may think lightly of these meagre relics of the bridge of *Cilurnum*, under the darker skies of Northumberland; but it may be affirmed, that the bridge over the river Gardon does not span a lovelier stream than the North Tyne, and that so much as remains of the masonry of the bridge at *Cilurnum* leads to the conclusion, that this bridge, as originally constructed, was not inferior, in solidity of material and excellence of workmanship, to the mighty structure reared by Roman hands in Gaul.'

So wrote John Clayton in a paper read to the Society of Antiquaries of Newcastle upon Tyne in 1861, (Clayton 1865) describing the east abutment of Bridge 2 at Chesters laid bare by his workmen in 1860. Modern opinion shows no alteration and in a recent edition of the *Handbook to the Roman Wall* (Daniels 1978) the bridge is still judged to be 'the most remarkable feature on the whole line of the Wall.'

Re-examination of the bridge in 1982–3 has shown that in its final form, probably as a result of the initiative of Severus, it was built entirely of stone, rather than partly of timber as was previously thought, and that it was embellished with a cornice, stone parapets, a series of columns, and possibly accommodated one or more shrines. That the bridge can now be seen to bear comparison with the more important road-bridges of the Empire does not mean that the remarks of Clayton and others have been mere hyperbole. Few could fail to be impressed by the remains of the great east abutment, partly shaded by mature oaks in a hollow by the river's edge, and reached from the modern road by a walk through lush meadows in the valley bottom.

The situation of the bridge at Willowford is scarcely less striking and, although its remains are less impressive, it is of an importance equal to that of Chesters. Indeed, the two sites are complementary: at Willowford the recent work has produced a much fuller picture of the bridge in its earlier stages than it has been possible to achieve at Chesters.

The opportunity to examine these bridges in advance of consolidation is the result of the foresight and vigorous administration of Dr Stephen Johnson, who at the time was the Inspector of Ancient Monuments with responsibility for Hadrian's Wall. The work at Chesters was directed by P T Bidwell and supervised in 1982 by Dr Jem Poster; in 1983 N Holbrook supervised the project and Stephen Speak was responsible for the planning of the site. Special mention must also be made of Anne Gibson Ankers, Margaret Finch, Nick Hodgson, Corinne Ogden, Stuart Sinclair and Margaret and Michael Snape; Hughie Grant and Ken McQueen organised the transportation of blocks of great weight across the site using the most rudimentary equipment.

The work at Willowford was also to have been directed by P T Bidwell but in the event the commitments of a full-time job elsewhere allowed him to spend only a very limited amount of time on site and N Holbrook assumed responsibility for the direction of the project. The supervisors were Stephen Speak (who was also responsible for all the photography), Paul Harrison, Martin Hicks, and Nick Hodgson. All who worked at Willowford will know how much help and kindness was shown by Mr Donald Dalrymple of Willowford Farm.

P T Bidwell was responsible for the chapters on Chesters and on the techniques of construction and the sections on the bridges at Newcastle and Corbridge; N Holbrook dealt with Willowford and the other bridges, principally Piercebridge, Carlisle, and Risingham. However, at every stage after the first season at Chesters, almost all the aspects of the bridges and their wider significance have been discussed at length by the authors, whether on site, in the study or in convivial surroundings, so that in every sense this is a joint publication.

The plans of Chesters were drawn by Jacqui Bayliss, and those of Willowford by Anne Gibson Ankers. Frank Gardiner of English Heritage contributed the fine watercolours of the bridges and Jim Thorn drew the dedication of Aelius Longinus and the possible counterweight stone from Chesters. Ralph Mills kindly supplied the plan of the bridge at Piercebridge. N Holbrook would like to thank Prof Peter Fowler, while both authors have benefited from discussions with Jim Crow, Charles Daniels, Nick Hodgson and Derek Welsby. They also gratefully acknowledge information received from Stuart Brown, Ian Caruana, the late John Gillam, Dr Lawrence Keppie, Norman Shiel, Colin Richardson, Raymond Selkirk, the late Peter Scott and Dr Grace Simpson. They offer special thanks to Tom Blagg and Stephen Johnson who read and commented in detail on the manuscript and Pamela V Irving who prepared it for publication.

P T Bidwell owes a special debt of gratitude to Adam Welfare who as a preliminary to a projected study of the bridge at Chesters had collected a comprehensive list of bibliographical references and excerpts from unpublished sources which he was kind enough to make available. Lindsay Allason-Jones kindly commented on some of the small finds, and made available for study fragments of lead tie-bars from Chesters and Corbridge in the Museum of Antiquities, Newcastle upon Tyne. The Trustees of the Clayton Collection (Chesters Museum) through Dr David Smith granted permission for the new drawings of the inscription of Aelius Longinus and the possible counterweight to be made. P T Bidwell also wishes to thank Stuart Brown for useful discussion of the Roman and medieval bridges at Newcastle upon Tyne.

Both authors acknowledge with gratitude the contributions of A D H Bartlett, L Bown, J C Coulston, J N Dore, K Hartley, N Shiel, P Wilthew and N B Hammo Yassi.

Paul T Bidwell
Neil Holbrook

Benwell – *Condercum*
Exeter – *Isca Dumnoniorum*
3 November 1987

Colour plates

List of figures

List of tables

1 Chesters: Introduction and bridge 1

Introduction

The remains of the Roman bridges at Chesters have been accessible to the public since they were first uncovered in 1860–3. By the beginning of this century they had become dilapidated and overgrown, as unpublished photographs in the John Collingwood Bruce Collection at South Shields Museum show. When in 1946 the remains were placed in the guardianship of the Ministry of Works landscaping of the site was carried out after limited excavation by F G Simpson (p 6). Although the site was subsequently maintained in good order, the unconsolidated remains of the wall and tower began to suffer damage which was mainly caused by visitors clambering on them. In 1982 the decision was taken to consolidate the remains, but only after a programme of archaeological investigation had taken place. The main objective of this programme was to make a complete record of the surviving fabric. This would also, it was hoped, distinguish between the original structural remains and blocks stacked on the remains of the bridge by the Victorian excavators (p 6).

At the beginning of the second season in 1983 these loose blocks were removed from the bridge for examination and display. This provided much information about the form of the Severan bridge (bridge 2). A limited excavation located the east abutment of the Hadrianic bridge (bridge 1) and recovered some information about the approach road to bridge 2 and the function of its tower.

It seems doubtful whether further excavation within the guardianship area would produce much more useful information. The study of the bridges, particularly of bridge 2, however, is far from complete. Excavation between the east abutment and east pier of this bridge, which lies largely outside the present guardianship area would probably recover many more architectural fragments and perhaps evidence for the date of the successive stages in the decay and demolition of the bridge (p 31–32).

On the west side of the river the approach ramp of bridge 2 is well preserved, and it is possible that just behind the river bank are the remains of another tower, matching that which lies behind the east abutment. The possibility that the approach ramp overlies buildings associated with the *vicus* of Chesters Fort should also be borne in mind; their excavation would offer the best chance of recovering dating evidence to establish a *terminus post quem* for the construction of bridge 2.

The setting

Hadrian's Wall crossed the River North Tyne by a bridge at Chesters, 4km upstream from the meeting of the waters, where the two branches of the Tyne unite and flow along a valley of increasing width into the North Sea, some 36km to the east. Immediately north of Chesters, the North Tyne flows through a wide valley but a short distance to the south it passes through a gap between Warden Hill to the east and higher land to the west (Figure 1).

The course of the river, at the point where it was bridged, has altered since Roman times. The east bank now lies approximately 15m west of the position it occupied in Roman times and this shift in its course has resulted in the east abutment of bridge 2 being engulfed in silt. Immediately above and below the bridge the change in the course of the river has been more marked. In the field north of the river and east of the bridge are a number of river terraces. It is uncertain which of these represents the Roman course of the river, but if the form of the west abutment of bridge 2 is correctly understood, this suggests that in Roman times the river flowed towards the bridge from further to the north-east (Figure 2, p 15). After bridge 2 was built, the south wing of the west abutment was affected by scour which was arrested by building an extension to the wing-wall (p 21). In the field south of the bridge the remains of an old channel of the river can be seen but it is impossible to say whether this represents its course in Roman times.

Where the river was bridged its width is now about 50m. It was perhaps a little wider in Roman times; bridge 2 was 58m in length (p 15) and its predecessor probably *c* 61m in length (p 14). The bed of the river is now covered with boulders and its depth during a reasonably dry summer is 1.5m at the most, but at present the river just below the bridge becomes wider and shallower, with many boulders protruding above the surface of the water except when the river is in spate.

The fort at Chesters, which lies 120m west of the river, was called *Cilurnum*, the cauldron pool; this name may refer to the Inglepool 'which, until partially filled up a few years ago, was very deep' (J C Bruce 1851, 192) rather than to a pool in the river. (The Inglepool lay to the south-west of the fort and has now been completely filled in.) Amongst the forts on Hadrian's Wall, Chesters, with an area of 2.3ha (5.75 acres) is only exceeded in size by Stanwix and Bowness. The original garrison was the quingenary *ala Augusta ob virtutem appellata* (Austen and Breeze 1979) and the fort continued to accommodate cavalry throughout most of its history, which would have enabled intensive and long-range patrols of the North Tyne valley to be carried out beyond the Wall.

The other defensive work in the vicinity of the bridge is the Vallum (Figure 2). East of the river its course is well established. A slight depression marks the line of the ditch and trial trenches dug in 1951 by Swinbank (1954, 120–1, 412–5) suggested that the Vallum had continued up to the east side of the old river-course and furthermore that it had swung slightly to the north as it approached this point. West of the river its course is less certain. A slight depression again shows the course of the ditch immediately west of the river but Swinbank (ibid, 62), contrary to earlier opinions, considered that the

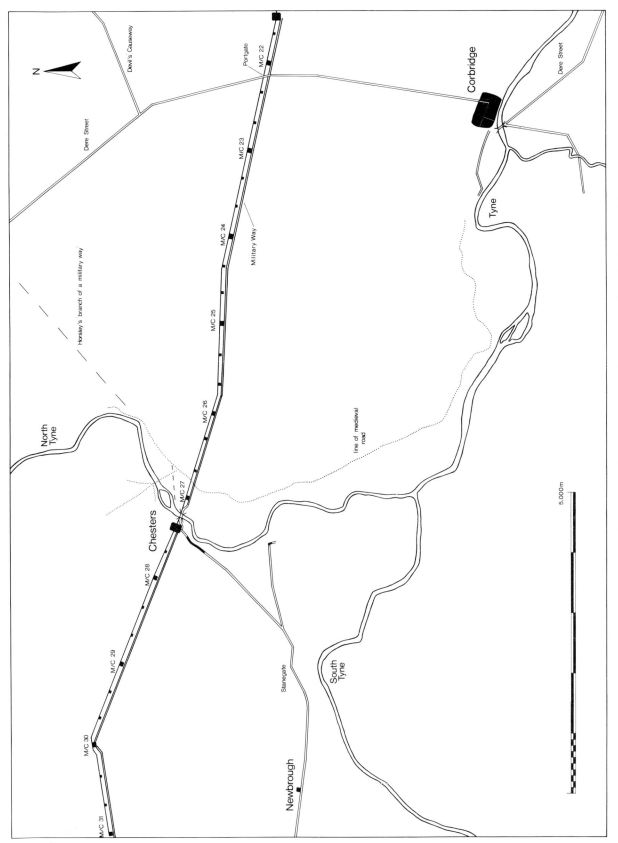

Figure 1   Chesters in its setting, showing the Wall and certain and assumed lines of Roman roads.   Scale 1:62,500

Vallum was diverted around the south side of the fort; large blocks of masonry visible in the surface of the field south of the south gate may mark the site of the Vallum causeway. The Vallum, whatever its exact course, was overlain, presumably no later than the third century, by a grid of streets shown by aerial photographs (eg University of Newcastle upon Tyne, Department of Archaeology Collection NY 9170/E and F).

Almost all the building materials required for the bridge were available in the immediate locality. Within 2.5km to the east there are outcrops of sandstone (Brunton sandstone) which could have yielded the large blocks used in the construction. J C Bruce (1867, 142) thought that the source of the stone was the Black Pasture quarry which was still being worked in his time. Another possible source is Fallowfield Fell, where until 1934 the face of the quarry bore the inscription *Petra Flaui Carantini* (the rock of Flavius Carantinus) (*RIB* 1442). Another inscription (*RIB* 1486; p 142), which had possibly fallen from the cliff above the east bank of the river south of the bridge, may indicate the site of a quarry, but the stone it would have yielded is unsuitable for forming large blocks. Petrological examination of the stone used in the bridge was not undertaken.

At Brunton there is an exposure of limestone known in the nineteenth century as the 'Big Limestone' which at that time was the principal source of lime in the district. Nearby there is ironstone which was also worked in the nineteenth century (G Tate in J C Bruce 1867, 445).

Antiquarian accounts

Few early writers who described the Wall omitted to mention the bridge at Chesters.

The earliest source is Camden who wrote that 'North-Tine...is crossed at Collerford [Chollerford] by a bridge of Arches' (Gibson 1695, 851). The reference to a bridge of arches does not mean that remains of the arches were to be seen; to Camden the stone piers no doubt necessarily implied the former existence of stone arches.

Gordon was the first writer to describe what could be seen of the bridge:

'Thence [from Brunton] to the Bank of the River called North Tyne at Chollar-Ford, are the vestiges of a Roman bridge to be seen; the Foundation of which consists of large square stones, linked together with Iron Cramps. But this bridge, however, is only seen when the Water is low.'

Gordon 1726, 23

Lingard, in notes on his 'Mural Tourification' of 1807 gave further details:

'The foundation stones are some of them still visible. They are large flags, 3ft [0.91m] by 18in [0.45m], with holes morticed in them. Mr [Nathaniel] Clayton says these holes were for a luis to raise them: an old gentleman in the neigh-

bourhood says they were joined together by iron bars: some of which he himself broke when a boy and carried off as presents to the schoolmaster.'

Bosanquet 1929, 147

Nineteenth-century survey and excavation

On 19 June 1848, J C Bruce paid his first visit to Chesters. He had intended to travel to Rome that summer but was prevented by the revolutions then taking place in Europe and instead devoted his holidays to an examination of the Roman Wall (G Bruce 1905, 110–12). Within a year or so of Bruce's visit his brother George Bruce had prepared a plan of the remains of the bridge on the river bed which was published in the first edition of *The Roman Wall* (1851, pl V; published here as Figure 13). In 1853 the position of the bridge was plotted by Henry MacLauchlan (1858, 26) who was puzzled by the differences in the alignment of the bridge and Wall; it seemed possible 'that a portion has been washed away, and that originally the foundations extended further in both directions.'

It was perhaps MacLauchlan's suggestion that the bridge extended beyond the present course of the river which led William Coulson in the spring of 1860 to begin the excavations which revealed the great east abutment of bridge 2.

The first mention of the excavations was on 4 April 1860 at the monthly meeting of the Society of Antiquaries of Newcastle upon Tyne when Clayton reported that

'Mr Coulson...was now excavating the approaches to the Roman bridge piers at Cilurnum, on the east side of the North Tyne. The works revealed a masonry larger than usual, and would settle the question of the exact direction of the bridge piers.'

Archaeol Aeliana, 2 ser, **6** (1865), 130

By the monthly meeting on 6 June 1860 drawings had been made by Mossman 'of portions of the massive masonry disclosed in excavating (the abutment)' and were exhibited to the meeting by Bruce (ibid, 135). Four drawings by Mossman are known which were 'executed at a period when the excavations were incomplete' (Clayton 1865, 82) and are reproduced here, (Frontispiece, rear cover, and Plate 1). These were bound into J C Bruce's copy of his third edition (1867) of *The Roman Wall* (now in the John Collingwood Bruce Collection at the South Shields Museum, Tyne and Wear Joint Museum Services).

Frontispiece A: This is a view from the west showing the entire length of the centre part of the abutment of bridge 2. The whole of the uppermost surviving course (course 5, p 19) and the top of the course below have been exposed. The overlying soil had been cleared back *c* 0.5m from the face of the

4

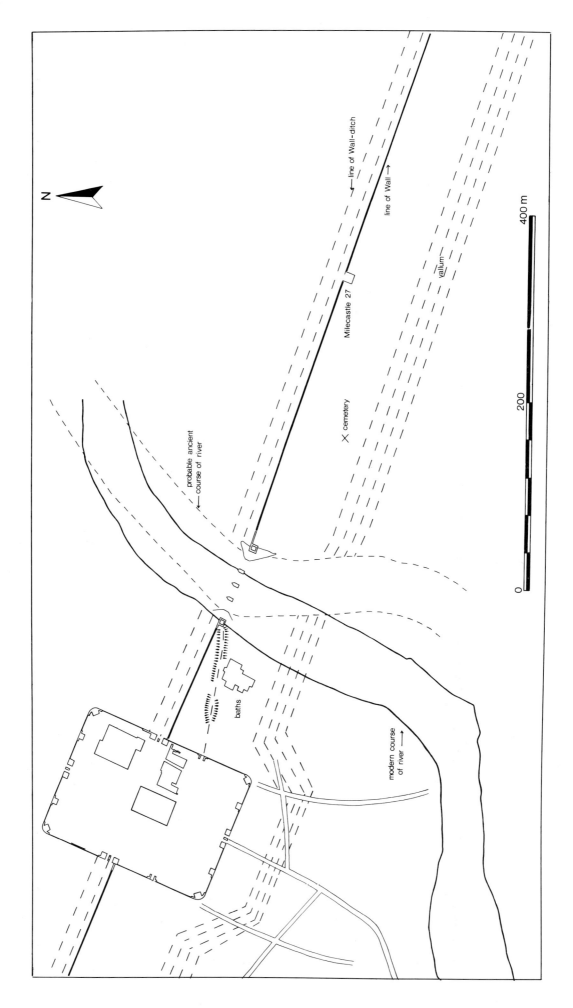

Figure 2 The site of the bridge at Chesters in relation to the line of the Wall and Vallum and the fort of Cilurnum. The course of the Vallum shown south of the fort is largely conjectural; the position of the streets of the vicus overlying the Vallum is after Salway 1967, fig 8.   Scale 1:4000

N

line of Wall-ditch
line of Wall →
Milecastle 27
vallum
cemetery
probable ancient
course of river
modern course
of river
baths

0   200   400 m

abutment. At the centre a trench had been cut back towards the west wall of the tower which it had not reached. A trench dug in the opposite direction is shown in the foreground (its position cannot lie far from Trench 2 dug in 1983, p 6). A continuation of the main trench had been started in order to trace the south wing of the abutment. To the north a large east–west trench was cut diagonally across the north wing. At right angles to this the drawing shows an area of shadow which may be a trench cut across the tower.

Frontispiece B: This drawing shows a detail in a later stage of the excavation. The trench cutting diagonally across the north wing had been enlarged to expose almost the full height of the masonry. The seated figure is so small that a misleading impression is given of the size of the masonry. The north-west corner of the tower and the opening through which the water channel passes are shown.

Plate 1: This view showing the interior of the tower from the south is later than the preceeding drawing which shows trees still standing over the tower.

Rear cover: (now in Tullie House Museum, Carlisle). This may be contemporary with Plate 1 or later when the excavations were at a more advanced stage. Almost the entire surface of the abutment had been exposed and trenches had been dug on either side of the Wall and eastwards from the south-east corner of the tower. An irregular north–south trench seems to follow the course of the water channel south of the tower. In the foreground the river is shown with the outline of the centre and west piers and the west abutment (probably taken from the plan published by J C Bruce in 1851). If these represent the sum total of the drawings done by Mossman those reproduced as the frontispiece at least must have been completed by 6 June 1860 when more than one drawing was exhibited. Indeed, all the drawings may have been made by this date: a letter marked 'from Joseph Fairless of Hexham' (bound into a copy of Bruce 1853, now in Durham University Library) to Bruce describes a visit to the site made on 9 June 1860 when clearance of the entire abutment seems to have been largely completed:

'[I was accompanied by] the inspector of works at Hexham Church, who is thought a first-rate mason; he was much surprised by the solid masonry, and says the jointed stones of the breastwork are the very strongest mode of building displaying great judgement in the art. The long narrow channels in the stones he believes would be fitted with lead and iron up and down to prevent any 'draw'.

'I believe there is a new feature made its appearance since we met together at the bridge, very interesting, the regular and distinct formation of the basement of a peir [sic] in the breastwork, strongly cramped together, the rest of the large masonry formed around it, as if of later date.

'I have given a sketch of the position of the peir on the breastwork, the dimensions of the peir from the extreme points 19 feet 8 inches [5.97m] breadth, across centre of ditto 9 feet 10 inches [2.98m] – distance between Guardroom wall and peir 5 feet [1.52m] from side of ditto – to front of breastwork 6 feet 8 inches [2.02m].

'Along the south wing of the breastwork a most interesting display of detached stones, various in form yet of design some chiselled out to receive or form a standing basement for something perhaps of wood.'

At the monthly meeting on 4 July 1860 Clayton (*Archaeol Aeliana*, 2 ser, **6**, (1865) 142–3) exhibited a plan made by Coulson. By this time the east river pier of the later bridge had been located and it was found that 'the vallum near the river has been filled with stones, at what period is uncertain.' An 'unsatisfactory fragment of an inscription', presumably the dedication to the nymphs (*RIB* 1547, see p 141), was also found.

No references to further work on the site were made until 2 October 1861 when Clayton read a paper on 'The Roman bridge of *Cilurnum*' to the Society of Antiquaries of Newcastle upon Tyne (Clayton 1865; reprinted virtually in full but without illustrations in *The Newcastle Daily Journal* for 3 October 1861, *Gentleman's Magazine* for November 1861 and *Archaeol J*, **19** (1862), 359–63). At the meeting a number of drawings were on the table, not only those by Mossman previously listed, but a further set by Henry Burdon Richardson, one of a family of distinguished Newcastle artists. He painted 64 pictures to illustrate the third edition of Bruce's *The Roman Wall* (1867) and it is possible that the four reproduced here as Plates 2–5 were all intended for that work although only Plate 2 was published (Welford 1907, 138). They are at present in the collections of the Laing Art Gallery, Newcastle upon Tyne.

Plate 2: A view of the abutment from the north-east. This is the painting published by Bruce (1867, facing p 143) in a poor reproduction of the original; in Bruce's engraving the figure examining the pier of the first bridge incorporated in the abutment is shown at half the size of the figure in the painting, giving an absurdly exaggerated impression of the size of the remains.

Plate 3: The north wing of the abutment from the west.

Plate 4: The south wing of the abutment from the south-west.

Plate 5: A view from the north painted at a later date than Plates 2–5, when the loose blocks on the bridge had been stacked in the position which they were to occupy until 1983.

Clayton's 1865 paper was accompanied by a fine

plan of the bridge by Robert Elliot and Henry Wilson (Figure 14).

The last reference to work on the bridge is in a letter from Clayton to Bruce dated 12 January 1863 (bound into a copy of J C Bruce 1853, in Durham University Library) which reports the discovery of *RIB* 1470. Clayton states that 'in a fortnight or three weeks the further exploration will be completed, when the bridge will be worth a visit.'

This work seems to have been at least partly concerned with digging west of the abutment in the river bed: the description of the inscribed block ascribes the erasure of the upper part of its text to its 'being buried in the bed of the river whilst the upper part has been exposed to the constant flow of the current.'

Victorian backfill over Trench 6 (p 7) indicated that at least half of the width between the abutment base and the east river pier had been cleared down to a level not far above the river bed, and the excavations in this area might well have extended as far as the pier, which lies under the present east bank of the river.

The first investigation of the bridge was thus spread over four years from 1860–3. More than 80 years were to elapse before excavations were renewed by F G Simpson. However in the early 1880s the structure was carefully examined by Sheriton Holmes, a civil engineer, who published drawings of various architectural elements and attempted to interpret their significance (1885–6; 1894; see further p 36).

Twentieth-century survey and excavation

Until 1946 no further work was carried out on the site but successive editors of Bruce's *Handbook to the Roman Wall* reinterpreted the structural sequence in terms of current Wall theories. During the Second World War German prisoners of war were set to work on tidying the site and it seems that they were responsible for digging the drain from the south end of the abutment face of bridge 2 (p 7; Davies 1974, 67).

In 1946 Captain Keith, the owner of the Chesters estate, which he had purchased from the Claytons in 1928, placed the east abutment of the bridge in the guardianship of the then Ministry of Works (now English Heritage). In the same year F G Simpson undertook excavations on the site on behalf of the Ministry. Work took place in three areas: the position of the east pier of bridge 2 was confirmed, the relationship between the Wall ditch and the water channel was determined, and finally the Wall was examined. A full report on the work has never been published but the extent of the excavations on the east part of the site can be seen from an aerial photograph (University of Newcastle upon Tyne, Department of Archaeology Collection, NY/9170/D). Simpson's work is referred to in *Watermills and military works on Hadrian's Wall* (Simpson 1976, 44–9). This adds little to the interim account published in 1947 (*J Roman Stud* **37**, (1947), 168) apart from

mentioning the investigation of a possible feeder for the water channel north of the guardianship area.

No further work was carried out on the site until 1982.

Survey and excavation in 1982–3

Two seasons of work on the eastern ends of the bridges were carried out by a small team in 1982–3. All the visible Roman masonry was drawn in plan and elevation at a scale of 1:20 and fair copies were made in pencil on drafting film. A system of numbering was adopted for all the stone blocks visible on the site, whether loose or in position; the former were numbered 1–122 and the latter were numbered 201–790; these numbers are retained in this publication.

The dimensions of the stones and any features of them, such as clamps, lewis holes and crowbar slots, together with general descriptions were recorded on a card index. Some of the more important stones are illustrated here (Figures 30–33, 78, 79, and 89) and the dimensions of the various types of stones and their features are set out in a series of tables (Tables 2, 3, 11, and 12).

These records will be held by the Hadrian's Wall Museums, with the archive drawings and an account of the limited excavations. The finds will also be stored there, and include mortar samples from the wall and tower which still await analysis. A continuous numbering system was adopted for the archaeological contexts. Full details of those not illustrated will be found in this archive.

The excavations of 1982–3 are discussed at various points in the descriptions of the two bridges but a summary account of the eight trenches is given below; Figure 3 gives their location and the overall layout of the area investigated.

Trench 1 was dug to test the theory that the Military Way had approached the later bridge diagonally from the south-east. No traces of metalling or paving were found but at a depth of between 0.55m and 0.70m below the present ground surface a thin layer of pebbles and brown clay-silt was encountered (context 51, not illustrated). This produced a copper alloy pendant (Figure 94, no 2) and the base of a Nene Valley colour-coated beaker of later second- or third-century date. This deposit which seems to represent the Roman ground surface overlay natural gravels.

Trench 2 was dug through Victorian and modern backfill in front of the north wing (Figure 17). Its northern side showed part of a layer of gravel (context 77; Figure 15) apparently deposited by river action after the construction of the first bridge (p 14) which was cut by a narrow construction trench for the north wing of the later bridge (context 76; Figure 15, p 19).

Trenches 3 and 4 (Figures 5, 7, and 8) represented an area extending from the east wall of the tower to

Plate 1   Watercolour by David Mossman of the interior of the tower of bridge 2 at Chesters, from the south, showing blocks forming the sides of the later water channel. (Reproduced by permission of Tyne and Wear Museums Service)

Plate 2   Watercolour by H B Richardson showing the east abutment of bridge 2 at Chester from the north-east.   (Reproduced by permission of Tyne and Wear Museums Service)

Plate 3   Watercolour by H B Richardson showing the north wing of the east abutment of bridge 2 at Chesters from the west.   (Reproduced by permission of Tyne and Wear Museums Service)

Plate 4   Watercolour by H B Richardson showing the south wing of bridge 2 at Chesters from the south-west.   (Reproduced by permission of Tyne and Wear Museums Service)

Plate 5 Watercolour by H B Richardson painted at a later date than Plates 2–4, a view of the east abutment of bridge 2 at Chesters showing loose blocks stacked on the surface of the abutment.   (Reproduced by permission of Tyne and Wear Museums Service)

Plate 6 Richardson's watercolour of Harrow Scar in 1848, showing the Wall and Wall ditch being undermined by the River Irthing. The large blocks in the river may represent the disturbed remains of the western bridge abutments

Plate 7   Possible reconstruction of Bridge 1 at Willowford, viewed from the south-west.   (Painting by Frank Gardiner)

Plate 8   Possible reconstruction of bridge 2 at Chesters, viewed from downstream.   (Painting by Frank Gardiner)

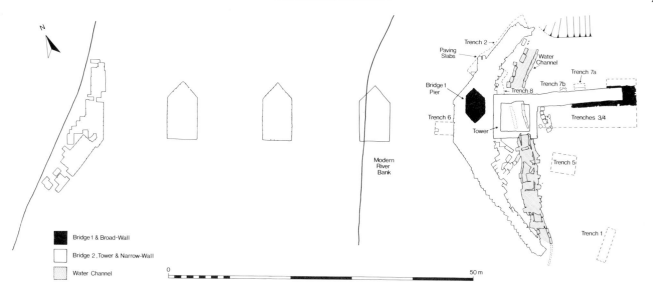

Figure 3   Composite plan to show the relationship of the 1982–3 trenches (see Figure 15) to the remains of the bridge as planned by George Bruce in c 1850 (Figure 13) and R Elliot and H Wilson (Clayton 1865) (Figure 14).   Scale 1:600

the top of the slope down to the river. Deposits associated with the first bridge are described on p 11 and the external construction trench of the east wall of the tower on p 23.

Trench 5 was dug to determine whether any traces remained of a revetment for the south side of the ramp approaching the later bridge. The natural gravels and sands under modern deposits were much disturbed by animal burrows and perhaps also the action of tree roots. No features or deposits of Roman date survived.

Trench 6 (Figure 4) was dug in front of the abutment base. A machine was used to clear a strip 4m in width along the length of the face; this work suggested that the bank of material between the abutment base and the present course of the river was wholly composed of redeposited silt, rubble and worked blocks (blocks nos 114; 117; 120, Figure 30, no 5; block no 121 ,Figure 30, no 8, and Figure 32; and block no 122), presumably spoil from the excavations of 1860–63. More recent disturbance had been caused by the construction of a drain running south-west from a point near the junction of the abutment base and south wing; this was probably constructed by German prisoners of war in the Second World War (p 6). At a height roughly level with the top of the third course of the abutment undisturbed deposits (context 352, Figure 4) were located in a trench dug by hand. These consisted of coarse river gravels set in a matrix of fine sand mixed with water-worn river boulders and blocks from the bridge (blocks nos 89; 118; 122). They immediately overlay natural gravel which was seen to extend beneath the abutment base.

Trenches 7A and B revealed the Broad Wall foundation on the north side of the Narrow Wall (see further p 9).

Trench 8 was excavated in the angle formed by the rear of the north wing of the abutment and the north side of the tower. The construction trench for these structures is described on p 19.

The discovery of bridge 1 and its relationship to Hadrian's Wall

Soon after the east abutment of bridge 2 was revealed, Joseph Fairless of Hexham described in a letter to Bruce (already quoted p 5) an earlier pier incorporated in the east abutment of bridge 2 (Figures 9, 10,and 12). Clayton (1865, 83), noting that 'its dimensions would scarcely admit of a superstructure wider than would be required for the march of foot soldiers' thought that the pier represented a bridge earlier than the Wall, showing that Chesters had been built under Agricola. At that time the Military Way was regarded as contemporaneous with Hadrian's Wall, in spite of indications that it was later than the Vallum noted by Horsley (1732, 99), and Clayton attributed bridge 2, constructed to take a road of some width, to Hadrian. In 1926, following his excavations at Willowford (p 52), Shaw (1926, 470–1) compared the earliest bridge at that site with the first bridge at Chesters which he implied had carried 'a continuation of the rampart walk on top of the Great Wall.' It was not until 1947 that the first bridge at Chesters was associated with the Wall in the *Handbook to the Roman Wall* (Richmond 1947, 79). In the previous year F G Simpson had found the Broad Wall foundation, which is of approximately the same width as the pier excluding the cutwaters (p 12), underlying the Narrow Wall immediately to the east of the bridge (*J Roman Stud*, **37** (1947), 168). Since then it has been accepted that the first bridge belonged to the original construction of Hadrian's Wall. Following the excavations of 1982–3, the excavated remains

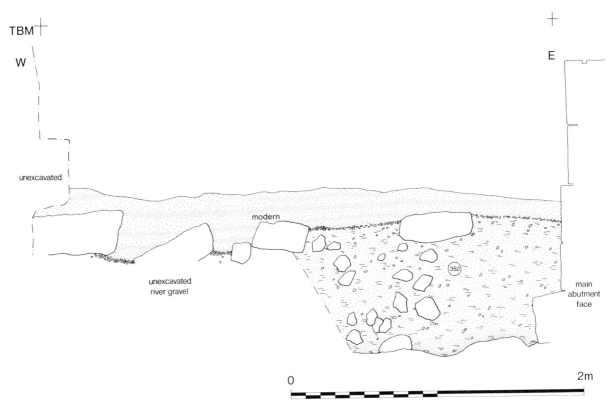

Figure 4   North-facing section of trench 6 showing deposits (context 352) accumulated against the main abutment face. For section and trench position see Figure 3.   Scale 1:25

of bridge 1 consist of the easternmost pier, the site of the eastern abutment, and lengths of the Broad Wall foundation and Narrow Wall, which have been traced eastwards from the abutment for a distance of 19m. The various elements are considered separately in the following sections.

The Broad Wall

Part of the remains of the Broad Wall were uncovered by F G Simpson in 1946 (*J Roman Stud* **37** (1947), 168) and the remainder in 1983. The footings consist of a single course of sandstone flagstones and whinstone cobbles set in yellow-grey clay. The width of the footing varies between 3.25m and 3.30m (Figure 8). The construction of the Narrow Wall has entirely removed the north face of the Broad Wall but two courses of the south face survive for a length of 5.2m (Figure 6B). The lower course, 0.3m in height, is set back by up to 0.1m from the edge of the footing; the upper course, 0.2m in height, is offset by 20–60mm from the lower, which represents construction to Standard A (Birley *et al* 1932, 255). Plant growth and weathering have removed any trace of the material used to bond these courses.

The south side of the Broad Wall footings ends abruptly 10.6m from the east edge of Trench 4 and 8.5m west of the estimated position of the bridge abutment face (Figure 8). The north side continues a

Figure 5   The Narrow Wall on Broad Wall foundation, showing the layers of unmortared rubble core corresponding to courses of facing stones, looking west.   (Photo: S C Speak)

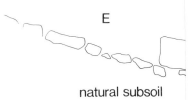

E

natural subsoil

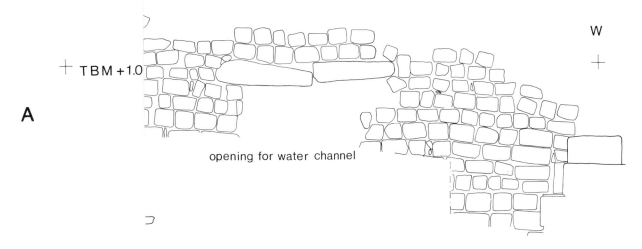

north wall of tower

W

+ TBM +1.0

A

opening for water channel

+ TBM +3.0m

W

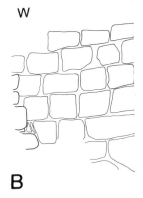

B

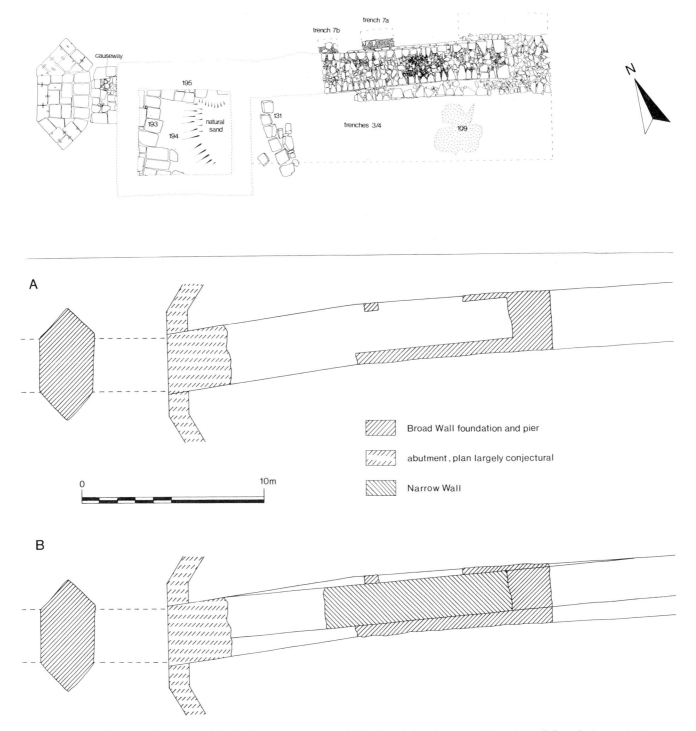

Figure 8   Bridge 1 at Chesters, with the later causeway, and the site of the abutment, Broad Wall foundation and Narrow Wall.   Scale 1:200
 Inset A shows a hypothetical form of the robbed east abutment and the divergence in alignment of the Broad Wall foundation and the bridge.
 Inset B shows the probable relationship between the Broad wing-wall of the bridge and the completed Narrow Wall.

Deposits south of Hadrian's Wall

In the area opened to the south of the Wall (Trenches 3 and 4, Figure 8) there were only two deposits of undoubted Roman date; unfortunately their relationship with the Broad Wall foundation had been destroyed by a modern trench dug along its face. Immediately above natural was a spread up to 0.18m deep of sand interleaved with mixed material: sandy loam, rubble, and patches of grey and yellow clay (contexts 110, and 118). It seems very probable that this layer was associated with the construction of the Broad Wall foundation; the sand and sandy loam would have been derived from the upcast of the foundation trench, the rubble from the dressing of the stone and the clay from the bonding of the flagged footing. Above this deposit was a layer of coal mixed with some smithing slag which had a maximum depth of 0.15m (context 109, Figure 8). This might well have resulted from the manufacture nearby of structural ironwork for the first bridge, especially the numerous dovetail clamps. A connection between this deposit and the construction of the later bridge can be discounted for it would appear

Figure 10   A detail of the west side of the pier of bridge 1 incorporated in the east abutment of bridge 2, showing sockets for dovetail clamps (two with lead still in position) and crowbar slots, 250 mm scale. (Photo: S C Speak)

that the area behind the Wall was probably covered by an earth ramp before work on the bridge itself had started (p 27).

The river pier

The pier (Figure 9) is 5.96m in length and has a maximum width of 3.1m (Figure 8). At each end it has cutwaters *c* 1.5m in length with sides at an angle of 45 degrees to the main body of the pier (for a discussion of piers with cutwaters at both ends see p 72). The lengths of its sides between the cutwaters are not quite equal, the eastern measuring 3.0m and the western 2.8m. Parts of two courses of blocks are visible. The lower, which was probably built immediately above the level of the paved river bed (cf Figure 11), is exposed on the west side of the pier. At this point the blocks along the edge of the pier are joined together with dovetail clamps of iron run in with lead (Figure 10). Dovetail clamps are also employed to join these edging blocks to the larger blocks in the centre of the pier (see p 125–6). Crowbar slots in the surface of this lower course show the

Figure 9   A pier of bridge 1 incorporated in the east abutment of bridge 2. To the right of the pier are the remains of the causeway, 1m scale.   (Photo: S C Speak)

position of some of the missing blocks in the course overlying it. Dovetail clamps are also used to join the blocks of the upper course where they form the cutwaters. They are however absent from the blocks on the east side which have been cut back slightly to accommodate the later causeway. At the tip of the north cutwater is a block which, unlike those in the original fabric, has a lewis hole and which was clearly an insertion perhaps replacing a split or shattered original when the pier was incorporated in the abutment of bridge 2 (Figure 9).

The site of the east abutment and its relationship to Hadrian's Wall

F G Simpson sought the abutment of bridge 1 behind the Wall east of the later tower, but evidently failed to find it (p 26). Its site therefore could only have lain beneath the later tower, and in 1983 the fill beneath the remains of its floor was removed, revealing to the west, paving (context 193, Figure 8) over the river bed, and to the east a bank of natural sand. The paving consisted of sandstone slabs with an average thickness of 0.2m, the largest measuring 1.15m by 0.65m. These were laid slightly askew to the line of the bridge. A number of slabs of similar dimensions were also seen partly underlying the front of the north wing of the abutment of bridge 2 and appear to represent a continuation of the paving extending 5.4m north of the pier (shown on Figures 3, 15 and 16). The bank of natural sand rose to a height of c 0.5m above the surface of the paving. Slabs or blocks appear to have been robbed from a gap between the base of the bank and the edge of the paving (context 194, Figure 8). To the north these slabs had apparently been laid up against an east–west foundation of large blocks (context 195, Figure 8), which to the east had been cut through the bank of sand. To the south the bank of sand was cut back diagonally.

The foundation (context 195) which cuts through the north edge of the bank of sand must have underpinned the north side of the Broad Wall as it approached the river, and its western end presumably marks the face of the abutment. A southern extension along the cut (context 194) in front of the bank of sand would have served to support the southern side of the Wall. The cut continues for another 1.5m beyond the line of the south side of the wall, suggesting that the base of the abutment was somewhat wider than the wall itself. The diagonal edge of the bank south of this point may indicate the line of a wing-wall revetting the bank, perhaps formed by a single line of blocks similar to those of bridges 1A and 2 at Willowford (see p 74–5, 83–4); Figure 11 shows an east–west profile through the remains of the east abutment and pier with a conjectural reconstruction of the vanished super-structure.

The surviving portions of the Broad Wall foundation and Narrow Wall do not share the same alignment as the bridge (Figure 8). The Broad Wall foundation approaches the bridge at an angle 4.5 degrees north-east of the long axis of the bridge as established by the position of the river pier, the Narrow Wall at an angle one degree further to the north-east. Fortunately there are other indications to show with which Wall the bridge was associated. G Simpson (1976, 48) noted that the length of the pier between its cutwaters is equivalent to the width of the Broad Wall and that they were 'intended to be associated.' The width of the pier is 3.0m and that of the Broad Wall foundation 3.25m; offsets on both faces of the Wall would have diminished its width to c 3m. The later causeway between the pier and abutment is of the same width (p 14).

The junction between the abutment and the Broad Wall to the east was probably intended to have been made at an angle, although it is doubtful whether work proceeded further than the construction of the Broad Wall foundation before the introduction of the Narrow Wall. Figure 8, inset A, illustrates this, showing the Broad Wall joining the abutment at an angle of 9.5 degrees. This angled approach to the bridge made by the Broad Wall also provides an explanation for the even greater angle formed between the Narrow Wall and the long axis of the bridge. Its north face is aligned on the estimated position of the north face of the abutment; the other end of this face of the Narrow Wall, if projected eastwards, would intersect the north edge of the Broad Wall foundation at the crest of the slope leading down to the river. It seems that the builders of the Narrow Wall had taken the opportunity to do away with the awkward realignment of the Broad Wall foundation and had laid out their Wall in a straight line between the abutment and the Broad Wall foundation at the crest of the slope (as shown in Figure 8, inset B).

We may consider possible reasons for this mis-alignment of the bridge and Broad Wall foundation. From the top of Brunton Bank, some 250m east of Milecastle 26, the Wall runs in a straight line to the North Tyne; at the turrets and at Milecastle 27 it was built to Broad gauge, but elsewhere it presumably consisted of Narrow Wall on Broad Wall foundations. West of the river the Wall, represented by Narrow Wall on Broad Wall foundations, runs on the same alignment as the bridge until it is overlain by Chesters fort. West of Chesters it runs at a slightly different angle and there must have been a change of alignment at some point under the fort, possibly at its junction with Turret 27a near the north-east corner of the *principia* (*J Roman Stud* **36** (1946), 134). The misalignment of the bridge and Broad Wall foundation to the east suggests that they were not of contemporaneous construction and it would seem that the construction of the Broad Wall foundation came first. The site of the bridge would have been visible to the gang laying the foundation of the Broad Wall from the east as soon as they reached the crest of the short slope down to the river; if the bridge was already under construction, it might be expected that the misalignment of the Broad Wall foundation would have been corrected at this point, thus avoiding the awkward angle. If the bridge was built

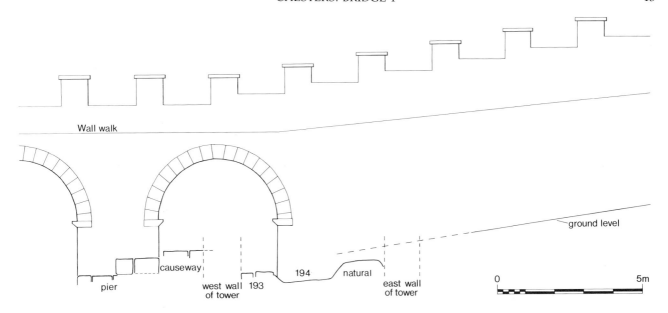

Wall walk

ground level

causeway

pier   west wall   193   194   natural   east wall
              of tower   of tower

0   5m

Figure 11   Conjectural reconstruction drawing of the south elevation of the east abutment of bridge 1 showing the position of excavated features and the position of the tower of bridge 2.   Scale 1:125

after the wall foundation was laid its alignment and position could not have been determined by the position of the Broad Wall foundation; more important to the builders would have been the direction of flow of the river, the contours of its bed, and the composition of its banks.

West of the river, as we have seen, the Broad Wall foundation and bridge share the same alignment as far as Chesters fort; the bridge is therefore likely to be contemporary with or earlier than this stretch of the Wall foundation, on which the Narrow Wall was built.

It is currently believed that the construction of the Broad Wall in the vicinity of the North Tyne began in AD 124 in the second full building season (Breeze and Dobson 1987,74 and table 7). There is evidence that the Sixth Legion was responsible for the Wall from Milecastle 22 to Turret 27a, but during that season the programme appears to have been disrupted by the decision to build forts on the line of the Wall. As a consequence some parts of the curtain wall were not completed until AD 126 at the very earliest, when the Narrow Wall was introduced. It has been supposed that the bridges at Chesters and Willowford were also begun in 124 but the new evidence from Chesters, suggesting that building of the bridge started only after the Broad Wall foundation had been laid as far as the North Tyne, would certainly allow a start in 125. The construction of the bridge was a major undertaking which would have required the skills of the most experienced masons in the legion. The start may perhaps have been delayed until the construction of milecastles and turrets was completed; since its purpose seems solely to have been to carry the Wall and its walk across the river (p 134), there would have been no need for the bridge until the completion of the curtain was in prospect.

One further matter requires consideration. In the earliest period at Willowford a tower gave access to the rampart walk just east of the east abutment and

it is argued that there was a second tower on the west side of the bridge (p 65). It might be expected that at Chesters there would also have been towers to serve the same function.

The stretch of completed Broad Wall associated with the abutment, as reconstructed on Figure 8, Inset A, is far too short to have accommodated a tower recess as at Willowford, but the alignment of the Narrow Wall indicates that the Broad Wall is most unlikely to have been of substantially greater length. However, the bridges could not have served their intended function as a continuation of the wall-walk across the river until the curtain wall was largely complete, and at Chesters perhaps the tower was to be situated east of the wing-wall. It should be noted that terracing of the general level south of the surviving portion of the Narrow Wall caused by previous excavations might well have removed all traces of the tower. Another possibility is that the site chosen for the tower was not immediately adjacent to the abutment but at the top of the slope down to the river where it would command a better view of the river upstream from the bridge.

The overall plan of the bridge

Holmes believed that the central river pier of bridge 2 incorporated a pier of the earlier bridge: the builders had not only reused the pier in the east abutment

> 'but had adopted and enlarged the other piers also, by adding a width of five feet eight inches [1.73m] to their western sides and lengthening them southwards. This is apparent on applying a tracing of the embedded pier (the dimensions of which can be exactly defined) to the plan of the second pier...where the different character of the masonry clearly defines the earlier and more recent work.'

Holmes 1894, 329, pl XXV

This pier is now mostly covered by gravel and boulders and cannot be re-examined at present. Holmes's identification of the earlier pier nevertheless seems doubtful; no mention is made of dovetail clamps and 'the difference in the character of the masonry' is not very striking for, although the rectangular blocks typical of bridge 2 are predominant in the western and central piers, there are also throughout their fabric a number of square blocks of similar dimensions to those used in bridge 1. In addition, the recent excavations have established that the space between the east abutment and the adjacent river pier is 4.0m in width. If the spacing of all the piers was the same, the blocks which Holmes identified as the remains of the piers of bridge 1 incorporated in the larger piers of bridge 2 are in the wrong position. In general Roman bridges which cross rivers of any width have equally spaced piers,although exceptions have occurred where a much deeper main river channel was more conveniently spanned by a single arch larger than the others (eg the Pont Julien: Gazzola 1963, 127–8). At Chesters the North Tyne flows in a channel which is of fairly constant depth across its width. It seems reasonable to suppose, therefore, that the piers of bridge 1 were equally spaced, like those of its successor.

The overall plan of bridge 1 is a matter for conjecture. Its successor, which was 58.0m in length, was constructed so that its great east abutment projected *c* 7.0m into the river (Figure 2). The east abutment of bridge 1 was of much slighter construction, associated with wing-walls that seem merely to have revetted the river bank with a single thickness of blocks (p 12). Assuming that when bridge 1 was built the width of the river was much the same as when it was spanned by its successor, and that as suggested above, the piers were equally spaced, a bridge of eight piers with a width of *c* 61.0m at the very least is indicated (cf Figure 12).

The piers of bridge 1 probably supported stone arches rather than a timber walkway. This is suggested by comparison with bridge 1 at Willowford (p 69), which was built entirely of stone, and which formed part of the same programme of construction. In addition, the close spacing of the east abutment and east pier, if repeated across the width of the bridge, would be strongly indicative of the existence of stone arches. As will be further discussed in Chapter 4, the design of bridge 1 is unsatisfactory from a technical point of view. A bridge with much more widely-spaced piers, as for example the contemporaneous bridge 1 at Willowford, would have been adequate and the additional labour and materials used were wasteful. Furthermore, the closely spaced piers, with their narrow waterways would have penned up water against the bridge, impeding the flow and much increasing the force of the current between the arches, thus threatening the stability of the structure when the river was in spate. These observations by no means undermine the reconstruction of the plan of bridge 1 proposed

above. Wide piers and narrow waterways, resulting from overcompensation for internal structural stresses, are typical of Roman bridges.

The later causeway

This feature has been visible since the abutment was first excavated but was not recognised until 1982 when a new plan of the remains was made (Figure 8). It consists of two lines of unmortared sandstone blocks retaining a core of sandstone rubble, also unmortared, with an overall width of 3.0m, and it runs eastwards from the pier of bridge 1 to the west wall of the tower which partly overlies it (Figure 9). At its west end the face of the pier seems to have been cut back slightly to receive it; further to the east it appears to have been removed when the abutment under the tower was robbed.

This fragment of masonry was probably part of a causeway between the pier and east abutment of bridge 1, constructed following the demolition or collapse of the arch. A similar feature occurs at Piercebridge and was inserted after the southern part of the river bed had silted up (p 112). Evidence for the accumulation of riverine deposits against the east bank of the river at Chesters, following the construction of bridge 1 and before its rebuilding, was detected in two places. The cut (context 371) for the rear of the north wing of the abutment of bridge 2, immediately north of the tower, had been dug through sand which appeared to have been deposited naturally; the top of this deposit was 1.1m above the sandstone paving of the river bed (which was not seen at this point) and its edge lay *c* 1.15m west of the estimated position of the first abutment (p 12 and Figure 15). Further to the west the front of the north wing of the later abutment was seen to cut through a bank of gravel (context 77), the edge of which was roughly in line with the east side of the pier of bridge 1 (Figures 3 and 15, p 19). Just west of the edge of this gravel there was a line of flagstones running from north to south and overlain by the north wing of the east abutment of bridge 2 (context 75, Figure 15); they perhaps served as the foundations of a revetment of the gravel bank, or of a wing wall associated with the river pier which now effectively served as the abutment of bridge 1.

Thus at some stage in the second century it seems that gravel and sand were deposited against the east bank over a width of *c* 4m, presumably by the action of the river. The arch was perhaps damaged by the same river action and, now redundant because of a slight shift westwards in the course of the river, was dismantled and replaced by a solid causeway. Dating evidence is lacking but the deposition of silt was more probably the result of a catastrophic episode rather than a gradual accumulation. Such episodes occur rarely in the history of a river and the same circumstances which brought about the destruction of bridge 1A at Willowford in the Antonine period, (see p 76), may have operated on the North Tyne at Chesters.

2   Chesters: bridge 2

Introduction

Bridge 2 consists of three piers 4.9m in width and 9.3m in length, spaced 10.8m apart (Figure 12). The overall width between the abutments, which are of unusually large size, is 58.0m. Only the east abutment is visible; the east pier is covered by the present east bank of the river and the remainder of the bridge lies in the river, which now also flows over the surviving courses of the west abutment. In this chapter the abutments, piers and other structures associated with bridge 2 are described and it is shown that the bridge was not as previously thought partly of timber but was wholly of stone. The evidence on which this depends involves not only the structural remains *in situ* but also many of the architectural fragments from the site which are considered in Chapter 3 rather than in a separate catalogue. Techniques of construction (stoneworking, the systems of clamping and the use of dowels, crowbar slots, the lewis and cranes,) are referred to only incidentally and are fully discussed in Chapter 8.

The west abutment and ramp of approach

Two antiquarian plans of the west abutment and the west and central river piers exist. The first (Figure 13) was drawn in about 1850 by George Bruce 'assisted in the minute detail by Mr [Robert] Elliot of Wall' (according to a notation in the third edition (1867) of the *The Roman Wall* in the John Collingwood Bruce Collection at the South Shields Museum, Tyne and Wear Joint Museums Services) and was reproduced in the first and second editions of *The Roman Wall* (1851, 1853). The second version (Figure 14) was drawn by Robert Elliot and Henry Wilson for Clayton's paper on the bridge (1865) and subsequently replaced the earlier version in the third edition of *The Roman Wall* (1867); it shows a little more detail but was perhaps no more than an amplification of the original with the addition of the newly discovered east abutment rather than an entirely new survey.

In September 1983 the west abutment was below only about 0.5m depth of water but much of what is shown on the nineteenth-century plans was concealed by debris. This description is therefore based on these plans, reliance being placed principally on the later plan which shows the detail more clearly.

The overall length of the abutment is recorded as 21.8m and it has two faces, the northern 12.2m in length and the southern 7.9m in length, joining at an angle of 132 degrees. Most of the blocks in the front courses of both faces are shown laid with their narrow ends towards the river and with lewis holes. At the southern end three blocks are shown laid with

their faces parallel to the river; the earlier plan shows four blocks in this position. These seem to represent a separate course. A groove shown running along the centre of these blocks was presumably to accommodate a lead tie-bar as elsewhere in the bridge (p 131). At the north end the coursing appears to be rather irregular and perhaps this represents a repair. If so, it is possible that the abutment originally resembled its counterpart on the east side of the bridge in having an angled north wing. On the other hand it may be that the river approached the bridge at an angle from the north-east (p 14), in which case a north wing which continued the line of the main abutment face might have presented the same angle to the direction of flow of the river as the north wing of the east abutment (cf Figure 12).

Between the abutment and the eastern *porta quintana* of the fort, a distance of some 125m, are the well marked remains of the road leading to the bridge (Figure 2). Just outside the gate the road is represented by a slight cutting but as it descends west of the bath house it begins to form a ramp which achieves a maximum width of 10–12m and continues to the edge of the sharp slope above the river. At this point the ground is broken away and retained by a modern wall. The top of the ramp is *c* 8.6m above the surface of the abutment.

There was thus direct access from the fort to the bridge. Only a brief reference to the excavation of the eastern *porta quintana* gate exists: '[it] was a single gateway, up to which was traced the road leading from the Roman bridge over the North Tyne' (Clayton 1876, 172). It is probable that there was also access to the bridge from the south, bypassing the fort. Aerial photographs (eg University of Newcastle upon Tyne, Department of Archaeology Collection, NY9170/E and F; cf Figure 2) show a branch leading eastwards from the road between the Stanegate and the fort some 70m south of the *porta decumana*. It can be traced to a point near the south-east angle of the fort beyond which it might well have swung north-east to join the road to the bridge, just to the west of the baths, which it might also have served.

The river piers

In 1983 the west pier was examined and found to be substantially in the same condition as in 1860, apart from the north-west part which was covered by boulders and gravel (Figure 12). It is 4.9m in width and has an overall length of 9.3m including on its north side a cutwater 3.3m in length, the two sides of which meet at a point forming an angle of 85 degrees. The plan of 1860 shows the block at the point of the cutwater bound to the block adjoining it to the south-east by what appear to be two exceptionally large bar clamps each *c* 0.65m in length (Figure 14). By 1983 erosion had removed all traces of these. In view of their large size they were perhaps of lead rather than iron (cf p 127). The east, west and south sides of the pier still preserve traces of the slots for lead tie-bars shown on the 1860 plan; their width is between 25 and 30mm.

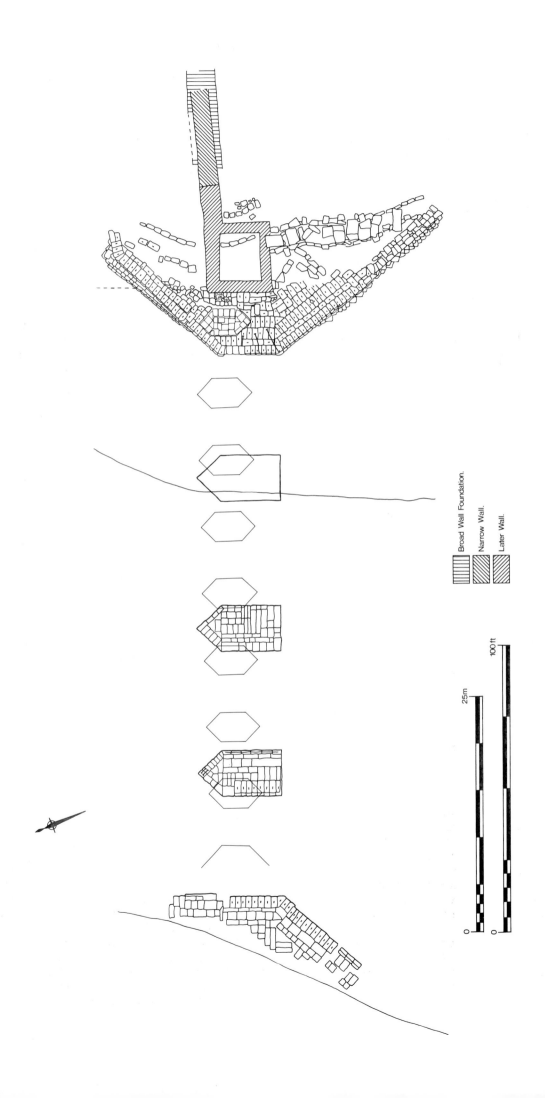

Figure 12 Bridge 2 with a restored plan of bridge 1 in red. Scale 1:400

Broad Wall Foundation.

Narrow Wall.

Later Wall.

25m

100 ft

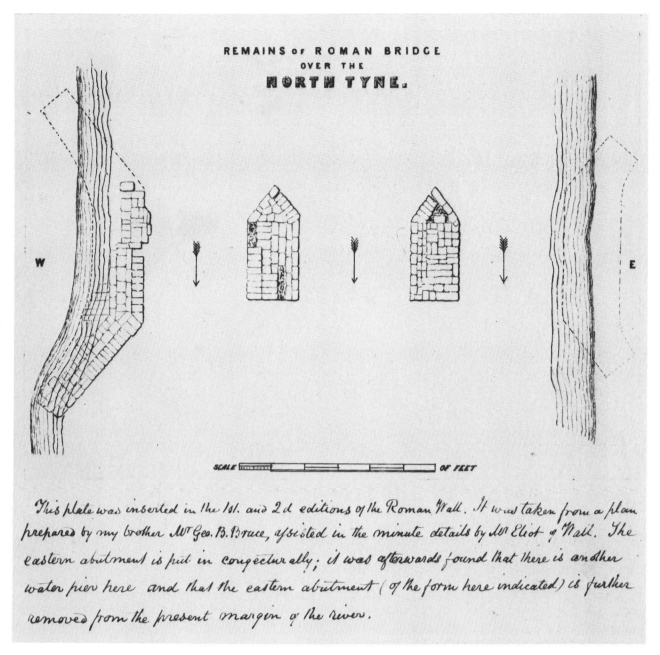

REMARKS of ROMAN BRIDGE
OVER THE
NORTH TYNE.

Figure 13 George Bruce's plan of bridge 2 of about 1850. A copy with J.C. Bruce's annotation bound into the third edition of The Roman Wall *in the John Collingwood Bruce Collection at South Shields Museum.   (Reproduced with the permission of Tyne and Wear Museums Service)*

In 1983 the central pier was largely concealed by gravel and boulders and the few blocks on its east side which when exposed were heavily eroded. To judge from the nineteenth-century plans, it was exactly the same size as the west pier. F G Simpson (*J Roman Stud* **37**, (1947), 168) stated that he found some remains of the east pier, which lies beneath the present east bank of the river, but gave no more detail.

Wallis (1769, 116–7) describes semicircular foundations under the piers but there is no corroboration of their existence from other sources; however a semicircular foundation certainly underlies pier 1 at Corbridge (p 104).

The east abutment

The east abutment (Figure 15), measuring 29.3m in length overall, was constructed throughout of stone blocks of regular size generally laid in alternating courses of headers and stretchers (that is, with their ends or sides alternately laid parallel to the face of the abutment). It consists of three elements: a central part, the main abutment from which the east arch of the bridge sprang, and two flanking wings. These taking the form of massive retaining walls, up to 5.7m wide at their base, but becoming narrower throughout their height by means of wide offsets at the rear,

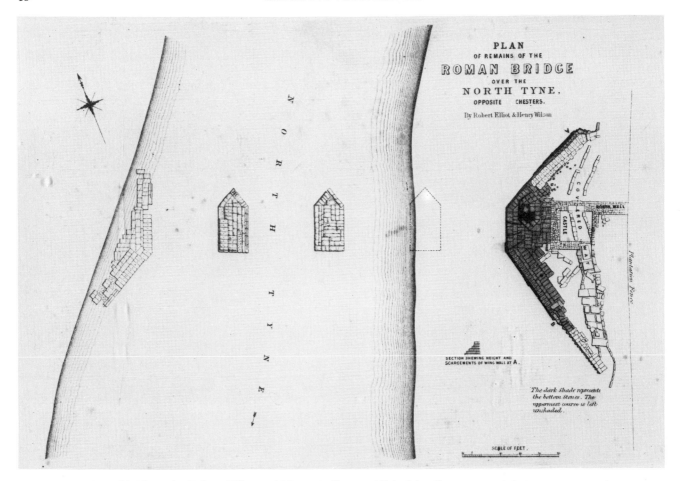

Figure 14   Plan of bridge 2 by Robert Elliot and Henry Wilson published in Clayton 1865, facing p 80.   Scale 1:580

and much narrower offsets at the front (Figure 15). The entire structure is not built level but shows a distinct incline towards the west; the coursing of the north wing falls 0.45m over its length, the south wing 0.24m and the main abutment 0.15m from east to west. Bruce thought that this was intentional although Holmes (1894, 331) attributed it 'to the dribbling away of material from under the abutment.' The even incline and absence of shear-cracks (other than those caused by the weight of the super-structure, shows that Bruce was correct. The face of the main abutment proper would have been eight courses high but the two lowest courses were omitted for most of the length of the wings. For ease of reference the courses are numbered 1–8 from the bottom upwards on the accompanying elevations (Figure 16).

The main abutment

The surviving height of the main abutment at its face is 2.0m (Figure 16, courses 1–5) and its length is 6.6m. The width from the face to the west wall of the tower is 6.55m. The blocks of the first course are laid as headers, but the next three courses are laid as stretchers. The fifth course consists of headers. The only surviving facing block of the sixth course, at the north end of the face, has been laid as a header;

crowbar slots show, however, that the rest of the sixth course consisted of stretchers (cf p 119). The position of crowbar slots also shows that the second row of blocks in the sixth course behind the south end of the abutment face had likewise been laid as stretchers. Apart from the single block of the sixth course at the north end of the abutment face, remains of courses 6–8 (Figure 16) only survive by the west wall of the tower. A block of the eighth course at the north-west corner of the tower had a rebate cut in its south-east corner so that it could fit around the angle.

The easternmost pier of the first bridge and the later causeway linking it to the abutment of bridge 1 were incorporated within the later abutment. This had involved some adjustment to its coursing, for the blocks of each of these three elements are at different levels, and of different thicknesses. At the north end of the pier the blocks of the cutwater are level with the sixth abutment course. It had proved necessary to cut back the north-west corner of the block abutting the pier in the north face of the causeway over a width of 200mm and to a depth of 340mm: this block was higher than the uppermost blocks of the pier and the recess was presumably formed to accommodate the end of a block belonging to the seventh course of the abutment covering the north-east angle of the pier. The north cutwater was thus apparently reduced to its existing level when the pier was demolished. The south cutwater, however, is

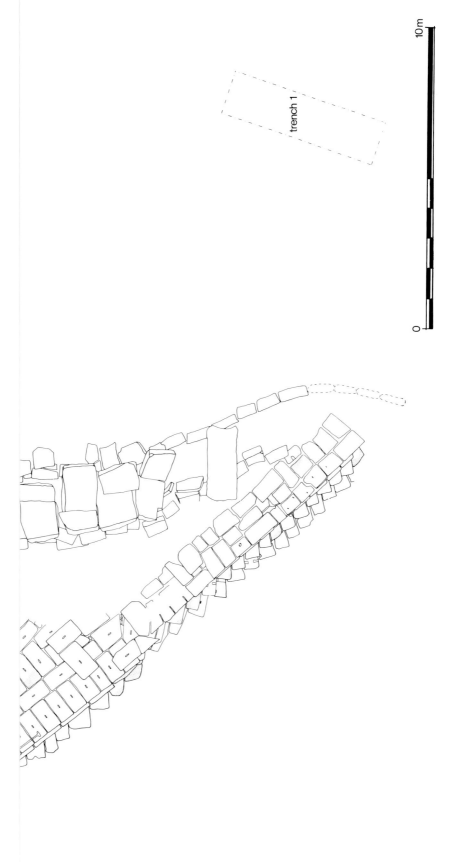

trench 1

0   10m

Figure 15   East abutment and tower of bridge 2. Blocks of the water channel which have been removed since 1863, restored in broken outline after Clayton 1865, fig facing p 80; 'c–h' indicates position of crane socket. For the floor levels inside the tower see Figure 22.   Scale 1:125

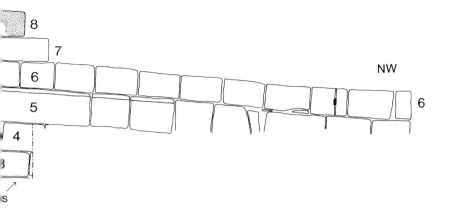

8

7

6

NW

5

6

4

3

s

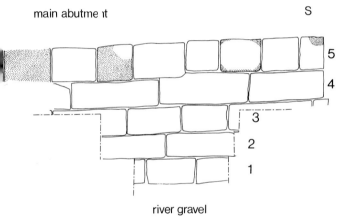

main abutment

S

5

4

3

2

1

river gravel

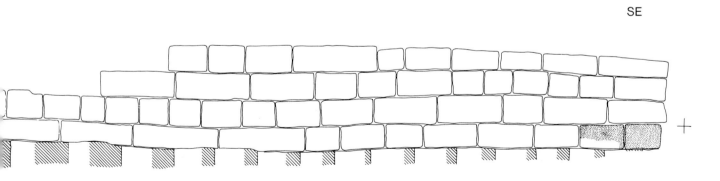

SE

+

later extension

outh faces of the blocks in

flush with the fifth course and the difference in level was perhaps compensated for by diminishing the depth of the blocks of the sixth course overlying the pier or by omitting them and increasing the depths of the blocks of the seventh course.

Trench no 6, (Figures 4 and 15, p 7) was cut in front of the abutment to locate any timberwork which might have been associated with it, for example a coffer dam, piles or horizontal timber strapping. It revealed that the lowest course of stonework sat directly on natural gravel and, although the trench extended 3.6m from the face of the abutment, no remains of timbers were seen.

The north wing

The length of the north wing at the top of the seventh course is 16.6m measured along its face. The wing consists of six courses with an overall height of 2.3m (Figure 16, courses 3–8, Figure 17), although the two lowest courses of the main abutment face were probably continued for a short distance along the north wing. The wing probably survives to its original height. The tooling of the surface of the uppermost course is rather rough and there are no crowbar slots or setting out lines to suggest the existence of a higher course which has been removed. The top of the wing is only 1.8m in width but below the seventh course its width is increased considerably by means of offsets at the front and rear (Figure 15). Those along the front are regular and diminish in width as they run south so that at a point 2.4m north of the junction with the abutment the wing has a continuous vertical face. The purpose of these offsets was probably to break up the force of the water hitting the face of the wing when the river was in spate. At the rear of the abutment the offsets were only seen to the north of the tower when the cut (context 371, Figure 15) for the rear of the north wing was partly excavated (see below). At this point the sixth course ran back to abut the north-west corner of the tower; 9m from the south end of the wing the sixth course had diminished to a width of 3.1m.

As has already been noted (p 14), at a point 8.5m from its south end the wing was seen to have cut through a bank of gravel apparently deposited after the first bridge was built. North of this point the bank must have rapidly gained height and this provides an explanation for the curious arrangement at the north end of the wing. The lowest three courses are roughly worked and were presumably below ground level but the upper three courses turn through an angle of 35 degrees and continue for a distance of 2.6m. They originally formed a vertical well-worked face without offsets and were presumably visible above the river bank. The blocks of the sixth and eighth courses which have been removed are probably those now forming the northern part of the water channel (p 28).

Part of the cut (context 371) for the rear of the north wing was excavated (Trench 8, Figure 15, p 6). It extended 1.6m east of the north-west corner of the tower and was cleared to a depth of 1.0m; its filling of rubble and sand (contexts 370, and 380) abutted

Figure 17   The full height of the north wing of the east abutment of bridge 2 at Chesters as revealed by trench 2 in the foreground, 2m scale.   (Photo: P T Bidwell)

the wall of the tower and lapped over the rough offsets at the rear of the north wing.

Most of the significant details of the masonry can be seen on the plans and elevations (Figures 15 and 16) but a few comments are required:

Course 3: this course includes four blocks with sockets for dovetail clamps reused from the first bridge.

Course 4: there is a setting out line for this course on the upper surface of course 3.

Course 5: the northernmost eight blocks are laid as headers, and then there are six stretchers, the largest surviving in position in the east abutment. On the face of the northernmost stretcher a phallus has been carved (Figures 16 and 18, p 141). The setting-out line for this course is up to 0.2m from the actual position of the face which demonstrates that the offset at the base of this course was originally intended to be narrower. The position of the crowbar slots shows that the blocks had been levered into position from the front. On the top of one of the blocks, at a point 6.3m from the south end of the wing, there is a socket filled with lead which, as probing established, extended for at least 100mm under an overlying block of the course above. This is probably the west end of the cross slot at the end of the tie-bar visible on the abutment and south wing.

Course 6: there are two setting-out lines for this course, one of which lies up to 0.37m beyond the face of the course at its north end. The latter is clearly a mistake but two crowbar slots in the tops of the fifth and sixth blocks from the north in course 5 show that some blocks were laid before the error was recognised; the position of the slots shows that the crowbars were being used to ease the blocks into position from the side. The south end of this course

Figure 18   Phallus carved on the fifth course of the north wing of the Chesters bridge 2 east abutment, 1m scale. (Photo: S C Speak)

for a distance of 4.95m from the north corner of the abutment has been exposed over its entire width by robbing and the slot for the lead tie-bar can be seen.

Course 7: the southernmost 5m of this course has been robbed. In the surviving portion the blocks are laid as stretchers but crowbar slots show that the missing portion of the face consisted of one further block laid as a stretcher and then another seven laid as headers. Along the rear of this course are a number of blocks of irregular size, some with sockets for dovetail clamps; they served as rough packing between the regularly sized blocks and the cut at the rear of the wing.

Course 8: as already noted (p 19), the rough working on the upper surface of this course and the absence of setting-out lines and crowbar slots suggests that, as now, this originally was the top course of the wing.

Figure 19   The dogtooth foundation at the base of the later extension of the south wing of the east abutment of bridge 2 at Chesters, 1m scale.   (Photo: S C Speak)

The south wing

The overall length of the south wing measured along the top of the fifth course is 12.8m (Figures 15 and 16). Robbing has exposed almost the entire upper surface of the fifth course which at its north end extends as far back as the tower; at its south end this course is at least four blocks in width but the presence of the water channel at this point prevented attempts to determine whether further blocks lay behind those visible. In any event the south wing is wider than the north wing although it is 3.8m shorter. At its south end the wing turns through an angle of 45 degrees; the original work is largely obscured by its junction with the later extension.

Detailed comments on the fabric of the wing are as follows:

Courses 1 and 2: the lowest course of the abutment presumably continues some distance along the face of the south wing but, because of lack of time, excavation was not carried down to a depth sufficient to establish this. The second course continues along the whole length of the wing but its presence was only established by probing at the south end, where the blocks seem to have been arranged in a dogtooth pattern in the same fashion as those of the overlying course.

Course 3: for a distance of 5.2m from the north end of the wing the blocks consist of stretchers. The remainder are set with their sides at an angle of about 45 degrees to the face of the wing in a dogtooth pattern set back from the underlying course which has been laid in the same way. The purpose of these two dogtooth courses was the same as that of the tapering offsets on the north wing: to break up the force of the water breaking against the wing when the river was in spate (see Figures 15 and 19).

Course 4: this consists of stretchers.

Course 5: this is offset from the underlying course by *c* 20mm at its north end increasing to 150mm at its south end. Crowbar and tie-bar slots and the socket for the vertical post of a crane (described on p 121) can be seen in the surface of this course (Figure 15).

Course 6: only two blocks of this course survive; they belong to the first and second rows behind the face. Crowbar slots show that the blocks which formed the face were laid as stretchers. There are two blocks at the level of this course at the south end of the wing; the southernmost belongs to the extension and perhaps also its neighbour. A setting-out line shows that at a point 7.0m from the north end of the wing the blocks of the face were set back at least 80mm from the front of the course below.

Courses 7 and 8: these have been entirely robbed. Each must have had a considerable offset for the face of the later extension is set back 0.4m from the face of the sixth course (see further below).

The extension to the south wing

The later extension to the south wing is 10.4m in length (Figure 15) and consists of six courses of blocks with an estimated overall height of about 2.1m. Only the top of the lowest course was seen and it is not shown on the elevation Figure 16. The top of the extension seems to have been at the same level as the missing eighth course of the south wing and thus survives to its full height (Figures 16 and 19). Uneven coursing, the absence of feathered tooling and the structural relationship of the extension with the south wing shows it to have been a later addition, its purpose to prevent or arrest scouring by the river at the end of the south wing. Excavation has also suggested that south of the abutment the Vallum had also been scoured away by the river (Swinbank 1954, 412–5). Some of the blocks in the extension have sockets for dovetail clamps, others sockets for bar clamps, showing that blocks from both bridges had been incorporated in the fabric (it seems unlikely that any of the blocks originated from the fort where no structures with clamped blocks are known).

The two lowest courses of the extension are constructed of blocks laid at an angle of 45 degrees to the face above, with the lower course projecting beyond the upper in the same fashion as the blocks of the second and third courses in the south wing (Figure 19). The top of these dogtooth courses is 0.55m higher than the corresponding courses in the south wing. On Figure 16 it can be seen how the top of the third course of the extension has been made to run through with the fifth course of the south wing, above which the coursing of the old and new work was presumably at the same level. Above the dogtooth foundation the face of the extension is without offsets and is set back 0.4m from the face of the fifth course of the south wing. Allowing for the offsets in the missing courses of the south wing, this presumably means that the faces of the top courses of the extension and wing were flush.

The tower

The tower was cleared in 1860 and until 1982 remained in much the same condition as when it was first exposed, apart from the displacement of some of the blocks of the water channel, and the insertion of blocks under the broken lintel of the water channel opening (Figure 20), replacing the timber props shown in Mossman's painting (Plate 1). In 1982 the blocks were removed and the lintel repaired (Figure 21).

The tower measures 7.17m from north to south and 7.27m from east to west externally (Figures 15 and 22). Its walls stand to a maximum height of 2.8m above the paving of the river bed associated with the first bridge, although much that remains of the walls would have been below the ground level associated with the later bridge.

The robbing trenches of the east abutment of bridge 1 and of the later causeway were enlarged to form a roughly square pit in which the foundations

Figure 20   *The tower, east abutment, bridge 2, Chesters, looking south, before the excavations in 1983. Modern blocking of the water-channel opening is still in position, 2m scale.   (Photo: S Sinclair)*

Figure 21   *The tower, east abutment, bridge 2, Chesters, looking west, after the removal of modern debris in 1983. The lintel over the opening for the water channel has been repaired and the modern blocking removed, 2m scale.   (Photo: S C Speak)*

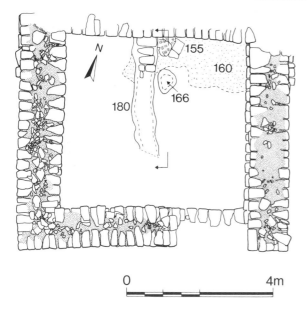

Figure 22   Remains of the floor-level (context 160), hearth (context 155) and partition (context 180) in the tower, east abutment, bridge 2, Chesters.   Scale 1:100

of the tower were set. First to be inserted were the foundations of the south and west walls; these were sealed beneath layers of sand and clay-silt (contexts 167, and 177–8, Figure 23; contexts 170–1, and 186–9 not illustrated), perhaps upcast from the digging of the foundations, and were in turn cut by the foundations of the north and east walls (contexts 175; and 176, Figure 23; contexts 179; and 168; not illustrated). The cut for the south foundation extended 0.4–0.5m beyond the face of the wall at its east end where it cut through the natural sand and the scarp left by the removal of the south wing of the earlier abutment; the filling of the south foundation cut was of clay, sand and pebbles (contexts 172–4).

West of this point there was no foundation trench, the south wall having been constructed on a base of large unmortared blocks 0.35m in height projecting 0.1–0.15m beyond the wall face and resting directly on the paving of the river bed (Figure 24). The west wall throughout its entire length was also built on a line of blocks laid on the paving of the river bed.

The north wall utilised the earlier foundation for the Wall just behind the abutment (context 195, Figure 8) and was set back 0.6m from its edge. The lowest course again consisted of unmortared blocks 0.35m in height (Figures 24 and 25). At the east end there was a foundation trench for the wall which cut through the natural sand; the lowest layer of fill consisted of mortar (context 179) overlain by sand (context 176, Figure 23) and sand mixed with sandstone fragments (context 175, Figure 23).

The foundations of the east wall were inserted last, cutting the foundations of the south and north walls. They consisted of thin boulders in a trench (context 168) cut through the natural sand. East of the wall there was a much larger cut (context 130), 0.9m wide at the north end and 1.35m in width further south, which was partly sealed by the line of blocks (context 131, Figure 15) associated with the ramp (see below). At its base was a layer of rubble (context 128) sealed by two layers, the lower one (context 122) of sand containing a few coal fragments probably derived from the deposit of coal and slag (context 109, Figure 8) to the east which was associated with the first bridge, the upper one of sand mixed with pebbles and lumps of clay (context 126). Above this a thin layer of pea-gravel and sand (context 113) was sealed by a thick constructional spread of mortar (context 112); this was at the same level as the constructional spread (contexts 164, and 165, Figure 23) inside the tower. The upper fill was of sand, pebbles and sandstone chippings (context 111).

The construction of the walls above their footings is of particular interest (Figure 24). They are of

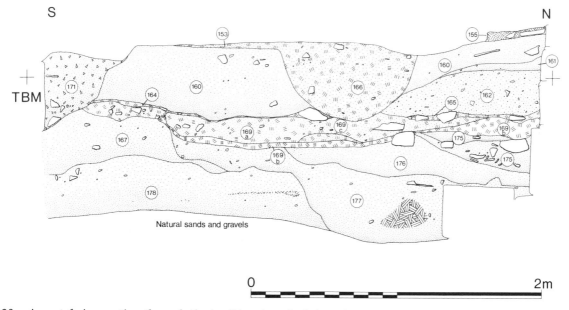

Figure 23   A west-facing section through the levelling deposits below the original floor-level of the tower, east abutment, bridge 2, Chesters, for position see Figure 24.   Scale: 1:25

Figure 24   Internal junction of the north and east walls of the tower, east abutment, bridge 2 at Chesters. The north wall is built on blocks which originally supported the north side of the Broad Wall, 2m scale.   (Photo: S C Speak)

similar to the mortar used to point the walls of the tower. This represents a construction level and was sealed by a levelling layer of sand and rubble (contexts 160–1, Figures 22–3; and context 163, not illustrated) which covered the offset on the interior of the east wall. Cut through the surface of the levelling was a small pit 0.45m deep and 0.95m across (context 166, Figure 22–3), the dirty sand filling of which spread over most of the surviving area of the levelling and formed a floor (context 153). It did not however extend as far west as a foundation (context 180, Figure 22) which divided the interior of the tower into two parts. The foundation consisted of a trench 0.6m in width and 0.25–0.3m in depth which was traced for a distance of 3.1m from the north wall of the tower. At the northern end a line of unmortared blocks laid across the width of the trench survived; they had presumably served to support a timber-framed partition. In the eastern angle of the partition and north wall was found a hearth consisting of a few flagstones set in clay (context 155, Figure 22–3); this yielded an archaeomagnetic date of A D 220±10 years (p 33). The hearth probably belonged to the primary occupation of the tower and might well have gone out of use when the entry to the tower was sealed during an early stage in the construction of the bridge. Above this level only isolated fragments of deposits survived the disturbance caused by the insertion of the water channel and by the nineteenth-century excavations (contexts 152, 154, and 156–8). One substantial feature cut through the levelling, a pit (context 171, Figure 23) containing a block measuring 1.05m by 0.7m by 0.6m, was isolated from these later deposits and was of uncertain date.

The tower appears to have been the first element of the later bridge to have been built. Its west wall is abutted by the blocks of the abutment, one of which in the eighth course fits round the north-west corner of the tower (p 18). The earth ramp of the tower will also have been later if the line of blocks (context 131, Figure 15) has been correctly interpreted as a retaining wall for the lowest level of dumping that formed the ramp (p 27); these blocks seal the east construction trench of the tower (context 130). (For details of the water channel which runs through the tower see p 28ff)

The function of the tower

A tower was associated with bridge 1 at Willowford (p 64ff), and possibly also with bridge 1 at Chesters, and it has been suggested elsewhere that the intended function was to give access to the bridges from south of the Wall (p 65). When bridge 2 was constructed at Chesters there would have been access from south of the Wall to the bridge by means of a ramp; the height of the bridge, estimated at 10.15m (p 44), was such that a tower with storeys at a yet higher level would probably not have been required for observation. The tower of bridge 2 at Chesters was evidently built to serve a purpose which differed from that of the towers associated with the earlier bridge at Willowford. Its notably massive construction would have been at least partly necessary

differing widths, (the north wall 1.45m wide, the east wall 1.1m wide) above an internal offset of 0.1m. The west and south walls are both 1.15m wide. All four walls consist of fairly neat coursing with blocks often of square elevation and rarely more than one and a half times as wide as they are high (Figure 25). On the exterior angles of the tower are alternating quoins twice as long as the facing stones. An exceptional feature is the length of the tails of the facing stones which are usually two or three times as long as the widths of their faces. This means that there is little space for a rubble core. The whole fabric above the footings is bound together with a strong whitish mortar with a coarse aggregate and is of great solidity.

At the east end of the south wall is an entry. It is now 1.85m in width but its west jamb had been removed when it was enlarged to accommodate the water channel. The neatly constructed east jamb with its quoin stones appears to be original, although elsewhere (p 28) it is shown that once the bridge was completed the entry was no longer usable.

Inside the tower a trampled level of sand, pebbles and mortar (contexts 164, and 165, Figure 23) sealed the foundations and over this was a pile of mortar (context 162, Figure 23) 0.35m high heaped against the north wall and showing two different mixes

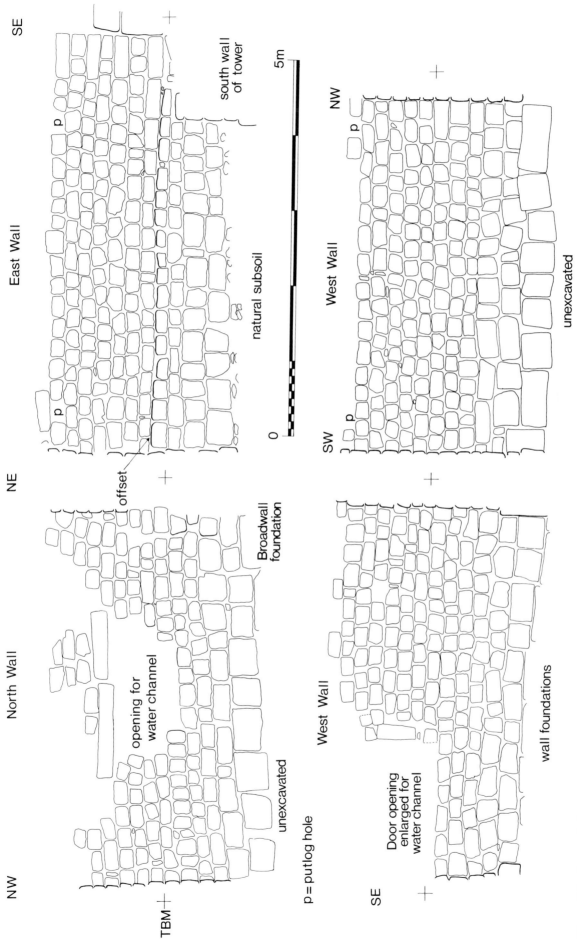

SE

South wall of tower

East Wall

natural subsoil

5m

NE

offset

Broadwall foundation

North Wall

opening for water channel

unexcavated

NW

TBM

p = putlog hole

0

NW

West Wall

unexcavated

SW

West Wall

SE

Door opening enlarged for water channel

wall foundations

Figure 25   Internal elevations of the walls of the tower ,east abutment, bridge 2 , Chesters.   Scale 1:50

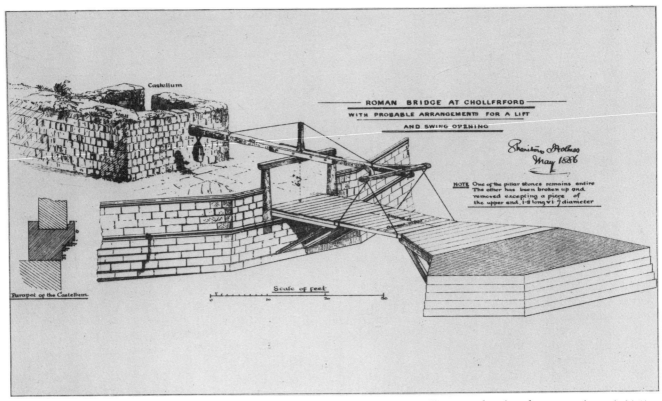

Figure 26   Holmes' reconstruction drawing of the east abutment of bridge 2 at Chesters, showing the approach-road skirting the tower (Holmes 1894, pl 27)

to withstand the weight of the ramp bearing on its eastern wall, even though some precautions were taken to reduce the amount of thrust from the mass of soil (p 27). The other three walls of the tower, however, are of equally sturdy construction which suggests that the tower perhaps supported a substantial superstructure at the level of the carriageway.

Common features of the larger Roman bridges were arches or other structures placed at one or both ends of the carriageway, or sometimes halfway along its length: for example the Römerbrücke at Trier (Cüppers 1969, 52–9 and Taf V showing a gate at the west end and an arch at the east end), Justinian's bridge over the *Sangarius* (Whitby 1985, 129, fig 1, an arch on the west side and another arch or perhaps a shrine on the east side) and the bridge of Alcántara over the Tagus in Spain (von Hagen 1967, 243, 245, with an arch in the middle of the bridge). At Chesters the existence of some form of gatehouse or an arch fitted with gates as on the Vallum crossing at Benwell seems probable.

The ramp and drain

In his paper given to the Society of Antiquaries of Newcastle upon Tyne in 1861, Clayton wrote that

> 'there is an apartment 24 feet [7.3m] by 23 1/2 feet [7.16m], under the platform of approach [ie the tower], and the roadway brought down to the bridge (including the parapets) is 22 feet wide [6.7m], and it is brought down to the bridge under the shelter of the Roman Wall.'

Clayton 1865, 82

Bruce however calls the tower 'a square building or *castellum' The Wallet-Book of the Roman Wall* (Bruce 1863, 75) and makes no mention of the roadway leading to the bridge 'under the shelter of the Roman Wall', implicitly rejecting Clayton's interpretation of the tower as a 'platform of approach'. For Holmes (1894, 331) the fact that the walls of the tower were well faced all round meant that it could never have been intended as an underground chamber. His reconstruction drawings show the road approaching the bridge around the southern face of the tower (Figure 26). F G Simpson (G Simpson 1976, 46) concurred with Holmes's views and in addition suggested that to the south of the tower the water channel had been covered with slabs because the Military Way passed over it.

In 1982–3 it was found that the area south of the Wall and east of the tower had been reduced almost to natural, leaving only a few traces of ironworking associated with the construction of the first bridge (p 11). This seems to have been the result of work carried out on three occasions:

Clayton's plan (1865, facing p 80, Figure 14) indicates that an area measuring roughly 5m east–west by 2m north–south in the angle between the tower and the Wall was excavated to a depth sufficient to reveal the line of blocks (context 131, Figure 15, see p 27), if not to natural.

Holmes states that

> 'Mr Clayton gave permission to have the face of the wall opened eastwards ... to a distance of sixty feet [18.3m] back with its junction with the *castellum'*.

Holmes 1894, 331

Further work in this area was undertaken by F G Simpson in 1946 (p 6). He was the first to note the existence of the Broad Wall foundation underlying the Narrow Wall (*J Roman Stud*, **37** (1947), 168).

Because of these investigations no traces remained of the roadway which Clayton seems to state was found behind the Wall. Unfortunately it is in fact very doubtful whether the roadway and its 'parapets' were actually found. The trench behind the tower was only 2m wide and can hardly have determined the existence of a roadway 6.7m in width. The figure of 22 feet (6.7m) which Clayton gives for the width of the roadway corresponds exactly to the width of the abutment between the wing walls and, although his assertion that the roadway was brought down to the bridge 'under the shelter of the Roman Wall' and over 'the platform of approach' (ie the tower) reads as if it were a statement of fact, it might have been no more than conjecture. Nevertheless, as will be shown, Clayton's conjecture was correct and he perhaps found some evidence such as metalling to suggest the existence of a roadway.

In 1982 an attempt was made to establish the exact direction from which the Military Way approached the bridge. Trench 1, (Figures 3 and 15) was dug along the east edge of the guardianship area across the line which a road approaching the bridge around the south side of the tower would probably have taken. At a depth of 0.55m at one end of the trench and 0.7m at the other, beneath brown sandy silt probably associated with the inundation of the river which covered the abutment, a thin layer of pebbles and clay-silt (context 51) was found which contained a copper alloy pendant (Figure 94, no 2) and the base of a Nene Valley colour-coated beaker of third or fourth century date (p 6). Beneath this deposit, which was probably the Roman ground surface, a layer of river gravel up to 0.3m deep was found. Its surface was not compacted or worn and excavation suggested that it was a natural deposit; subsequently the same stratum was observed 15m to the north where it was cut by the Broad Wall foundation. The interface between this material and the underlying clay-silt mixed with river-worn boulders, which seems to have been naturally deposited, was uneven and uncompacted with pockets of bright orange clay-silt on the surface of the underlying deposit.

The lack of evidence for a road in this position confirms what seems obvious from a glance at the plan of the abutment: that the tower would have stood directly in the path of traffic passing over the bridge. Its presence might have required vehicles to make a sharp turn which, if its purpose was merely surveillance of the bridge, could have been avoided by siting the tower further up the slope. However in the preceding section (p 26) the very solid construction of the tower has been taken to indicate that it supported a substantial superstructure at the level of the carriageway of the bridge, probably some form of gatehouse or arch. The road approaching the bridge would thus have been carried up to the level of the carriageway by a ramp east of the tower, similar to that which survives west of the abutment (p 15).

Four features on the site suggest the existence of such a ramp, immediately behind the Wall and abutting the east wall of the tower, which would bear out Clayton's notion that the Military Way approached the bridge directly behind the Wall:

First, just to the east of the tower there is a line of roughly squared stone blocks (context 131, Figure 15) partly sealing the east construction trench of the tower (context 130; p 23). The northernmost block seems to have been laid up against the south face of the Wall, which at this point is a rebuild contemporary with the construction of the later bridge. These blocks might have served as a kerb or rough retaining wall designed to relieve the east wall of the tower from the weight of material forming the base of a ramp behind it.

Second, the capping of the later water channel had been specially strengthened for a distance of 4.5m south of the point at which it issued from the tower (p 30), presumably because it was intended to carry a greater weight than the capping over the rest of the channel. This greater weight might well have been the base of the ramp fanning out around the south side of the tower.

Third, south of the tower and running from north-east to south-west is a drain (context 132, Figure 15) with a channel 0.35–0.45m in width by 0.45m deep. This was massively constructed of irregularly-sized blocks with one capping stone, a rectangular block 0.33m thick, still in position. Four of the six blocks which form the sides of the channel have cut-away corners or one or two sides cut at an angle. They have been roughly worked to shape with lines of diagonal tooling carried out with a point; none has lewis holes, sockets for clamps, or crowbar slots, and they are perhaps roughouts from the quarry, originally intended for use in the fabric of the bridge. The purpose of the drain which they formed was probably to collect water from a system of gullies and ditches alongside the Military Way and at the base of the ramp.

Lastly, when the water channel was constructed, the drain was cut through and some of the blocks from it were reused in the walls of the channel. A line of three blocks ran from the south-west corner of the tower towards the southern end of that part of the channel which had a specially strengthened capping. The northernmost is from a flight of steps (block no 123; Figure 30, no 2) but the other two are roughly worked in the same fashion as those used to form the drain and perhaps originally formed part of it. These blocks probably served as a kerb at the base of the ramp which may have been partially reconstructed at this point when the water channel was cut through it.

These features make sense if they are interpreted in connection with the existence of a ramp. No alternative explanation of them is obvious and there is only one objection to the existence of a ramp: the presence of an entry at the east end of the south wall of the tower which is apparently an original feature. In the preceding paragraphs it has been assumed that the ramp was of earth and not retained on the south side by masonry, the lower courses of which might be expected to have survived since neither the Wall nor the tower had been robbed below the ground level as it existed in 1860. The height of the ramp where it met the tower can be estimated at c 5.5m (cf Figure 36, south elevation) and the degree of batter on its south side would have meant that the lower part would extend some distance along the south side of the tower thus blocking the entry. Two explanations can be proposed for this. First it might quite simply have been a mistake. The tower was built before the ramp and its builders might have overlooked the fact that the base of the ramp would block the door; perhaps it might even have been originally intended to provide a retaining wall along the south side of the ramp. An alternative explanation is that the entry was provided for the convenience of the builders so that they could gain access to the interior of the tower from ground level during its construction and that it was sealed up as soon as the tower was completed and the ramp constructed. Subsequently access to the base of the tower would have been only from the level of the carriageway and ramp of bridge 2.

Dating evidence

Evidence for the date of bridge 2 is supplied by finds from the recent excavations and by the earlier find of an altar. None of the finds from construction levels offers any help in establishing the date of bridge 2. Finds from primary occupation levels in the tower included a corroded plated copy of a *denarius* of Septimius Severus (coin no 2, p 142). From disturbed material derived from the same levels came pottery representing a type in use in the first half of the third century (Figure 95, nos 3, and 4).

Fired clay from a primary hearth in the tower produced an archaeomagnetic date of A.D. 220±10 years (see end of chapter). The pottery and archaeomagnetic date establish a *terminus ante quem* for the construction of the bridge but not the date of its actual construction.

The lettering of the dedication made by Aelius Longinus, prefect of cavalry (RIB 1470; Figure 93, and p 141) was considered to be Hadrianic by Collingwood (1933, 75). Eric Birley however, put forward several reasons why it was probably considerably later:

'the absence of *praenomen*, filiation and tribe does not accord with a date earlier than the third century, nor should we expect to find an Aelius in a senior equestrian appointment at so early a date: the earliest datable examples of Aelii serving in equestrian posts in Britain are two commanders of the *ala Augusta* at Old Carlisle, P Aelius Septimianus Rusticus in AD 185 [*RIB* 903] and P Aelius P F Ser Magnus in AD 191 [*RIB* 894], while the other seven instances are all assignable to the third century.'

Birley 1939, 251

It should be noted that the upper part of *RIB* 903 was lost before 1785 and the editors of *RIB* restore the letters recorded before its loss as *cu]i p[r]aee[st]* | *Septimenus* | rather than *..P.Ael[ius] Septimianus..*

The forebears of men bearing the name Aelius will have received citizenship under Hadrian or Antoninus Pius and even their most successful descendants were unlikely to have achieved equestrian rank until the second or third generation. The dedication is therefore almost certainly of late second-century date at the earliest. What remains doubtful is whether it is necessarily associated with the construction of bridge 2. It will be argued elsewhere (p 47), however, that it was set in the parapet of the bridge and also that it was unlikely to have been the principal inscription recording its construction. It might perhaps be a record of later repairs, but an association with the original construction work remains a strong possibility. The bridge will almost certainly have been built by legionaries, but just as on the bridge over the Cendere Çay in Turkey, (Figure 28), built by the Sixteenth Legion, the four *civitates* of Commagene erected columns honouring the Severan dynasty (p 43; Humann and Puchstein 1890, 393–7), so at Chesters a dedication might have been made by the commander of the unit which would have had charge of the bridge upon its completion.

The dating evidence for the bridge is thus far from satisfactory because none of it can be indisputably linked with its construction. But the weight of the evidence, such as it is, favours a late second or early third century date and other factors discussed on p 138ff make a construction date in Severus' reign during the governorship of Alfenus Senecio (c 205–7) very probable.

The water channel

Apart from the extension to the south wing which has already been described (p 21), the only modification in the area of the abutment was the construction of a water channel, which runs from north to south across the site behind the abutment, passing through the base of the tower. F G Simpson (*J Roman Stud* **37**, (1947), 168) found that it had continued across the bottom of the Wall ditch north of the abutment. No traces of this stretch are now visible but most of the remainder survives *in situ*. Between the Wall ditch and the tower is a stretch 8m in length and 1.65m in width. The channel sides are formed by large blocks set on edge. Three of these on the west side at the north end have lewis holes and are probably blocks which were robbed from the north end of the abutment (p 19); the remainder are roughly worked and display no signs of previous use.

The channel passes through an opening in the base of the north wall of the tower. A massive lintel slab (2.45m by 1.15m by 0.33m) had been inserted to cover the opening which was c 1.8m in width and 0.7m high. A large block, probably removed from one side of the channel to the north, had been inserted into the opening. A thinner slab had been wedged into place above it to support the lintel, which had broken. It has been claimed that this 'systematic walling-up' of the opening is of Roman date (Simpson 1976, 46) but this is not so. A drawing by Mossman (Plate 1), shows no sign of any blocking but rather two lengths of timber supporting the broken lintel. The blocking therefore seems to have been inserted during the excavations of 1860–3.

As part of the programme of consolidation in 1982–3 the blocking was cleared away and the lintel and wall above dismantled and then reinstated with a steel beam supporting the lintel (further details of this are contained in the site archive). The work provided an opportunity to examine the sides of the opening. Remains of a refacing three courses high survived on the east side of the channel but on the west side there was only a tumble of collapsed facing stones.

The insertion of the lintel, when the water channel was originally carried through the tower, had required the reconstruction of the wall above. The north face of this reconstruction was flush with that of the earlier work but the south face was set back 0.4m from the inner face of the tower and the uppermost of the three surviving courses was set back a further 0.16m giving the wall above the lintel a width of 0.9m. The facing stones employed in the rebuild were without the exceptionally long tails of those in the original construction of the tower (Figure 27).

The course of the channel across the floor of the tower appears on the plan by Elliot and Johnson accompanying Clayton's paper (1865, facing p 80: Figure 14) and is shown very clearly on the Mossman drawing (Plate 1). Both sides were two courses (c 0.9m) high, the lower courses consisting of large blocks set on edge, the upper of smaller slabs about half the thickness of the blocks beneath. In 1983 only the lower courses on the east side of the channel survived in position. The blocks on the west side had

Figure 27   Broken lintel from the water channel, looking north, showing the walling above set back from the face of the original north wall of the tower, east abutment, bridge 2, Chesters, 2m scale.   (Photo: P T Bidwell)

collapsed into an excavation trench dug between the channel and the west wall of the tower. None of the blocks showed any signs of previous use. No deposits associated with the water channel survived within the tower.

The water channel was built directly on the original floor of the tower and putlog holes indicate that a wooden floor was inserted above it. Only one (Figure 25), at the north end of the east wall of the tower, survives intact. The base of the opening is *c* 1.1m above the original floor and measures 0.3m by 0.2m by 0.55m deep and is capped by a flat slab. Immediately opposite, a gap in the coursing of the west wall must mark the position of the corresponding putlog hole. At the south end of the east wall there is also a gap in the coursing which almost certainly represents one of a second pair of putlog holes. The purpose of the beams which would have been inserted in the putlog holes was presumably to support the ends of a series of joists running from north to south with planking above.

The water channel crosses the tower at an angle and passes through the south wall through the door in the south-east corner, perhaps previously blocked (p 28), which had been cut back on the west side to accommodate the width of the channel.

South of the tower the channel is visible for a length of 17m (Figure 15) and the plan published by Clayton (1865, facing p 80: Figure 14) shows that it had continued at least a further 4m to the south. Throughout most of its length the channel is covered by slabs of considerable size, the largest measuring 2.3m by 1.25m by 0.35m and weighing about 2.5 tonnes. Only four blocks show any signs of previous use. One is a fragment of an upright slab, block no 93, probably from a water tank (Figure 30, no 1). The other three have sides cut at an angle and surfaces with rough diagonal lines of tooling; they have been reused from the drain cut by the water channel (p 27).

For a distance of 4.5m south of the tower the sides of the channel are constructed of two courses of blocks; as in the tower the upper course is about half the thickness of the lower. This part of the channel had been covered with slabs, most of which remain in position. They were all supported not by the side walls of the channel but by upright slabs laid against the walls and of such a height that the covering slabs supported on them were flush with the top of the channel walls. It has been argued elsewhere (p 27) that this portion of the channel was buried by the tail of the earth bank which formed the ramp leading through the tower to the bridge. For a distance of 10m to the south of this specially strengthened length the walls of the channel consists of one course of blocks, supporting a covering of slabs, only two of which are missing. All the slabs laid lengthwise across the channel are broken, presumably because of the root action of trees; remains of the plantation which covered the site until 1860 can be seen in Mossman's drawings (frontispiece). The remaining 7.5m length of the channel preserves no traces of a covering. In this part of the channel one block of the southern wall overlies a block in the later extension of the south wing.

The purpose of the water channel

Clayton described the water channel as
> 'a covered passage, which has been carried across the ruins … obviously of a date posterior to the Roman occupation of the country, and many of the stones of the bridge have been used in its formation'.
> Clayton 1865, 83

Bruce adds a little to Clayton's account, noting that the 'covered way' went
> 'beyond the extent of the excavations in both directions.' and
> 'as it is founded on a bed of silt at least a yard thick, its construction cannot have taken place until the works of the bridge had been overwhelmed by some terrible devastation'

(the silt is either packing behind the wings of the abutment or represents the earlier river bank). The notion that the covered way was a water channel was rejected by Bruce because
> 'the joints of the passage are by no means close, and, though covered on top, the bottom of it consists simply of the sandy alluvium of the river.'
> Bruce 1863, 77

Nearly fifty years elapsed before further observations concerning the water channel were made. Rye (1911, 166) suggested that it was a mill race and compared the size of the tower to that of an ancient mill with a horizontal wheel which he had seen in the north of Scotland. A water supply could have been obtained from a small burn which flows into the North Tyne 200m upstream from the bridge. Rye speaks of this burn as a 'quick running stream' but today it is a sluggish trickle. Collingwood seems to take account of this interpretation in the ninth edition of the *Handbook to the Roman Wall* (1933, 75) for he writes of the 'channel or water course'. In the subsequent edition the relevant passage is largely rewritten as follows:
> [the channel] 'entering the tower by a prepared opening … must have served an undershot water-mill placed therein, to which the stone axle-tree noted above may have belonged. The wheel would work a geared wheel, described by Vitruvius'.
> Richmond 1947, 79–80

This follows F G Simpson's views that the channel was 'in reality a leat for a water-mill housed in the ground floor of the tower' (*J Roman Stud* **37** (1947), 168; see also Simpson 1976, 44–6). The 'stone axle-tree' is the stone which elsewhere has been tentatively interpreted as a counterweight employed as part of a crane (Figure 87, p 123). G Simpson (1976, 48) has taken Richmond to task for suggesting that the stone was the hub of a watermill wheel. Richmond's interpretation as given in the *Handbook to the Roman Wall* does seem improbable, for to serve the function of a hub the stone should have had some means of attachment to the shaft it was supposed to drive and there are neither recesses nor tenons in the ends of the stone. However, Moritz, citing a letter from Richmond, writes of the stone as part of 'a composite hub of wood, stone and iron'. This interpretation is worth consideration and can only be doubted because, as is argued below, the tower could not have been used as a mill. In the same letter which Moritz cites it is stated that

> 'the mill is, according to Professor Rich-mond, an integral part of the tower and abutment, and not the later insertion it was once thought to be'.
>
> Moritz 1958, 136

Apart from the recognition that the covered way was a water channel, for which Rye (1911) may take credit, there is nothing amongst these previous interpretations which stands scrutiny. The water channel is certainly not contemporary with the construction of the bridge: it passes through the base of the tower through openings which are secondary and overlies occupation levels on its floor. Indeed it appears to be later than the extension to the south wing, for one of the blocks on its south side overlies a block in the rear of the extension. But it is probably not 'of a date posterior to the Roman occupation of the country' as Clayton believed. Only three blocks rather than 'many stones of the bridge' have been used in its construction and those stones were taken from the north end of the north wing. The water channel was presumably constructed when the bridge was still in use and being maintained in good order. The approach ramp seems still to have been in use, for the channel was strengthened to take its weight.

The suggestion that the water channel had served as a mill race does seem probable. It is too small to have served as a relief channel for the river and is at too low a level to have formed part of an aqueduct serving the fort across the river or buildings in its *vicus*. Far less probable, however, is the notion that the tower itself housed the mill. A considerable force of water is required to drive a water wheel (Landels 1978, 21) and at Haltwhistle Burn Head there was a sharp fall in the channel before the wheel (Simpson 1976, 34, pl I). At Chesters the construction of the water channel is such that the force of water would be diminished as it passed through the tower. As it enters the tower the channel changes direction and the narrowing of the channel south of the tower by the slabs supporting the covering would tend to pen up water to the north. It seems rather that the water channel was brought through the tower because that was the only course it could take: to the east lay the Wall with a wide earth ramp behind it and to the west the great stone abutment of the bridge some 7m in width. The mill, which the water channel very probably served, would have lain south of the bridge and might yet survive in an exceptional state of preservation beneath the silts deposited by the river along its east bank in post-Roman times. A constant supply of the large volume of water required to drive the mill wheel could have been obtained by con-structing a weir across the river above the bridge to

feed water into the channel.

Finally, the covering of the channel has been thought

> 'to prove the Roman character of the work, for the Military Way in approaching the bridge would pass over the covered-in watercourse'
>
> (Simpson 1976, 46)

The narrowing of the channel immediately south of the tower so that it could be covered by shorter slabs capable of carrying a greater weight than those further south is explained by the existence of the ramp, the base of which will have continued around the south side of the tower (p 27). The contours of the area further south of the tower suggest that much of the remaining length of the channel would have been well below the contemporary ground level; the slabs covering this portion of the channel probably therefore merely supported a covering of earth.

The destruction and decay of the bridge

There are no signs that the bridge fell into disuse or disrepair during the Roman period. No masonry in the fort, particularly in the commanding officer's house, where later Roman modifications are evident, can be identified as material reused from the bridge. The causeway leading to the west abutment is still prominent and shows no surface signs of having been encroached upon by later buildings. The roads which the bridge served, the Stanegate and the Military Way, were both maintained until the end of the Roman period, as far as is known, and certainly until at least the early fourth century, as milestones show (Stanegate: *RIB* 2292, 2297, 2301–2; Military Way: *RIB* 2311).

The only published reference to the possible destruction of any part of the bridge is by Bruce (1863, 75) who mentioned that 'several lairs [layers] of wood-ashes were found' when the interior of the tower was cleared. The letter to Bruce from Fairless already cited (p 5) has a sketch plan of the bridge with an annotation next to the tower stating 'in excavation [of] this chamber 4 lairs of wood-ashes were found.'

However, from the presence or absence of various architectural elements, a certain amount can be deduced about the destruction and decay of the bridge. There seem to have been at least four stages in this process.

First, only one parapet slab (block no 121, Figure 30, no 9 and Figure 32) has been recovered. In view of the large number of other elements from the superstructure probably found between the east abutment and pier, this suggests that most of the parapet slabs had been removed from the bridge for reuse elsewhere. Their thickness of between 100mm and 170mm would have made them suitable for paving slabs.

However many of the blocks which, it is argued elsewhere (p 39) formed a projecting moulded cornice below the parapet, have been recovered, perhaps as many as half the number required to form the length of carriageway between the tower and the east river pier. More of these blocks possibly still lie on the old river bed, along with other elements of the super-structure. As will be noted elsewhere (p 35), voussoir blocks are almost entirely absent and yet, if the bridge had collapsed when the parapet blocks were still in position, the voussoirs would have underlain these elements of the superstructure on the river bed. It seems probable, therefore, that the parapet blocks were deliberately dislodged and pitched into the river while the bridge was still standing. This might well have been an act of purposeful destruction, for the course underlying the parapet blocks might well have been clamped together with iron and lead and also bonded with lead tie-bars. Many Roman buildings which employed these building techniques have suffered from the attentions of robbers intent on recovering iron and lead, which have usually left the surfaces of such structures pockmarked with small holes where the metal clamps have been chiselled out. At Chesters the robbers would have been able to recover several hundredweight of lead and iron merely by levering the parapet blocks out of position. Traces of medieval ironworking at Willowford were probably associated with this kind of activity (p 105).

Even after these two stages in the dismantling of the bridge, its essential fabric was perhaps still intact. Many Roman bridges survive today in a similar state, with their parapets removed or rebuilt in later times but with their arches still standing (eg the *Pons Aelius* at Rome). It is difficult to determine whether the destruction that placed the bridge at Chesters beyond repair and led to its demolition was brought about by the agency of man or by the river itself. However, a collapse of the western side, following an en-croachment by the river seems likely. This would have been a culmination of the process which began after the construction of bridge 1 when the river shifted its course far enough to the west to render the easternmost river arch redundant.

Finally, robbing of the fabric of the bridge followed. In view of the very large quantities of stone involved, this might well have been carried out over a considerable period of time.

There thus seem to have been distinct stages in the decay and destruction of the bridge but the dates of these stages are uncertain. There are however, a few indications that little of the bridge was visible by the later medieval period. The earliest known medieval crossing of the river in the vicinity was at Chollerford Island where the stone bridge probably dated from the thirteenth or early fourteenth century (p 32). By that time the Roman bridge must have been at least beyond repair and was quite possibly already demolished. None of the existing later medieval buildings in the area show reused Roman masonry, which raises questions about which structures were built from the masonry of the bridge. Amongst earlier buildings in the neighbourhood only the church at Warden contains material which might have come from the bridge: a block with a lewis-hole, set on its side to serve as a quoin in the eleventh-century tower (J Gibson 1934, 218). But in addition to Warden, there are other churches in the neighbourhood which

originate in the Anglo-Saxon period but where no fabric of that date remains visible: St Oswald's is mentioned in Bede (III, 2 ; *NCH* iv, 179–80) and Chollerton is perhaps pre-Conquest (ibid, 262); St John Lee is also mentioned by Bede, assuming that it is the church associated with St John of Beverley (V, 2; *NCH* iv, 12). Anglo-Saxon builders favoured construction with large blocks when they were available and the Roman bridge at Corbridge was a probable source of blocks for the crypt of Wilfrid's church at Hexham (p 105). It is even possible that the bridge at Chesters was also a source of stone for other phases at Hexham Abbey. Several of the reused inscriptions must certainly have come from Cor-bridge (e.g. *RIB* 1151, 1172) but others could equally have come from other sites.

Later crossings of the North Tyne at Chollerford

The present bridge is *c* 750m upstream from the Roman bridge and was opened for traffic on 21 April 1775 (*NCH* iv, 169). It was a replacement for a bridge carried away by the great flood of 1771. Two piers shown on the Ordnance Survey 1:2500 map im-mediately south of the present bridge are presumably the remains of this earlier bridge which is shown on the *Original Survey of the Military Road* of *c* 1746 (Lawson 1966). The remains of a third bridge have been found on the east side of Chollerford Island *ic* 250m downstream from the existing bridge. They were first seen in *c* 1865 and then in 1913 were measured by T Hepple and photographed by F G Simpson (G Simpson 1976, 157–8, text fig 19a–c). The masonry seems to represent the east abutment and the whole length of the bridge probably lies on the island.

In 1333 an indulgence was granted by Bishop Skirlaw of Durham for labour or money contributed to the repair of a bridge at Chollerford (*NCH* iv, 169). This was probably the bridge on Chollerford Island for in the medieval period few stone bridges were constructed before the thirteenth century, even on major routes or in cities. It is scarcely conceivable that the bridge which lay just south of the present bridge had been in existence in 1333 for sufficiently long to require major repairs, if it was the successor of the yet earlier stone bridge now on Chollerford Island.

Archaeomagnetic dating of samples from the hearth in the tower of bridge 2, Chesters

by N B Hammo Yassi

Archaeomagnetic dating is based on the fact that the geomagnetic field directions are stored in fired archaeological materials which have remained in position after cooling down from firing. The variation in the directions of the geomagnetic field has been recorded for the last four centuries using observations on suspended magnetised needles. In addition to these direct observations the geomagnetic field directions were recorded using structures which are well dated either by archaeological chronology or by other dating methods (radio-carbon, thermoluminescent etc). The British archaeomagnetic curve covers a period between 50 BC and AD 1600 and the directions after AD 1600 until the present are recorded using direct observations.

Nine samples were collected from an irregularly shaped hearth (context 155, Figure 22–3), of presumed late Roman date, about 0.3m across, in the tower of bridge 2 at Chesters. The hearth comprised of fired clay with colour ranging from red to black. The natural remnant magnetisation of these samples was measured using a Digico magnetometer (Molyneux 1971). The intensities ranged between 16–399 mAm^{-1} and their directions were consistent with each other. AC-demagnetization was carried out at steps of 7.5, 15, 30 and 40mT. The behaviour during demagnetisation was stable as indicated by high

stability indices (Tarling and Symons 1967). The most stable directions were consistent with each other and their mean values where corrected and plotted on the Meridan archaeomagnetic curve (Hammo Yassi 1983) giving an age for the hearth of AD 220 ±10 years.

Table 1   Archaeomagnetic samples from the hearth in the tower of bridge 2 at Chesters

Sample no	Initial Dec	Inc	Most Dec	Inc	stable SI
1	0.2	60.2	1.8	62.2	2.8
2	−7.2	0.3	−3.5	60.0	2.9
3	5.4	57.9	2.4	61.0	2.6
4	7.8	58.7	0.9	62.4	2.8
5	−2.9	58.8	−4.8	62.8	5.2
6	1.5	62.9	0.8	62.1	4.4
7	2.6	56.4	1.8	63.8	2.6
8	7.9	58.5	3.9	64.5	3.0
9	5.5	61.5	2.8	61.4	2.9

Mean value Decrease = 0.2 Increase = 62.2 95 = 1.2 k = 1717
Mean corrected to Meriden Decrease = 0.3 Increase = 60.1

3 Chesters: The superstructure of bridge 2

Introduction

Not a single stone of the superstructure of bridge 2 remains in place but most of the large collection of loose blocks stacked on the wings of the east abutment by the Victorian excavators can be shown to have originated from it. The cataloguing and analysis of these blocks which was carried out when they were moved to a new position in 1983 (p 6) produced enough information to determine the general character of the superstructure and to elucidate some details of its design. A separate catalogue of the blocks is not presented here; their dimensions are set out in Tables 2–3 and where relevant they are described in the following discussion.

One preliminary observation is necessary. The blocks from the superstructure display methods of construction not encountered in the surviving portions of the abutment or river piers: principally band anathyrosis, a method of working the sides of blocks to achieve tight joints (see p 118 and Figure 83), and the use of wooden dowels and of bar clamps of iron set in lead or wholly of lead. There is no reason to take this as evidence of extensive repairs or partial rebuilding. The blocks in addition have features such as feathered tooling and slots for lead tie-bars which also occur in the bases of piers and the abutments. The builders presumably decided that when construction of the bridge had reached a certain height additional methods of securing the solidity of the structure were required.

Previous writers have been unanimous in stating that the piers of the bridge carried a timber carriageway. In 1861 Clayton wrote that

> 'neither amongst these ruins nor in the bed of the river have been found the voussures [sic] of an arch. The inference is that the passage over the river has been upon a horizontal platform.'
>
> Clayton 1865, 84

Clayton was presumably thinking of a wooden platform and J C Bruce soon after declared that

> 'the platform of this bridge was undoubtedly of timber, [adding that] several of the stones ..... have grooves in them for admitting the spars.'
>
> Bruce 1863, 76

In the most recent edition of the *Handbook to the Roman Wall* (Daniels 1978, 108), it is said that the bridge 'undoubtedly carried a timber superstructure' and the same arguments that Bruce and Clayton employed are advanced in justification.

Study of the loose blocks of the superstructure in fact demonstrates that the bridge was wholly of stone.

Voussoirs

The apparent absence of voussoirs amongst the loose blocks from the site is one of the main reasons why it has been thought that the superstructure of the bridge was of timber. But the matter is far from straightforward. In an arch with a span of 10.5m, the voussoirs are likely to be proportionately narrower than in arches of smaller size; they will therefore show less taper and will be more difficult to identify. At Milecastle 37 where the north gate has a span of 3.1m, a voussoir found in position was 0.6m in length and tapers over that distance from 0.33m to 0.48m (Simpson 1976, pl XI). Many other voussoirs of a similar size are lying nearby: 15 would have been required to construct the arch, each voussoir comprising a 12 degree segment of the 180 degrees of the arch. If at Chesters bridge the widths of the voussoirs was comparable to the depth of the blocks used in the east abutment (0.3–0.45m) between 37 and 55 voussoirs, each comprising between 3.3 and 4.9 degrees of the circumference of the arch would have been required. Long, thin voussoirs which taper only slightly are common in the construction of Roman bridge-arches. In Turkey the bridge over the Cendere Çay Figure 28, (in Roman times the *Chabinas*) consists of one great arch 34.2m in width with a ring of about a hundred voussoirs each with a maximum thickness of 0.6m (Humann and Puchstein 1890, 394, Taf XLIII; for smaller arches with thin voussoirs at Rimini and Vaison la Romaine, see Gazzola 1963, 74 (fig) and 129 (fig)). The dimensions of the voussoirs were probably not dictated by the size of the arch but rather by the requirement that they were not too heavy to raise into position.

The differences between voussoirs with these dimensions and blocks used in horizontal courses will be slight. In the east abutment the blocks are generally accurately cut square but there are exceptions and it is common for blocks in structures on Hadrian's Wall to have been cut two or three degrees out of square (Hill 1981, 14–20). In addition in parts of the bridge the lower or upper beds of horizontal courses will have been deliberately cut at an angle to the horizontal, for example in the sixth or seventh course of the east abutment at the point where accommodation is made to incorporate the pier of the earlier bridge within the fabric (p 18). Furthermore, it is unlikely that the voussoirs would have been cut to exactly the same angle. Their thicknesses will have presumably varied according to the size of the rough-outs which the quarry was able to supply (p 117) and this of course will have affected the degree of taper. In spite of these considerations there are six possible voussoirs from Chesters (Block No 30, Figure 30, no 3; and Table 2). They show a tapering of their sides markedly in excess of the divergence from the square of blocks from horizontal courses and are fairly carefully worked. One (block no 52) has been cut down from a larger block; in one of its tapering sides there is a lewis hole, not placed centrally but very close to one edge. Another (block no 53) has three sockets for bar clamps with expanded ends, one containing a fragment of iron set in lead. This block,

Table 2   Possible voussoirs and their dimensions

Number	Length in metres	Depth in metres	Width in metres	Angle of taper
2	0.85	0.38	0.51–0.52	2.5
9	0.87	0.49	0.33–0.41	6.0
30	0.92	0.43	0.33–0.43	6.5
52	1.01	0.34	0.32–0.36	2.5
53	0.81	0.44	0.35–0.41	4.5
97	1.23	0.49	0.23–0.28	3.0

if it is a voussoir, must have been used at the base of the arch; otherwise the sharply inclined angle of the face would have made it impossible to run lead into the sockets for clamps.

Taking the average dimensions of these six possible voussoirs (width 0.43m, tapering at their narrow end to 0.35m), the number of voussoirs needed to construct each arch can be calculated. Given an intrados with a circumference of 16.5m, about 47 voussoirs would be required for each ring. The width of the bridge is 6.6m, so a total of about 730 voussoirs would be required for each arch. This of course assumes that the entire width of the intrados was formed by voussoirs, which is probable but by no means absolutely certain. Occasionally ribbed construction is encountered, as in a bridge at Narbonne (von Hagen 1967, 204–5).

This calculation throws up another problem. Although only six voussoirs have been recognised, a far greater number of cornice blocks, 33 in all, have been recovered. When measured against the number of such moulded stones which originally existed, these form 50 per cent of such blocks required for both the upstream and downstream faces of the bridge between the abutment and the nearest river pier (p 40). It might thus have been expected that a very much larger number of voussoirs would have come to light. If the notion that the superstructure of the bridge was of timber is discounted (see also p 40), only one other explanation for their scarcity seems possible and that is concerned with the history of robbing, demolition or collapse of the bridge already discussed in full in chapter 2.

The preceding discussion has indicated that there are a few blocks from the site which might well have

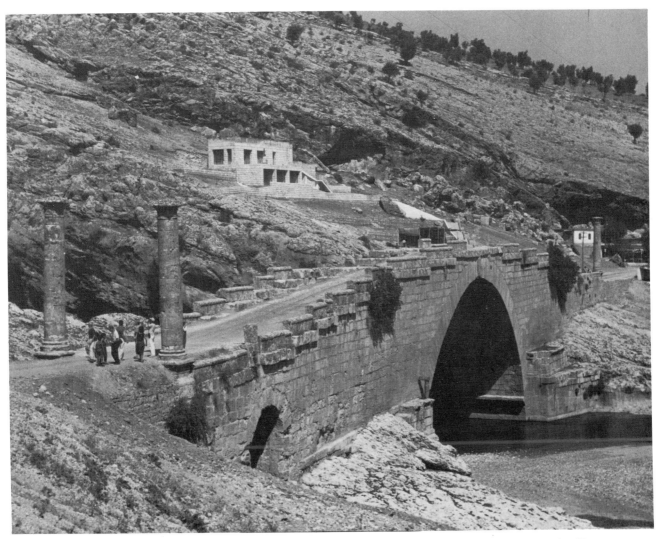

Figure 28   Bridge over the Cendere Çay in Cappadocia showing the downstream side.   (Photo P T Bidwell)

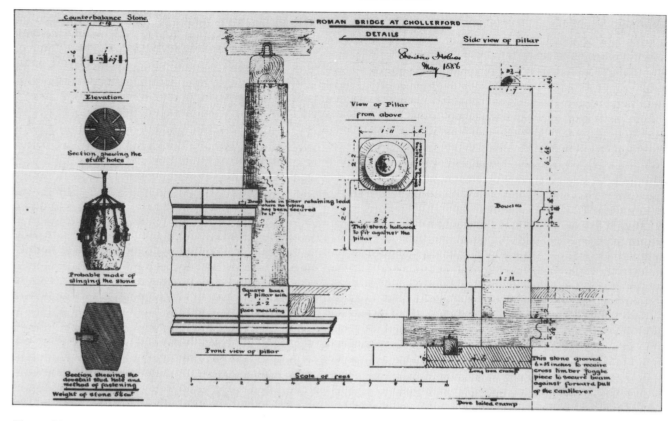

Figure 29   Holmes' reconstruction of the parapet and other details of bridge 2 (Holmes 1894, pl 26)

been voussoirs, and that in any event there is a possible explanation for their virtual or complete absence. To follow Clayton (1865,64), and Bruce (1863,76) in arguing that the superstructure of the bridge was of timber because of the absence of voussoirs would clearly be wrong but the evidence presented above hardly proves beyond reasonable doubt that it was of stone. The true character of the superstructure is determined by the cornice blocks and other architectural elements considered in the sections below.

Cornice blocks

In addition to the absence of voussoirs, Bruce further reasoned that the superstructure of the bridge had been of timber because

> 'several of the stones which lie on the ground have grooves in them for ad- mitting spars.'
>
> Bruce 1863, 76

Bruce could only have been referring to a group of 33 blocks loose on the site which have mouldings cut along one of their short sides or exceptionally along one of their long sides. On many of these blocks there are grooves on the upper surfaces parallel to the mouldings. To Holmes (1894, 333, pl XXVI and XXVIII) these blocks

> 'apparently formed an ornamental string course along the face of the abutment.'[cf Figure 29]

Bruce ignored Holmes's views and retained Bruce's

description until Richmond (1957, 85) conjectured that the grooves were 'for admitting the rails', later amended to 'timbers' (Daniels 1978, 108). However, close examination of all these blocks, which was not possible until 1983, has yielded sufficient information to show that none of these previous interpretations is satisfactory. That the mouldings formed a project- ing cornice or string course is not in doubt but the purpose of the grooves and position the blocks occupied can be seen to have been very different from those previously suggested.

The blocks are in general very carefully worked. Six have band anathyrosis (p 118) and when this technique is not employed the sides of the blocks have been dressed flat with a point or punch. By far the largest number have mouldings cut across their ends and these blocks have generally been worked so that their length is almost exactly twice their width (eg blocks nos 7; 25; 28; 31; 43, Figure 30 no 3; 82; 96, Figure 31; and Table 3), their dimensions corresponding more or less to a measurement of four Roman feet by two. Only two blocks have sockets for clamps in their upper surfaces but a number have dowel holes in their undersides (p 128ff). Seven blocks have lewis holes, all traces of which may have been removed from the other blocks by dressing of their surfaces after they were set in position (p 120) and by subsequent wear. The mouldings are generally *c* 150mm deep with fillets delimiting their upper edges. They generally extend between a third and a half of the thickness of a block. Two types can be distinguished.

In the first (type 1), the moulding is of a

pronounced reversed S-shape (*cyma recta*) with the upper part cut back further than the projecting belly of the basal recurve (blocks nos 83; 43; 120, Figure 30, nos 4–6). Thirteen examples of this type are known and this moulding also occurs on the base of the complete column (Figure 33, no 1, and Figure 34). The second type of moulding (Type 2) can be distinguished by the shallow profile of its upper part which is not cut back further than the basal recurve. Eighteen examples of this type are known.

There are two further fragmentary blocks (blocks nos 35 and 72, Table 3) with grooves on their upper surfaces, but with their front ends broken away.

The blocks can also be sub-divided according to the presence or absence of grooves. Twenty-two of the blocks have grooves on their upper surface, nine with mouldings of Type 1, eleven with Type 2, and two where the mouldings are missing. The grooves continue across the whole width of the blocks at a distance of between 0.18 and 0.28m from the edges

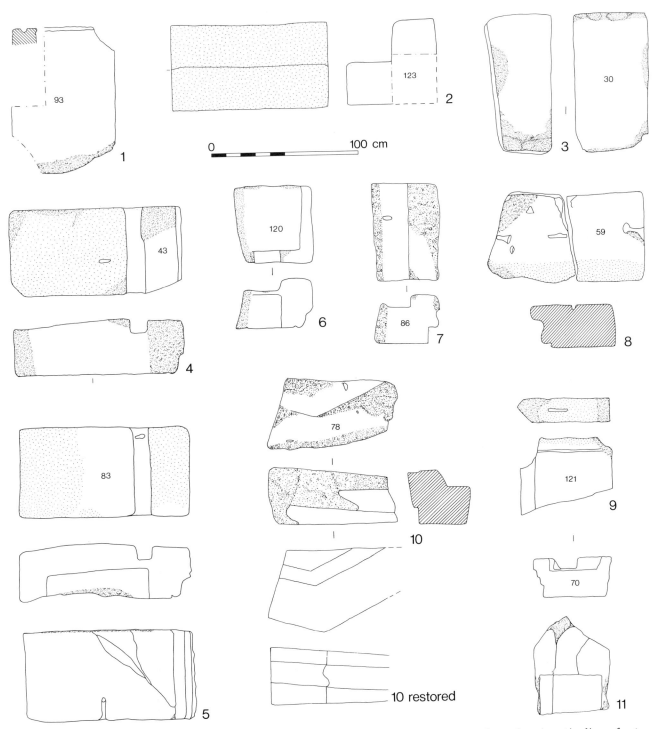

Figure 30 Blocks from bridge 2 at Chesters. Areas of light stipple denote worn surfaces; heavier stippling, fractured surfaces. Scale 1:25

Table 3 Dimensions and details of cornice blocks from Bridge 2, Chesters

Block no	Mouding Type 1	Type 2	Groove	Wear	Lewis	Complete ?	Band Anathyrosis	Dowel	Length m	Width m	Thick m	Groove Width m	Groove Depth m
7	-	*	-	-	-	*	-	*	1.17	0.55	0.32	-	-
25	-	*	-	-	*	*	*	*	1.13	0.57	0.38	-	-
28	-	*	-	-	-	*	-	-	1.22	0.60	0.31	-	-
31	-	*	-	-	-	*	-	-	1.10	0.58	0.34	-	-
35	?	?	*	*	*	-	*	-	1.13	0.61	0.32	?	?
41	-	*	?	?	?	-	?	?	0.24+	0.52	0.32	?	?
43	-	*	*	*	*	*	*	-	1.16	0.60	0.33	0.13	0.10
57	*	-	*	?	?	-	?	?	0.35+	0.30+	0.26	?	0.10
58	*	-	*	?	?	-	?	?	0.35+	0.28+	0.28	?	0.095
59	*	-	-	-	*	-	-	-	0.56	1.02	0.28	-	-
64	*	-	*	?	?	?	?	?	0.50+	0.45+	0.24	0.17+	0.095
72	?	?	*	-	*	-	-	-	0.87+	0.67	0.24	0.15+	0.10
75	*	-	*	?	?	-	?	?	0.40+	0.45	0.26	0.145	0.095
77	*	-	*	-	*	-	-	?	0.56+	0.57	0.37	0.15	0.10
78	*	-	*	-	-	-	-	-	0.92	0.55	0.23	0.25+	0.095
79	-	*	*	*	-	*	-	-	1.12	0.63	0.37	0.13	0.09
80	-	*	*	?	?	-	-	?	0.54+	0.52	0.36	0.11	0.08
81	*	-	*	-	-	*	-	-	0.54	0.64	0.27	0.16	0.10
82	-	*	*	-	-	-	-	-	0.80+	0.55	0.34	0.13	0.09
83	-	*	*	-	?	*	*	-	1.17	0.57	0.38	0.10	0.09
85	-	*	*	?	-	-	?	-	0.78+	0.37+	0.34	0.13	0.09
86	*	-	*	?	?	-	?	?	0.46+	0.63	0.29	0.16+	0.10
87	-	*	*	*	-	*	*	-	1.16	0.63	0.30	0.13	0.095
88	-	*	*	?	?	-	?	?	0.43+	0.55	0.29	0.15	0.095
90	-	*	?	?	-	-	-	-	1.10+	0.54	0.38	?	?
91	-	*	*	?	-	-	-	?	0.70+	0.55	0.39	0.09	0.055
96	-	*	*	*	-	*	*	-	1.12	0.56	0.37	0.12	0.065
98	*	-	*	?	?	-	?	?	0.48	0.40	0.29	0.16	0.09
101	*	-	*	?	-	-	-	-	0.55	0.65+	0.29	0.15	0.10
115	*	-	*	?	?	-	?	?	0.60+	0.66	0.24	?	?
117	*	-	-	?	*	-	?	-	0.69	0.68+	0.29	-	-
120	-	*	*	-	-	-	*	-	0.58+	0.50+	0.35	0.17	0.095
122	-	*	?	?	?	-	?	?	0.62+	0.37+	0.26+	-	-

* = present, - = absent, ? = uncertain

Figure 31 Underside of block no 96 from Chesters, with moulding of Type 2, scale 0.5m. (Photo: P T Bidwell)

above the mouldings. Only one block, of Type 1, has a moulding cut along its length (block no 101, Table 3). The grooves have vertical sides with flat bases, their widths varying from block to block between 100 and 170mm and their depths between 90 and 100mm with three shallower examples (55mm, 65mm and 80mm deep). Some grooves have shallow sinkings in their bases which appear to be crowbar slots (eg block no 86, Figure 30, no 7; block no 83, Figure 30, no 5; blocks nos 64; 82; and 101, Table 3).

Of the six examples without grooves, four (blocks nos 7; 25; 28; and 31; Table 3) have mouldings of Type 2 cut across their ends. The other two have mouldings of Type 1 (Block no 59, Figure 30, no 8; and no 117). Block no 117 has a moulding cut across its end but on block no 59 the moulding is cut along the side of the block, one end of which is cut at an angle presumably reflecting a change of direction in the line of the cornice. On the upper surface a zone extending *c* 150mm back from the side with the moulding is heavily weathered; beyond this zone the original tooling is preserved. None of the other blocks displays weathering although some are slightly water-worn.

Most of the moulded blocks with grooves display considerable wear on their upper surfaces, confined entirely to the area behind the grooves and usually more pronounced towards the inner ends of the blocks. The surfaces between the grooves and the outer edges show only slight wear consistent with natural weathering. Given this contrast, the wear behind the slots would seem to have been the product of traffic. There is no difficulty in distinguishing it from the action of water on some of the blocks; in these examples the edges are rounded and the wear extends over all or part of two or more surfaces.

The purpose of the grooves in the cornice blocks

The previous interpretations of the use to which these blocks were put, already noted above, can be discarded. Bruce's belief that the grooves were 'for admitting spars' (1863, 75) to support a timber platform takes no account of the evident wear on the upper surfaces of the blocks. Holmes' interpretation was more elaborate (1894, pl XXVI and XXVIII, cf Figures 26 and 29). His illustrations show blocks with mouldings of Type 1 forming a string course immediately below the upper course of the abutment and blocks with mouldings of Type 2 forming the ornamental top of a parapet *c* 0.75m in width. Once again, this does not account for the wear on the blocks nor does it explain the purpose of the grooves.

That the blocks with mouldings and grooves formed the uppermost course of some part of the bridge or its east abutment is clear from the pattern of wear on their upper surfaces. The presence of what seem to be crowbar slots on the bottom of some of the grooves suggests that they held upright slabs rather than the rails suggested by Richmond (1957, 85). One fragment from the site is almost certainly from one of these upright slabs (block no 121, Figure 30, no 9 and Figure 32). It measures 0.64m in width and is 0.17–0.18m thick; the lower part has been broken away but its height was originally at least 0.5m. The top has a simple curved moulding along either side and shows some wear; in the centre is a lewis hole (see further p 121). One face of the slab has bold diagonal tooling delimited on one side by a margin 50mm wide which has been dressed flat. The opposite side has been cut diagonally to form a mitred joint with a neighbouring slab of the same thickness and the outer edge is bevelled. The other face of the slab has been dressed flat across its whole width. These features are in accord with the use of the slab as part of a parapet slotted into the grooves in the upper surfaces of the cornice blocks. The width of the slab is greater than many of the grooves but those in block nos 64; 78, Figure 30, no 10; 86, Figure 30, no 7; and 120, Figure 30, no 4 are wide enough to accommodate it. The angle of about 45 degrees at which one side is cut roughly matches the angle of the face on block no 78 (p 40).

The purpose of the cornice blocks is now clear. They formed the uppermost course on some part of the bridge and the grooves found on the majority of the blocks accommodated the upright slabs of a parapet (cf Figure 91). The use of large slabs to form parapets seems to have been common in Roman bridge construction to judge from surviving examples but the few detailed illustrations do not show them bedded in slots. For example at Rumkale in Turkey the parapet was formed by blocks 0.88m in height and 0.5m in width which were sufficiently wide in proportion to their height not to require any form of seating (Wagner 1972, 681, Abb 4 citing three other bridges with similar parapets in Turkey). Durm (1905, Abb 535) gives sketches of two rather more elaborate parapets from the Pont de Vaison (see also Gazzola 1963, 129) and the Ponte Salario, consisting of long, fairly wide blocks of no great height alternating with uprights of square section, their tops elaborately carved. In other structures on the northern frontier of Britain methods of constructing parapets or screens in the same fashion as at Chesters occur commonly, particularly in headquarters buildings to screen the openings between the *aedes* and its flanking rooms and the cross hall (the best example is at *Vindolanda*, see R Birley 1977, pl 50; other examples listed in Bidwell and Speak forthcoming). The cornice blocks which surmounted the fortress wall at Chester also had grooves on their upper surfaces to accommodate the base of a crenellated parapet (Strickland 1982, 1983; the parapet was presumably of small coursed masonry).

The position of the parapet and cornice

The principal evidence for the position of the parapet is furnished by the large number of cornice blocks which have been recovered; it can be calculated that together the cornice blocks represent a length of just under 21m. The complete blocks form a run 15.185m in length to which must be added the width (0.57m)

Figure 32   Parapet slab, block no 121, from Chesters, scale 0.5.   (Photo: P T Bidwell)

Conversely there are too many cornice blocks to have belonged solely to parapets on either side of the carriageway between the west face of the tower and the abutment face, a distance of 6.55m.

The only other conceivable position for the cornice blocks is flanking the carriageway of a bridge with stone arches. The principal objection to the positions discussed above, that there are too many cornice blocks, does not apply in this instance. The length of the bridge which fell within the area of the excavations in 1860–3 extended from the west face of the tower probably as far as the east river pier (p 6), a length of about 22m. That half of the original number of cornice blocks should have been recovered from this length might seem remarkable in view of the thorough robbing of certain parts of the bridge but an explanation probably lies in the history of the destruction of the bridge, as already noted (p 32).

The cornice blocks could only have formed the parapet of the bridge and they thus provide the principal reason for considering the bridge to have been built entirely in stone.

of the moulding on the cornice block to which the column is attached (Figure 33, no 1, and Figure 34). Seven further though fragmentary blocks, if all regarded as of the type with the moulding cut across the end of the block, would represent an additional run of 4.165m (the average width of complete blocks of this type is 0.595m). For the purposes of this calculation the fragmentary block with a moulding cut along its length (block no 101) is regarded as having an original length of 1.02m, the same as the complete block of this type (block no 59, Figure 30, no 8). The total length of the run represented is 20.94m. It is of course impossible to guess how many more blocks are to be found on the old river bed. The discovery of five blocks (nos 90–1; 117; 120, Figure 30, no 6; and 122) in front of the abutment during the limited excavations of 1982–3 suggests that the number is likely to be considerable.

Four possible positions for the parapet can be suggested. Clayton (1865, 82) mentions a parapet on his 'platform of approach' but as already noted (p 27) he seems to have assumed rather than proved its existence. In any event the blocks seem all to have come from the river bed between the east abutment and pier.

Holmes's alternative interpretation (1894, 333) of the cornice blocks as a string course along the wings of the abutment and as the capping stones of a parapet wall has already been rejected (p 36). His view that the Military Way approached the bridge from the south-east, skirting the tower, has also been doubted (p 27). In addition, the length of the south wing (excluding the later southern extension) is 12.8m which is far too short for all the cornice blocks. His suggestion that the parapet also ran along the north wing has nothing to recommend it. Such a parapet would serve no useful purpose for the north wing was there to protect the bridge and not to form the base of a sort of esplanade. Furthermore, the north wing seems to survive to its full height (p 19).

Other types of cornice blocks

Having established the positions which the cornice and the parapet occupied, it is now possible to suggest the purpose of some other blocks with mouldings which do not belong to the types already discussed.

Block no 78 (Figure 30, no 10), a much damaged block, was originally at least 0.92m in length, its width at least 0.55m, and its thickness 0.37m. There had been a groove on its upper surface, although only the side nearest the moulding survives. The width of the groove seems to have been at least 0.25m. Near the centre of the block the groove turns through an angle of about 40 degrees which is the same as the angle made by the faces of the wings and the abutment at their points of junction. The moulding is poorly preserved but sufficient remains to show that it was of Type 1 and that it also turned through an angle. Another notable feature of this block is that the moulding is not cut horizontally across the two angled faces but at an angle of about 6 degrees, that is, at the same angle as the moulding cut across the base of the column (p 46). This shows that at least part of the cornice and parapet was on an incline but it is significant that these sloping mouldings are only to be seen on two blocks with special functions. The easiest way to form a continuous moulding on an incline is to cut at an angle the upper surface of the course below the blocks with mouldings. The upper course along the face from which the moulding was to be cut would then consist of rectangular blocks of regular thickness, their angle achieved by their position on the bridge not from special masoncraft in the cutting of the mouldings. This was the method which was adopted in the Ponte Nascoso at Civitatomasso and in a bridge at Pollenza (Gazzola 1963, 55, 76). An alternative method was employed in the bridge over the Cendere Çay in Turkey, where the cornice and parapet were stepped

The columns

up at regular intervals as the carriageway ascended to pass over the single great arch of the bridge (Humann and Puchstein 1890, Taf, XLIII, and Figure 28).

Block nos 70, Figure 30, no 11; and 71 both have stepped mouldings with identical profiles cut across two adjacent faces which meet at an angle of about 135 degrees . Their upper surfaces have grooves of the same general dimensions as those on the cornice blocks with mouldings of Types 1 and 2. They were presumably likewise intended to accommodate parapet slabs. On both blocks the grooves lead into larger rectangular recesses which are probably seatings for steles. On the undersides of both blocks are holes to receive the upper ends of wooden dowels (cf p 128). The blocks have been carefully tooled with a point or punch.

Both blocks were illustrated in watercolour by Mossman (unpublished: interleaved in a copy of Bruce 1867 in the John Collingwood Bruce Collection at South Shields Museum) and a section through block no 2 was published by Holmes (1894, pl XXVII). The latter considered that the blocks were from a cornice below the 'parapet of the castellum' (tower) but this does not account for the angle formed by the two faces with mouldings. The significance of these blocks is discussed further on p 47 Block no 120 (Figure 30, no 6) was found immediately in front of the south wing of the abutment at a point 4.0m south of the angle of the main abutment, in modern material which had accumulated against the face of the wing since its excavation in 1860–3. It has a moulding of Type 2 cut across its face; the width of the block is 0.5m, its thickness 0.35m and its length has been in excess of 0.585m (the rear of the block is broken away). Most of the upper surface is occupied by a recess 0.10m in depth and measuring 0.42m across the width of the block; its length has been in excess of 0.37m. On one side the recess either continued across the surface of the adjacent block or the adjacent block formed the side of the recess. On the opposite side the recess does not extend as far as the edge of the block but the higher surface beyond the recess ends in a vertical face 0.09m in height, 0.18m from the front of the block; this is almost certainly the outer edge of a groove to accommodate a parapet slab.

The recess was presumably to accommodate the base of some feature such as a column or stele which was set in the line of the parapet. The presence of a crowbar slot in the base of the recess suggests that whatever the feature, it was probably a later insertion. The slot would have been covered by the object placed in the recess but it is in line with the groove on the opposite side of the block; crowbar slots occur in the base of the grooves for parapet slabs (p 20) and it seems probable that on this block the groove originally extended across the whole width of the block and was removed when the slightly deeper recess was cut.

For the significance of these blocks in a possible reconstruction of the bridge see p 46–7.

By far the largest architectural fragment from the site is a roughly cylindrical column attached to a rectangular block which has a moulding of Type 1 cut across its face at an angle of four degrees to the horizontal. The lower part of another column was recovered from the river bed in front of the abutment in 1983 and fragments of a third column are mentioned in the account of the excavations in 1860–3, one such fragment being found on the south wing of the east abutment in 1983. A fragment of a fourth column mentioned by Holmes (1894, 334) is now stored behind the baths on the west side of the river. Before these fragments are described in detail, it should be noted that they are not columns in the usual sense. They lack mouldings at either the base or the top, they are not completely circular in section. Figure 33, no 1, and Figure 34 a complete column (or section of a column) attached to a base which has a moulding of Type 1 cut ross one face. Overall length 2.828m; maximum diameter of column of top 0.564m, increasing to a maximum diameter of 0.632m at the base; overall height of column 2.01m and of base 0.66m. Much of the surface is weathered but the marks of a chisel or axe are in evidence near the base. In one side of the column there is a dowel hole containing the remains of a lead bar 52mm by 20mm in section.

The column was first mentioned by J C Bruce in the *Wallet-Book of the Roman Wall* (1863, 78) and was presumably found in the excavations between the east abutment and east pier of bridge 2 which took place in late 1862 or in January 1863 (p 6).

The feature that allows us without hesitation to allocate the column a place in the parapet is the moulding of Type 1 cut across the block forming its base. Details of the way in which it was fitted into the cornice and parapet are readily apparent. The moulding is not cut across the lower edge of the base as are the mouldings on the cornice blocks; instead the bottom of the moulding is 100–135mm above the lower edge of the base which probably sat in a recess cut into the top of the course below the cornice blocks. Other differences are that the face is stepped back above the moulding by 20mm and that the height between the moulding and the base of the column itself is 0.32m, considerably higher than the depth between the mouldings and upper surfaces of the cornice blocks.

Figure 33, no 2 this fragment was found in Trench 6 (Figure 15) on the river bed in front of the abutment lying in gravel deposited by the river (context 352, Figure 4). Its overall height is 1.17m including a base 0.34m in height which is roughly square in section (0.55m by 0.52m). The column is not circular but, as in the case of Figure 33, no 1, has a square section with rounded corners. Its maximum width is 0.585m, its minimum width 0.52m. In the sides of the column are two irregular recesses, one measuring 70mm by 70mm by 60mm in depth, the other 100mm high, 50mm wide and 30mm in depth. These probably held dowels for the adjacent slabs of the parapet. They are disposed so as to suggest that the column stood at a point where the parapet changed its alignment through an angle of about 25 degrees. This is rather less than the angle of about 40 degrees made by the junction of the wings and the abutment and also the corresponding angle of the cornice block no 78 (Figure 30, no 10) described above. However, the position of the dowel holes would only be a reliable guide to the angle made by the two lengths of parapet if they were set out so that their alignments converged at the centre point of the column and this might not have been so.

Holmes also noted fragments of a second column found in 1860–3

> 'there are also portions of a similar column [i e similar to Figure 33, no 1] which has been broken up. The upper end of it is now on the abutment amongst the ruins, and what appears to be a portion of the shaft, about four feet [1.2m] long, with a dowel hole cut in a similar manner to that in the entire column, is now placed in an angle of the building on the west side of the river.'

Holmes 1894, 333–4

The building referred to is the baths and the fragment is still there lying in the corner formed by the recess for the hot bath and the apse of the *caldarium*. It is 0.9m in height and measures 0.5m by 0.47m in its section which resembles those of Figure 33, nos 1–2 in being squarish. Both ends are fractured and there is a socket 60mm in height, 30mm in width and 30mm deep in the side of the column 300mm from one end.

The fragment on the abutment to which Holmes was presumably referring was found again in 1983; it was 0.55m in height and 0.5m thick but preserved rather less than half of the width of the column.

Whether Holmes was correct in assuming that these two fragments were from the same column is uncertain. It is difficult to understand why the undistinguished fragment stored by the baths was selected from the large number of architectural fragments on the east side of the river for removal; it might perhaps have been found on the west bank of the river. On the other hand the small fragment noted above might perhaps have come from the missing upper part of column no 2. All that can be said is that in addition to the complete column two other columns are probably represented by the fragments and quite possibly three.

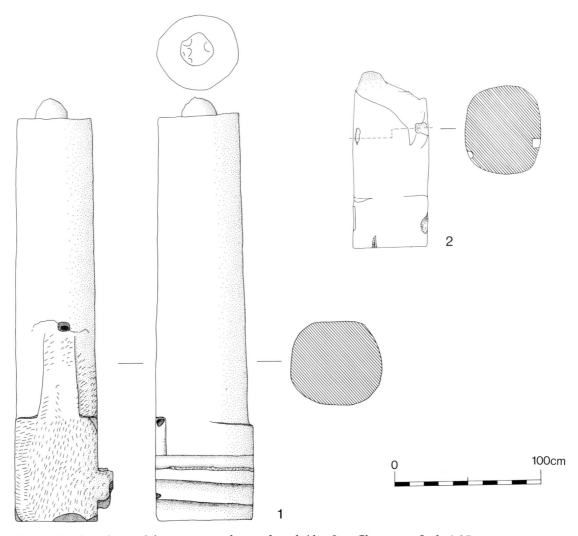

Figure 33   Complete and fragmentary columns from bridge 2 at Chesters.   Scale 1:25

Figure 34   Column no 1 from bridge 2 at Chesters, scale 10.5m.   (Photo: P T Bidwell)

Bridges with parapets incorporating columns and other elements

Few Roman bridges with arches still standing preserve remains of their parapets but of those which do there are a number which incorporate columns and sometimes other elements. In some cases at least, the columns carried statues.

The only bridge where columns still remain standing is that over the Cendere Çay (the ancient *Chabinas*) in Turkey (Humann and Puchstein 1890, 393–7, Taf XLIII) (Figure 28). Pairs of columns stood at either end of the parapets, each inscribed with a dedication made in AD 200 to one of the Severan imperial family: dedications to Septimius Severus, Julia Domna and Caracalla survive (Leaning 1971); the column that is missing no doubt carried the name and titles of Geta and was probably destroyed following his *damnatio memoriae*. The columns stand on square bases and have an overall height of 8.51m, the width of the shafts tapering from a diameter of 1.0m to 0.9m. They are surmounted by capitals with simple palm-leaf decoration and are thought to have each carried a statue of a member of the imperial family. The parapets also incorporated four steles, three of which survive in position. They carry imperial dedications and record the construction of the bridge by the Sixteenth Legion during the governorship of L Alfenus Senecio. By the side of each is a small altar. L Alfenius Seneco was later governor of Britain in *c* 205–7 when bridge 2 at Chesters was probably built (pp 28, 138ff).

A medallion of Hadrian bearing the obverse legend **HADRIANVS AUG COS III PP** has on the reverse a representation of the *Pons Aelius* across the Tiber at Rome. It shows a bridge with three main arches and smaller arches under ramps of approach on either side. Above the springings of the main arches are tall columns on either side of the carriageway, numbering eight in all and surmounted by statues (Gnecchi 1912, vol 2, tav 42, no 4)

The *Pons Aemilius* at Rome is apparently portrayed on an ancient wall-painting which came to light on the Esquiline in 1668, this shows two double arches and two pairs of columns surmounted by statues on the carriageway of the bridge (Hülsen 1896).

The bridge across the Mosel at Trier originally consisted of nine stone piers carrying a timber carriageway (Cüppers 1969). An engraving of 1670 shows it with a column of square section and a projecting cap on the third pier from the west on the upstream side and a pair of columns of similar type on the fifth pier (ibid, Abb 10). The text of the work in which this engraving was published mentions that the columns had carried spheres and statues (ibid 18–19). An earlier description in 1584, gives more detail

> *'columnae..semiquadratae ex singulis lapidibus altero alteri superposito, quae paullum exstant supra pontis marginem; in his deorum olim fuisse simulacra referebant'*
> (half-square columns of single stones laid on top of each other, which project slightly beyond the edge of the bridge; on top of these there were formerly statues of gods.)
>
> ibid 17

Whether columns had once stood on other piers is uncertain but presumably for reasons of symmetry there were columns on the downstream side of the third and fifth piers from the west.

In 1835 two columns were found standing on the north side of the bridge over the Rede at Risingham. They were removed but still survive and one is illustrated here (Figure 81, and see p 113). Two columns were also found in 1813 and 1815 on the north side of the road bridge over the Eden at Carlisle, and in 1951 a column was recovered from near the site of the road bridge (p 109; Caruana and Coulston 1987, 49).

A series of glass flasks showing views of *Baiae* and *Puteoli* include among the representations of various buildings piers or moles carried on arches. These had pairs of columns surmounted by statues. Painter (1975, 64) in his consideration of these flasks wrote that it is 'likely that the views show buildings which really existed and not generalised scenes.'

These examples are sufficient to show that free-standing columns on bridges were a widespread form of adornment: the examples cited above range from Britain to Turkey and include not only two of the principal bridges of Rome but also the two much smaller bridges at Risingham and Carlisle in a distant frontier area. Whether these columns always supported statues as in the case of the *Pons Aelius* and the *Pons Aemilius* and apparently of the bridges at Trier and over the Cendere Çay (Figure 28) is impossible to determine; some perhaps were merely surmounted by decorated capitals.

In the light of these examples the columns at Chesters can now be recognised as decorative elements; they were not, as Holmes (1894) suggested, part of a curious drawbridge system (cf Figure 26) and neither were they

> 'bollards [which may have been] to carry gratings, chains or hecks, slung across the river downstream from the bridge, to catch anyone passing below it'

Richmond 1966, 82

(elaborating an idea first proposed in Collingwood 1933, 74–5)

The tenon on top of the column, Figure 33, no 1 and 34, was presumably to secure an additional length of column; the existing length is too short to have supported a decorative capping if an approximation to the usual proportions of classical architecture was intended. This method of joining two lengths of column is unusual; dowels were generally employed for this purpose (Lugli 1957, fig 59). However several examples of mortises and tenons can be seen at Nemrud Dǎg in eastern Turkey, the *hierothesion* of Antiochus I, King of Commagene, where they were used to join together not only lengths of column, as in Figure 35, but also various elements of the colossal statues which lined one side of the east and west terraces.

Of the decorative cappings of these columns, no remains have been recovered. By analogy with columns of other bridges (p 43), we might expect that they supported decorated capitals perhaps surmounted by statues; these might still lie in the river bed if they were thrown in when the parapets were demolished (p 32). There is a Corinthian capital from Chesters, first described by Hodgson (1840, 183), but the diameter of its shaft (0.385m) is too small for the

columns of the bridge. Blagg (1980–1, 31–33) described it as an evolved form of an east Mediterranean fashion which was probably carved after the middle of the third century.

A possible reconstruction of bridge 2

In the preceding sections much has already been established about the overall form of the bridge: the piers supported arches and the carriageway over the arches had parapets of upright slabs set in the tops of cornice blocks; at intervals the parapet was interrupted by columns and perhaps other features. The tower, it has been suggested, served as the base of a gate-house or arch at the level of the carriageway. But with the evidence to hand it is possible to go further: the minimum height of the bridge can be established; details of its plan at the level of the carriageway can be suggested and there are also possible indications of the positions occupied by some architectural fragments which have not yet been considered in detail (Figures 36 and 37, Plate 8 and the front cover).

The height of the bridge will have been the sum of the radius of the intrados of the arches (5.25m), the depth of the voussoirs (c 1.2m, the largest example in Table 2), the depth of the cornice blocks and of an underlying course (c 0.7m) giving a total of c 7.15m. The only other factor to be considered is the position from which the arches sprang and this would seem to be indicated by the construction technique of the east abutment and its wing-walls. Unfortunately at

Figure 35   Length of column with a tenon cut in the top of the drum; from Nemrud Dag, Cappadocia, mid first century BC.   (Photo P T Bidwell)

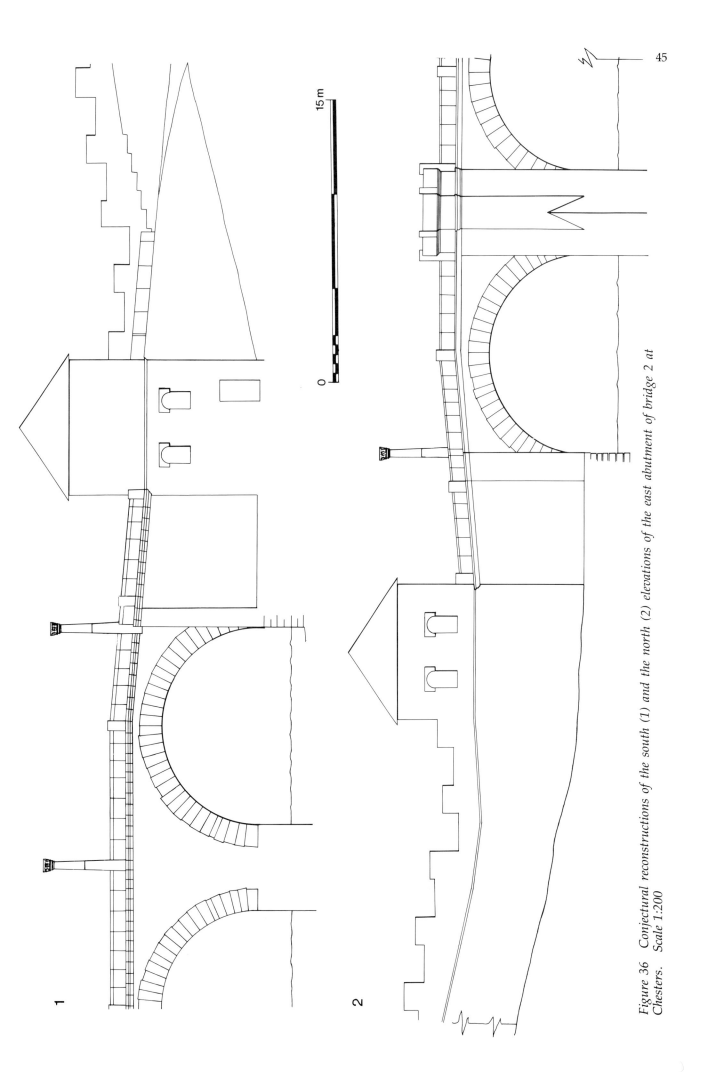

1

2

15 m

0

45

Figure 36   Conjectural reconstructions of the south (1) and the north (2) elevations of the east abutment of bridge 2 at Chesters.   Scale 1:200

the front of the east abutment base only five courses of blocks have survived later robbing, although the position of crowbar slots shows that the sixth course had consisted of stretchers (p 18). The arch might perhaps have been constructed from immediately above the sixth course but the remains of the seventh and eighth courses by the tower consist of blocks of the same type as those used in the rest of the abutment base and wing-walls. It will be argued elsewhere that different construction techniques, including the use of dowels, clamps and band anathyrosis, occurred in the superstructure (p 117). Because of this the arch is likely to have been built above the level of the abutment base, which would have had an overall height of 3.0m. To this figure can be added the height of c 7.15m allowed for the arch, voussoirs and cornice (see above) to produce an overall estimated height of c 10.15m for the bridge from the river bed below the abutment base to the level of the carriageway. It should be noted that the ramp leading to the west abutment still survives to a height of c 8.6m above the river bed (p 15).

There are two architectural fragments from the east side of the bridge with cornice mouldings cut across their faces at an angle. One is the column with its attached base (Figure 33, no 1, and Figure 34, p 41) which probably stood above the point where the arch sprang from the east abutment . The moulding of Type 1 is cut across the base at an angle of 4 degrees to the horizontal. The second fragment (block no 78, Figure 30, no 10) which is poorly preserved also has a moulding of Type 2, cut along two faces. These meet at an angle corresponding to that which would have been formed at the point where the abutment began to narrow to accommodate itself to the width

of the bridge (cf Figure 36). The angle of the moulding to the horizontal is about 6 degrees. A slope of about 5 degrees is thus indicated by the angles of the two mouldings; as can be seen from Figure 36, south elevation, an incline of precisely 5 degrees is required to take the Military Way from the top of the slope above the river up to the level of the carriageway above the easternmost arch. It is thus possible to restore in outline the elevation of the bridge with some confidence.

Some of the architectural fragments raise difficult questions about the superstructure of the bridge above the level of the carriageway which can only be settled, if at all, by the recovery of more blocks from the river bed. One problem concerns the positions which the two types of cornice mouldings occupied. On the base of the complete column the moulding, which is of Type 1, slopes down from left to right showing that the column was set in the southern parapet. This might be taken to suggest that the cornice blocks with mouldings of Type 1 also came from the south side of the bridge, and those with mouldings of Type 2 from the north side.

However, there is a second cornice block with a moulding of Type 1 cut across an angled face (block no 59; Figure 30, no 8). The moulding is horizontal, so it cannot have come from a position corresponding to that suggested for block no 78 (Figure 30, no 10) on the north side of the east abutment. But block no 78 has been attributed to the only acute angle which occurs on the south side of the bridge at its east end (cf Figure 36, south elevation, and Figure 37). If the possibility that block no 59 had been transported from the west abutment is excluded, which seems justifiable, the only possible position for it would be

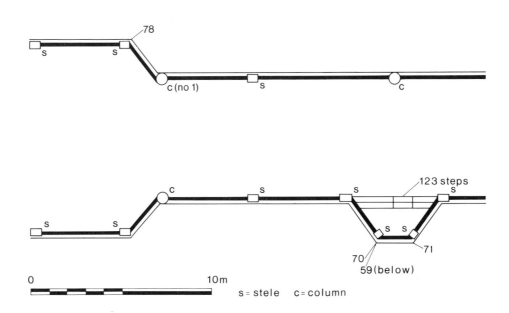

Figure 37   Plan of the carriageway of Bridge 2 at Chesters, (numbers are block nos).   Scale 1:200

on the north side of the bridge. As will be suggested in the following paragraphs, it may have formed part of an elaborate structure over one of the cutwaters, the presence of which could account for other unusual features occurring on a number of other cornice blocks. At the outset it should be noted that if block no 59 came from the north side of the bridge, the simple explanation which has been proposed above for the presence of two types of cornice mouldings, that Types 1 and 2 came respectively from the south and north sides of the carriageway, fails.

Block no 59 has no slot to accommodate parapet slabs and at either end of the block are sockets for T-shaped clamps. This shows that above this cornice block there were further courses of masonry. Five other cornice blocks exist which lack slots for parapet slabs (block no 117 with a moulding of Type 1; blocks nos 7; 25; 28; and 31 with mouldings of Type 2) and two of these (blocks nos 25 and 117) have sockets for T-shaped clamps. They suggest that at some point at the east end of the bridge there was a considerable mass of masonry above the level of the cornice which perhaps had coincided with the junctions of mouldings cut to slightly different profiles by two sets of masons. A possible indication of the position occupied by this structure is supplied by a pair of blocks with stepped mouldings quite different to those of Type 1 and 2 (block no 70, Figure 30, no 11). These have dowel holes on their undersides and on their upper surfaces. In addition to slots for parapet slabs they also have large square sockets, presumably to accommodate upright stone blocks or steles. Each block is a mirror image of the other and they clearly came from the same structure. They seem to have come from the ends of a length of straight wall joining two angled walls. The possibility that they came from the junctions of the abutment with the wing-walls can be excluded (see above)

The only position for such an arrangement would seem to be over the cutwaters of the piers (Figure 36, north elevation, and Figure 37). In many Roman bridges the cutwaters do not rise to the full height of the superstructure but finish above the level of floodwater at which point the fronts of the piers rise flush with the front of the arches; occasionally the junction between the top of the cutwater and the flush, vertical face of the pier is masked by a pyramidal cap, as in the case of a bridge over the Wâdi Zedî in Syria (Butler 1919, 304, ill 271–2). There are other bridges, however, with cutwaters extending through the full height of the superstructure, for example at Trier where pairs of columns had risen from above some if not all of the cutwaters (Cüppers 1969, Abb 10). In the reconstruction the front of the cutwater is truncated above the level of floodwater but not cut back flush with the arches. Figure 36, south elevation shows the proposed arrangement in elevation: the cutwater rises to the top of the parapet along the carriageway, the main cornice being carried around its three sides, and then at a higher level has its own parapet and cornice with small steles at the front angles and larger steles at the junctions of the cutwater and carriageway. There is one further architectural fragment which might have been

associated with this part of the bridge, the block with two steps cut in it (no 123; Figure 30, no 2) reused in the kerb (context 131, Figure 15) south of the tower which was built to retain the base of the ramp following the construction of the water-channel (p 27). The block is only 1.07m in width and its sides are worked to a very smooth surface, as if it had been part of a wider flight of steps constructed of a series of blocks. It is quite possible that this block was originally used in such a flight leading up from the carriageway to a higher level above the cutwaters.

The purpose of these platforms above the cutwaters cannot be established with certainty. One of them might have accommodated a small shrine to the nymphs of the river, the existence of which is suggested by a fragmentary dedication by a vexillation of the Sixth Legion from the area of the east abutment (*RIB* 1547; see p 141). The statue of the reclining river god found in the baths next to the commanding officer's house (Coulston and Phillips 1988, 35, no 94) might perhaps also have originally come from here.

The *Pons Aelius* at Newcastle provides another possible example of a shrine on a bridge, where the two altars to Oceanus and Neptunus (*RIB* 1319–20) were set up (p 101). This aspect of the discussion of the superstructure of the bridge is to some extent speculative but one point seems firmly established: that there were considerable masonry structures above the level of the carriageway, most probably above the cutwaters.

Two more comments on the restored elevations and plan (Figures 36, and 37) are required. It has been assumed that the stele bearing the dedication made by the prefect of cavalry, Aelius Longinus (*RIB* 1470; Figure 93, p 141), was one of a series, not all necessarily inscribed, set in the parapet. The gatehouse is shown as a simple structure of one storey at the level of the carriageway with a pyramidal roof (p 26). The principal building inscription was perhaps set above one of the gate-arches.

Quantity survey

In the preceding section arguments have been set out for the height of the arches and the angle of the ramps of approach. The ground-plan of the bridge is not in doubt and thus it is possible to estimate the volume and weight of the masonry in its various constituent parts, see Tables 4 and 5 below.

These calculations exclude the stone required for the gate-tower (or towers if there was also one on the west side of the bridge), for the rebuilding of the Wall and for the parapets, columns and other features above the carriageway.

Using estimates of the amount of time required to quarry and dress stone before the introduction of power-assisted tools, it is possible to proceed further with this quantity survey. The figures given below are taken from I A Baker's *A Treatise on Masonry Construction*, tenth edition (1909), which contains tables showing the time taken to quarry, prepare and lay the stone in a number of public buildings and works in the United States. In some respects, later nineteenth-century methods had advanced far beyond those of the ancient world, for example in the use of explosives, which probably means that more time should be allowed for quarrying than Baker gives. But the remainder of his figures seem to be for work carried out by hand, even in raising the blocks into position (steam cranes seem to have been used only when blocks were raised to a height of more than 20 feet (6.1m) (ibid, table 50). The estimates of time required for the various processes are as follows:

Table 4 Estimate of the volume and weight of masonry in the constituent parts of bridge 2 at Chesters

	No of Blocks	Volume in cubic metres	Weight in tonnes
West abutment	1200	288	720
Wings and base			
Abutment	1583	380	950
Pier	1538	370	925
Arch	833	200	500

These figures are based on the following assumptions:
1 The average size of the blocks employed is 1.2 × 0.5 × 0.4m = 0.24 cubic metres.
2 The density of the sandstone is 2500kg per cubic metre (cf Everett 1981, 104, table 37)
3 Construction was of cut stone blocks throughout. There is no evidence for a fill of mortared rubble behind the arches or in the core of the abutment.

Using the figures above an estimate of the total amount of stone used in the entire bridge can be made. It is assumed that the volume of stone used in the west abutment and its wings was the same as in the east abutment.

Table 5 Estimate of the total volume and weight of stones in bridge 2 at Chesters

	No of blocks	Volume in cubic metres	Weight in tonnes
Abutment (two)			
Wings and base	2400	576	1440
Abutment (two)	3166	760	1900
Piers (three)	4614	1110	2775
Arches (four)	3332	800	2000
Total	13,512	3246	8115

Quarrying, Baker (ibid, 297) only sets out the time required to quarry a given quantity of gneiss, a much harder stone than sandstone but this difference can be offset against the use of explosives. The workmen include a foreman, drillers, labourers, blacksmiths, a tool boy and men managing the horse-teams to move the stone. The amount of time taken to quarry a cubic metre of stone is 3.37 man-days. For the bridge at Chesters 3246 cubic metres of stone was required to which should be added 20 per cent for wastage in cutting the stone, giving a total of 3895 cubic metres. The number of man-days required to quarry this amount of stone will thus have been 3.37 + 3895 = 13,126.

Cutting, ie preparing the blocks from the quarry rough-cuts. Baker (ibid, 299) only states the time required to cut granite for headers and stretchers, which is 5.69 days per cubic metre but he gives the cost of cutting sandstone as two-fifths of the cost of granite; the time taken to cut sandstone will thus have been 2.276 days per cubic metre According to these figures the man-days required to cut the stone required for the bridge will have been 2.276 + 3895 = 8865.

Laying, Baker's figures (ibid table 50) are for laying the cut stone masonry of a dam with the blocks hoisted by hand up to a height of 20 feet (6.1m). The time required to lay a cubic metre is 1.793 man-days and thus 5820 man-days would have been required to lay the stone in the bridge.

The fourth important element in the work programme at Chesters would have been the transport of the stone. Modern methods are not comparable with those that would have been used at Chesters but fortunately there is a certain amount of information about ancient methods. Carts pulled by yoked oxen would probably have been used and in temple-building at Epidaurus carts with a capacity of 1100kg seem to have been employed[1]. This is roughly equivalent to the average size of four blocks employed at Chesters, allowing an additional twenty per cent for the material to be removed from them in their roughed-out state. The number of journeys needed to transport the blocks from the quarry to the bridge would have been 8893 (8115 tonnes plus 20 per cent divided by 1.1 tonnes, the size of a cartload). In calculating the amount of work this would involve, it is assumed that loading at the quarry and unloading at the bridge was carried out by the gangs working there and that each journey would merely require the time of a carter. The quarry at Black Pastures (p 3) is c 2km from the bridge and the time allowed for a journey is half an hour with twenty minutes for loading and unloading: thus seven journeys could be made in just over eight hours.

The number of man-days involved would be 8893 divided by 7 which is 1270. An additional three men should be allowed for: a harnessmaker, a wheelwright and a man to arrange the supply of forage and the watering of the animals.

The total amount of labour required during the principal stages in the construction of the bridge is therefore as follows:

Quarrying:	13,126 man-days
Cutting:	8,865 man-days
Laying:	5,820 man-days
Transport:	1,270 man-days (including the services of three men for the teams throughout the duration of the work)
Total	29,081 man-days

It is impossible to be certain about the number of working days in a year, but a tentative estimate can be made. For perhaps as much as four months during the winter and early spring, building work would be hindered by weather conditions and the high level of the river would have prevented any work on the base of the bridge. It seems best to exclude these months which leaves an effective working year of 243 days; during this period there would have been a number of military festivals and rest-days and the maximum number of days actually worked in a year would seem likely to be around 200. The number of man-days cited above is equivalent to about 145 man-years which means that about 75 men (including three extra men for the teams) could have carried out the principal work of construction on the bridge in two years.

No claims can be made for the accuracy of the figures given above but they establish an order of magnitude. They bear comparison with the period of time required to construct Justinian's bridge over the Sangarius in Turkey, a structure 429m in length with seven main arches and five smaller ones, which Whitby (1985,140–1) has argued amounted to about three years, commencing in the autumn of 559.

Footnote

1 Burford 1969, 187; see also Burford 1960 for a rebuttal of the pessimistic view of the capacity of draught animals and the inefficiency of their harnessing in antiquity. The figure of 1100kg is rather more than twice the load for wagons (500kg) assumed in G C Boon's analysis of the building of the town wall of Silchester (1974, 101, 319, n 10); his estimate was based on the limits on loads for long distance transport in the *Codex Theodosianus*.

4 Willowford: Bridges 1 and 1A

The setting

The Roman bridge at Willowford, Cumbria is situated at the point where Hadrian's Wall crossed the river Irthing (Figure 38). The bridge lies within the current bounds of Willowford Farm and is 1km west of the Poltross Burn, the present border of Northumberland and Cumbria.

The position of the bridge seems to have been determined solely by the line selected for Hadrian's Wall. After leaving the crags of the Great Whin Sill near Carvoran the next natural feature the Wall could utilise was the Irthing gorge. The Wall was made to run along the northern side of the valley (unlike the earlier Stanegate system which kept mainly to the south of the river) and this made a river crossing necessary. The Wall was sited on the northern sumit of the Irthing gorge in order to avoid the mosses of Midgeholme and Spadeadam which lay immediately to the north, and it was this necessity that determined Willowford as the crossing point. The precise line taken by the Wall across the river appears to have been decided by first fixing the site to be occupied by Milecastle 49 (Harrow's Scar) and then sighting across the valley to the eastern scarp just west of Turret 48b (Willowford West). It was therefore as a consequence of strategic factors that the bridge came to be situated at a point which from an engineering viewpoint was far from suitable (p 70).

In the initial scheme the stone curtain wall was only constructed as far west as the Irthing, the remaining 31 miles to Bowness-on-Solway being built in turf. Whether the stone curtain terminated at the eastern abutment of the bridge or at the top of Harrow's Scar, a carboniferous limestone scarp immediately to the west of the river, is not known with certainty. However, excavations at Milecastle 49 on the summit of the scarp have found no trace of the Broad Wall to the east of the milecastle, so it is likely that the Turf Wall descended the slope to the western abutment of the bridge (Richmond 1956a). The scarp would have been less steep in Roman times than it is at present (p 52) and a system of stepping, such as that noted in some places on the Antonine Wall, may have been used to bring the Turf Wall down the slope (Hanson and Maxwell 1983, 81). All traces of the Turf Wall (and its subsequent replacement in stone) on the face of the scarp have now been destroyed. The reasons for the use of turf instead of stone at the Irthing are not fully understood. The idea that it was because of a lack of good building stone in Cumbria is now discredited and a current suggestion is that turf was used to ensure a speedier completion of the building programme (Breeze and Dobson 1987, 32–3).

The River Irthing

Willowford Bridge lies 33 km downstream from the head of the Irthing, which rises at the confluence of two upland streams on Paddaburn moor. The river has a very meandering course before it joins the Eden at Warwick and forms several waterfalls where it crosses harder rock strata above the bridge. The most noticeable aspect of the river is the great seasonal variation in its flow: while it runs almost dry in the summer in the autumn and winter it can become a violent torrent, and frequently breaks its banks and floods the valley bottom. It is this tendency to flooding which has discouraged settlement in the Irthing valley and prevented the establishment of routes along its line. The Stanegate, for example, was forced to follow a route over the higher broken ground west of Nether Denton because of the unsuitability of the valley bottom.

One of the most striking aspects of the bridge site today is the fact that the Irthing now lies some 72m west of the abutment of the Roman bridge (Figure 38). This movement of the river channel has been a continuing process over a number of millennia, both before and after the Roman period, for the river originally flowed beneath the scarp to the east of the bridge. Its westward passage has left a flat terrace of coarse gravels and sandy alluvium and it is upon these deposits that the bridge and Wall immediately east of it are founded.

The bank upon which the eastern abutment of the Hadrianic bridge was constructed was discovered in the recent excavations (context 1001, Figure 45, section 5). It was found to be equivalent to the bank discovered by Shaw (1926, 487) a little to the south of the bridge, which he stated curved back south-eastwards towards the line of a river terrace preserved in a field. In the Roman period therefore, the river meandered sharply eastwards immediately south of the bridge, the apex of the bend lying just to the north of the bridge. Since the construction of the Hadrianic bridge, westward movement by the river has 'smoothed out' this meander, a process which can to some extent be reconstructed from contemporary maps. The earliest one available is Howard of Naworth's survey of the Barony of Gilsland in 1603 (lodged in the Department of Palaeography, University of Durham, reference C 713/15). This map is of particular interest as it also seems to be the earliest accurate representation of the line of Hadrian's Wall (referred to as 'The Pight Wall') which is shown crossing the Irthing and ascending Harrow's Scar. The 1603 map indicates a still very pronounced meander although to the south of the bridge some westward movement has occurred. The line of this course is largely fossilised in the present parish boundary between Upper Denton and Lanercost. It was therefore in the period after 1603 that the bulk of the westward movement of the Irthing occurred, heavily eroding the soft limestone of Harrow's Scar. In 1732 John Horsley wrote of his visit to Willowford

'the bank of the River Irthing on the west side, to which the Wall points, is very steep and high, but it seems to have become more so of late years from the falling away of the sandy bank.'

Horsley 1732, 152

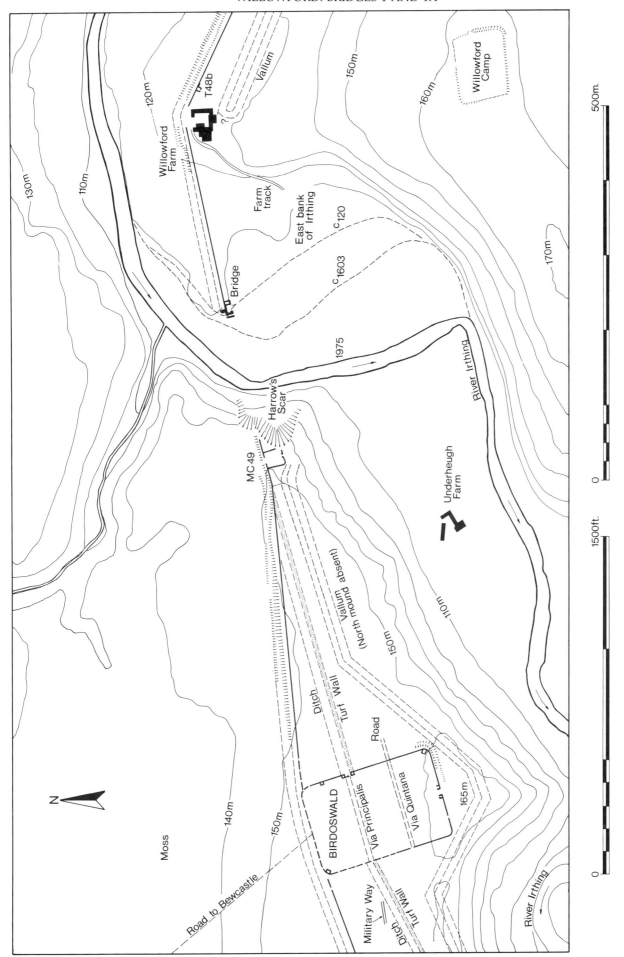

Figure 38 The site of the bridge at Willowford in relation to the line of the Wall, Vallum and fort at Birdoswald. Broken lines indicate previous courses of the River Irthing. Scale 1:5000

H B Richardson's watercolour of Harrow's Scar (Plate 6), painted in 1848, clearly shows the Wall mound and ditch being undermined by the river. Today Harrow's Scar has a gradient of approximately 50 per cent (1:1) and all traces of the Wall on its face have been destroyed. In the Roman period the gradient was probably in the region of 27.5 per cent (1:3.5) assuming an even slope from the summit to the western bank of the river.

Antiquarian accounts

William Camden was the first person to record a visit to Willowford, which was made in the course of his northern tour of 1599 to collect information for the 1600 edition of *Britannia*:

> '... and hard by the wall Burd Oswald [Birdoswald]. Beneath which, where that Picts wall passed over the river Irthing by an arched bridge, was the station of the first band Aelia Dacia'   trans Holland 1637, 785

Howard of Naworth's survey of 1603 indicates that at the time of Camden's visit most of the bridge would have lain in the river and the piers would presumably have still been visible. This may explain the reference to an arched bridge, which need not be taken literally: the presence of stone piers probably suggested to Camden that stone arches had once existed.

Nineteenth-century survey and excavation

After Camden's time the westward movement of the river covered the piers with silt and although the line of the Wall was visible as a tree covered mound, both Gordon (1726) and Horsley (1732) do not mention anything of the bridge. Bruce likewise records no trace of the bridge in the first edition of *The Roman Wall* (1851) and Henry Jenkinson was the first person to make detailed observations:

> 'Fortunately on our last visit, we meet at Birdoswald with Mr John Armstrong, a master mason, residing at Gilsland, and he assured us that when the old Peel house at Willowford was pulled down, thirty six years since [ie *c* 1836] and the present farmhouse built, the foundation of the bridge was visible, and a great number of very large stones, beautifully shaped, and with luis [sic] holes in them, were taken from the bank of the river, close to where the Wall evidently crossed, and were broken and used in building the house. From the quality of the stones, it was evident that they came from the Lodges Quarry, near the Low Row railway station. He was also of the opinion that they only got a part of the stones and that many more would be found in their original positions if the sand were removed'
> Jenkinson 1875, 199

It is probable that the stones 'taken from the bank of the river' were those that can be seen in Richardson's watercolour of 1848 (Plate 6) and that they represent the disturbed remains of the western abutments which lay in the course of the Irthing at that time. Bruce also met John Armstrong, probably as a result of Jenkinson's publication, and in the third edition of *The Handbook to the Roman Wall* (1885) added that there was a land breast lying 60 yards (*c* 55m) from the river which was about 20 feet (6.1m) long and three or four courses high (J C Bruce 1885a, 195). This 'land breast' is the pier of bridge 3 and Shaw (1926, 473) found evidence of its robbing during his excavations. If it is accepted that the stones in the bank were derived from the western abutments this would indicate that the bridge was roughly 60 yards (*c* 55m) in length. The width of the river is *c* 25m at present so the bridge in its latest phase will have extended for some distance either side of the river, bridging a length of the flood plain to accommodate the frequent inundations of the river.

Twentieth-century survey and excavation

Despite the impressive results obtained by Clayton at Chesters, and the extensive work in the Gilsland to Birdoswald sector around the turn of the century, the bridge was not excavated until 1924. An excavation had been planned in 1886 by the Cumberland Excavation Committee as part of a programme of investigating river crossings made by the Wall, although it never came to fruition (*Trans Cumberland Westmorland Antiq Archaeol Soc* o ser **9** (1888), 163). The excavations in 1924 were directed by R C Shaw. He had first become interested in Hadrian's Wall during World War I as a result of a friendship with F G Simpson and this led to the production of their joint paper on the Vallum in 1922 (Simpson and Shaw 1922, G Simpson 1976, 5).

Shaw (1926) excavated two turrets on Willowford Farm in 1923 (Turrets 48a, 48b) and then excavated for two months at the bridge from September 1924. Shaw recorded and published his results with exemplary thoroughness for his time, although his interpretations of the structural sequence and relationship between Turf and Stone Walls are now known to be incorrect. R G Collingwood, the editor at that time of the Transactions of the Cumberland and Westmorland Antiquarian and Archaeological Society, was evidently responsible for the incorrect captions of some figures and plates in the report (Simpson 1976, 61). In April 1927 F G Simpson undertook a study of the bridge fabric, which had been left open after Shaw's excavations and he subsequently produced a modified version of Shaw's plan (reproduced in Simpson 1976, text fig 7a). The only new point of any substance in Simpson's plan is that he deleted Shaw's 'Military Way'. This has now been shown to be a natural gravel deposit (p 95) and Simpson had probably realised this in 1927.

The site became overgrown after Shaw's excavation

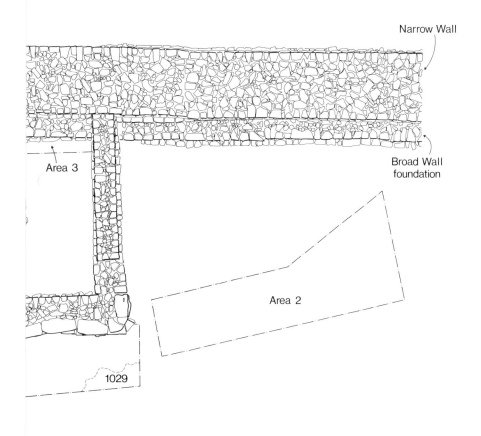

1924 Ditch section ◁

Narrow Wall

Area 3

Broad Wall
foundation

Area 2

1029

25m.

SCS/AMG

5

W

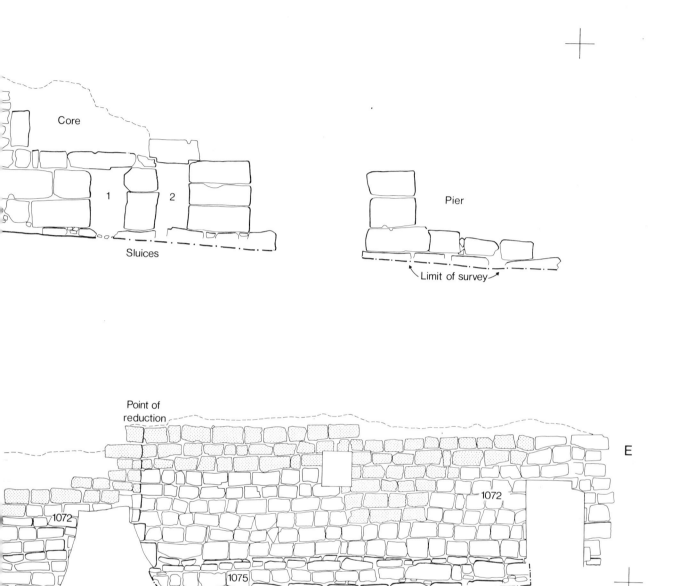

Core

1   2

Sluices

Pier

Limit of survey

Point of
reduction

E

1072

1072

1075

1105

1099

ural

15 metres

50 feet

the south face of Hadrian's Wall.

and in the summer of 1939 Lord and Lady Henley placed the bridge in the guardianship of the then Office of Works (now English Heritage), which undertook its consolidation. As part of this programme F G Simpson returned to excavate. He reported in 1941 that:

'On September 3rd [1940], water-piers of the bridge, sought for in vain in 1924, were at last discovered. The remains of two piers, consisting of masses of fallen stones, surrounding masonry still in position, were located nearly ten feet [3m] below the present surface. The stonework was exceptionally massive, comparable to the largest blocks reused in the later reconstructions of the eastern abutment.

'Before the height of the standing masonry, or the shape of the piers could be ascertained, bad weather caused the Irthing to rise above the bottom of the trenches, making further work impossible until the river returned to its summer level' Simpson 1941, 214

Simpson mistakenly believed, as a result of these excavations, that a stone reused in the tower of bridge 2, (block no 372, Figure 50, no 5) indicated that the Hadrianic bridge had had segmental rather than semicircular arches. This would have had the disadvantage that the lateral thrust created by the structure would not have been channelled downwards as efficiently as it is in a normal semicircular arch. The segmental arch is known in Roman architecture but its use was not particularly widespread, nor is its use likely here.

During consolidation of the bridge the turf and trees which had been left on top of the Wall during Shaw's excavations were removed and this revealed the 'turret' recess of bridge 1. This was included by Richmond (1947, 165) in his reappraisal of the bridge in the tenth edition of the *Handbook to the Roman Wall*. The previous edition, edited by R G Collingwood

(1933), gave only a brief and erroneous account of the bridge. The structural sequence Richmond proposed for the bridge has been generally accepted although some have doubted its validity (Breeze and Dobson 1972, 197, n 67). Table 6 provides a concordance of the present and previous structural sequences.

Survey and excavation in 1984–5

By 1984 the consolidated remains at Willowford had begun to deteriorate. It was decided that a limited amount of archaeological investigation should be carried out at the site before the necessary remedial work was begun. This investigation was to have two principal objectives: first to record the standing masonry before further consolidation occurred, and secondly to attempt to research the development and design of the successive bridges through selective excavation within the guardianship area.

The work was carried out in two eight-week seasons in the autumn of 1984 and 1985. Initially a detailed survey of the remains was undertaken, plans and elevations of all the standing masonry were prepared at 1:20 scale. A system of numbering all the blocks visible on the site was adopted, and these numbers are retained in this publication. The exact dimentions of features such as clamp sockets and lewis holes were recorded in a card index, retained with the site archive.

When the survey had been completed excavation commenced in six separate areas (Figure 39).

Area 1 Work here concentrated on defining an abutment wing-wall (subsequently identified as the southern wing-wall of bridge 1A) which was clearly visible on the site before work commenced, but which did not appear on any previously published plan. A series of dumps to the south of this wing-wall were also examined and in this area the original medieval ground surface (context 1008, Figure 45, section 5) was preserved.

Table 6 Concordance of structural sequences at Willowford

	1984-5	Shaw 1926	Richmond 1947
bridge 1	Broad Wall	wall A	Broad Wall
	tower recess	not known	Turret 1
	Narrow Wall	wall B	Narrow Wall
	pier	not known	not known
bridge 1A	southern wing-wall	'line of cobbles' (fig 5) was the easternmost (rear) limit of the wing-wall core	no mention
bridge 2	reconstructed curtain wall	wall C	'drastic reconstruction'
	abutment	abutment 2	phase 2 abutment
	southern wing-wall	wing of abutment 2	abutment 1
	northern wing-wall	abutment 1	masonry apron
	tower	tower	tower II
bridge 3	abutment	abutment 3	later abutment
	pier	pier	later pier

Area 2 was excavated to investigate the structure of the road marked on Shaw's plan (1926, fig 5). In the event it was conclusively demonstrated that this feature was a natural gravel deposit which marked a pre-Roman river bank. The only archaeological feature in this area was a small pit (context 1083, Figure 71) associated with medieval activity on the site.

Area 3 was a small area of turf and backfill within the tower which was removed to fully expose a length of the footings of the Broad Wall foundation.

Area 4 was examined to test Richmond's theory (1947, 165) that the mass of masonry to the north of Hadrian's Wall (the northern wing-wall of bridge 2) revetted the berm between the Wall and ditch as it approached the river. Excavation showed this to be incorrect, the wall ditch terminating *c* 3m to the east of the wing-wall.

Area 5 was excavated in an attempt to locate the first pier of the Hadrianic bridge. In fact nothing of the pier was found *in situ* although its position was indicated by a mass of worked blocks which had been deposited above the river bed following the destruction of the pier by river action (Figure 42).

Area 6 here a length of the consolidated capping of Hadrian's Wall was removed and excavation took place between the consolidated faces. As a result the extent and nature of the previous consolidation work on the Wall became clear. In a number of places a considerable amount of modern mortar was found on the inside of the Wall faces. This clearly cannot have been the product of simply grouting out the Roman mortar and resealing the joints with modern mortar, and it would appear that at least some lengths of the Wall face had been dismantled and rebuilt. These rebuilt areas are stippled in Figure 40, elevations 1 and 2.

All these areas were backfilled at the end of the second season.

The programme of investigation solved many of the outstanding problems posed by the site, and for the first time a clear appreciation of the structural development of the eastern abutments is possible. Future work would most profitably be concentrated outside the present guardianship area. In particular the location and full excavation of the two piers briefly uncovered by F G Simpson would be especially useful. It is also likely that excavation to the west of the guardianship area would uncover a considerable amount of architectural material derived from bridge 3, which could have had a superstructure as elaborate as that suggested for bridge 2 at Chesters (p 44ff).

During post-excavation work Dr G Simpson kindly supplied a series of coloured drawings prepared by Shaw from his original records. A set of photographs taken by J Gibson during the 1924 excavations was also obtained from the Northumberland County Record Office. These are included in the site archive, along with full records of the 1984 and 1985 seasons work, which has been deposited in the RCHM(E) National Monuments Register. The finds have been deposited in the Tullie House Museum, Carlisle.

The structure of Hadrian's Wall at the bridge

Shaw's excavations had revealed that Hadrian's Wall consisted of a number of elements at the bridge. (Shaw 1926, 453–63; Figure 40) Above the footings four courses of curtain wall were constructed, almost 10 Roman feet (*pes monetalis*, hereafter RF) wide (now generally referred to as the Broad Wall foundation). Above the foundation, and extending for *c* 11.6m east of the postulated position of the abutment of bridge 1 the curtain was completed to a similar width (Shaw's Wall A; ibid, 454–8, here the Broad Wall). As the bridge was built before the rest of the curtain wall had been completed in this sector, this length of the Broad Wall was constructed to facilitate subsequent bonding in. Similar wing-walls were also built at turrets and milecastles. When the curtain wall was eventually brought up to the bridge it was now constructed to a narrower gauge, 7.8 RF wide (Shaw's Wall B; ibid, 458–61, here the Narrow Wall). This narrower curtain was constructed on top of the existing foundation and so is described as Narrow Wall on Broad Wall foundation.

The Broad Wall

The footings of the Broad Wall consist of large water-worn stones and boulders of sandstone and granite, with smaller stones filling the voids. They were constructed directly above the natural alluvium. East of the bridge the footings generally consist of a single course, *c* 0.2m in depth, above which the first course of the Broad Wall foundation was laid (context 1099, Figure 41, sections 1, and 3). In the south face of the Wall, however, from a point *c* 13.6m east of the probable position of the abutment (p 66), the depth of footings increases westward with extra courses added, consisting of a mixture of boulders and small stones (context 1099, Figure 40, elevation 2). Above these deeper footings an additional course was laid, consisting of fairly thin, roughly dressed stones, to make a level base upon which to place the Broad Wall foundation proper (context 1105, Figure 40, elevation 2). The Broad Wall foundation is 2.94m (9.93 RF) wide and while the north face (context 1074, Figure 40, elevation 1, and Figure 41, section 1) is fully preserved, many of the courses of the south face (context 1075, Figure 39, elevation 2, and Figure 41, section 1) have been removed. The foundation was originally four courses (*c* 0.5m) high. The probable reason for the deeper footings is that as the Wall descended the river bank the top of the Broad Wall foundation remained level while the footings were stepped into the slope. Consequently the foundation and footings may have risen to over 3m in height when they met the abutment. This strengthening of the wall would have been necessary to provide an abutment of sufficient stability to absorb the thrust of the first arch and also to withstand any flooding of the river.

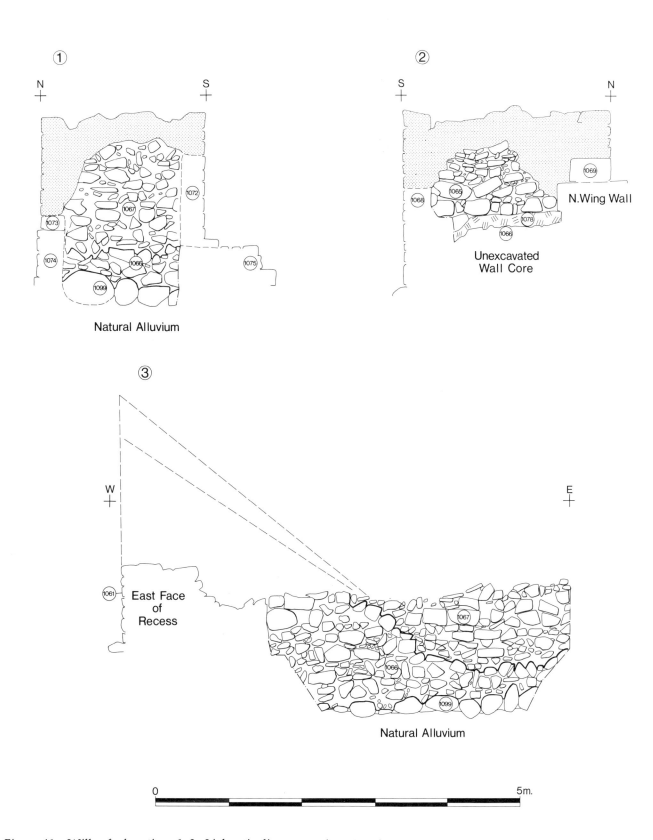

Figure 41   Willowford sections 1–3. Light stippling on sections 1 and 2 denotes walling rebuilt in consolidation.   Scale 1:50

From the top of the river bank eastwards much of the Broad Wall foundation would have lain below ground level. Shaw recorded the height of the Roman ground level to the north of the Wall:

> 'In front of the north face a number of potsherds and bones were found lying in a black deposit close to the Wall and extending for about 7 feet [2.13m] along its face. The upper level of this stratum coincided with the sixth course and the lower with the bottom of the fourth... Below the black layer lay fairly clean sand containing very few water-worn stones. No sherds or bones were found at this level, which shows that the Roman surface corresponded with the third course.'
>
> Shaw 1926, 460

On the south side of the Wall the ground was evidently *c* 0.4m lower; the top of the alluvium corresponded to the lower part of the second course of the Broad Wall foundation near the west wall of the tower of bridge 2 (ibid, 480, fig 7, ii).

Above the foundation the Broad Wall was constructed (context 1103, Figures 39, and 40, elevation 1; context 1104, Figure 40, elevation 2). Although there was a relatively greater proportion of charcoal, lime and masons' chippings in the core filling the foundation compared to that of the Broad Wall, no firm division could be distinguished within the core, so it is likely that the foundation, and the Broad Wall were constructed together (context 1066, Figure 41, section 3). The mortar used in the foundation (sample 8; p 97) was also identical to that used in the Broad Wall (sample 7; p 97). The Broad Wall stands nine courses high above the top of the foundation and to a total height of 1.96m above the top of the footings. Above the offsets at the top of the Broad Wall foundation (up to 0.1m on the north side and 0.15m on the south) the wall was 2.78m (9.39 RF) wide. Shaw described the masonry before consolidation:

> 'The stones in the [south] face are very mixed in character; sandstones, limestones, shale and cobbles all occur within the comparatively short space of 17 feet [5.18m]. The shale stones are a pronounced feature of this phase, not occurring in the work of the two later periods to anything like the same degree.
>
> '... The dressing of the face work is of a very indifferent type, even in the courses which must have been well above the surface level. Most of the stones appear to have been roughly fashioned with the hammer, but not pick or chisel dressed. Consequently the joints are wide, but are sealed with a fairly good mortar...
>
> '... one is immediately impressed with the peculiarly small size of the facing stones, which are of poor quality and badly dressed, leaving wide joints. Many of these stones measure only 4 by 5 inches (0.1m by 0.13m) on their outer faces, and some are even smaller.'
>
> ibid, 456–8

A coarse lime mortar with aggregate was used in the faces of the Broad Wall (sample 7, p 97).

The Wall core consists of a mass of stones of widely varying size (largest stones *c* 0.3m × 0.5m in area; context 1066, Figure 41, sections 1 and 3). The only bonding material in the core is a silty sand, mortar being restricted to the dressed faces. Stone types represented are hewn and river derived sandstones, granites and appreciably more whin than in later constructions.

The stones are less well compacted than the subsequent Narrow Wall core, although a rough coursing is still evident. At the eastern end of the Broad Wall the core is stepped, with larger than normal stones laid across the width of the Wall, to serve as a rough kerbing (context 1066, Figures 39; 41, section 3; 42; and 43). This ensured the stability of the core in the period before the construction of the curtain wall. The facing stones at the eastern end of the south face of the Broad Wall also terminate in a stepped arrangement (Figure 40, elevation 2), and this presumably matched the gradient of the core. The relevant portion of the north face has been destroyed by a subsequent refacing. The stepping of the eastern end of the Broad Wall can be paralleled at the wing-walls of Turrets 26b (Brunton) and 29a (Blackcarts, Charlesworth 1973, 98). They differ from Willowford in their relationship to the Narrow Wall however, for in both cases when the Narrow Wall was constructed it simply rode over the stepping, the south face of the narrower curtain sitting upon the core of the Broad wing-wall. At Willowford the south face of the Narrow Wall formed a projecting vertical point of reduction where it met the eastern end of the Broad Wall (p 59). To the east of the stepping of the Broad Wall the Broad Wall foundation was filled with core up to *c* 0.2m below the top of its uppermost course (context 1066, Figure 41, section 1).

There is a perceptible difference in the alignment between the length of Broad Wall at the bridge and the Broad Wall foundation to the east of it. This is most clearly observed to the east of the (later) point of reduction where the south face of the Broad Wall foundation is on an alignment 2–4 degrees south of that taken by the Broad Wall (Figure 39). The junction between the Broad Wall and Broad Wall foundation may perhaps be discerned in their north face (Figure 40, elevation 1) although no corresponding distinction could be recognised in the core. It seems probable that the Broad Wall foundation was laid from west to east in this sector (Breeze and Dobson 1987, 74, 76) and this is supported by the reduction in height of the foundation from four courses to three between Turrets 48b and 48a, for this probably reflected a decision to construct the foundation to a shallower depth once it had passed from the soft alluvium of the flood plain onto firmer subsoil (see below). The misalignment of the Broad Wall and the Broad Wall foundation is presumably a consequence of the sequence of construction, and this raises the question of which was built first; the bridge and length of Broad Wall, or the Broad Wall foundation? Although the evidence is not conclusive it is more probable that work had at least started on the bridge, and that the length of Broad Wall to the east had been

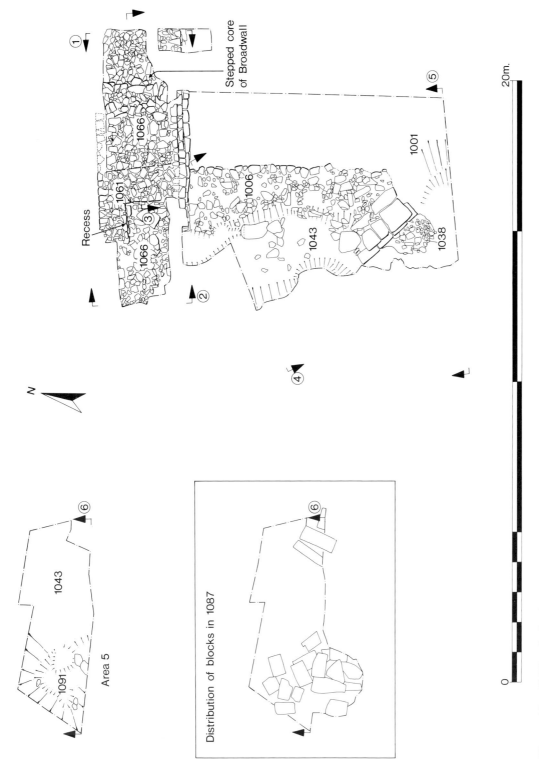

Figure 42 Willowford, abutment of bridges 1 and 1A, showing the position of the stepped core at the eastern end of the Broad Wall. Inset: the distribution of worked blocks in the river gravels which were deposited there after the destruction of bridge 1A. Scale 1:125

completed, before the Broad Wall foundation was laid. If this had not been the case, and the foundation had been constructed first, it would have been necessary for work to have commenced some distance from the river bank and for the bridge abutment and Broad Wall to have been subsequently fitted in; some means of retaining the core of the foundation until this occurred might also be expected if this were so (none was discerned in excavation). The southward deviation of the Broad Wall foundation was necessary to make a straight alignment onto the summit of the scar to the east of the bridge. The reason the bridge itself was not on this alignment could be that it was aligned on the Turf Wall to the west of the river (Breeze and Dobson, (1987, 74) consider that the Turf Wall was largely completed before work commenced on the stone wall in the sector to the east of the Irthing), or simply that the position of the bridge was shifted slightly from its planned position due to factors in the local topography, such as the nature of the river bed.

It is of note that the proposed Willowford sequence is the opposite of that suggested for Chesters, where it is considered that the laying of the Broad Wall foundation preceded the construction of the Hadrianic bridge (p 12) This is not a problem however, for there is no need to suppose that work on both these bridges had to commence at exactly the same time, and there is also ample evidence that the rate of wall construction varied considerably between sectors (ibid, 76)

The structure of the Broad Wall

The Broad Wall and foundation at the bridge are of poor construction with crudely worked facing stones and an unmortared core. Construction of the Broad Wall where it survives between Newcastle and the Irthing is not everywhere homogeneous. In a number of places between Denton Bank (Wall mile 7) and Chesters bridge (Wall mile 27) the Broad Wall has a clay bonded core with mortar confined to the faces (Bennett 1983, 44). Further west in Wall miles 46–48 at Longbyre, Gilsland Vicarage and now Willowford Bridge, the core of the Broad Wall foundation has been found to consist of a mass of stones with at most only a matrix of sandy soil, the use of mortar once again being confined to the faces (Salway 1959, 212; G Simpson 1976, 64, text fig 8, *contra* Simpson 1928, 385). Elsewhere, most noticeably in some sections in Wall miles 7–12, the Broad Wall has been found to possess a concrete core often associated with abnormally large facing stones (Birley 1960, 55). Whether this is original work or a subsequent rebuilding from the foundations is not clear although the latter is a distinct possibility.

Further variation in the Broad Wall is created by the number of courses in the foundation: one (so-called Standard A); three (Standard B) and four (Standard B variant) (Breeze and Dobson 1987, 67, fig 15). The four course foundation is confined to a short section of curtain wall to the east of Willowford Bridge, ending at an undetermined point between Turrets 48b and 48a (Turret 48b has four courses

Figure 43   Stepped core at the eastern end of the Broad Wall at Willowford looking west, 2m scale.   (Photo: S C Speak)

below the offset in its northern face while Turret 48a has three, the normal Standard B; Shaw 1926, 431, 438). It is noticeable that the evidence from Willowford Bridge and Gilsland Vicarage indicates similar Broad Wall construction throughout this length so variation in the foundation does not seem to be in accordance with the use of different core materials.

The height of Hadrian's Wall

The stepping of the core at the eastern end of the Broad Wall provides an opportunity to estimate its minimum height. This is determined by projecting the gradient of the stepping upwards to the point where it would have met the eastern wall of the recess (context 1066, Figure 41, section 3). If it is assumed that the stepping was of a constant gradient, despite some doubt about precisely which gradient to use, a value for the height of the wall above the top of its footings of between 3.5m and 4.00m can be calculated. However the Roman ground level to the north of the Wall would have lain level with the top of the third course of the Broad Wall foundation so some of this height would not have been exposed above ground level.

The minimum height of 3.5m at Willowford can be compared with other estimates for the height of Hadrian's Wall. The highest surviving portions of curtain are on Hare Hill (Wall mile 53, 3.00m high, which is a Narrow Wall replacement of the Turf Wall;

Daniels 1978, 221) and just east of Milecastle 39, (Castle Nick; 3.3m high, substantially rebuilt Narrow Wall; *Britannia*, **16** (1985), 271). For other evidence of the height of Hadrian's Wall see Birley 1961, 81–3, Breeze and Dobson 1987, 23. A height of 3.5m–4.0m is probably a reasonable estimate.

The Narrow Wall

The curtain wall constructed upon the Broad Wall foundation and brought up to the Broad Wall at the bridge is 2.3m (7.8 RF) wide and is known as the Narrow Wall (Figure 39). It utilises the existing four courses of the north face of the Broad Wall foundation, the new work commencing above that level, slightly offset (context 1073, Figure 40, elevation 1). The south face of the Narrow Wall rests directly upon the top of the Broad Wall foundation core (context 1072, Figures 40, elevation 2, and 41, section 1). The Narrow Wall exhibits a conspicuous northward kink over 8.6m as it approaches the completed length of Broad Wall from the east (Figure 39). This reflects the slightly different alignment of the Broad Wall foundation, upon which the Narrow Wall sits, from that of the completed length of Broad Wall discussed above (p 56). This slight adjustment in the line of the Narrow Wall does not occur in the lowest course of the south face however, which becomes offset by up to 0.2m from the coursing above it as the wall approaches the junction with the Broad Wall. This suggests that this course was laid before the need to modify the alignment of the Narrow Wall was realised. East of this kink as the first offset became less apparent, another, *c* 0.06m wide, develops above the second course. It is not possible to state with certainty in this sector whether the Narrow Wall was built eastwards from the bridge or westwards towards it.

Construction of the Narrow Wall left the four courses of the south face of the Broad Wall foundation free standing, 0.7m from the south face of the new curtain. It is difficult to understand why some of these courses were not removed and the stones reused in the new work. The bottom two courses revetted the foundation core but the third and fourth courses would have projected above the ground and served no function. Shaw does not record that the gap between the two faces was deliberately filled and so, as Charlesworth (1973, 98) noted, water could have penetrated between the two faces and when frozen would have broken up the footings.

At the point where the Broad Wall meets the Narrow Wall the width of the curtain wall is reduced by 0.63m (a point of reduction). This was effected by removing the third and fourth courses of the south face of the Broad Wall foundation. A large sandstone block at least 0.76m long and 0.32m high was then placed at right angles to the axis of the Wall, resting upon the second course and core of the Broad Wall foundation (Shaw 1926, plate ii, B). Coursing, slightly offset, was constructed above it, which is clearly of uniform build with the south face of the Narrow Wall. To the west, coursing was carried up to the

stepped south face of the Broad Wall.

The south face of the Narrow Wall (context 1072, Figure 41, section 1) stood nine courses (1.66m) high when first excavated. Within the area enclosed by the tower of bridge 2 its south face was found to have been extensively damaged by medieval industrial activities (ibid, 459; p 97). This section was subsequently rebuilt in the course of consolidation as was much of the north face above the top of the Broad Wall foundation (context 1073, stippled areas in Figures 40 elevation 1, and 41, section 1). Shaw described the masonry of the Narrow Wall before its consolidation:

> 'The masonry of the south face of the Wall and its eastward continuation is not of equal merit to that found in many parts, the joints are wide and the dressing crude. It is, however … decidedly superior to that in Wall A [Broad Wall]. The stones are more uniform in size, especially in depth. The material is a sandstone similar to that worked in the Lodge[s] quarries near Low Row, and harder that the sandstones in Wall A, which are similar to that from Lanerton quarry a short distance down the river. Lastly there is the distinct difference already mentioned in the quality of the mortar, that in Wall B containing a greater admixture of sand.'

ibid, 459–60

A coarse light brown lime mortar with gravel aggregate and traces of charcoal was used in the faces of the Narrow Wall. While distinct from that used in the recess it is difficult to distinguish visually from the mortar used in the Broad Wall (sample 6, p 97).

The core of the Narrow Wall consists of a mass of stones with very little trace of mortar except immediately behind the faces; the core can therefore be described as unmortared like that of the Broad Wall. Hewn and riverine sandstones and some granite are present in the core. The average area of the stones is 0.2 by 0.3m although some are as large as 0.6m by 0.3m. The core directly overlies that of the Broad Wall foundation and no humic deposits could be recognised between them. The Narrow Wall core displays clear coursing consisting of layers of stones *c* 0.1–0.15m thick with small stones and masons' chippings filling the voids. A thin layer of sandy silt covers each layer. This coursing is far more apparent than in the Broad Wall core and indicates that in the construction of the Narrow Wall the laying of the core kept pace with the construction of the faces.

It has been stated (Daniels 1978, 16) that the Narrow Wall always has a mortared core. Recent work in the vicinity of Milecastle 39 (Castle Nick) however has indicated the extent of later rebuilding and has shown that the original core of the Narrow Wall was unmortared. Where a mortared core has been found in this sector it is the result of later repairs (*Britannia* **14** (1983), 290). At Chesters bridge the core of the Narrow Wall also contained very little mortar and this probably derived solely from the mortaring of the faces (p 9). Willowford is thus not alone in

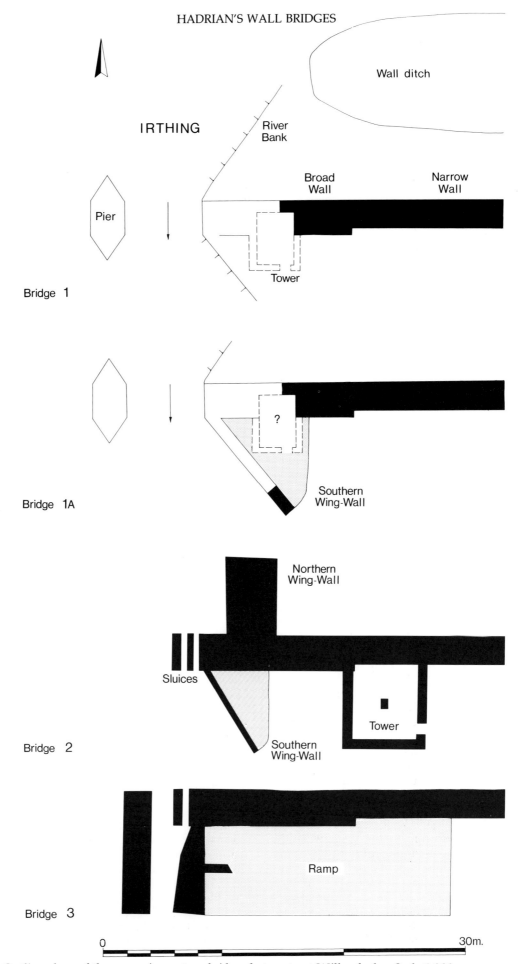

Figure 44   Outline plans of the successive eastern bridge abutments at Willowford.   Scale 1:300

having an unmortared Narrow Wall core. Closer at hand at Gilsland Vicarage Garden, less than a kilometre to the east of the bridge, F G Simpson cut a trench across the Broad Wall foundation and the superimposed Narrow Wall in 1927. The cores of both structures contained a mass of unmortared stones and Simpson considered that they were homogeneous. This section thus not only demonstrates the unmortared nature of the Narrow Wall core, but if Simpson's observation of the relationship between the core of the Broad Wall foundation and the Narrow Wall is correct, it is also

> 'The clearest possible evidence that there was no interval of time between [the construction of the] Broad Foundation and the change to Narrow Wall'
>
> G Simpson 1976, 64–7, text fig 2

F G Simpson therefore considered that it was at this very point that the Wall builders (who were working from west to east) decided to cease construction of the Broad Wall foundation and commence work on the Narrow Wall (a view succinctly expressed in Richmond 1939, 266).

Just how much reliance can be placed on the evidence from a single narrow trench is open to question. At Willowford similar materials were used in the cores of the Broad Wall foundation and the Narrow Wall and the division which existed between them could only be detected by carefully excavating a length of the Wall core in plan. In section the boundary between the cores was by no means clearly apparent and had only a narrow trench been dug across the Wall at Willowford it is possible that the erroneous conclusion, that both cores were one and the same, may well have been reached. If Simpson was correct and the decision to construct the Narrow Wall was taken at Gilsland Vicarage, this is difficult to reconcile with the presence of fully constructed Standard B Broad Wall foundation c 150m further east, immediately west of Milecastle 48 (Richmond 1929, 314, fig 3), and also at Longbyre in Wall mile 47 (Salway 1959, 212).

It can thus be suggested that at Willowford and also at Gilsland Vicarage Garden the Broad Wall foundation and Narrow Wall were constructed as distinct and separate operations. What interval of time elapsed between their construction is not known with certainty. One possibility is to associate the change from Broad to Narrow Wall with the decision to place forts upon Hadrian's Wall which is known by inscriptions to have occurred under the governorship of Platorius Nepos (122–c 126; RIB 1340, 1427; Breeze and Dobson 1987, 57–8). In this case the Narrow Wall at Willowford may have been built only a year or so after the construction of the bridge and the Broad Wall foundation.

A large number of centurial stones are known from the sector from Willowford Bridge to Milecastle 48. There are at least 18 (13 listed in Stevens 1966, 118, with the addition of RIB 1957, apparently from the burn west of Gilsland Vicarage, RIB 1862, 1864, 1865, and Britannia 18 (1987), 369, no 11 built into Willowford farmhouse). Although they were found lying either in the Wall tumble or reused in buildings it is probable that they came from the original Narrow Wall or a later reconstruction of it. The auxiliary inscription of Petta Dida, found 48.2 m east of the point of reduction at the bridge, may perhaps fall in this latter category. None of these stones mentions a legion although R P Wright (1940, 165) has suggested that RIB 1867, found 20.7m east of the point of reduction, is comparable with RIB 468 found at Chester and is therefore almost certainly attributable to legio XX Valeria Victrix. In the general model proposed by Breeze and Dobson (1987, 77) the sixth legion was mainly responsible for the completion of the Narrow Wall between Milecastle 22 (Errington Arms) and the Irthing.

The Wall ditch

Shaw (1926, 487–8, fig 9) sectioned the Wall ditch 3.5m east of the east wall of the tower of bridge 2. The ditch was 19.14m (30.9 RF) wide with a 5.28m berm and a maximum depth of 1.52m below the level of the Wall footings, although as Roman ground level was at the height of the third course of the Broad Wall foundation on the north side of the Wall, its overall depth would have been c 2.00m (6.8 RF). Shaw stated that the inner slope of the ditch was 'carefully banked with hewn stone' and that the bottom of the ditch was filled with organic material. The recent excavations examined a further portion of the ditch (context 1058, Figures 39, and 45, section 7) and demonstrated that the ditch became shallower and gradually faded out as it approached the river bank. No trace of any stone packing was found on the inner edge of the ditch and it is very probable that Shaw's statement reflects a misinterpretation of rubble filling the ditch which had become embedded in the soft sandy natural (context 1071, Figure 45, section 7).

As the ditch was carried right up to the eastern river bank it would have filled with water when the river was in flood. This arrangement can be contrasted with that of the Vallum which evidently terminated on top of the scar to the east of the bridge, probably beneath the site of Willowford Farm. No trace of the Vallum has been seen descending the scar and this can be paralleled on the west bank of the Irthing where Richmond (1956a, 24) found that the Vallum terminated just west of Milecastle 49. The Wall ditch, to judge from Richardson's watercolour (Plate 6), descended Harrow's Scar and probably ran right up to the western abutment of the bridge. In the Irthing valley greater importance was therefore attached to the Wall ditch than to the Vallum. This is not a general rule however and the opposite is true at Limestone Corner (Wall mile 29) where the Vallum was dug through solid rock and yet the ditch was abandoned when only half completed (Daniels 1978, 21). At Chesters both the Wall ditch and Vallum were carried right up to the eastern bank of the North Tyne (p 1). It is slightly surprising that the Vallum was not constructed in the valley bottom at Willowford as it would have prevented unsupervised access to the bridge from the south. Perhaps the unsuitability of the Irthing valley for settlement and communication

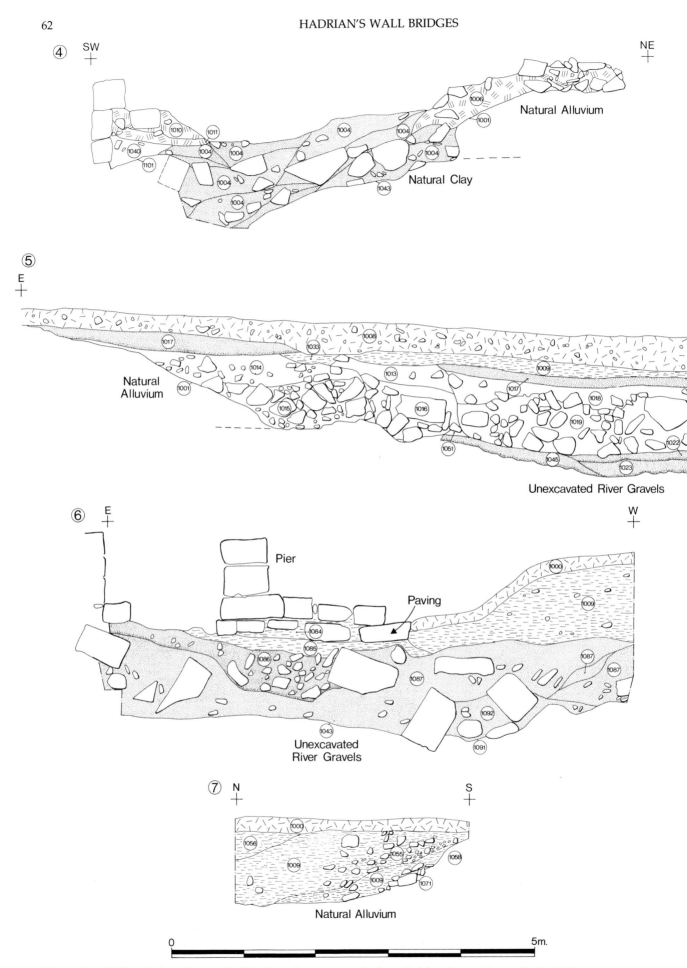

Figure 45   Willowford sections 4–7. Stippling denotes gravels deposited by river action.   Scale 1:50

convinced the Roman engineers that access from the civil zone was unlikely to be a problem in this particular case.

Bridge 1

Bridge 1 was constructed to carry the Broad Wall across the Irthing. Within the Broad Wall part of a dressed faced recess was discovered; this was probably associated with a small tower which provided access to the bridge from the bank. At some date the bridge was damaged by flood action and this may have included the collapse of at least one arch of the bridge. When repairs were carried out (bridge 1A; Figure 44) a southern wing-wall was added to the abutment to protect the bank from river scour. This repaired bridge was subsequently heavily ruined by another major inundation of the river. Although the dating evidence is not conclusive, the construction and destruction of bridge 1A both probably fell within the second half of the second century and perhaps more specifically c 160–80 (p 96)

The bridge was constructed mainly of sandstone. Most of this was quarried rather than derived from the river, which appears to have been the source of most of the other stone types represented. Sandstone is a difficult rock to characterise to individual quarries and so Shaw's (1926, 460) identifications of the source of the sandstones used in the Broad and Narrow Walls should not be regarded as certain. Shaw thought the sandstone used in the Broad Wall was similar to that from the Leap quarry at Lanerton (NY 595 649), 3 km downstream from the bridge, while that in the Narrow curtain derived from the Lodges quarry, Low Row (NY 592 632), 4.4 km to the south-west. This is the same source which John Armstrong (p 52) identified for the blocks robbed from the water pier of bridge 3. There is no conclusive evidence that the Romans exploited the Lodges although Lanerton was certainly used. Hodgson (1840, 440) records that Roman inscriptions and the carved figure of a deer once existed on the quarry face, although they were subsequently destroyed by workmen.

It is apparent that there was a deliberate exploitation of carboniferous sandstone, rather than the more ubiquitous limestone of the region, in the construction of the bridge. This must indicate that sandstone was considered to be a better building material and Hill (1981, 2) has stated that it is often easier to work than limestone.

Evidence suggests that the blocks arrived from the quarry in a roughed-out state and were finished on site prior to their incorporation in the structure (see below). Typical blocks in the piers weighed between c 130 and c 290 kg.

The bridge site and evidence for construction

The eastern abutment of the Hadrianic bridge (bridge 1) was built on the fine sandy alluvium of the river bank (context 1001, Figure 45, section 4, and section 5). As well as running down into the river the ground surface also fell away southwards across the width of the bridge, dropping by c 1m in the area covered by the bridge abutments. The alluvium overlay a heavy grey-pink clay which comprised the bed of the river and which was only c 0.1m thick in places (context 1043, Figure 45, section 4, and section 6). This in turn overlay extensive deposits of coarse gravels, over 1m deep, which had been laid down by river action. Bedrock was not reached in the excavations.

Shaw (1926, 479) recorded that there was an extensive layer of sandstone chippings directly overlying the natural river bank. The layer was c 0.15m thick and covered the area beneath the tower of bridge 2 as well as extending to the west and south. Westward the chippings faded out at the back of the core of the southern wing-wall of bridge 1A. To the south more chippings were found to extend for 6.1m from the south wall of the tower (ibid, 486, fig 5). Shaw thought the latter distinct from the other chippings and interpreted them as the base of a branch road of the Military Way. His descriptions do not make clear how the chippings were different however, and the interpretation of them as a road is unlikely. Shaw records no trace of kerb stones or any other feature which might definitely distinguish a road, and in any event what he took to be the Military Way is now known to be a natural gravel deposit (p 95). The likelihood is therefore, that the chippings which underlay the tower and those to the west and south of it were the same deposit and that they covered an area of approximately 12.5m by 11.9m. The layer was not recorded to the north of Hadrian's Wall.

Shaw stated that the chippings 'definitely touched' the foundation of the tower and he considered them to derive from the dressing of the blocks incorporated in that structure. Upon re-examination, the chippings (context 1029, Figure 39), which had been heavily disturbed since their discovery, were found to extend beneath the angular rubble which filled the construction trench of the western wall of the tower. As the construction trenches lay on the interior of the tower, it is probable that the blocks used in the foundation were placed flush with the outer face of the trench, which may account for Shaw's observation. This point could not be examined further as all the stratigraphy on the outside of the tower foundation has now been removed by previous excavation and consolidation.

The chippings are therefore earlier than the construction of the tower of bridge 2 and so the most likely explanation is that they are associated with the construction of bridge 1. Where it survived the deposit varied from a crushed powder to angular offcuts clearly derived from stone dressing. This suggests the presence of a stoneyard on the river bank where blocks, having arrived from the quarries in a roughed-out state, were finished for incorporation in the bridge.

Shaw (ibid, 459–60) also recorded finding sandstone chippings 25.3m south-east of the tower of bridge 2. It is not clear whether these are further indications of construction work.

Figure 46   Recess within the Broad Wall of Willowford bridge 1.   (Photo: S C Speak)

The tower

In the south side of the Broad Wall, 4.5m west of the point of reduction, there is a recess faced mainly with split-faced stones. Initially discovered during consolidation in 1941, the recess had been exposed by the removal of the core of the reconstructed curtain of bridge 2 which infilled it. The top three courses of the recess were consolidated at that time and during the recent excavations the recess was once more fully exposed by the removal of rubble filling (Figures 42, and 46)

Only the eastern face of the recess and a fragment of the northern face 1.16m in length are intact; the western side of the recess has been destroyed and the original length cannot now be determined. The recess is 1.8m deep. The dressed faces survive to a maximum height of eight courses; the bottom course rests on the core of the Broad Wall foundation which has been levelled off with unusually large stones to produce a solid platform (Figure 47). The bottom course consists of water worn whin cobbles and sandstone fragments above which, and offset by up to 0.13m, the main walls of the recess were constructed (context 1061, Figure 41, section 3). The walls consist in the main of sandstone blocks with undressed split faces although some unworked whin cobbles are also present. Gaps of up to 0.14m existed within (and to a lesser extent, between) courses owing to this irregular finishing. These were filled with a light brown mortar (sample 1, p 97). This was

found to be too degraded for chemical analysis although it could be seen to contain an abundant aggregate of small pea gravel and charcoal flecks, the latter derived from the burning of lime. The core of the Broad Wall abutted the back of the dressed faces of the recess, indicating their contemporaneity.

If the recess existed in isolation from a structure to the south of the Wall one possibility is that it housed a flight of steps (*ascensus*) to provide access to the bridge. A flight of stone steps, 4.67m long and 1.62m wide, is known from Milecastle 48 (Poltross Burn, Gibson and Simpson 1911, 418). In this case the steps abut the south face of the north wall of the milecastle, rather than being recessed into it, and this is the usual arrangement where *ascensus* are found within forts, as at the Lunt (Hobley 1972, 19) and Annetwell St, Carlisle (*Britannia* **16** (1985), 274). At Willowford the recess diminished the width of the curtain to 0.96m, which, allowing *c* 0.5m for the width of a parapet, would have effectively obstructed access to the bridge from a wall-walk. The very existence of bridges on the Wall in the Hadrianic period strongly suggests that a wall-walk did exist (p 134ff) so that the presence of steps built within the recess is unlikely.

Another possibility suggested by Richmond (1947, 165) is that the recess formed part of a turret. There are, however, a number of objections that can be raised to this hypothesis if a turret of similar design to the others on the Wall is envisaged. Firstly, it is doubtful if there was enough room to fit a turret onto the bank at this point. The portion of unscoured river bank to the south of the bridge indicates that the bank roughly occupied the line subsequently taken by the southern wing-wall of bridge 1A (context 1001, Figure 42). Assuming that the turret was built right up to the edge of the bank, the maximum dimensions possible would have been *c* 3.88m by 3.68m. Turrets on Hadrian's Wall are usually in the region of *c* 4.27m square internally although the Willowford turrets (48a and 48b, which were presumably built as part of the same legionary work length as the bridge) were slightly smaller: Turret 48a was slightly irregular in shape, but had minimum dimensions of 4.04m by 3.57m while Turret 48b was 4.19m east–west (Charlesworth 1977, 15; Shaw 1926, 438, 431). Even if the turret was slightly smaller than normal the south-west corner of the structure would still have rested on the very edge of the bank and, in time of flood, water would have flowed against the corner of the turret, not only flooding the ground floor, but also threatening the safety of the structure. There is secondly, absolutely no evidence on the ground for the presence of a turret. The recess commenced above the top of the Broad Wall foundation, and yet this was *c* 0.5m above the height of the Roman ground level recorded by Shaw (1926, 480, p 55). Had a normal turret existed it would have been necessary for the foundations of its eastern wall to have been carried down to at least this level and probably further; the evidence from Turret 10a (Throckley: Bennett 1983, 32) shows that the foundations of turret walls were dug to a greater depth than those of the curtain. Excavation revealed no traces of foundations or robber trenches for any walls, nor was there any scar visible in the south face of the Broad Wall foundation immediately east of the recess, of the kind that might have been expected had the east wall of a turret been demolished. It is clear that there was no refacing of this portion of the Broad Wall foundation, the later masonry blocking of the recess only having been built from above the foundation (context 1068, Figure 40, elevation 2).

Despite these objections to Richmond's theory the purpose of the recess is difficult to explain unless there was some form of tower at this point (no other recesses are known on Hadrian's Wall which are not connected with a turret). If a tower did exist, its primary function must surely have been to provide access to the wall-walk and so it need not have extended much above the top of the parapet. Surveillance of the bridge and the river valley to the north was already provided by Milecastle 49 and Turret 48b, and so there may have been little need for an elevated lookout at the bridge itself. Such a tower could thus have been a comparatively slight structure, which may in part account for the lack of evidence which it has left. The principal problem for the hypothesis remains Shaw's record of the Roman ground level (Shaw 1926, 480), and this can only be overcome if dumping occurred after the construction of the Broad Wall to raise the ground surface to a point level with the top of the Broad Wall foundation (and the base of the recess). The (presumably shallow) foundations for the tower walls could then have been sunk into the dump and have abutted the

Figure 47   The ragged end of the Broad Wall core following the destruction of Willowford bridge 1A; in the background, large coring beneath recess. 2m scale. (Photo: S C Speak)

south face of the Broad Wall foundations (this would account for the absence of a scar in the south face of the foundation, and the absence of foundations in the underlying alluvium). If the tower held only a ladder or wooden steps it could have been considerably smaller than a normal turret and so be set back from the edge of the river bank. The existence of a tower on the western side of the bridge also is probable.

The pier

Within the area of excavation no part of the first pier was found *in situ* as it had been destroyed in the flood which led to the collapse of bridge 1A (p 76). The approximate position of the pier can be reconstructed however by reference to the evidence for its destruction.

Twenty worked blocks were found in a layer of riverine gravel which was deposited following the destruction of the bridge (context 1087, Figures 42, and 45, section 6). While all the blocks were disturbed from their original positions a clear concentration was apparent in their distribution and examination of the individual blocks indicated that they were from a stone pier. The three blocks found to the east of the main concentration probably derived from the eastern abutment.

A clearly defined but irregularly shaped depression in the natural clay and underlying gravel of the Roman river bed represented a scour pit directly underneath the concentration of blocks in the river gravel (context 1091, Figure 45, section 6). The depth of the depression was at most 0.56m below the level of the surrounding river bed. It extended some distance north (upstream) of the postulated position of the pier although this is to be expected in the formation of scour pits around submerged structures (p 66). The fill of the scour pit (context 1092, Figure 45, section 6) consisted of gravel set in a fine light-blue silt matrix which was very distinct from the other riverine fills around it.

A possible reconstruction

Some features of bridge 1 can be reconstructed by a study of the loose blocks which were derived from it. Eighty-six have one or more features in addition to plain dressing and fall into two groups: those excavated from the riverine gravels associated with the destruction of the bridge and those reused in bridge 2. In addition there were other blocks found reused in later contexts or loose on the site which have features in common with those firmly attributable to bridge 1 and so were probably also derived from it. It is worth stressing that only a very small area of the riverine gravels was excavated and so a large number of blocks may still await discovery. Their recovery would permit a much more detailed reconstruction.

Evidence for two different types of clamp is represented by the loose blocks which can be associated with the bridge destroyed by the inundation of the Irthing. Thirty-two of them have dovetail clamp sockets although unlike the Hadrianic pier at Chesters no trace of iron or lead was found in any of the sockets and nor were there extraction scars visible in the reused blocks. Consequently the clamps were almost certainly of wood. Seven other blocks have bar clamp sockets and a number from the riverine gravels still retained iron clamps with their lead settings (Figures 48, and 57). There are no examples of dovetail and bar clamp sockets on the same block. It seems unlikely that two methods of clamping would have been utilised in the main body of the pier: although different techniques of construction were used in different parts of bridge 2 at Chesters (p 117). No examples are known of wooden dovetail clamps and iron bar clamps being used alongside each other in the same part of a structure. Consequently two periods of construction appear to be represented, the small number of blocks with bar clamps probably representing later repairs to the original fabric. The blocks with sockets for bar clamps are therefore considered separately below (p 75).

Although no trace of the eastern abutment survives *in situ* its location can be determined as the later southern wing-wall of bridge 1A butted up against it. A projection of the alignment of the surviving blocks

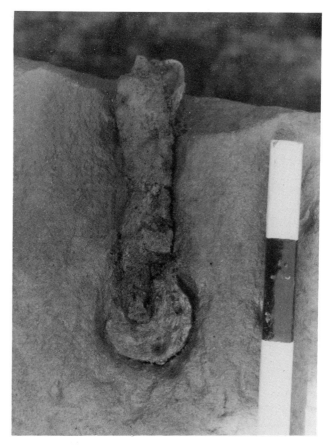

Figure 48   Fragment of an iron bar clamp set in a lead filled socket in block no 544, from Willowford bridge 1A, divisions on scale 50mm.   (Photo: S C Speak)

at the south-eastern end of the wing-wall therefore indicates its position (Figure 47). No blocks can be attributed with certainty to the abutment although it presumably consisted of an *opus quadratum* (p 117) termination to the curtain.

Three angled blocks came from the cutwater of a pier: block no 520 (Figure 50, no 1) formed the point of a cutwater and had sides at angles of 50 and 52 degrees to its base, while block 537 (Figure 50, no 2) and block no 363 (not illustrated) came from the shoulders of a pier and were angled at 59 and 69 degrees to their bases respectively. In the pier reconstruction (Figure 49, A) a mean angle of 57 degrees has been used for the cutwater which compares with angles of 45 degrees on the Hadrianic pier at Chesters. It is argued below that the pier would probably have lain a little to the south of the northernmost extent of the scour pit and so, assuming that the cutwater met the main body of the pier on the same line as the northern face of the curtain, the width of the pier can be calculated at *c* 2.6m. The Chesters pier has a maximum width of 3.1 m.

As noted above, the evidence for the position of the first pier of the bridge relies principally on a concentration of loose blocks and the presence of a scour pit. However, the positions occupied by a pier and, following destruction, a resultant scour pit are not fully coincidental. The effects of scour around a bridge pier with a pointed cutwater lead to erosion

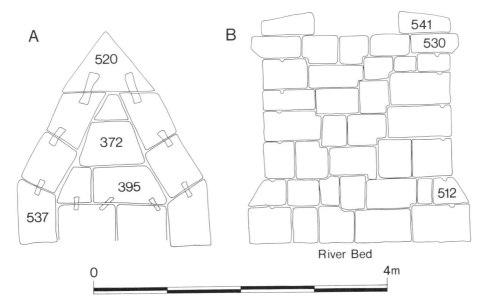

Figure 49
    A: *reconstructed plan of a cutwater of a pier of Willowford bridge 1*
    B: *reconstructed elevation of the pier below the level of the arch springing.*   Scale 1:50

of the river bed upstream and subsequent deposition downstream. In addition when a pier is built diagonally to the current, as at Willowford (p 72), scouring also takes place along the side of the pier exposed to the current (Robinson 1964, 44, 50). Consequently at Willowford, although the scour pit extended for a distance of 2.8m north of the projected line of the Wall, it is unlikely that the pier was as elongated as this. Furthermore, the edge of the scour pit may also have lain slightly to the west of the site of the pier because of the angle of the current. Taking these considerations into account, and working from a pier width of 2.6m, it can be calculated that there would have been a distance of *c* 6.55m between the first pier and the postulated position of the eastern abutment. If it is also assumed that the spacing of the piers was regular (by no means always true of Roman bridges, see p 112) then two piers and three arches would have had an overall width of 24.85m, sufficient to span the Irthing for most of the year, although the bridge would have then been very vulnerable during the winter floods.

Conjectural architectural reconstruction

An architectural reconstruction of the bridge has been attempted employing the evidence supplied by the loose blocks derived from it (Figures 50–54, and Plate 7).

In common with Chesters and Piercebridge no evidence for a timber coffer dam was found in the excavations although because of the low water-level in summer such a dam may not have been necessary. Their use may have been generally confined to bridge constructions in much larger rivers. The body of the piers below the level of the arch springing was constructed of *opus quadratum* to judge from the large quantity of sizeable dressed and squared sandstone blocks reused in the structures of bridge 2. The

dressing of these blocks is generally of good quality with the chisel and point being used as well as the pick for some of the cruder dressing.

An initial foundation course for the pier has been restored by reference to the Römerbrücke at Trier (Cüppers 1969, Abb 59). Above this there was probably a chamfered course. A group of at least seven blocks are known at Willowford with a chamfer of 55 to 86 degrees to the horizontal (producing an offset 0.14–0.20m in width). Where visible each block has at least one dovetail clamp socket, as would be expected with an external course below water level (block no 512, Figure 50, no 3; blocks nos 212; 213; 214; 215; 217; and 533), although none of the blocks exhibited much water wear. At least five of the blocks were reused in the chamfered north face of the northern wing-wall of bridge 2. The main body of the pier was constructed from solid masonry with the exterior blocks once again securely fixed together by dovetail clamps, as in the Hadrianic pier at Chesters (block no 550, Figure 50, no 4; blocks nos 225; 308; 397; 510; 540; and 549). Within the body of the cutwater the reconstruction has utilised block no 372 (Figure 50, no 5), considered by Simpson (1941, 214) to have been a springer or haunch for a segmental arch. There is now no reason to believe that the bridge did not possess normal semicircular arches (see above p 53). Block no 371, similar to block no 372, was also reused in the tower of bridge 2.

Two other groups of chamfered blocks have been recognised, which are distinguished by the angle and dimensions of the chamfer. One group consists of four blocks (no 530, Figure 50, no 6; no 320, Figure 50, no 7; no 40, Figure 50, no 12; and no 327). The presence of a crowbar slot in block no 530 and lewis holes in blocks nos 320 and 327 clearly indicates which were the upper surfaces of these blocks and so demonstrates that they originally formed a projecting course chamfered on the underside. The angle of the

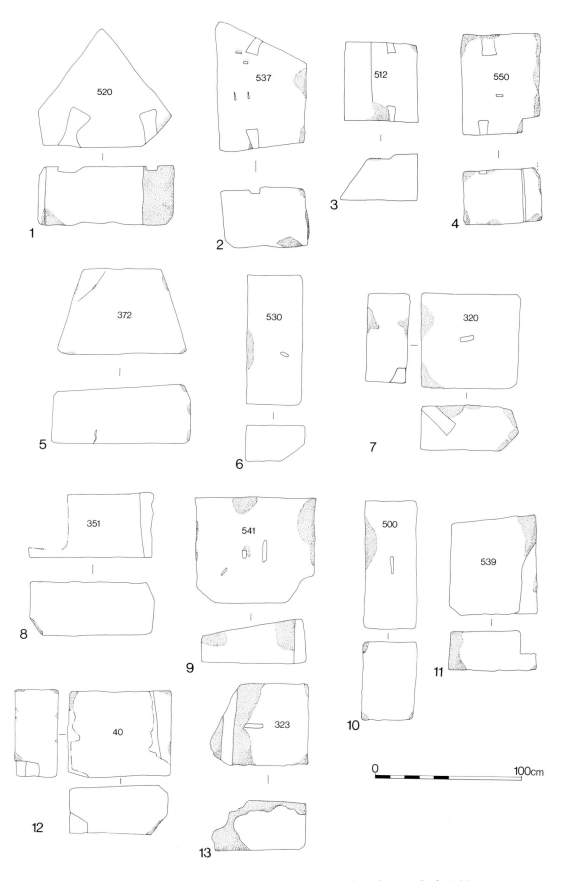

Figure 50   Blocks from Willowford bridge 1. Stippling denotes fractured surfaces.   Scale 1:25

chamfer varied from 35 to 50 degrees, producing an offset of 0.11–0.17m. None of the blocks have clamp sockets and this may suggest that they were positioned above water level on the bridge. Consequently in the reconstruction the blocks are suggested to have projected immediately below the springing of the arch, as in the imposts of some Roman fort gateways, for example at Housesteads (Richmond and Child 1942, 141). Where the springer is set back from the front of the projecting chamfered block, the resulting ledge could have been used for seating timber centering for the arch. The other group of chamfered blocks consists of two examples (block no 351, Figure 50, no 8; and block no 350) with small chamfers, 0.1m in height and at angles of 34 and 48 degrees. Both are reused and heavily obscured in the foundations of the tower of bridge 2, but they probably belonged to an offset course on the piers or abutments or a string course at the level of the bridge walkway on the north face of the Wall.

An arch springer (block no 541, Figure 50, no 9) and one voussoir (block no 172) were reused in bridge 2 and demonstrate that bridge 1 probably possessed semicircular arches. In addition there are two unstratified voussoirs (block no 500, Figure 50, no 10; which is almost identical to block no 172; and block no 323, Figure 50, no 13). All four blocks have lewis holes in their upper surfaces which probably indicate that a crane was used to place the voussoirs into position in the arch ring. The springer block no 541 also has a sub-rectangular hole in its upper surface which probably held a wooden dowel. The position of the lewis holes indicates that block no 323 was laid almost in a horizontal position just above the springing while block no 500 came from nearer the crown of the arch. The degree of taper on these two voussoirs is 60mm over a length of 0.64m and 45mm over a length of 0.51m respectively. This small amount of taper is due to the large (c 6.55m) diameter of the arch (cf p 34). It can be calculated that there must have been approximately 28 voussoirs in each arch ring and as each vault would have been 3 voussoirs thick this produces a total of c 84 voussoirs in each vault, and 252 in the whole bridge. Considering this number of voussoirs existed it is surprising that only three are known at present although more may still lie undiscovered in the river gravels to the south of the bridge.

Eleven blocks which can be assigned securely to bridge 1 (and nine that cannot) display evidence of joggling. On nine of these a recess of either square or rectangular section has been cut from one corner (blocks nos 550, Figure 50, no 4; 541, Figure 50, no 9; 205; 303; 332; 378; 527; 531; and 546). Matching projections on adjacent blocks would then fit into these recesses to provide a further method of preventing slippage within a course. Another six blocks have recesses which run the full length or width of a block, yet do not pass through the full thickness (blocks nos 539, Figure 50, no 11; 323, Figure 50, no 13; 99; 144; 247; and 534). Their function was to joggle joints vertically between blocks in adjacent courses, as illustrated in the suggested reconstruction of the bridge river pier (Figure 49, B)

Figure 51   Carved relief of a phallus on block no 99, reused in the abutment of Willowford bridge 3, 300mm scale.   (Photo: S C Speak)

The recess in the back of voussoir block no 323 (Figure 50, no 13) probably facilitated the bonding of horizontal coursing into the voussoirs in the arch ring. Block no 99, reused in bridge 3, has a recess cut through its full length and also has a phallus carved in relief on one of its faces (Figure 51, p 142, no 2). The phallus might have been carved when the block was reused.

Three blocks contain sockets of varying dimentions at various angles whose function remains unknown. Two of these (blocks nos 320, Figure 50, no 7; and 40, Figure 50, no 12) had chamfers on the face opposite to that with the socket. The third block (no 54), reused in the pier of bridge 3, has its other faces obscured.

Two fragments of different mouldings are associated with the bridge (block no 394, Figure 52, no 14, and Figure 53; and block no 524, Figure 52, no 15, and Figure 54), but insufficient lengths of them survive to make any interpretation of their original position within the bridge possible. The moulding on block no 394 closes up at the right hand margin of the block indicating that it terminated at this point. Both mouldings are small and fairly finely dressed and are thus unlikely to come from below the springing of the arches, often a favoured location for mouldings on bridges (as on the Augustan bridge at Narni on the *Via Flaminia* in Italy; Ballance 1951, 92).

The bridge-walk would almost certainly have been continuous with the curtain wall-walk. The latter has been estimated to have been at least 3.5m above the footings at the east end of the Broad Wall (p 58). Assuming that the crowns of the arches were virtually at the level of the bridge walkway, probably just leaving enough room for a string course above, it can be calculated that the arches would have sprung from a height of at least 3m above the river bed. This elevation would have been sufficient for the arch springing to have lain above the river level, even when in flood. The body of the pier, some 3m in height and probably representing seven or eight courses below the arch springing, has been shown to have been of *opus quadratum* construction. It is unlikely that this construction was continued above that level, however, because the vaults above the arches would not have needed to have been of massive construction. The only load they had to carry was the walkway, and thus the bridge was probably constructed of small facing-stones above the arch springing, with a rubble core infilling the spaces between the arch rings. The bridge walk would have been *c* 2.3m wide if a width of 0.5m is allowed for a crenellated parapet.

Three blocks have had recesses cut from more than one face, the function of which is unclear. Block no 331, (Figure 52, no 16) has two slight recesses running along either side of its long axis. Block no 330 is similar to block no 331. Block no 367 (Figure 52, no 17) has two recesses in its front face which pass through the full thickness of the block, while in the rear face there is an irregular sinking, which is only 100mm deep.

Two unusual blocks have been reused in the abutment of bridge 2. Block no 253 (Figure 52, no 18) has a roughly semicircular recess of unknown purpose cut through its full thickness. The two dovetail clamp sockets are secondary and relate to the use of the block within the abutment. Block no 254 (Figure 52, no 19) has a V-shaped slot cut into one side. In the top of the block there is a lewis hole which may be contemporary with the slot and a dovetail clamp socket which is connected with the

reuse of the block. The function of these blocks is uncertain.

Design of the bridge

The design of a bridge needs to take two factors into account: the internal stresses created by the structure, and the effects of a river upon it. Scour by the river is the most serious threat and also the most difficult to assess and compensate for. Two kinds of scour can be defined: general, when the whole river bed is deepened, and local, caused by the disturbance of water currents when they come into contact with a submerged structure. These currents cause a limited area of deeper scour around an obstruction. Unlike general scour, qualitative work using hydraulic models has shown that local scour is directly affected by the design of the bridge and Laursen (1960, 44) has concluded that the length–width ratio of piers (including the presence or absence of a cutwater), the angle of attack of the currents against the piers, and the degree of encroachment of the abutments are the key parameters. The width of the piers, and the encroachment of the abutments are of importance, as the greater these become the more the bridge resembles a dam. Blockage of the river flow leads to a building up of the water level above the bridge and a lowering downstream, so that the velocity of the river increases as it passes beneath the bridge. As a consequence the river bank immediately downstream from the abutment becomes a particularly vulnerable area for scouring. A bridge constructed diagonally to the current reduces the area of unimpeded flow usable by the river and so increases local scour.

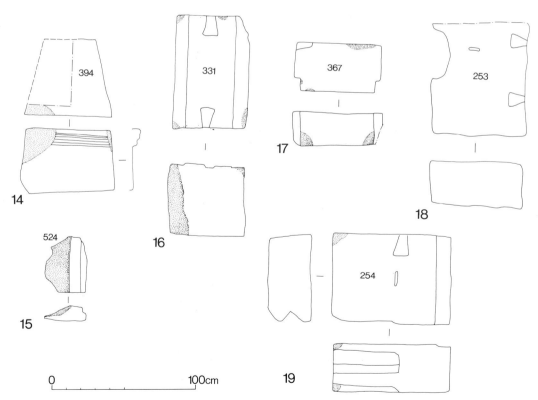

Figure 52   Blocks from Willowford bridge 1. Stippling denotes fractured surfaces.   Scale 1:25

Table 7 Blocks from bridge 1 at Willowford mentioned in the text

Block	Illustration	Context	Notes
40	Fig 50, no 12	RU: 3,P	front: offset, chamfered on the underside, 140mm high, 50° to horizontal. Back: socket at an angle of 31° to the horizontal, length 130mm, depth 120mm, width at rear 70mm expanding to 140mm at front
54		RU: 3,P	side: triangular profiled socket, length 145mm, depth at face 120mm, width at face 60mm
99	Fig 51	RU: 3,A	recess cut through full length of block, width 390mm, depth 120mm. *Front:* carved phallus
144		RU: 3,A	recess cut through full length of block, width 80–100mm, depth 190mm
172		RU: 2,NWW	voussoir: Top, lewis hole, depth 60mm. Angle of taper obscured
205		RU: 2,NWW	recess cut from one corner, full depth of block, length 135mm, width 120mm
212		RU: 2,NWW	front: chamfer, 65° to horizontal. Top, obscured
213		RU: 2,NWW	front: chamfer, 67° to horizontal. Top, obscured
214		RU: 2,NWW	front: chamfer, 86° to horizontal. Top, obscured
215		RU: 2,NWW	front: chamfer, 72° to horizontal. Top: two dovetail clamp sockets
217		RU: 2,NWW	front: chamfer, 72° to horizontal. Top: obscured
225		RU: 2,NWW	top: two dovetail clamp sockets
247		RU: 2,C	recess cut through full width of block, width 200mm, depth 90mm
253	Fig 52, no 18	RU: 2,A	semi-circular recess, full depth of block, length 280mm, width (max) 100mm. Top: crowbar slot, two dovetail clamp sockets (secondary)
254	Fig 52, no 19	RU: 2,A	side: triangular-profiled recess, length 460mm, width 150mm, depth 70mm. Top: lewis hole, 90mm deep, dovetail clamp socket (secondary)
303		RU:2,SWW	recess cut from one corner, full depth of block, length 160mm, width 130mm
308		RU: 2,SWW	top: two dovetail clamp sockets, two crowbar slots
320	Fig 50, no 7	U	front: offset, chamfered on the underside, 125mm high, 50° to horizontal. Top: lewis hole, 95mm deep. Back: socket, 45° to horizontal, length 250mm, depth 98mm, width 102mm at rear tapering to 73mm at front
323	Fig 50, no 13	U	voussoir: angle of taper 3°. Top: lewis hole, 70mm deep. Back: recess cut through full width, width 60mm, depth 70mm
327		U	front: offset, chamfered on the underside, 130mm high, 47° to horizontal. Top: lewis hole, depth 60mm
330		U	recesses cut along both margins of upper surface of block. RHS: width 160mm, depth 15mm. LHS: width 90mm, depth 10mm
331	Fig 52, no 16	U	recesses cut along both margins of upper surface of block. RHS, width 90mm, depth 10mm. LHS, width 80mm, depth 30mm. Two dovetail clamp sockets
332		U	recess cut from one corner, full depth of block, length 120mm, width 110mm
350		RU: 2,T	front: chamfer, 100mm high, 34° to horizontal
351	Fig 50, no 8	RU: 2,T	front: chamfer, 100mm high, 48° to horizontal
363		RU: 2,T	cutwater block, side angled at 69° to its base. Dovetail clamp socket opens onto angled face
367	Fig 52, no 17	RU: 2,T	front: recesses cut from both corners, full depth of block: RHS, length 60mm, width 40mm; LHS, length 90mm, width 40mm. Back: irregular sinking, length 120mm, width 20mm, depth 100mm
371		RU: 2,T	pier block, two angled faces
372	Fig 50, no 5	RU: 2,T	pier block, two angled faces
373		RU: 2,T	top: lewis hole, depth 50mm, dovetail clamp socket
378		RU: 2,T	recess cut from one corner, full depth of block, length 230mm, width 50mm. Top: lewis hole, 65mm deep
394	Fig 50, no 14	RU: 2,T	front: moulding, 130mm high, two inward chamfers with a fillet below and a groove along the top. Closes up at RHS of block see also Fig 53
395		RU: 2,T	pier block, two dovetail clamp sockets at angles of 30° to front face but in diverging directions
397		RU: 2,T	top: lewis hole, depth 35mm, two dovetail clamp sockets
500	Fig 50, no 10	U	voussoir, angle of taper 5°. Top: lewis hole, depth 58mm
510		RU: 2, Context 1016	top: two dovetail clamp sockets, crowbar slot
512	Fig 50, no 3	RU: 2, Context 1016	front: chamfer, 55° to horizontal. Top: two dovetail clamp sockets
520	Fig 50, no 1	RG	cutwater block, sides at 50° and 52° to base. Top: two dovetail clamp sockets
524	Fig 52, no 15	RG	small moulding see also Fig 54
527		RU:3, Context 1019	recess cut from one corner, full depth of block, length 150mm, depth 60mm
530	Fig 50, no 6	RG	front: offset, chamfered on the underside, 130mm high, 35° to horizontal. Top: crowbar slot
531		RU:3, Context 1019	recess cut from one corner, full depth of block, length 140mm, width 60mm
533		U	front: chamfer, 69° to horizontal. Top: dovetail clamp socket
534		U	recess cut through full length of block, width 120mm, depth 110mm
537	Fig 50, no 2	RU: 2, Context 1013	cutwater block, side angled at 59° to base. Top: two dovetail clamp sockets, two crowbar slots
539	Fig 50, no 11	RU: 2, Context 1013	recess cut obliquely across full width of block, width (max) 130mm, depth 120mm
540		RU: 2, Context 1015	top: two dovetail clamp sockets
541	Fig 50, no 9	RU: 2, Context 1015	springer, angle of taper 10°. Top: lewis hole, depth 73mm; dowel hole, length 61mm, width 41mm, depth 90mm. Recess cut from one corner, full depth of block, length 150mm, width 110mm
546		RG	top: crowbar slot; hole, length 65mm, width 15mm, depth 21mm, just possibly base of a large bar clamp socket. Recess cut from one corner, full depth of block, length 200mm, width 60mm
549		RG	top: two dovetail clamp sockets
550	Fig 50, no 4	RG	top: two dovetail clamp sockets; crowbar slot. Recess cut from one corner, full depth of block, length 130mm, width 115mm

KEY: RG = found in riverine gravel; U = unstratified (blocks excavated by Shaw the contexts of which are unknown); RU = reused, 3 = bridge 3, 2 = bridge 2, P = pier, A = abutment; T = tower NWW = northern wing-wall, SWW = southern wing-wall. Contexts 1013, 1015, 1016, and 1019 Fig 45, section 5.

Figure 53   Willowford block no 394, 300mm scale.
(Photo: S C Speak)

Figure 54   Willowford block no 524, 300mm scale.
(Photo: S C Speak)

At Willowford the location of the bridge was far from ideal. As noted above (p 50) it appears that the bridge was located a little downstream from the apex of a meander, a position dictated by the line of the Wall. Meanders produce disturbed patterns of flow and immediately downstream from a bend the main stream line of the water flow leaves the concave bank and moves across the river. Consequently at Willowford the main stream line would have met the bridge piers obliquely, which in addition to the disturbed currents created by the meander, must have accentuated the problem of scour (Figure 55).

Many problems would have been overcome if the river had been spanned by a single arch. Roman engineers certainly had the technical ability to do this, for the largest Roman bridge arch known is the Ponte San Martino, near Aosta in Italy, diameter 35.65m (Briegleb 1971, 318, n 945: cf the arch of the bridge over the Cendere Çay in Turkey, width 34.2m: Humann and Puchstein, 1890, 394, and Figure 28). Such a solution, however, was not practicable at Willowford for enormously high abutments would have been required, along with a heightened stretch of wall adjacent to the bridge.

From the estimated dimensions of the piers it can be calculated that the bridge would have had a ratio of pier width to arch width of *c* 1:2.5. This is a very high ratio (medieval bridges had a ratio between *c* 1:2 and 1:3, eighteenth century bridges *c* 1:5) caused by the great thickness of the piers (Robinson 1964, 16). The comparative width of Roman piers generally is probably due to the method of construction, for it is likely that the arches were built one at a time, and so after the construction of one arch but before the completion of the adjacent one, each pier would have had to act as an abutment and contain the stresses created. Once the adjacent arch had been completed, however, many of the forces on the pier from the two arches would have been equal and opposite and so effectively cancelled out. This over-compensation for the forces created by the bridge explains why some extant Roman bridges are still capable of bearing up to the stresses of modern traffic passing over them (for example the *Pons Aelius* and *Pons Fabricius* in

Rome). On the other hand the massiveness of Roman piers meant that an increasing proportion of the width of the river became blocked, so accentuating the problem of scour. At Willowford about a fifth of the width of the river (at *c* 25m) would have been blocked by the piers, and at Chesters about 33 per cent of the river was obstructed by the first bridge.

In the reconstruction (Figure 55) cutwaters have been placed on both the upstream and downstream sides of the piers, as was the case with the Hadrianic pier at Chesters. Cutwaters downstream were not always present in Roman bridges however (cf the piers of the later bridges at Chesters and Corbridge). In tidal rivers the purpose of a cutwater on the downstream end of a pier is obvious although Whitby (1985, 133) has emphasised that cutwaters in this position also reduce turbulence, and hence scour, immediately below the bridge. He further suggested that a rounded cutwater upstream is better than an angular one for it too reduces turbulence (although the results of Rhebock's hydraulic models would not appear necessarily to support this statement; Robin son 1964, 44; Terzaghi and Peck 1967, 476, fig 53.3). A few examples are known of Roman and Byzantine bridges which possessed a rounded cutwater upstream and a pointed end downstream (p 104–5) but the opposite arrangement with the point upstream was far more commonly used (as at the Römerbrücke in Trier, Cüppers 1969, Taf 1).

Roman engineers attempted to protect river piers from scour in a number of ways. If possible they dredged away the soft alluvial deposits until a solid stratum was reached and then founded the piers upon this. Such an operation normally required the construction of coffer-dams around the site of the piers, the interior of which would have been pumped out so that dredging could begin. Vitruvius (V, XII, 5) described such coffer dams and remains of them were found at the Römerbrücke at Trier where the foundations of the piers were sunk to a depth of as much as 4m below the bed of the river (Cüppers 1969, 70–3). Where no suitable stratum could be reached, the usual method was to sink a timber pile-work into the river bed and then found the masonry piers on a wooden platform constructed upon the piles. There are numerous examples of this method of con struction such as the Pfahlrostbrücke at Trier, the Rhine bridge at Mainz and the bridge over the Enns at *Lauriacum* (ibid, 42–50, 185–7, 194–7). Despite the use of pile-works to modern times, Robinson (1964, 62) is critical of their ability to protect piers successfully from scour and notes that not a single medieval bridge built in France upon timber piles has remained intact.

At Willowford a pile-work might have been expected as no solid stratum was present in the river bed. No trace of any timber piling was found in the area examined beneath the northern point of the pier and so presumably none existed (it is perhaps unlikely that all traces could have been obliterated by scour). Nor is there is any evidence that the foundations of the pier were sunk to any appreciable depth below the surface of the river bed. Even allowing for the fact that the excavated profile of the river bed (context 1043, Figure 45, section 6) has been affected by scouring it is noticeable that at most the base of the scour pit was only 0.56m below the surrounding bed. It would therefore appear that the pier at Willowford was constructed more or less directly upon the river bed with little or no preparation. This lack of provision against the effects of scour is surprising and indicates a poor level of engineering (as opposed to architectural) design.

Another method of scour protection utilised in Roman bridges was to pave the unstable beds of rivers with heavy blocks. This device (which presumably derived from the paving of fords) appears to date back to early Imperial times at least as Ballance (1951, 102) recorded paving associated with the Ponte Fonnaia on the *Via Flaminia*. Although paving was employed in the Hadrianic bridge at Chesters (p 12) there is no evidence that this was the case with bridge 1 at Willowford. Bridge 1 at Willowford thus appears to have been poorly designed from an engineering point of view, perhaps because the military architects were not experienced in the construction of stone bridges (the Hadrianic Wall bridges may well have been the first stone bridges to be constructed in Britain).

Building of the bridge

In the absence of a building inscription it cannot be certain which unit constructed the bridge although Breeze and Dobson (1987, 82) have considered it to be the work of the Twentieth legion. The construction of the bridge was a major undertaking which would have required greater masoncraft than the building of the curtain wall. For this reason there may well have been a far greater concentration of specialists working here than elsewhere. Possibly a specialist unit may even have been involved. Individual units building specific structures are known elsewhere on the Wall as at Benwell where a detachment of the British Fleet built an exceptionally well constructed granary (Simpson and Richmond 1941, 17).

A temporary camp of 0.8ha has been located on top of the scar to the south-east of the bridge and it is possible that this may have been a construction camp for the bridge (Figure 38). The date of the camp is uncertain but it is possibly associated with bridge 1 for during the construction of bridges 2 and 3 the workers could have been accommodated at Bird oswald, if indeed they were not actually part of the normal garrison there.

Bridge 1A

There is evidence that bridge 1 underwent modific- ation and repair. The southern wing-wall appears to be a later addition and the seven blocks associated with the bridge which have bar clamp sockets are not considered to be part of the original fabric and most probably belong to a major repair (p 66).

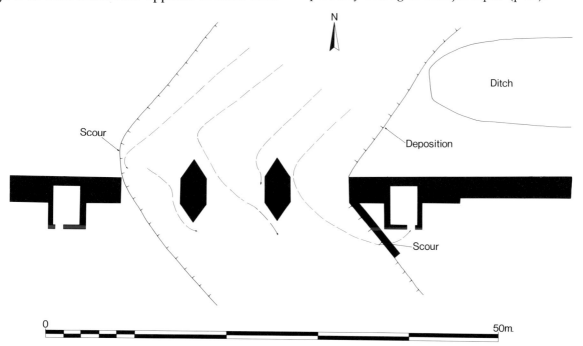

Figure 55   Schematic plan showing the river currents of the Irthing at the bridge.   Scale 1:400

Figure 56   The southern wing-wall of Willowford bridge 1A, with the partially excavated scour pit to the left; in the background, the junction of the southern faces of the Broad Wall foundation and the reconstructed curtain wall of bridge 2, 1m scale.   (Photo: S C Speak)

The southern wing-wall

The southern wing-wall consisted of a row of large, roughly tooled, sandstone blocks which revetted a core of clay and stone (Figures 42, 56). The dressed facing had an estimated overall length of c 10.6m and ran at an angle of 50 degrees to the line of the curtain wall. Only the south-eastern end of the wing-wall now remains, four blocks in length and two courses high. At this point the wing-wall had been terraced into the front of the gently sloping river bank and the three blocks at the end are founded upon a layer of sand and stones up to 0.3m thick (context 1038, Figure 42) which had been deposited as levelling. The bottom course is represented by four blocks, on average 0.26m high, and above these, and inset by 0.1–0.2m on the north-western side, three blocks remain. The end block of the upper course is particularly large measuring 0.84m by 0.70m by 0.37 m; as there is no trace of any extension south eastwards it clearly represents the original end of the wing-wall. The next block to the north-west has a dovetail clamp socket in a useless position on its south-east face and has clearly been reused. The socket is quite shallow (33mm) so the face of the block may have been cut back when reused. Two of the faces of the third block of the upper course had been

crudely fractured into shape (in contrast to the fairly fine tooling on the other faces) and so this block may also have been reused.

The front faces of the blocks show little trace of water wear although wear is present on the top surfaces of the blocks of the second course for a distance of 0.12m from the front faces; the tooling on the rest of the surfaces is much fresher. This indicates that there had originally been a third course inset from the face of the second. Assuming that this course was of a similar height to those still remaining the face of the wing-wall would have been brought up to a height level with the top of the river bank immediately to the south-east. The Roman ground level dropped by c 0.8m from the south face of Hadrian's Wall to just south of the wing-wall so it is probable that the face of the wing-wall was stepped up with the addition of one or more courses as it approached the abutment.

The masonry face of the wing-wall revetted a core of clay and stone which was terraced into the bank (context 1006, Figure 42). The core consisted of a mass of stones, mostly sandstone river cobbles, mudstones and granites, set in a clayey loam. Immediately behind the face there were stones of larger than average size and the westward limit of the core was marked by a kerb of rounded river cobbles (the 'line of cobbles' marked on Shaw's plan, 1926, fig 5. The maximum surviving depth of the core was 0.44m although it would have been deeper at the back of the masonry face (these areas were subsequently destroyed). The construction trench for the core had been dug down against the southern face of the Broad Wall foundation so that the core would have abutted the Wall. This demonstrates that the Broad Wall foundation had been completed before the construction of the wing-wall.

The core stabilised the bank although it is probable that it also served as a foundation for a masonry capping. Shaw recorded that the sandstone chipping layer (context 1029, Figure 39) faded out where it met the back of the core (p 63) and it is apparent that the surviving height of the core was *c* 0.6m below the level of the chippings. The most likely explanation for this disparity in levels is that the core was originally capped by dressed blocks which would have been level with, or higher than, the sandstone chippings. After the destruction of the bridge the surviving blocks must have been robbed out for reuse and the trench then filled, Shaw failing to identify the fill of the robber trench in his excavations. A well tooled rectangular block (no 522) was found in the riverine gravel which overlay the slumped core of the wing-wall and could have been disturbed from the capping. The purpose of such masonry would have been to prevent flood water scouring away the soft bank immediately behind the face of the wing-wall.

The construction of the wing-wall would have necessitated the demolition of the tower because the core was terraced into the river bank to a depth below the level at which the tower walls would have been constructed. It is not known if a new structure was built to replace it although this is a probability as there would still have been a need for access to the bridge from the bank. Any such structure could have been built directly upon the masonry capping, and would thus have left no trace.

Repair work

Five of the blocks which possessed bar clamp sockets were recovered from the gravel layer above the scour pit (context 1087, Figure 45, section 6). Three of these blocks (nos 544, Figure 57, no 20; 548, Figure 57, no 21; and 553, Figure 57, no 22) have one side cut at an oblique angle which varies from 52 to 79 degrees, cf 57 degrees for the original cutwater. Block 553 has a type of bar clamp socket (wedge shaped rather than circular) which differs slightly from those in the other blocks from the river gravels, although this type of socket is also found in a block (no 258) reused in the sluices of bridge 2. Crowbar slots in the upper surfaces of the blocks indicate the presence of superimposed blocks. Block no 544 has also had a recess cut from one corner for the joggling of joints (cf p 69). Block no 528 (Figure 57, no 23) was found in the river gravels (context 1004, Figure 45, section 4) west of the southern wing-wall, although as there is no evidence for the use of bar clamps in the existing fabric of the wing-wall it might have originated from the eastern abutment. In the upper surface of the

block there is a recess which does not pass through the full thickness.

The extent of the damage to bridge 1

Five of the seventeen blocks catalogued from above the scour pit of the pier have bar clamp sockets and this suggests that at the very least major repairs were undertaken at the northern end of the pier. As none of the other blocks with dovetail clamp sockets display any signs of reuse, some of the original fabric presumably remained intact after the repairs took place. It is unlikely therefore that the pier was completely destroyed and rebuilt. The first arch might well have collapsed, however, for otherwise it would have been very difficult to carry out substantial repairs to the pier as some of the blocks in the cutwater would also have extended beneath the arch springing. A possible cause of the destruction of the arch may have been erosion of the eastern bank leading to the undermining and collapse of the eastern abutment. Block no 528 has been cited as possible evidence for the reconstruction of this abutment. Certainly the addition of the southern wing-wall indicates that the scouring away of the eastern bank immediately downstream from the bridge was considered to be a serious problem.

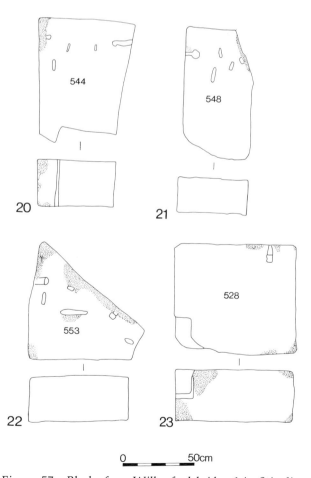

Figure 57   Blocks from Willowford bridge 1A. Stippling denotes fractured surfaces.   Scale 1:25

Table 8   Blocks from bridge 1A at Willowford mentioned in the text

Block	Context	Notes
522	River gravel	well tooled featureless block, length 0.75m, width 0.63m, depth 0.24m
528	River gravel	bar clamp socket; recess cut from one corner, length 145mm, width 125mm, depth 150–180mm, Fig 57, no 23
544	River gravel	two bar clamp sockets, one with iron bar clamp set in lead still *in situ*, other heavily fractured. Three crowbar slots. One long side cut at 79° to the other. Recess cut from one corner, full depth of block, length 370mm, width 130m, Fig 57, no 20
548	River gravel	two bar clamp sockets, one with iron bar clamp set in lead still *in situ*, other heavily fractured. Three crowbar slots, two with a row of three small holes at the bottom of the slot, presumably from the teeth of the crowbar. One short side cut at an irregular oblique angle to the other, Fig 57, no 21
553	River gravel	two bar clamp sockets, unusual profile, wedge-shaped rather than circular. Lewis hole, heavily fractured, depth 30mm; two crowbar slots. One side angled at 52° to the opposite face, Fig 57, no 22
555	River gravel	block only partially exposed. One bar clamp socket, iron bar clamp set in lead *in situ* (= Fig 90, no1)

It is likely that the pier and abutment were repaired at the same time as the southern wing-wall was added. The wing-wall contained at least one reused block which possessed a dovetail clamp socket and may have originally been used in the piers or abutments of bridge 1. If this was the case it indicates that the wing-wall must have been constructed after damage had occurred to the bridge and further suggests that the two activities were part of the same operation.

The destruction of bridge 1A

Bridge 1A was extensively damaged and perhaps entirely destroyed by an inundation of the Irthing. During what must have been an exceptionally heavy flood scouring took place to such an extent that the northern end (if not the whole) of the first pier, a large proportion of the southern wing-wall, and c 6.3m of curtain and abutment were destroyed. The increased erosive power of the Irthing also led to a westward shift in its course which may well have seriously damaged the western abutment. All three arches of the bridge probably collapsed as a result of the flood. The damage to the structures on the eastern bank was a result of the line of the main stream crossing back across the river from the concave (western) bank as it left the meander, and so causing increased scouring of the eastern bank immediately downstream from the abutment (Figure 55). The shape of the resulting scour pit on the eastern bank suggests that after scouring away the face of the wing-wall the river cut back northwards destroying the bridge abutment (Figures 42, 46, 47). The full extent and maximum depth of the scour pit could not be established, although the river cut at least 0.77m deeper than the bottom of the extant blocks of the wing-wall. The destruction of the masonry front of this structure led to the collapse and slumping into the river of the clay bonded core which it revetted (context 1006, Figure 45, section 4).

The full extent to which the river shifted westwards has not been established although after the flood the eastern bank of the river lay at least 10m west of the site of the original abutment (the new bank was not located in Area 5 and so it must have lain

further to the west). It is not certain whether this movement was entirely the result of geomorphological processes or whether the partial damming of the river by collapsed masonry also played a part. The action of water passing through a meander will always lead to erosion upon the concave (in this case the western) bank and during heavy flood this process is accelerated, thus increasing the likelihood of significant channel change. The degree to which the Irthing has shifted its course at Willowford is clearly visible (Figure 38) and it may be that a significant proportion of this movement was caused by sudden changes as a result of heavy flooding. For example, Shaw (1926, 451) recorded that in 1897 when the Irthing was in spate it broke its banks at Willowford and shifted the width of its course within a single flood.

As the velocity of the flood waters dropped gravel deposits began to be laid down. The primary fill of the pier scour pit was gravel set in a distinctive fine, light-blue silt (context 1092, Figure 45, section 6). Above this a thickness of up to 1.2m of coarse gravels was deposited, the lowest level of which contained blocks dislodged from the pier (context 1087, Figure 45, section 6). Nearer to the bank the riverine layers contained greater proportions of sand (context 1004, Figure 45, section 4), and a patchy layer of fine, light blue silt, up to 0.2m thick, accumulated above the gravels (context 1045, Figure 45, section 5).

The evidence suggests that bridge 1A at Willowford was destroyed by a particularly catastrophic inundation which was of greater intensity than the normal winter floods of the Irthing. Widespread and serious flooding of abnormal intensity is known to have affected a number of rivers in northern England in historic times. Two such instances are the flood of November 1771 which swept away nine bridges on the Tyne and caused widespread flooding from the Eden to the Tees, and the flood of December 1815 which also caused extensive damage in the North. Movement of river channels is recorded in a number of places as a direct result of these floods, as at Piercebridge on the Tees in 1771 (Scott 1982, 80) and Shotley Bridge on the Derwent in 1815 (Denham 1816, 7). It is therefore possible that the destruction of bridge 1A at Willowford could have been a consequence of a similarly widespread episode of flooding and that other bridges in the North might have been damaged. At Chesters the North Tyne shifted westwards and a solid causeway was constructed from the abutment of bridge 1 to the first pier (p 14). This movement could have occurred as a result of flooding which also damaged the first pier. The causeway was perhaps constructed to replace the fallen first arch and was founded upon the gravel deposits laid down when the flood waters receded. At Piercebridge the stone bridge discovered in 1972 (p 110) seems to have superseded a bridge on the original course of Dere Street. There the bridge was rebuilt some distance downstream from its predecessor, perhaps at a point where the course of the river widened to lessen the danger to its fabric when the river was in spate (Scott 1982, 77). It is not impossible that the damage caused to the bridges at Willowford, Chesters and Piercebridge could have been as a consequence of a single catastrophic flood. The destruction of bridge 1A at Willowford is not particularly well dated although it certainly occurred within the second half of the second century, and perhaps in the period c 160–180, although this is less certain (p 96).

5   Willowford: bridge 2

Following the destruction of bridge 1A a new bridge was built (Figure 44, bridge 2). Its construction can be dated to the second half of the second century, possibly the period *c* 160–80. A new length of curtain wall was built westwards from the ragged scar of the Broad Wall and this terminated in a dressed stone abutment pierced by two sluices. The bridge possessed two wing-walls: to the north a quadrilateral mass of masonry projected from the curtain wall, while to the south a single row of blocks revetted a clay and stone core. New stone piers also appear to have been constructed, although their positions are unknown. Unlike bridge 1, bridge 2 apparently possessed a timber superstructure.

Sources of materials

Most of the blocks in the eastern abutment of bridge 2 were reused from bridge 1 and 1A, but some blocks reused in bridge 3 and probably derived from the piers of bridge 2 appear to have been newly cut. John Armstrong (p 52) considered that blocks robbed from the pier of bridge 3 derived from the Lodges quarry near Low Row. This structure however was almost entirely composed of material reused from bridge 2 and so it can be reasonably suggested that the Lodges quarry was utilised in the construction of bridge 2, as well as bridge 1 (p 63). There is in addition one block reused in bridge 2 which may have come from a different source, block no 307 (Figure 58, no 24) reused in the southern wing-wall. The block (dimensions 10.85m+ long by 0.65m wide and 0.34m deep) has a large pivot hole, one side of which has been broken through when the block was fractured. The pivot hole has a diameter at the top of 140mm and a depth of 115mm. At the bottom of the hole, and slightly off centre, is a smaller sinking, 65mm in diameter and 35mm deep. The sides of the pivot hole have been worn smooth with no trace of original tooling remaining. The upper surface has an area of wear consistent with its use as a threshold; this is partly obscured by later working.

The pivot hole is much larger (0.85m+ long by 0.65m wide and 0.34m deep) than those used in milecastle gateways and a better parallel for the Willowford block is the pivot slab of the monumental gateway at the Benwell Vallum crossing (Birley *et al* 1934, 177). This slab measures 0.89m by 0.71m with a pivot hole 120–130mm in diameter and 70mm deep. A chase for the insertion of the gatepost runs from one side of the pivot hole to the edge of the slab; such a chase on the Willowford block would have been cut across the missing portion. Block 307 therefore seems to have come from a gate of considerable size. There is no evidence or indeed reason for the existence of such a gate at the bridge and a possible source in view of the resemblance to the Benwell slab is the Vallum crossing at Birdoswald excavated in 1932 (Simpson and Richmond 1933, 247). The foundations for the revetting walls of the causeway, consisting of large squared blocks with lewis holes, were all that

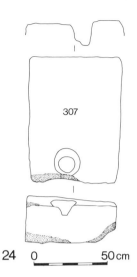

Figure 58   Willowford block no 307, possibly reused from the Vallum crossing at Birdoswald. Stippling denotes fractured surfaces.   Scale 1:25

survived intact. The rest of the structure, presumably including a monumental gateway of the same type as at Benwell, had been dismantled when the Vallum ditch was filled with peat and capped off with a layer of clay. This filling was considered to have occurred very quickly after the construction of the crossing on the strength of botanical analysis of the sediments found in the bottom of the Vallum ditch in an earlier section at Birdoswald. In that section the sediments were found to contain seeds of weeds which colonise newly disturbed ground and the analysis concluded

> 'I think we may assume that the Ditch could only have been open a year or two before the re-filling with the peat'
>
> Richmond 1929, 309

However, similar results would have been obtained if the Vallum ditch had been thoroughly cleaned out a couple of years before its filling. Such cleaning may have been associated with routine maintenance of the Vallum, or else may have occurred on the return from the Antonine Wall when at least certain lengths of the Vallum were probably reinstated (Breeze and Dobson 1987, 128). The advantage of allowing a later date for the demolition of the causeway is that the pivot block, perhaps along with other less distinctive stones, could have then been taken straight from the dismantled gateway to Willowford for incorporation in bridge 2. The date in the late 120s proposed by Gillam and Swinbank (1950, 61) for the demolition of the Vallum causeway necessitates a stockpiling or other use of the block for at least thirty years beforehand, a somewhat less probable situation. Pottery in the clay capping of the filled in Vallum ditch has been published as a group from a securely dated later Hadrianic context (Swinbank and Gillam 1950; Gillam 1970, group 36. AD 130–140), but could be as late as the Antonine period.

The reconstructed curtain wall and abutment

As a result of the destruction of bridge 1A the Broad Wall ended in a ragged scar where it had been scoured through by the river. The northern wall of the tower recess had been completely broken through while the Broad Wall foundation beneath it gradually petered out westwards (Figure 46). Following the destruction a new length of curtain wall was built (Figure 59) which terminated in a dressed stone abutment 9.3m west of the scar (Figure 60). The new curtain wall bonded into, and continued, the line of the Broad Wall above its offsets, and is 2.74m (9.3 RF) wide at the junction with the fractured wall, although this increases by a kink in the north face to a width of 2.90m where it meets the abutment sluices. Neither face exhibits any offsets. The Wall runs obliquely across the edge of the scour pit which, even after it had been filled with riverine deposits, remained as a depression. Consequently in some places the bottom of the southern face of the curtain wall is up to 0.64m below that of the northern face (Figure 41, section 2). Where this difference in level is most pronounced, the southern face is founded upon a course of large river boulders, up to 0.52m in height (Figure 40, elevation 2). In the northern face

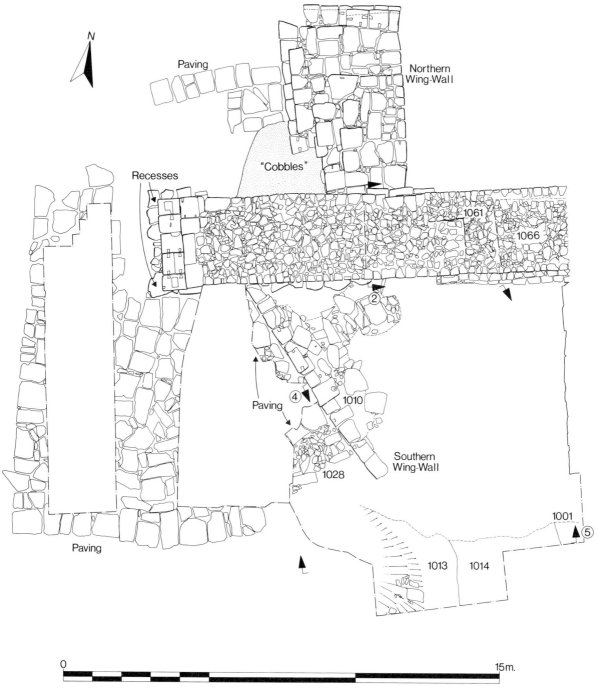

Figure 59   Willowford bridge 2 and subsequent modifications. The extent of the 'cobbles' after Shaw 1926, fig 5.   Scale 1:125

Figure 60   Abutment of Willowford bridge 2 with dovetail clamp sockets and two recesses; abutted right by abutment of bridge 3.   (Photo: S C Speak)

these only occur beneath the abutment sluices. The boulders not only partly compensate for the difference in level between the faces but also form a firm foundation above the soft gravel infill of the scour pit.

When first excavated the south face survived to a height of fourteen courses above the boulders, a total height of 3.04m. The lowest course of this face contains stones larger than average (height *c* 0.3m). Shaw described the masonry above as being

> '... of very heterogeneous description, many of the stones being river cobbles, others pieces of flag-stone mixed with better-dressed blocks. Throughout the face the squaring of the masonry is very poor, and the joints wide.'
>
> Shaw 1926, 462

Shaw also thought that he could recognise an area of refacing in the south face, 3.66m east of the end of the abutment, occurring above the sixth course and extending for 1.22m. However much of the southern face of the curtain wall was rebuilt during subsequent consolidation work, obscuring all trace of this refacing.

The footing and bottom two courses of the fractured end of the southern face of the Broad Wall foundation were left *in situ* when the new curtain wall was constructed, but above this a large dressed block 0.62m by 0.32m was placed to form a regular termination to the masonry (context 1068, Figure 40, elevation 2; Figure 56). The next course is inset by 0.13m and consists of four squared stones which are carried back eastwards above the masonry of the Broad Wall foundation, not only to block the tower recess, but also to bond securely into the existing fabric. As the new curtain wall was laid on an alignment fractionally different from the Broad Wall, a slight southward deviation is apparent at their junction (Figure 59).

The north face of the curtain wall has two distinct types of masonry (Figure 62). At the junction with the Broad Wall three large roughly tooled blocks, 0.36m in height and 2.26m in length, overlie the remaining second course of the Broad foundation and two blocks of the northern wing-wall. Above, and inset by 0.2m–0.28m, four courses of large masonry survive, one block in the uppermost course being clearly reused (context 1106, Figure 40, elevation 1). At their western end the blocks step down to bond with the other type of masonry, which consists of smaller work similar to that used in the south face. This smaller masonry is used in the rest of the face as far as the abutment (context 1069, Figure 40, elevation 1). The mortar used in the two types of masonry is identical thus demonstrating that the whole face is of one build and secondary to the Broad Wall. This disproves Richmond's assertion (1947, 165) that the larger masonry represents the original construction and the smaller work a refacing. The reason for the use of unusually large masonry in a restricted portion of the northern face remains unclear.

Excavation within the core of the curtain wall indicated that immediately above the truncated remains of the Broad Wall foundation there was a dirty compacted layer of clayey loam, 0.15m thick, with inclusions of charcoal, lime, and decayed sandstone (context 1078, Figure 41, section 2). This appears to be a layer of constructional trample associated with the northern wing-wall, one block of which sits directly upon it. The northern wing-wall and the new length of curtain wall were probably built at the same time: some blocks of the wing-wall pass beneath the northern face of the curtain wall (although only as far as the inner edge of the facing stones; Figure 41, section 2) while others abut the completed face. The construction layer within the curtain wall is level with the top of the third course of the south face and these three courses must have been cut into the side of the remaining core of the Broad Wall foundation. Above the construction level

is a wall core consisting of a mass of river-derived sandstone and whin boulders and some quarried angular sandstone (context 1065, Figure 41, section 2). The stones are set in a matrix of dirty gravelly soil which also contained some sandstone chippings (Shaw 1926, 461, stated incorrectly that the Wall had a core of rubble and mortar).

As in the cases of the Broad and Narrow Walls the mortar was restricted to the faces of the curtain wall, but it was hard and white and very distinct from that used in the other structures, (samples 2 and 4, p 97). Hard white mortar has been recognised at a number of places along Hadrian's Wall and has been generally associated with Severan rebuilding since the discovery that it was employed in the wall blocking the recess of Turret 54a Garthside, (Simpson *et al* 1934, 142; for the pottery, Welsby 1985). The occurrence of this mortar in an Antonine context at Willowford, however, suggests that it was not confined to a single period of building on the Wall.

The curtain wall terminates in a masonry abutment with two sluices; these allowed the free passage of flood water through the structure (Figures 60, and 61). Immediately east of the eastern sluice (sluice 1) larger masonry blocks bond into the face of the curtain wall while the abutment itself is composed of large reused blocks. All the reused blocks had been previously well dressed although some fairly crude secondary dressing occurred when the blocks were utilised in the abutment. This is particularly evident in the central support between the sluices where the

Figure 61　The northern face of the abutment of Willowford bridge 2 showing the two sluices. 1m scale. (Photo: S C Speak)

Figure 62   The northern wing-wall of Willowford bridge 2 with chamfered northern face; in the background, the two types of masonry used in the northern face of the reconstructed curtain wall of bridge 2, 2m scale.   (Photo: S C Speak)

northern face has been roughly battered into shape and bears a very crude chamfer. The abutment is founded upon a course of large river boulders which form a firm foundation above the soft riverine gravels, as was the southern face of the curtain wall. The two sluices are 0.45m wide at their bases and the abutment terminates in a solid plinth, 3.04m wide, 0.85m long and 0.94m high, surviving to a height of three courses (Figure 60) which represents the original height at this point. The upper course not only supports the cover slab of the western sluice (sluice 2) but also has a pair of recesses cut into its surface. These are spaced 2.24m apart and have been cut into the two corner blocks of the plinth. The northern recess measures 280mm by 270mm by 65mm deep and the southern 330mm by 250mm by 50mm deep although the level of the base rises abruptly by *c* 10mm, 95mm from the northern edge, perhaps representing a recut as Shaw (1926, 466) suggested. The uppermost course of the plinth was bound together by dovetail clamps, which to judge from the lack of extraction scars, were of wood rather than of iron set in lead. The northern recess is cut through the rear of a dovetailed clamp socket

although there is no reason to doubt that they are contemporary and associated with the use of the block in this position. The abutment is the only place on the bridge where dovetail clamp sockets can be seen *in situ*. Shaw (ibid) recorded that he lifted one of the blocks in the upper course and found empty dovetail clamp sockets in the underlying block and it is very probable that clamping occurs in all three courses of the plinth.

Both sluices are covered with slabs *c* 0.3m thick and of considerable weight (one block weighs *c* 500kg). The underside of the slabs covering sluice 2 have rebates, 80mm–130mm wide and 40mm–90mm deep, where they rest upon the side walls of the sluices (Figure 40, elevations 1 and 2). In order to maintain a level seating for the most northerly slab of sluice 2 an additional stone was inserted above the central support to compensate for the difference in height between the top of the support and the top of the plinth. Above the cover slabs of sluice 2 a single block measuring 1.04m by 0.47m by 0.33m remains. The core of the curtain wall extends westward as far as this block but no further, and when discovered by Shaw its upper surface was covered with mortar (ibid, 468). The block probably formed part of a dressed stone face at the end of the curtain wall. Sluice 1 is of similar construction to sluice 2 although the visible cover slabs only have a rebate along their western margins.

The abutment wing-walls

The northern wing-wall

The northern wing-wall consists of a mass of masonry projecting northwards from the reconstructed curtain wall, with which it has been shown to be contemporary (p 80; Figures 59, 62, and 66 elevation 3). Its function was to form a solid revetment for the soft sandy river bank, an area of which adjacent to the north face of the curtain wall it completely enclosed. North of the wing-wall the river bank cut back eastwards (context 1001, Figure 39). The dimensions of the wing-wall are *c* 6.2m by 4.1m and it is slightly trapezoidal in plan, the eastern (landward) face running at right angles to the line of the curtain wall while the western face is slightly splayed. It is constructed without mortar and almost entirely of reused blocks from bridge 1/1A, many fractured or redressed. The northern and western faces are composed of coursed and dressed blocks which retain a roughly-laid core of large worked blocks and smaller fragments. On the eastern side the core simply abuts the river bank although at the north-east corner a single block has been terraced into the bank so as to prevent the river from scouring around the back of the north face. The level of the core steps down from the face of the curtain wall towards the north face of the wing-wall, which survives in places to its apparently original height of two courses (Figure 66, elevation 3). The north face is chamfered at an angle of 55–70 degrees to the horizontal; of the nine blocks still in position five seem to have been reused from the chamfered course of the bridge 1 piers while four were newly cut for the purpose. There is little trace of water wear on their faces.

The west face survives for a length of 4.44m from the north-west corner of the wing-wall, the missing length of 1.3m having been removed during a subsequent modification (p 89). The face has offsets of *c* 0.28m and *c* 0.64m between courses. The faces of the blocks in the lowest course are slightly inclined from the vertical and their upper surfaces show secondary working to form a level seating for the large course above. The lowest course shows clear signs of water wear although tooling is still fresh upon the second course so presumably the Irthing only flowed against the face in times of heavy flooding which can rarely have exceed a depth of *c* 0.5m. Abutting the west face of the wing-wall is an area of large sandstone paving slabs.

Shaw (1926, 485) recorded that a carved block was found lying loose near the wing-wall. Although the block had probably been built into the wing-wall it might well have been reused from bridge 1/1A, as were many of the other blocks in the structure. The

Figure 63   A Block found by Shaw near the northern wing-wall of Willowford bridge 2 depicting a horned god. Reproduced by permission of Carlisle Museum and Art Gallery.   (Photo: N Franklin)

block which is now in the Tullie House Museum, Carlisle,(Wright and Phillips 1975, 74, no 198) is crudely carved to show a naked figure, 0.33m high, with a pair of horns and his left arm raised (Figure 63; p 142).

The southern wing-wall

The southern wing-wall of bridge 2 is similar in form to the wing-wall of bridge 1A which it replaced and consists of a masonry face revetting a core of clay and stone. Its face is 8.00m long and is aligned at an angle

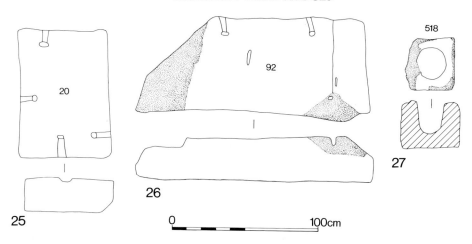

Figure 64   Blocks from Willowford bridge 2. Stippling denotes fractured surfaces.   Scale 1:25

of 58 degrees to the curtain wall, which it abuts immediately east of sluice 1 (Figure 59; Figure 66, elevation 4). The wing-wall face is composed of a single thickness of worked blocks, very many, if not all, reused, and survives to a height of four courses (1.36m) in one place. The lowest course of blocks is cut into the river gravels which filled the scour pit following the destruction of bridge 1A (context 1101, Figure 45, section 4). The only remaining block of the fourth course, which is reused, displays heavy wear upon its upper surface, particularly along the front edge and this suggests that the face survives to its full height at this point, although the number of courses probably reduced towards the south eastern end of the wing-wall (see below). The core consists of large river boulders and fragments of worked blocks set in a clayey loam (contexts 1011, and 1010, Figure 45, section 4); originally it filled the depression which remained above the natural filling of the scour pit and extended eastward as far as the broken end of the Broad Wall (Shaw 1926, 470). It is not certain whether the core was capped with masonry, as the core of the southern wing-wall of bridge 1A seems to have been (p 75) although Shaw's section (ibid, fig 7,i) shows that the core did not extend above the top of the third course of the face.

The south-eastern end of the wing-wall of bridge 2 was constructed 0.6m west of the remaining portion of the wing-wall of bridge 1A. In order to fill the gap between them and prevent the river scouring around the back of the new wing-wall, dumps of gravel were laid down against the river bank. These extended the ground surface westwards by at least 5.4m and encased the end of the new wing-wall (contexts 1015; 1014; 1016; and 1013; Figure 45, section 5). The dumps, which contained many loose blocks from bridge 1/1A, were c 1.0m deep and built up the ground to the same level as the top of the second course of the wing-wall. If this was the full height of the wing-wall at this point, the face must have stepped up by at least two courses as it approached the curtain wall.

Immediately west of the wing-wall face, and within the same cut, there was a crude foundation of large river boulders (context 1028, Figure 59), only part of

which was exposed during the excavations. The boulders were covered by c 0.3m of gravel (context 1021) which was in turn overlain by heavy sandstone paving slabs, these being visible in the area between the wing-wall face and the back of the abutment of bridge 3. This paving originally extended further to the south-east as demonstrated by the pattern of wear on the vertical face of one block in the lowest course of the wing-wall. This block lies 2.06m from the south-east end of the wing-wall and for a height of 0.12m above its base the face displays clear traces of tooling with a point. Above this level the block has been water worn. The other blocks in the lowest course of the face are also slightly water worn. This supports the evidence of the wear on the western face of the northern wing-wall, that the Irthing only flowed against the eastern side of the bridge during periods of heavy flooding.

Paving of the river bed beneath bridges with large slabs to protect the underlying river bed from scour during flooding is associated with bridge 1 at Chesters (p 12). It also occurs at Piercebridge in the later stone bridge over the Tees where the whole river bed was paved, and the bridge piers rested directly on the paving (p 112). At both bridges the slabs ran up to the front faces of the abutments.

Reconstruction and discussion

Only one block with a bar clamp socket was found reused in bridge 2 and it is argued elsewhere that this came from a repair of bridge 1; twenty-one such blocks found reused in bridge 3, however, suggests that bar clamps had been widely employed in bridge 2. The bar clamped blocks fall into two categories: first, there are rectangular blocks with clamps frequently in more than one side and sometimes in all four (block no 20, Figure 64, no 25), and eighteen other blocks listed in Table 9; second, there are two chamfered blocks (no 92, Figure 64: no 26; and block no 102), the position of the sockets indicating that the chamfers project outwards from the top of the blocks. The chamfers on the two blocks are cut at an angle to the horizontal of 40 and 47 degrees respectively.

Block no 92 also has a lewis hole, and a crowbar slot at the top of the chamfered face. If primary, as seems likely, the slot indicates the existence of masonry above the chamfer. This block is particularly massive, weighing c 725kg.

One block (no 39) reused in the pier of bridge 3 possesses a pair of dowel holes. In its upper surface (which also has two bar clamp sockets) there is a circular hole, diameter 40mm and 45mm deep, while on the underside there is a socket with a groove running from the face of the block to a deeper hole, diameter 40mm and 60mm deep. This socket is more deeply cut than is usual for bar clamp sockets and its dimensions compare well with the dowel sockets used in bridge 2 at Chesters (Table 12). This is the only example of a block with a dowel socket at Willowford, although another block subsequently reused as an altar has been noted in Nether Denton churchyard. The altar had been cut from a rectangular block which had a lewis hole in the (original) upper surface and a dowel socket, identical to those at Chesters, in its base. When it was reused as an altar, the block was turned on its side, and the central portions of three of the faces cut back to leave pronounced mouldings at the top and bottom. The surfaces of the altar are heavily eroded, and only one or two letters of the inscription can be made out. There can be little doubt that the altar was cut from a block which had originally been used in the bridge at Willowford, which lies only 3.2km to the northeast of Nether Denton. It cannot be certain that this block was originally used in bridge 2 however, for dowels may well have been used in bridge 3 as well. The block was probably removed from the bridge as part of repairs or alterations and then reused (probably at some date in the third century as inscribed altars are very rare after this period). If this is the case it is unlikely that the altar would have been dedicated at Nether Denton. The fort, which the churchyard overlies, probably predates the construction of Hadrian's Wall, although occupation in the *vicus* may have continued until later in the second century (Daniels 1978, 209–11). A more likely origin is the paradeground to the east of Birdoswald, which has produced a number of third-century altars (p 95). If this is the case, presumably it was carried to Nether Denton subsequently for reuse within the fabric of the church.

It is argued above (p 82) that the abutment of bridge 2 stands to its full height and so the blocks reused in bridge 3 must have come from elsewhere, most probably the piers. The absence of reused cutwater blocks in bridge 3 might suggest that the larger piers of that bridge incorporated the extant piers of bridge 2. If so it may have only been necessary to demolish the upper part of the piers and the reused chamfered blocks perhaps came from a string course around the top of the piers. There is no firm evidence for the number, dimensions or spacing of the piers although a resistivity survey (p 96) encountered a positive anomaly c 16m west of the abutment, centred slightly to the north of the projected line of the north face of Hadrian's Wall. The anomaly 'would not be inconsistent with the presence of masonry at depth' and may be a ruined pier,

although its identification as such is far from certain.

Although bridge 2 seems to have had stone piers as well as stone abutments, it differs from bridges 1 and 1A in that it must have had a timber superstructure. This is suggested by the eastern abutment where the curtain wall terminated in a dressed stone revetment only 0.7m from the end of the abutment which possesses two shallow recesses in its upper surface (p 82). They probably held timber uprights which were morticed into horizontal beams supporting the bridge walkway. These beams would have run between the pier and abutment and presumably passed into sockets in the masonry termination of the curtain wall. If the bridge walkway was of the same width as the curtain wall the sockets would have lain very close to the faces of it, a possible explanation for the additional support provided by the timber uprights. The morticed joints between the uprights and the horizontal beams could have been further strengthened by diagonal struts.

The simple construction proposed for the walkway of bridge 2 contrasts strongly with the superstructure of the bridge over the Danube at Drobeta depicted upon Trajan's Column, the elaborate nature of which was made necessary by the exceptionally wide spacing of the piers (c 32–33m; Choisy 1873, 162; Richmond 1935, 32–34; Tudor 1974). Even large bridges sometimes had simple superstructures as is demonstrated by the Römerbrücke at Trier (Cüppers 1969, 65–70, Abb 151) which had a maximum pier spacing of 21.3m. In this bridge the horizontal timbers which linked the stone piers were supported by six diagonal struts. Recesses in the sides of the piers which held the struts are still visible in some cases and in Pier 2 they are c 0.5m wide and spaced at intervals of 0.7m–1.0m . The bridge walkway at Willowford would probably have been planked with cross railed timber parapets on either side, such as are shown on a mosaic of a timber bridge over the Rhone in the Foro delle Corporazione at *Ostia* (Becatti 1961, no 108).

The two sluices in the abutment have sometimes been taken as evidence for the presence of a watermill a little downstream from the bridge (see p 94 for discussion). There is no firm evidence to support this hypothesis however and the sluices are better interpreted as being designed to relieve flood water building up against the north face of the abutment and curtain wall. The pattern of wear on both the northern and southern wing-walls indicates that water flowed against them only in times of flood. While it might be considered that the sluices were unnecessary because a width of only 0.85m separated sluice 2 from the end of the abutment beyond which water could flow freely, such arrangements can be paralleled. At the bridge over the Wâdi Zedî on the road between Kharaba and Bosra in Syria, the eastern abutment was pierced by two sluices, 0.95m and 0.99m wide, the western sluice separated by only 2.3m of masonry from the end of the abutment (Butler 1919, 304). The base of the sluices lay c 3m above the bottom of the wadi and their function can only have been to allow water to pass through the abutment during flash floods. Numerous other examples also exist of small arches piercing abut-

Table 9   Blocks from bridge 2 at Willowford, mentioned in the text

Block	Context	Notes
5	reused in bridge 3 pier	three bar clamp sockets, all show iron staining
7	reused in bridge 3 pier	south side: dovetail clamp socket; bar clamp socket, base of lead clamp *in situ*. East side: bar clamp socket, traces of iron staining
9	reused in bridge 3 pier	two bar clamp sockets
20	reused in bridge 3 pier	four bar clamp sockets (Fig 64, no 25)
24	reused in bridge 3 pier	three bar clamp sockets; base of iron clamps remain in two of them
26	reused in bridge 3 pier	bar clamp socket, traces of iron staining
34	reused in bridge 3 pier	bar clamp socket; crowbar slot
38	reused in bridge 3 pier	bar clamp socket; rest of block heavily osbscured
39	reused in bridge 3 pier	top, west (short) side: bar clamp socket; dowel hole, diameter 40mm, depth 45mm, 200mm from west face, 100mm from north face. North (long) side: bar clamp socket. Bottom, west side: dowel hole, channel, length 140mm, width 40mm; hole, length 40mm, width 40mm, depth 60mm
41	reused in bridge 3 pier	bar clamp socket
52	reused in bridge 3 pier	bar clamp socket
82	reused in bridge 3 abutment	bar clamp socket, base of iron clamp *in situ*
88	reused in bridge 3 abutment	two bar clamp sockets, one traces of iron staining, the other heavily fractured
90	reused in bridge 3 abutment	east side: dovetail clamp socket, heavily scorched; south side, bar clamp socket
91	reused in bridge 3 abutment	two bar clamp sockets, two crowbar sockets
92	reused in bridge 3 abutment	three bar clamp sockets, one heavily fractured; lewis hole, depth 40mm; crowbar slot. Front, chamfer 150mm high, 40° to horizontal (Fig 64, no 26)
94	reused in bridge 3 abutment	bar clamp socket
95	reused in bridge 3 abutment	bar clamp socket, heavily scorched
102	reused in bridge 3 abutment	bar clamp socket; crowbar slot at top of chamfer. Front, chamfer 100mm high, 47° to horizontal
116	reused in bridge 3 abutment	heavily obscured, mouth of one bar clamp socket visible
143	reused in bridge 3 abutment	heavily obscured, mouth of one bar clamp socket visible

ments and piers to prevent a build up of water against the bridge (Ballance 1951, 99).

The tower

A tower was constructed against the south face of the curtain wall 14.5m east of the end of the abutment (Figures 39, 65, and 66, elevations 5, 6). It was positioned so that the inner face of its western wall was roughly coincident with the vertical point of reduction between the Broad and Narrow Walls The large number of blocks from bridge 1/1A reused in its foundations indicates that it was contemporary with the construction of bridge 2. The tower has external dimensions of 6.80m by 6.94m and is substantially larger than a normal Wall turret (internal area 32.9 square metres, cf 18.2 square metres or less for a Wall turret).

The natural subsoil in this area consists of a deposit of coarse gravels which formed a pre-Roman river bank. The level of this stratum drops away to the west and is overlain by soft alluvial sand (context 1001, Figure 45, section 5). When the tower was built the foundations were constructed so that they rested upon the gravel. While the east wall of the tower could be placed directly upon the gravel, the foundations for the west wall had to be dug to a depth of *c* 1.2m below the surface of the sand in order to reach it. The foundations for the south wall (Figure 66, elevation 6) were laid upon the slope of the stratum.

The foundations on the western and southern sides of the tower consisted of large blocks reused from bridge 1/1A and they were placed one upon another

with small stones infilling any gaps. No mortar was used in the foundations; that for the west wall was four courses (1.56m) high with only the uppermost course visible above ground level. There was an offset of *c* 0.18m above the third course and the blocks in the fourth course showed much tighter jointing than those in the underlying courses (Figure 66, elevation 5). The foundation where it meets the south face of the Broad Wall foundation, was roughly laid and river cobbles had been used to pack the gaps between the two structures. The block in the fourth course however, was flush with the curtain wall, its upper surface level with the offset above the Broad Wall foundation. The south wall foundation was similar to that on the western side, although it was only three courses high at its eastern end however, because the gravel deposit there was *c* 0.22m higher than at the south-west corner. Its face had no continuous offsets. Construction trenches for the foundations exist behind their inside faces and are packed with angular rubble (Shaw 1926, 479). The outside faces of the blocks were probably laid flush against the sides of the construction trenches and this might explain the relationship with the sandstone chipping layer (context 1029, Figure 39) which was incorrectly observed by Shaw (p 63).

The south and west walls of the tower rested directly upon the foundations. There was a single footing course, 0.74m in width, above which the walls were offset by 0.06m–0.16m from both faces. The walls consisted of facing stones retaining a core of rubble and mortar. The east wall which stood to a maximum height of seven courses (1.14m) was carried across the Broad Wall foundation to make a straight butt joint with the south face of the Narrow Wall. Within the tower the Broad Wall foundation

Figure 65 Willowford bridge 2 tower, looking north. NB reused blocks from bridge 1/1A in the foundation, 2m scale. (Photo: S C Speak)

stands two courses high, the upper two courses presumably having been removed when the tower was built. The interior face of the west wall meets the south face of the curtain wall 0.11m west of the point of reduction. The footing and first course abut a large sandstone block used at the point of reduction and the next two courses above this also make a straight joint with the curtain wall. Above this level alternating facing stones of the Narrow Wall were removed and stones of the inner face of the tower wall projected into the cavities to produce a firmer bond (ibid, plate B).

In the centre of the tower there is a rectangular base, 0.88m by 0.72m, which stands two courses high. It was constructed from worked stone and overlies a rough footing course which was originally level with the primary floor of the tower (Shaw 1926, 483). The footing rests upon a clay and cobble foundation. All stratigraphy within the tower has been removed by previous excavation and consolidation work but Shaw (ibid) recorded that the primary floor consisted of worked clay up to 0.08m thick. This floor came up to the top of the footing course of the tower walls and passed over the remaining courses of the Broad Wall foundation, extending up to the south face of the Narrow Wall. A hearth consisting of burnt flagstones set in clay was found upon this surface (ibid, fig 5). Shaw also recorded that there was a seperate deposit of coal in the north-west corner of the tower. Although coal was extensively utilised by the Romans in north Britain it was perhaps here associated with the medieval industrial use of the tower (Figure 67): Shaw found a similar deposit of coal in the same

position 'overlying' a subsequent floor level, and the 33 iron nails found on the earliest floor are probably better associated with the medieval occupation (p 97). The entrance into the tower was at the southern end of the west wall. The north jamb remains, standing three courses high, while the southern one has been completely destroyed. Shaw (ibid, 482) found a stratum of gravelly sand 0.13m thick which overlay the continuous footing and had a width of 0.76m in the entrance. He was able to associate this deposit with the primary floor level. No trace of a pivot stone for a door was found. There can be no question that block no 307 (p 78) originally formed the threshold of the tower; the block is too long to fit the entrance, and the pivot hole is far too large for this small doorway.

The masonry base in the centre of the tower (Figure 67) was probably for an upper floor support, either a stone pillar or perhaps a wooden post. Supports of this type are rare within Roman towers of the second century, particularly in such places as the turrets on Hadrian's Wall or the towers on the German and Raetian *limes* (which were up to 8m square: Baatz 1976, 26). However, internal supports are found in the later fourth century Yorkshire signal stations; Goldsborough for example was 9.91m square internally and possessed six padstones for wooden posts (Hornsby and Laverick 1932, 209). There is no direct evidence for the height of the Willowford tower, although in view of its large floor-area and the strength of its foundations, it may well have stood higher than two stories. In the demolition debris above the uppermost floor in the tower Shaw (1926, 484) found fragments of stone slates and a bevelled

N   S

3   ↖ Top of paving

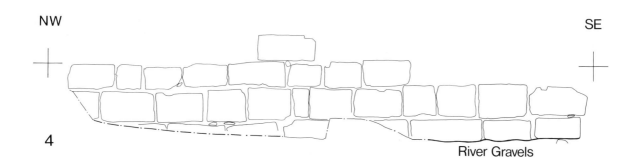

NW   SE

4   River Gravels

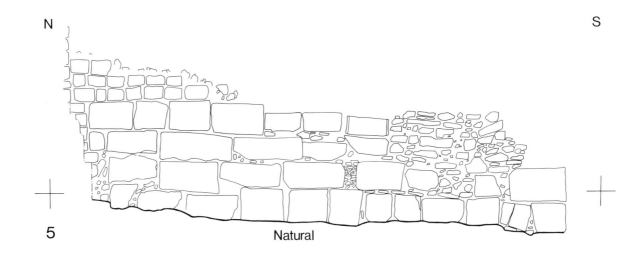

N   S

5   Natural

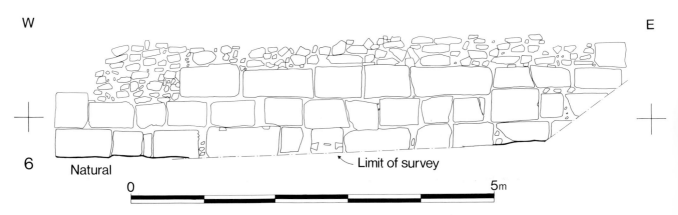

W   E

6   Natural   ↖ Limit of survey

0   5m

Figure 66   Willowford Bridge 2 elevations:
   3   west face of northern abutment wing-wall;   *5   west wall of tower;*
   4   south-west face of southern abutment wing-wall;   *6   south wall of tower.   Scale 1:50*

flagstone. Clay tiles or stone slates have only been noted at four of the Wall turrets, two of which are the Willowford Turrets 48a and 48b (Bennett 1983, 48, n 43). It is therefore possible that this tower was several stories high with a pitched slate roof.

The function of the tower was presumably to provide access to the bridge from the south and prevent unauthorised crossing beneath the bridge-arches. The bridge itself also had to be protected because damage to it would have disrupted lateral communications along the Wall. The presence of a hearth, detected by Shaw, suggests that the ground floor was used as a messroom by the soldiers on duty at the bridge.

Activities associated with bridge 2

Bridge 2A?

North of the curtain wall and west of the northern wing-wall Shaw found

> 'a mass of cobbles and clay, laid against the lower courses of the Great Wall beyond the point where the abutment [of bridge 2] masonry finishes. The cobble 'penning' extends for about 8 feet [2.44m] from the Wall face.'
>
> Shaw 1926, 469, (Figure 59)

His elevation (ibid fig 7, iii, west) shows that the top of the cobble layer was level with the top of the fourth course of the curtain wall with a depth of c 0.90m. All traces of this layer have since been removed but

it is clear from Shaw's record that the cobbles must have abutted the west face of the northern wing-wall, and presumably also filled the area where the wall face had been robbed. The cobbles also sealed an area of paving to the west of the wing-wall.

The extent of the cobbles is consistent with the possibility that they formed the core behind the masonry face of a wing-wall of similar design to the southern wing-walls of bridges 1A and 2. If the masonry face was subsequently robbed out, and its presence not detected in excavation, only the edge of the core would have remained to indicate the line of the wing-wall. The masonry face of this new structure would have met the north face of the curtain wall immediately east of sluice 1 (mirroring the arrangement on the south side of the Wall) at an angle of c 70 degrees. At its north-east end the new face would have abutted the west face of the original northern wing-wall of bridge 2. The blocks robbed from the original structure might have been used in the facing of the new work. The new wing-wall was probably built because the original wing-wall lay too far east and, in times of flood, water washed against the footings of the curtain wall threatening to undermine it.

The postulated wing-wall is considered to be an addition to bridge 2 rather than part of bridge 3 because it respected the northern opening of sluice 1. Both openings of sluice 1 were blocked when the abutment of bridge 3 was constructed, so if the wing-wall was associated with the later bridge there would have been little point in it respecting an inoperative sluice (p 91). It is also noted that sluice 1 contained a 0.30 depth of river silt when it was blocked (Shaw 1926, 468). Shaw makes no mention

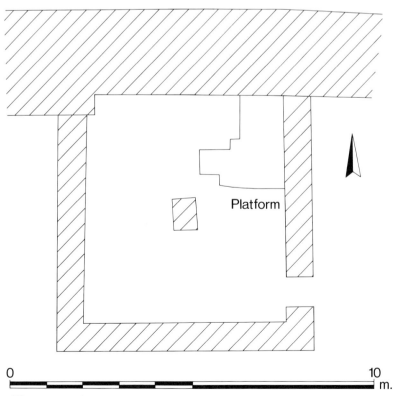

Figure 67   Outline plan of Willowford bridge 2 tower, platform after Shaw 1926, fig 5.   Scale 1:100

of any silt beneath the cobbles and the alluvium may have accumulated against the face of the wing-wall.

Coin no 7 found beneath the cobbles indicates that the wing-wall was constructed after AD 190 (ibid, 499–500; p 142), although it apparently precedes the construction of bridge 3, which it is argued occurred in the governorship of Alfenus Senecio (AD 205–7; p 139ff).

Natural processes

While silt was being deposited north of the bridge, erosion took place to the south. The gravel deposits (contexts 1013,and 1016, Figure 45, section 5) laid down to extend the ground surface westwards at the south end of the southern wing-wall were scoured back slightly, although this never seriously threatened the stability of the structure (Figure 59).

The curtain wall

An area of the north face of the curtain wall showed evidence of refacing. It is undated but is considered here for convenience. Shaw (ibid, 460) recorded that immediately east of the facing associated with the Broad Wall 'exceptionally large masonry' occurred in the face and his original site illustration indicates this to have consisted of blocks with average dimensions of c 0.4m by c 0.35m (context 1102, Figure 40, elevation 1). This section of facing has since been rebuilt but elevation 1 reproduces the blocks shown in the original drawing. Shaw considered that this facing was part of the fabric of the Narrow Wall but recent examination of the core revealed a thin spread of hard, white mortar immediately behind the now rebuilt face. This is very distinct from the mortar of

the Narrow Wall and the blocks thus appear to be an addition. Analysis of the mortar indicated that it was also distinct from that used in the reconstructed curtain wall of bridge 2 (sample 5, p 97). The original extent of the refacing is unknown as it extended beyond the area of Shaw's elevation.

Shaw also noted (ibid, 462) refacing on the south side of the reconstructed curtain wall of bridge 2 but evidence for this has also been completely destroyed by consolidation.

The tower

A second floor was laid down within the tower at a date probably within the second half of the second century (p 96). Shaw (ibid, 484) found that the primary floor was overlain by 0.05m–0.08m of debris consisting of 'dark material and a few stones'. Above this was a new floor of sand, 0.10m thick. At the entrance this stratum was represented by a flat stone (which may have served as a threshold) and adjoined by two disturbed flagstones, although this does not necessarily indicate that the whole floor was originally flagged (ibid, 482). A platform in the north-east corner of the tower was contemporary with the new floor. It consisted of a line of five dressed stones laid outwards from the south face of the Narrow Wall, upon which rested the western edge of a pavement of heavy flagstones (ibid 484; Figure 67). Upon excavation the paving was found to have been disturbed; if the platform was originally rectangular it would have covered an area of c 2.3 square metres. A number of similar platforms built against the north walls of turrets are known and they may have served as areas for meal preparation (Charlesworth 1977, 18).

6 Willowford: bridge 3 and later activities

Bridge 3 consisted of the following elements: a large abutment built against the south face of the curtain wall, with an earth ramp behind it, and a narrow rectangular pier, 1.68m west of the abutment of bridge 2 (Figure 44). The dimensions of the new structures indicate that for the first time the bridge was designed to carry a road, the Military Way. The construction of bridge 3 can probably be dated to the first quarter of the third century (p 96), and it is argued elsewhere, (p 139ff) that the conversion of the Wall bridges to road bridges carrying the Military Way occurred in the governorship of Alfenus Senecio, *c* 205–7.

The abutment

Before the construction of the abutment of bridge 3 dumps of gravel and river boulders, 0.90m in depth, were deposited to make up the ground surface to the south of the bridge (contexts 1018, and 1019, Figure 45, section 5). These dumps filled a depression scoured out by the river from material previously deposited to the south of the southern wing-wall of bridge 2 (context 1013, Figure 59). The full extent of the depression was not determined.

The new abutment constructed against the south face of the curtain wall is 7.4m in length and varies in width from 2.58m at its southern end to 1.50m where it abuts the Wall (Figures 39, 68 and 69, elevation 7). This narrowing is caused by the west face curving back eastwards as it approaches the Wall to allow sluice 2 to remain in operation. The face meets the Wall immediately east of sluice 2 and completely blocks the southern opening of sluice 1. The northern opening of this sluice was also blocked at this time; Shaw recorded that the blocking consisted of

> 'a large tightly-fitting stone and another smaller one, the wider joints laterally being packed with clay and small stones.'
> Shaw 1926, 468

The three faces of the abutment are composed of masonry blocks, very many, if not all, reused and they retain a core of rounded river pebbles and angular sandstone fragments set in mortar. The west face of the abutment survives to a maximum height of seven courses (1.94m) and displays no offsets (Figure 69, elevation 7). On the south face there is an offset of 0.16m above the first course. The east face is much more irregularly constructed than the other two but it would have been concealed by the earth ramp which lay behind the abutment.

Figure 68   Willowford bridge 3 pier and abutment looking east. NB the paving in the foreground was relaid during consolidation.   (Photo: S C Speak)

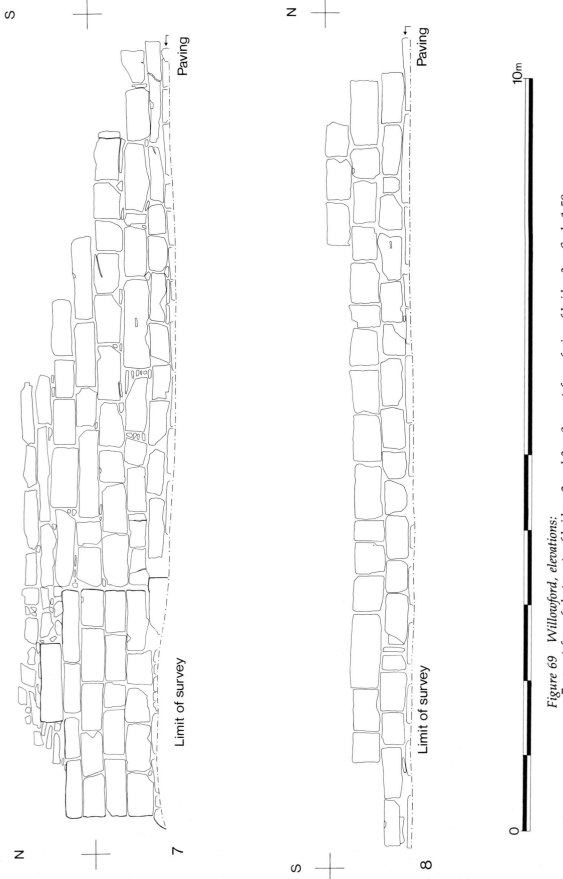

Figure 69 Willowford, elevations:
7 west face of abutments of bridges 2 and 3; 8 east face of pier of bridge 3.   Scale 1:50

Filling the triangular space between the rear wall of the abutment and the face of the southern wing-wall of bridge 2 is a layer of large river boulders set in clay which probably served as a foundation for the earth ramp. Two blocks supported upon this foundation continue the line of the south face of the abutment eastwards. On one of these (block no 99, Figure 51), which is clearly reused (see p 142), a phallus has been carved in relief. These two blocks are probably the remnants of a revetting wall for the south side of the ramp, the north side of which was retained by the curtain wall. Approximately halfway between these blocks and the south face of the curtain wall there is a row of four blocks also supported upon the boulder foundation. The blocks run from the rear wall of the abutment to the face of the southern wing-wall of bridge 2 and may have formed a spine wall to provide greater stability within the ramp. Traces of the ramp, which consisted of a 'great mass of earth,' were discovered by Shaw (ibid, 472) although they have been heavily disturbed by subsequent activity, and all remains of the ramp have since been removed.

Both the abutment and the pier are founded upon large paving slabs. Paving of the flood plain below the bridge first occurred when bridge 2 was built, although the area covered may have been enlarged during the construction of bridge 3. The slabs are *c* 0.12m thick and still preserve clear traces of tooling in some cases. One slab near the north-west corner of the pier, has a crowbar slot on its underside which may indicate that it was reused. To the west of the pier many slabs were found to be disturbed upon discovery and were relaid during consolidation (ibid, fig 5).

The pier

The pier lies 1.68m west of the abutment of bridge 2 and measures 10.24m by 2.34m (Figure 39, Figure 68). Its construction of large reused blocks retaining a core of clay-bonded rubble is similar to that used in the abutment. The pier has been heavily robbed and survives only to a maximum height of three courses (1.08m). The east face (Figure 69, elevation 8) has no offsets but on the west face there is an offset of 0.20m above the first course. A similar offset of 0.11m above the first course exists on the north face and the position of a crowbar slot in the middle block of the first course of the south face suggests the missing blocks of the second course were offset by *c* 0.16m. The north-west corner of the pier has been completely robbed but on the underlying paving slab there is an area of tooling which is less waterworn than that on the remainder of the slabs. This fresher tooling indicates the original existence of superimposed masonry and thus shows that the pier was originally rectangular (*contra* Shaw, ibid, 474).

Richmond (1947, 166) distinguished two phases of construction within the pier: the northern part of the pier which corresponded in width to the curtain wall, being contemporary with the abutment of bridge 2, while the remainder was an extension associated with bridge 3. Detailed examination of the fabric of the pier shows it all to be of one build however, and there can be no doubt that it was part of bridge 3. The reused voussoir identified by Collingwood (*J Roman Stud* **14** (1924), 216) within the pier could not be located and Shaw's culvert through the width of the pier proved to be merely a void created by the fracture of one of the blocks in the east face (Shaw 1926, 473).

Reconstruction of the bridge

Shaw (ibid, 471) considered that the abutment survived to its original height (ie 1.94m) where it joined the south face of the curtain wall. This seems impossible because there are no remains of an arch springing or slots for timber struts to support a carriageway linking the abutment and the pier. The abutment may in fact have been of considerably greater height. Behind the abutment an earth ramp carried the Military Way up to the level of the carriageway (as also occurred at the eastern abutment of bridge 2 at Chesters p 27–8). The dimensions of the ramp are uncertain: the slope indicated on Shaw's section Z–Z (ibid, fig 7) is incorrect as it assumes that the abutment stands to its full height. It is quite possible that the ramp was of considerable length and incorporated the demolished remains of the tower. Pottery suggests that occupation of the tower did not continue beyond the earlier third century at the latest (p 96) and Shaw noted that

> 'The evenness with which the east wall [of the tower], both face and core appears to have been reduced indicates a purposeful demolition rather than the work of "stone-seekers." '

> ibid, 484

It is quite possible therefore that the tower was levelled to the seventh course when the ramp was built. Within the tower Shaw (ibid) found 0.91m of 'soil' above the latest floor which might represent deliberate filling during construction of the ramp. If this was so, and assuming the abutment to have been built up to the estimated height of the wall walk, the ramp would have been at least 26m in length and would have had a gradient of 14 per cent (1:7) or less. Such a gradient could be negotiated with ease by horse drawn traffic. The *Pons Aelius* in Rome had ramps on either side of the Tiber with gradients of *c* 25 per cent (1:4) (Platner and Ashby 1929, 397). The bridge over the Cendere Çay in Turkey had ramps up to 43.6m in length with gradients of *c* 12 per cent (1:8), (Humann and Puchstein 1890, 394, Taf XLIII; Figure 28). The ramps of both these bridges were constructed of dressed stone blocks which has the advantage of reducing the amount of pressure exerted upon the abutment. This can be quite considerable: in the case of an earth ramp between 30 and 40 per cent of the pressure exerted upon the ground by the weight of the ramp is also exerted upon the rear face of the abutment (Robinson 1964, 109). The thickness and massiveness of the Willowford abutment was therefore necessary to withstand the thrust from the ramp.

Shaw recognised that the pier lay too close to the abutment to be an ordinary water pier and thought it was associated with a watermill (p 94). It is in fact likely that the pier and abutment were part of an elevated causeway carrying the Military Way over the flood plain; the paved area between the two structures acting as a flood channel. Such channels passing through abutments and ramps occur at a number of Roman bridges and were intended to prevent a build up of water against the structures, as for example at the bridge over the Cendere Çay where a channel 3.82m wide and 4.5m high to the crown of its arch pierced the southern ramp (Humann and Puchstein 1890, 393). At Willowford the flood channel would have acted in conjunction with sluice 2 which continued in operation when bridge 3 was constructed. There is no conclusive evidence to show whether the carriageway passed over the flood channel on a stone or a timber superstructure but in the light of the presence of stone arches in bridge 2 at Chesters the former may be more likely. The pier is quite narrow (2.12m above offsets) but can be compared with the stone arched bridge on the *Via Flaminia* at Spoleto which had piers 1.5m wide and the Ponte Romano at Ceggia on the *Via Annia* which had piers 1.6m wide (Ballance 1951, 114; Brusin 1949–50, 121–3). Moreover, on its west side the Willowford pier may not have supported one of the main bridge arches but merely another flood arch. F G Simpson excavated to the west of the visible pier at Willowford in 1940 (Simpson 1941, 214) and found two further piers at a depth of nearly 3.05m (p 53). He was unable to record their dimensions or spacing although in view of their depth below the present surface both piers probably lay within the main Roman channel of the Irthing. One of these piers might be represented by the anomaly observed in resistivity survey (p 96) *c* 12m west of the visible pier although this is far from certain. If this possible pier was associated with bridge 3 its distance from the known pier to the east is probably too great to have been spanned by a single arch, considering its narrow width, so another intermediate pier would have been required.

The fact that probable traces of the western abutments were noted at a distance of *c* 55m from the known east pier indicates that at some stage a considerable length of the Irthing flood-plain was bridged (p 52). By the time bridge 3 was constructed therefore the main course of the Irthing was perhaps quite some distance west of the eastern abutment of bridge 2. If so more than one of the bridge arches could have lain completely to the east of the main river channel. Such an arrangement occurs at the Ponte di Porto Torres in Sardinia (Gazzola 1963, 117, no 152). which has five arches (ranging in width from 5.0m to 5.4m) traversing the flood plain on one side of the river while the main channel of the Mannu is crossed by two larger arches (widths 12.5m and 19.5m). The height of the bridge increases by 6.5m over its length of 112.5m and it is conceivable that a similar arrangement existed at Willowford with the carriageway passing onto the slope of Harrow's Scar at a higher level than the top of the eastern abutment. At the Ponte di Porto Torres the pier on the edge of

the river channel was about twice the width of those on the flood plain.

Cornice blocks, columns and other architectural fragments similar to those recovered from Chesters have not been found at Willowford. This does not necessarily mean that such features were absent from bridge 3, however, as all the blocks recovered by Clayton at Chesters were apparently found in excavation beneath the main bridge arches, an area hardly examined at Willowford.

The watermill?

Shaw (1926, 468, 476) thought that the sluices, paved channel and pier were associated with a watermill, an interpretation subsequently taken up by Richmond(1947,166), and more recently Spain (1984, 109–111). The plan of a Romano-British watermill has been clearly demonstrated by Simpson's excavations at Haltwhistle Burn Head where a millhouse associated with a waterwheel was located next to a leat (Simpson 1976, 32–42). There is not enough space to accommodate a millhouse east or west of the paved channel between the abutment and pier at Willowford and the channel is most unlikely to have functioned as a wheelrace because no trace of a leat was found to the south of the bridge. Shaw's (1926, 477) tentative identification of the river deposits between the pier and abutment 2 which were laid down after the destruction of bridge 1A as the filling of an 'undershot pit' is clearly mistaken. Richmond (1947, 166) considered that a socketed stone found at the bridge may have been a spindle bearing for a waterwheel but this has been (rightly) challenged by Dr G Simpson (Simpson 1976, 50). The stone (block no 518, Figure 64, no 27) has a socket in its upper surface 0.20m in diameter and 0.22m deep, and its sides display clear traces of tooling with a point. There is no trace of wear consistent with the socket having housed a rotating member so the stone probably held a timber post. While there is no evidence for a watermill at the eastern abutment of the bridge, the existence of such a structure elsewhere at Willowford cannot be ruled out.

The course of the Military Way in the vicinity of the bridge

The course of the Military Way as it approached the bridge on either side of the Irthing is not known with certainty. To the east of the bridge F G Simpson (1913, 389–93) discovered the Military Way immediately west of Poltross Burn and by means of seven sections traced its course as far as the Gilsland to Low Row road. In this sector the road ran along the north berm of the Vallum and consisted of large angular stones topped with gravel, with kerbs of larger stones on either side. The road varied in width from 4.88m to 6.71m. No physical investigation of the Military Way has taken place at Willowford Farm, although it is highly probable that the road continued along the north berm of the Vallum as far as

Willowford farmhouse. The Vallum terminated at the top of the scar to the east of the bridge, presumably beneath the present farmhouse (p 61). Horsley is the only source for the course of the Military Way between the farmhouse and the east bridge abutment.

> 'At Willowford on the east side of the river the military way seemed to be south of both walls [ie Hadrian's Wall and the Vallum], and at the head of the bank on the west side near Burdoswald, there seemed to be a military way on the north of them both ... the declivity on each side of the water must probably have always been considerable; because the military way here fetches a compass, and goes sloping down the one side and up the other.'
>
> Horsley 1732, 152

Horsley's observations are best explained if the Military Way, having previously run along the north berm of the Vallum, turned south-westwards at the point where the Vallum terminated to follow the course now occupied by the farm track, which lies to the south of a projected westward course of the Vallum (Figure 38). In view of the steepness of the slope a course which runs obliquely down the scar seems most probable. On the alluvial plain at the base of the scar all trace of the road has probably been ploughed away. Shaw's (1926, 486) interpretation of a layer of sandstone chippings some distance south-east of the abutment as the base of the Military Way is not convincing. However the Military Way presumably curved northwards from the base of the scar and ran behind the south face of Hadrian's Wall as it approached the ramp leading to the bridge. Shaw (ibid, 485) encountered what he thought was the Military Way immediately south-east of the tower but excavation has proved conclusively that this is a natural gravel deposit marking a pre-Roman river bank.

The course of the Military Way on the west side of the Irthing is even more uncertain. Maclauchlan (1858, 53) thought he could see traces of a road winding down the scarp towards Underheugh Farm but Haverfield (1899, 185) discounted this, considering it to be the result of a landslip. Considering the amount of erosion which has occurred on Harrow's Scar since Roman times it is unlikely that any trace of the road would survive. Once it reached the summit of Harrow's Scar the Military Way would have been aligned on the *porta principalis dextra* of Birdoswald, a course which necessitated the crossing of the already obliterated Vallum. The parade ground which is known to have lain to the east of Birdoswald probably lay along the south side of the Military Way (Daniels 1978, 198).

Later activities

Following the construction of bridge 3 the westward movement of the Irthing must have continued, because the paved channel between the abutment and pier was blocked. Shaw (1926, 475) found several large stones wedged across its northern entrance and the channel was filled with a c 1.08m depth of gravel and stones. A single sherd of pottery from the filling suggests a third-century or later date.

There is no direct evidence for how long the bridge was maintained. Milestones show that the Stanegate and Military Way were maintained until at least the early fourth century (p 31). Occupation of sites on either side of the Irthing certainly continued into the later fourth century, if not beyond. Both Milecastle 48 (Poltross Burn) and Birdoswald have produced pottery of the second half of the fourth century and the latest coin from Birdoswald is of 389+ (Gibson and Simpson 1911, 453; Birley 1961, 259). Recent excavations at Birdoswald have confirmed that the site was occupied until the very end of the Roman period, and probably beyond (A Wilmot personal comment). The importance of a road bridge at Willowford for communications with Birdoswald probably ensured its upkeep as long as organised occupation continued at the fort. Once Hadrian's Wall ceased to have a military function the bridge at Willowford presumably no longer served any useful purpose. In the medieval period the main crossing of the Irthing was at Lanercost, where there was the gentler landscape of the Old Red Sandstones to the north of the river rather than the steep scarp of the Irthing valley.

Excavation has produced some evidence for the destruction and decay of the bridge. Shaw (1926, 475) found a layer of mortar overlying the gravel filling of the paved channel which had probably weathered from the decaying fabric of the bridge. The mortar layer was overlain by a thin black humic stratum which was in turn covered by a mass of collapsed masonry. Similar debris was also recorded to the north of the curtain wall by Shaw and excavation of the ditch terminal to the north of the Wall revealed a small amount of stone compacted into the soft sand of the scarp face; (context 1071, Figure 45, section 7). The latter material consisted mainly of undressed coring with only the occasional facing stone and was presumably robbing debris rather than collapsed walling.

The eastern abutments became gradually engulfed in riverine deposits. To the south of the bridge a layer of gravel, up to 0.3m thick, was laid down over the Roman ground surface (context 1017, Figure 45, section 5). Thereafter the bridge began to be covered with fine silt and this process continued throughout the medieval period. In the Wall ditch terminal up to 0.48m of silt accumulated before the deposition of a thin rubble layer associated with medieval pottery, while to the south of the bridge up to 0.2m of silt was found beneath the medieval ground surface (context 1009, Figure 45, sections 5 and 7).

The dates of the bridges

Bridge 1 was designed to carry the Broad Wall across the Irthing and therefore belongs to the early stages in the building of Hadrian's Wall (probably between c AD 122 and 124–5). The dating of the later bridges and the modifications made to them is more complex. There is only a small amount of stratified dating evidence which can be associated with the construction and destruction of the various bridges. Inevitably therefore, much of the proposed dating depends upon chronological probabilities rather than firm evidence.

The important dating evidence can be cited thus:

Construction of bridge 1A: from the slumped core of the southern abutment wing-wall (context 1006, Figure 44, section 4) came a sherd of a mortarium (Figure 95, no 7) of a type datable to c 150–200.

Occupation within the tower of bridge 2:   on the first floor: one samian vessel datable to c 150–90. The coarse pottery would fit a date in the second half of the second century, although there is nothing that need necessarily be late second century.

On the second floor/rubbish to the north of the wall: one samian vessel datable to the late second to third century, and two black burnished ware cooking pots (Figure 90, no 21, Figure 91, no 33) which can be dated to the late second century. The absence of black burnished ware cooking pots with obtuse-angled lattice decoration indicates that the group was closed before the second quarter of the third century.

Modifications to bridge 2: from the core of a possible secondary northern wing-wall, coin 7, of AD 190–1.

As bridge 1A cannot have been built before c 150, bridge 1 was presumably partially destroyed during the occupation of the Antonine Wall (c 139–63) or subsequently. In the former case rebuilding will presumably have been delayed until Hadrian's Wall was refurbished for re-occupation. The earliest record of rebuilding on the Wall is *RIB* 1389, probably from near Heddon-on-the-Wall, dated to AD 158. The mortarium (Figure 95, no 7) of c 150–200 only provides a *terminus post quem* for the construction of bridge 1A, and in order to fix the period in which construction probably occurred it is necessary to refer to the pottery on the lowest floor of the tower of bridge 2. This is clearly a second-century group, and so the construction and destruction of bridge 1A, and its replacement by bridge 2 must all have occurred within the second half of the second century. This is all that can be said with confidence. If the absence of specifically late second-century types of pottery from the tower group is considered significant however, and the construction of bridge 1A is placed after the return of troops from the Antonine Wall, then a closer date range of c 160–80 could be proposed for the above events.

Bridge 2 shows no sign of having been damaged by river action and its replacement by bridge 3 can be related to its change of function from a wall bridge to a road bridge. This rebuilding can be associated with a wider alteration in the road system of the northern frontier which is discussed in chapter 9 and Appendix 1. There are two pieces of evidence for the date of the replacement of bridge 2 by bridge 3. The latest pottery from the tower, demolished when bridge 3 was constructed, can be dated to the late second, or the first quarter of the third century (although probably no later than this). Cobbles which apparently formed the core of a secondary northern wing-wall of bridge 2 contained a coin (no 7) of Commodus issued in AD 190–1. Water wear on the face of the primary wing-wall behind the cobbles suggested that a considerable period had elapsed between the construction of the two wing-walls. Unfortunately this coin has now been lost and its state of wear is unknown, but it is a remote possibility that it was lost in its year of issue, and this coin is here taken to indicate a *terminus post quem* of c 200 for the alterations to bridge 2. The construction of bridge 3 can thus probably be placed in the first quarter of the third century. This is important because it apparently excludes the possibility that bridge 3 is to be associated with the Commodan restoration of Hadrian's Wall (p 138). Although it is possible that bridge 2 was associated with this Commodan restoration, its construction followed the destruction of its predecessor by flood action of the river and there is no need to place its building in a general scheme of renovations of the Wall.

Bridge 3 was constructed as part of a wider programme of bridge building on the northern frontier which it is argued (p 139) took place in the reign of Septimius Severus during the governorship of Alfenus Seneco (c 205–7).

Resistivity survey

by A D H Bartlett

(The following is a summary of AM Lab Report G13/85)

An area of 60m by 25m was surveyed to the west of the guardianship area using the twin electrode probe configuration which provides a depth of penetration equivalent to (or slightly exceeding) the probe separation. Surveys with probe separations of 1m, 2m and 3m were undertaken with readings taken at 1m intervals along the transects on the 1m probe separation (2m intervals on the 2m and 3m separations). The survey readings have been plotted as contours which show the results after numerical filtering and so allow localised features to be seen against a uniform background.

Three main anomalies (A, B and C) were visible in all three plots and so the features causing them must have extended from near the surface to a depth of at least 3m. The most likely interpretation is that they were the result of deposition on the inside of the meander during previous courses of the Irthing. There were only relatively weak and ill-defined anomalies in the eastern half of the survey, although one anomaly (D) was slightly more pronounced at the 3m separation, which would not be inconsistent with the presence of masonry at depth. The anomaly lay slightly to the north of the projected line of Hadrian's Wall although it could possibly represent the disturbed remains of a pier (p 85).

Mortar analysis

by P Wilthew

(The following is a summary of AM Lab Report 4786)

Seven samples of mortar were examined visually and using low power optical microscopy. Six of these samples were then treated with dilute hydrochloric acid to determine the proportion of acid-soluble material. The acid-insoluble residues were also examined.

Broad Wall: three samples were examined: sample 7 from the inside of the south face of the Broad Wall to the east of the tower recess; sample 8 from inside the north face of the Broad Wall foundation, and sample 1 (which proved to be too degraded for analysis) from the facing of the tower recess.

Narrow Wall: one sample (6) was examined from inside the north face of Narrow Wall.

Analysis showed all the samples to be coarse lime mortars with an aggregate which varied from stones several centimetres in diameter to fine sand. The acid-insoluble residues also included some clay, but this may have been largely due to contamination. Examination of the original samples and of the acid-insoluble residues did not indicate any significant differences between the samples, although the proportions of acid-soluble material did differ between the Broad Wall mortar (samples 7 and 8, 15 per cent by weight) and that used in the Narrow Wall (sample 6, 20 per cent by weight). These results should not be regarded as conclusive, however, in view of the degraded nature of the samples.

Reconstructed curtain wall (bridge 2): two samples (2 and 4) were examined from the inside of both faces of the curtain wall. Analysis showed the samples to be a lime mortar, with an aggregate of stones, sand, charcoal, and old mortar. The proportion of acid-soluble material was 31 per cent by weight although this is not an accurate reflection of the proportions of lime and aggregate in the original mortar as the aggregate contained some calcareous material.

Refacing: one sample (5) was associated with the refacing of the north face of the Narrow Wall (context 1102, Figure 40, elevation 1, p 90). This sample was also a lime mortar but differed from the mortar in the reconstructed curtain wall of bridge 2 in certain respects. It contained a lower proportion of acid-soluble material (27 per cent by weight), and the acid-insoluble residue was apparently contaminated with iron compounds and contained a significant proportion of clay. These differences do not prove that sample 5 was not originally essentially the same as samples 2 and 4. The differences could be the result of degradation and contamination during burial, although strong additional evidence would be required before it would be safe to conclude that sample 5 and samples 2 and 4 were part of the same phase.

Medieval activity

In the medieval period industrial activity took place on the site of the tower of bridge 2 (Figure 70). The tower itself would not have been a visible feature at this time, either being covered by the ramp of bridge 3, or perhaps already largely robbed out. Up to 1.83m of the south face of the Narrow Wall was demolished, and in the Wall ditch terminal a small quantity of discarded wall core material was found associated with medieval pottery (context 1055, Figure 45, section 7; Shaw 1926, 459). On the eastern side of a hollow formed in the curtain Shaw (ibid, 481) found a low wall of rubble and facing stones, 0.46m wide and 0.91m long, constructed at right angles to the line of the Wall. Adjacent to this a scoop dug into the underlying Roman levels was filled with 0.76m of soot containing 'iron scoriae' (cinder). All the stones within this area were heavily scorched. Deposits of soot debris, up to 0.3m thick, were found to extend to the south and west beyond the perhaps already robbed walls of the tower. Part of a small pit (context 1083, Figure 70) containing charcoal, soot and burnt sandstone chips was found in the recent excavations.

Shaw considered that the tower was reused as a bloomery in the Elizabethan period. Strictly defined a bloomery hearth is for removing residual slag still present after the initial smelting but Shaw probably used this term for iron smelting in general. His interpretation can be rejected for two reasons. Firstly there are no iron bearing ores in the vicinity of the site and there is no evidence for similar activity in the area (Tylecote 1965, fig i). Secondly there is no mention of slag, the chief by-product of a bloomery, in Shaw's description. Consequently the medieval remains at Willowford are more probably from smithing than smelting. Tylecote has stated that:

> 'The minimum equipment for this purpose [smithing] is a pile of burning charcoal with a tuyère inserted to raise the temperature locally. If this is done in the open a few stones are needed to prevent the winds from blowing away the light charcoal. But the most important piece of equipment may be protection for the bellows. This can be provided by making a bowl hearth, with the bellows placed above and to one side of the hearth.'
>
> Tylecote 1981, 42

The depression against the south face of the Narrow Wall is therefore likely to have been a bowl hearth, with the low wall serving as a crude windbreak. The source of iron for the smithy was probably the iron bar clamps used in bridge 2 and probably bridge 3 as well, parts of which were presumably being robbed or demolished at this time. The clamps would have been initially heated until the lead could have been separated from them (the lead itself was a valuable commodity) and the iron then further heated until molten. One of the products of the smithy was probably iron nails. Nine nails of varying dimensions were found in the medieval ground surface to the south of the bridge and the 33 iron nails found 'on'

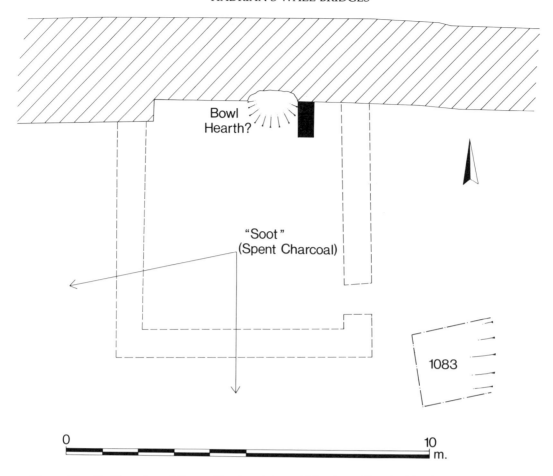

Figure 70   Outline plan of the medieval activity within the Willowford bridge 2 tower.   Scale 1:100

the first floor of the tower might have been intrusive from the smithy (context 1008, Figure 45, section 5; Shaw 1926, 485).

The date of the medieval activity at Willowford cannot be fixed with precision. Medieval pottery recovered from both Shaw's and the recent excavations includes one sherd which could date to the eleventh or twelfth centuries, while the bulk falls into the period of the thirteenth to the fifteenth centuries (p 148). The possible Saxo-Norman sherd may be associated with earlier robbing of the bridge, perhaps

evidenced by a block with three dovetail clamp sockets built into the north wall of the eleventh- or twelfth-century church at Over Denton. The industrial activity on the site of the bridge cannot be associated with the construction of nearby buildings. A pele house, demolished in 1836, did exist on the site of Willowford Farm: its foundation date is unknown, but it probably falls within the main period of pele construction which occurred after the smithy had gone out of use (Jenkinson 1875, 199; Dixon 1979, 249–50).

7 Other stone bridges on Hadrian's Wall and in northern Britain

Introduction

The bridges at Chesters and Willowford should not be viewed in isolation: much of their development will doubtless have been matched at the third Wall bridge at Stanwix, and it is argued elsewhere (chapter 9 and appendix 1) that their modification into road bridges was part of a more extensive programme of bridge construction which certainly included the bridge at Corbridge, and probably others besides. The techniques employed in the bridges at Chesters and Corbridge are so similar as to suggest that they may have been constructed under the direction of the same architect. There is also a concentration of evidence for stone bridges in northern Britain (Figure 71) which is so far unparalleled in the civilian parts of the province (p 138), and a review of these structures has provided further evidence for the techniques of construction discussed in Chapter 8.

Other bridges on, or in the environs of, Hadrian's Wall

Newcastle upon Tyne

Pons Aelius appears as a fort *per lineam valli* in the *Notitia Dignitatum*, listed between *Segedunum* (Wallsend) and *Condercum* (Benwell), and its garrison is given as *cohors I Cornoviorum*. A recently discovered inscription dating to AD 213 from the fort at Newcastle was dedicated by a different unit, *cohors I Ulpia Traiana Cugernorum CR* (Daniels and Harbottle 1980) but there is no reason to doubt the traditional identification of *Pons Aelius* with Newcastle.

It has long been thought that the site of the bridge was the same as that of the medieval bridge and its successors; indeed some have stated that the medieval bridge actually incorporated some of the fabric of its Roman predecessor (eg Brand 1789, 37–8). The medieval bridge was extensively damaged by the flood of 1771 and replaced by another bridge between 1773 and 1781. In 1872 the demolition of this later bridge laid bare the remains of earlier work which were seen and described by J C Bruce (1885b). The removal of the third pier from the south, of the eighteenth-century bridge revealed structures which he claimed represented the piers of the medieval and Roman bridges. His plan (Bruce 1885b, pl II; Figure 72) seems to show the timber substructure of a large pier with a width of 11.6m enclosing the timber substructure of a smaller pier with a width of 7.1m. The smaller pier 'must have been the bridge of Hadrian' and the larger pier therefore represented the medieval bridge. Thus for the first time some vestiges of the *Pons Aelius* had apparently been seen and considerable public interest was aroused. One form which this interest took was the salvaging of timber from the substructure which was then made into souvenirs and items of furniture; the latter included a magnificent bookcase commissioned by Bruce, now in the possession of Tyne and Wear Museums (at present held at South Shields Museum) and still housing many of his books (G Bruce 1905, 157–8; see Allason-Jones and McKay 1985, 52, pl XIV a–b, for the bronze eagle cast out of 'defaced coins' from Coventina's Well that surmounted the pediment of the bookcase).

Recently Mr S Brown while studying records of the medieval bridge at Newcastle has pointed out (personal comment) that there are obvious discrepancies between Bruce's identification of the medieval pier and a plan made of the bridge soon after the great damage it sustained in the flood of 1771 (Mylne 1772, plan attached to the printed report; Figure 73). The medieval pier in question was the fourth from the south side in which was set the Blue

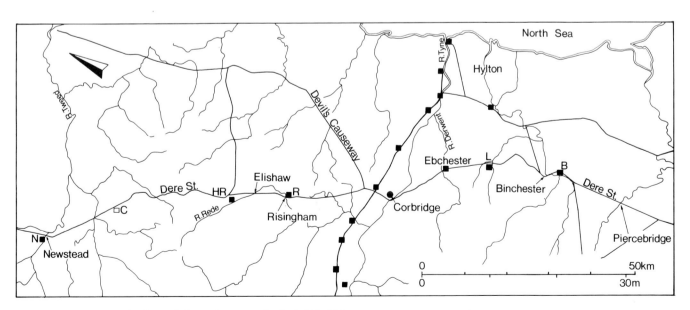

Figure 71   Roman bridges on Dere Street.   Scale 1:850,000

Stone marking the boundary of jurisdiction between the Bishop of Durham and the City of Newcastle upon Tyne. On Mylne's plan the width of the pier is given as 23 feet (7.0m) and it is shown to have been completely enclosed by a starling (a protective timber piling) with an overall width of approximately 39 feet (11.8m). A comparison of Bruce's plan with Mylne's makes it immediately apparent that Bruce had mistaken the starling for the medieval pier, and the medieval pier for a Roman pier. The dimensions given by Bruce tally almost exactly with Mylne's and the misalignment of the timbers on the south side of Bruce's 'medieval pier' was probably the result of scouring in the flood of 1771 which, as Mylne's plan shows, damaged the starling and destroyed the two piers to the east. Bruce was misled by the construction of the medieval bridge which is well described by Smeaton and Wooler in another contemporary report. They state that the bridge

> 'having been erected some centuries ago, upon the principles that were in common use for such Edifices [was constructed on] a great number of piles driven down into the Bed of the River, supporting a timber platform or framing under each Pier, a little above the lowest water of the river, upon which the Masonry is established; and those stilts being surrounded with a row of close piling, at the distance of several feet, and the Interval filled up with Gravel and other Stone Materials, thrown down at Random, and the whole connected with proper timbers, and paved down at the Top with large Stones, a few feet above low Water Mark, forming the Footing or Basement, for the security of the pier, which is called a *sterling*.'
>
> Smeaton and Wooler 1772, 3–4

J C Bruce also mentions the discovery of what he supposed was Roman work when the third pier of the eighteenth-century bridge from the Newcastle side was removed

> 'The river here seems to have been very deep, and the Romans have had considerable difficulty in getting a foundation. They have, first of all, thrown in a quantity of quarried freestone and then laid upon it a mass of concrete nineteen feet [5.6m] thick. Imbedded in this concrete were found some piles of black oak, on which was planted a horizontal framework of oak. The medieval foundation had lain upon this mass.'
>
> Bruce 1885b, 10

There seems no reason why the mass of concrete should not itself have been medieval rather than Roman.

It must be concluded that no definite remains of the Roman bridge have ever been seen. Unfortunately, topographical considerations offer little help in fixing even the approximate position of the bridge.

There is nothing to indicate the line which the

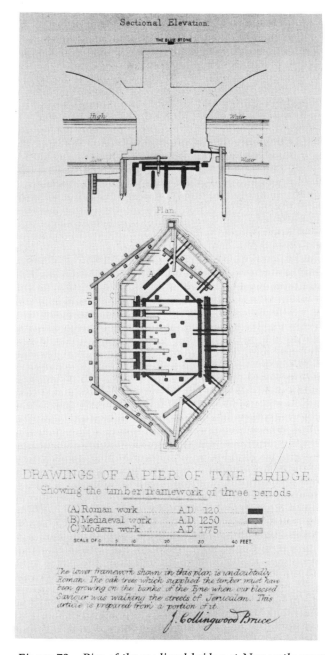

Figure 72   Pier of the medieval bridge at Newcastle upon Tyne after Bruce 1885, pl 2 (cf Figure 73). Pulls of the original block in the John Collingwood Bruce Collection at South Shields Museum include the following note cropped from the bottom of the plate in the article: 'The lower framework shown in this plan is undoubtedly Roman. The oak trees which supplied the timber must have been growing on the banks of the Tyne when our blessed Saviour was walking the streets of Jerusalem. This article is prepared from a portion of it. J Collingwood Bruce'. The last sentence presumably means, either that the quarto-sized off-print which Bruce issued with additional illustrations was printed on paper prepared from wood-pulp derived from the 'Roman' timbers, or that the blocks were made from wood from the bridge

Broad Wall took as it ran down to the river. The later Narrow Wall has been seen 600m east of the fort, at the junction of Grenville Terrace and Blaydon Street. The Wall ditch has been traced to within a short distance of the east side of the fort, but it may be merely following the line of the Narrow Wall (Spain and Simpson 1930, 496–500).

The discovery in the river, near the medieval bridge, of three important inscriptions which probably came from the Roman bridge might seem to support the traditional identification of its site. The first is an altar inscribed *Neptuno le(gio)* | *VI Vi(ctrix)* | *P(ia) F(idelis)* (*RIB* 1319) which was 'dredged up when the works of the Swing Bridge were in progress' in 1875. In 1903 a dedication to Antoninus Pius was recovered during clearance of the river channel near the Swing Bridge; it mentions a vexillation either sent to the three British legions from the two Germanies or sent to the two Germanies from the British legions (*RIB* 1322; Wilkes 1985 but cf Frere 1986). At the same time an altar was also found, inscribed *Ociano leg(io)* |*VI Vi(ctrix* | *P(ia) F(idelis)'*; (*RIB* 1320), it is without doubt a companion to the altar dedicated to Neptune. The exact circumstances of the discovery of this altar, and of the dedication to Antoninus Pius, are the subject of conflicting reports. In one account R O Heslop stated that the altar was 'recovered from the debris of the Roman structure in the river bed' *Proc Soc Antiq Newcastle*, 3 ser, **1** (1903–4), 112 but in another that it was 'embedded in the river bottom' (Heslop 1904, 134).

According to Bosanquet (1930, 512) who quotes from an unreferenced source which it has not been possible to identify, the altar was 'embedded in the masonry remains of an old pier.' These three inscriptions might therefore have been reused within the fabric of the medieval bridge and if so the place

of their discovery offers no clue to the location of the Roman bridge.

Besides the question of the exact position of the *Pons Aelius*, there are a number of problems concerning its date and purpose. It has not always been assumed that it belonged to the original construction of the Wall. Haverfield (1904, 143, n 4) proposed the possibility that the dedication to Antoninus Pius (*RIB* 1322) might in some way have been associated with the building of the bridge, for Aelius was the *gens* of Antoninus as well as of Hadrian; for that matter it was also the *gens* of Commodus. The general opinion, however, has been that the bridge was part of the original plan for Hadrian's Wall and that since work on the Wall began at Newcastle, it was one of the first structures to have been built (Breeze and Dobson 1987, 73). The two altars from the bridge dedicated by the Sixth Legion (*RIB* 1319–20) have been thought to mark its construction. As the names of Neptune and Oceanus are inscribed on the capitals of the altars, however, a feature most frequently found on third-century altars in north Britain (Kewley 1973), they might possibly have been erected long after the reign of Hadrian.

We have already seen that at Chesters and Willowford bridges which merely served to carry the Wall across the river were replaced by large road bridges in the third century; at Carlisle separate bridges carried the Wall and Hadrianic service road or extension of the Stanegate across the Eden. The bridge at Newcastle must have stood near the eastern terminus of the Wall as it was originally planned, although within a few years, (but perhaps after the bridge was completed), the Wall was extended to Wallsend. From the south the bridge was approached by a road which ran parallel to, and no great distance to the east of, Dere Street all the way from the vicinity

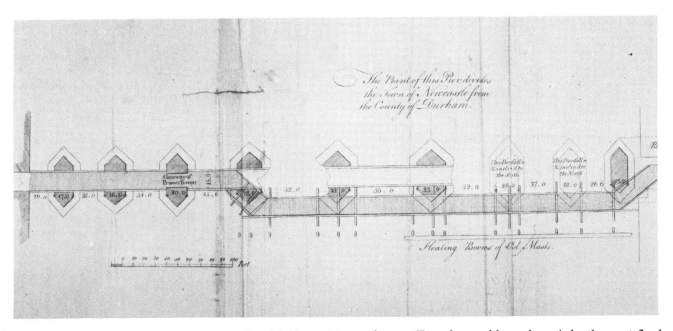

Figure 73   Robert Mylne's plan of the medieval bridge at Newcastle upon Tyne damaged beyond repair by the great flood of 1771 (Mylne 1772, frontispiece). The fourth pier from the right is that planned by Bruce and claimed by him as a pier of the Pons Aelius *(cf Figure 72). Scale 1:1000*

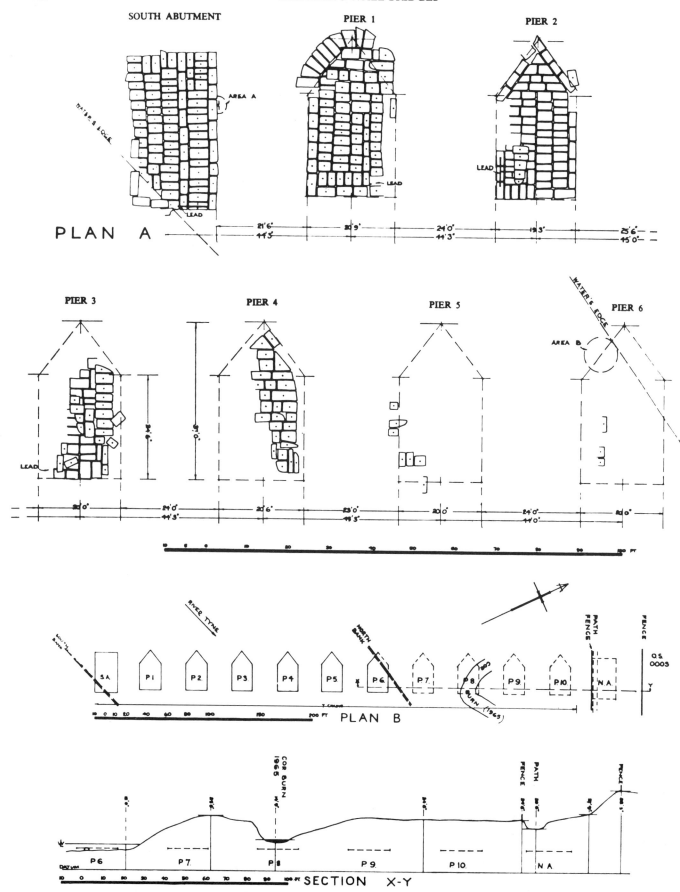

Figure 74   Plan of the bridge at Corbridge after Bourne 1967, plans A and B. It is possible that pier 6 represents part of the north abutment; the evidence for the existence of piers 7–10 is very thin.   Scales: Plan A, 1:265;Plan B, 1:960; Section, 1:528

of York. There is only one fort known on its entire length, at Chester-le-Street, which appears to have been built in the second half of the second century (Gillam and Tait 1968, 85, 95). This suggests it was a route of only minor importance; other roads in northern Britain have forts at frequent intervals along their length, and the road from the south once it had crossed the Tyne at Newcastle could apparently only have connected with the Hadrianic service road for Hadrian's Wall. Throughout the Roman period the main eastern route from southern Britain into Scotland remained Dere Street which crossed the Tyne at Corbridge. Although it has been suggested that a road ran north from Newcastle to join the Devil's Causeway (Hafemann 1956, 150), there is no evidence for its existence.

It remains to be explained why the bridge on this unimportant route was of such note that it was named *Pons Aelius* and lent its name to the fort constructed at Newcastle later in the second century. Most likely perhaps is that the bridge stood at the original terminus of the Wall and was therefore of a monumental design which bore no relationship to its modest purpose.

Corbridge

The site of the Roman bridge is 6.2km downstream from the meeting of the North and South Tyne (Figure 71) and lies just beyond a wide meander at a point where the river valley is almost a kilometre wide, see Figure 1. A little downstream, just below the present eighteenth-century bridge, the valley narrows sharply.

In the earlier sixteenth century, according to Leland (1964, vol 5, 57), there were 'evident tokens yet seen wher the olde brig was' and later writers such as Horsley, Wallis and Hodgson mention its remains. The first investigation took place in 1861 when William Coulson uncovered traces of what he took to have been the north abutment of the bridge (*Archaeol Aeliana*, 2 ser, **6** (1865), 18). The principal source, describing the bridge before much of its stonework was removed in 1840 for use elsewhere by the agent of the Greenwich Hospital Estates, is Robert Forster. Unfortunately the account of the bridge in his *History of Corbridge* (1881) is difficult to follow, and perhaps not accurate in some points of detail, since he relied on his memory of the remains as they had existed some forty years earlier. In 1906–7 excavation and survey was carried out by another Robert Forster (Robert Henry) (Forster 1907), apparently no close relation of the other Robert Forster who had died in 1885.[1]

An unpublished survey carried out shortly after the Second World War by the late J P Gillam suggested errors in the 1906–7 survey, while work in 1963–6 for the first time produced a detailed plan of the surviving fabric of the bridge in the river (Figure 74) and confirmed the unreliability of the earlier survey (Bourne 1967, also noting J P Gillam's work on p 24).

The principal route which the bridge carried was Dere Street which approached the south abutment from the south-east and on the north side ran directly towards Portgate after curving around the west side of the Roman site (Figure 1). A minor road seems to have approached the bridge from the south-east; MacLauchlan (1852, 20) traced it to a point a little beyond Dilston, which is just over a kilometre south-west of the Roman bridge (see also R Forster 1881, 8, n 2). On the north side about a hundred metres from the bridge there is a junction of the Stanegate approaching from the west and Dere Street (the form in which the Stanegate may have continued to the east is discussed on p 153).

The bridge thus stood at the junction of one minor and two major routes. However, only one of the roads has been investigated in the immediate vicinity of the bridge. In 1907 a length of Dere Street was exposed at a point about 40m north of the river bank and about 10m north of the postulated position of the north abutment (R H Forster 1908, 208–15, pl III). The road was originally 11.4m in width and was laid over make-up 1.2m thick. After the road was re-metalled once, a third surface at a height of 2.4m above natural was laid down. In a sewer associated with this surface was an illegible third-century coin and another coin, of Constantine II, which 'according to the workmen who found it, came from beneath the surface of this third road' (ibid, 214).

The later surface was 13m in width, but to the north it was reduced abruptly to 8.2m by means of two offsets 2.4m in width. To Salway (1967, 58–9), this narrowing could be explained by the existence of a gate at this point, its *spina* and the foundations of its flanking towers or arch-supports presumably having been entirely robbed. Whether the evidence recovered by R H Forster will bear this interpretation is doubtful. The final surface with which Salway associated his suggested gate lay 2.3m above natural clay and the considerable depths of makeup associated with the various surfaces suggests that the road was embanked to provide a level approach to the bridge. The section drawn by Knowles (Forster 1908, 211) shows neither disturbance of the earlier metalling underlying the position which would have been occupied by the side walls of the carriageways of the suggested gate, nor any disturbance in the later surface caused by the removal of a *spina*. It might be expected that the foundations of a gate would have penetrated through these deposits down to the natural ground surface. The widening of the road as it approached the bridge might have been merely to give space for traffic waiting to cross when the carriageway over the river was congested.

William Coulson had also located this road in 1861 and followed it until he came upon what he thought was the north abutment which

> 'presented itself in very great decay. Only the core remained, all the facing stones having been removed.'
>
> *Archaeol Aeliana*, 2 ser, **6** (1865), 18

Excavations at the same spot in 1906 revealed 'large stones' which Coulson had apparently regarded as the core of the abutment; R H Forster judged them to have perhaps once

> 'formed part of the abutment, but ... to have been put in their present position to

strengthen the bank and to support the arable land above it.'

Forster 1908, 208–9

The south abutment and southernmost four piers (nos 1–4) of the bridge are known in some detail as a result of the survey carried out by Bourne (1967; Figure 74); the same survey also located the very fragmentary remains of two further piers (nos 5–6). The south abutment is 10.97m in length but the piers are shorter, between 7.31m and 7.62m in length with cutwaters between 3.76m and 3.96m in length. The widths of the piers range from 5.87m to 6.32m and the spaces between them from 7.31m to 7.77m except between the abutment and pier 1 where the width is 6.55m. The dimensions of piers 5 and 6 are quite uncertain. These remains of the bridge lie about half a metre below the surface of the water when the river is low; a few blocks at the rear of the abutment can be seen exposed in the river bank.

In restoring the plan of the bridge Bourne placed the north abutment somewhat to the south of the position where Coulson found what he took to be its remains. This restoration gives a bridge of ten piers with a length between the abutments of 132.5m. But Bourne (1967, 26) readily admitted that there was little evidence to establish the position of the north abutment and rightly placed little reliance on borings carried out in 1907 which were claimed to have located the remains of other piers north of pier 6. The present width of the river at the point where the bridge crosses it is about 65m, rather less than half the width of the bridge indicated on Figure 74. At Chesters the width of the bridge corresponds approximately to that of the river as it is at present. If the same were the case at Corbridge, the observed remains of 'pier 6', consisting of three blocks *in situ*, might quite possibly represent part of the north abutment. The overall width of the bridge between its abutments will then have been 74m.

There are several notable features in the construction of the bridge. R Forster, calling upon his 'early recollections' of the visible remains of the bridge some forty years before writing his *History of Corbridge* (1881), described the piers at the south end of the bridge as follows: the base of the piers

'might be three or four feet in height [c 1.0m]; from this base the pillars [piers] had risen. The base widened considerably towards the bottom and resembled so many steps, which consisted of three or four courses of stones, each course or layer projecting out beyond the higher something like the distance of a foot [0.3m], the lowest course being embedded in the solid masonry.'

He mentions earlier that there was visible

'the base of two or three pillars [piers], with all the firm and massive stonework betwixt them as well as below, but more especially above them.'

Forster 1881, 11

This is a description of the remains before about 1840 when much of the stonework was removed on the orders of the agent of the Greenwich Hospital Estates to build the case of a waterwheel at Dilston and for other purposes.

Although some aspects of R Forster's description are vague, it is clear that the bases of the piers had a number of offsets, one of which is still apparently preserved on the south side of pier 5; the curved foundation under pier 1 also seems to indicate the existence of an offset and it was presumably the stonework above the 'stepped bases' which was removed in about 1840 (*contra* Bourne 1967, 21). The 'solid masonry' in which the bases of the piers were embedded might perhaps have been paving of the river bed, which also occurs at Chesters, Willowford and Piercebridge. R Forster (1881, 11) also cites in a footnote an observation by Mackenzie that

'the foundations of the piers [of Roman bridges] were constructed of an horizontal arch made of stones in the form of a wedge, as appears by the remains of the bridge here'[ie at Corbridge]

Mackenzie 1825, 328

Mackenzie here is following Wallis who wrote that

'the arches of their [ie Roman] bridges were usually wide over such rivers [as the Tyne], formed with the greatest geometrical nicety, the pillars multangular, the base of each secured by horizontal arches gradually contracted, every stone in them of a vast length and wedge-like, laid level with the water. Such stones are now lying in the river by both these stations [Corbridge and Chesters], with iron cramps in them.'

Wallis 1769, 116–7

What Mackenzie and Wallis were presumably referring to at Corbridge was the semicircular offset recorded by Bourne on which the cutwater of pier 1 was built and which was presumably repeated under the cutwaters of the other piers. Bourne was perhaps correct in suggesting that it was a repair but it still remains a notable feature which finds few parallels amongst other Roman bridges. The Ponte dei Ladroni on the *Via Traiana* between *Brundisium* and *Beneventum* (cf p 140) as shown in plan by Ashby and Gardner (1916, fig 10) has a pier with a rounded end upstream, but it is impossible to determine from the plan whether this rounded end was merely the foundation of the cutwater as at Corbridge or whether the cutwater itself was rounded. At Trier the downstream ends of the piers of the stone bridge are rounded through their whole height (Cüppers 1969) but the Byzantine period furnishes us with another example of a bridge with rounded upstream cutwaters, Justinian's bridge over the *Sangarius* (the modern Sakarya) in western Turkey, completed in AD 562 (Whitby 1985). At present the river flows from south to north and the presence of rounded cutwaters at the south ends of the piers and pointed cutwaters at the north ends (giving piers of the same plan as those at Trier mentioned above) has been traditionally explained by postulating the existence of a canal constructed by Justinian which had reversed the natural direction of flow during the Byzantine period. The purpose of this suggested canal had been to divert the flow of the river from the Black Sea into Lake Sophon. Whitby (*ibid*, 129–36) maintained that there was no evidence for the existence of this canal and as further support for the idea that the flow of the river has always been from south to north argued that a structure on the south side of the river was a breakwater. Piers with the plan apparently occurring in the *Sangarius* bridge are well designed to reduce turbulence in the flow of water around the piers and thus reduce the amount of scouring on the downstream side of the bridge. The evidence from Corbridge and the Ponte dei Ladroni shows that this method of reducing scouring was known to some Roman engineers.

In addition to the information about the construction of the bridge recorded by R Forster and Bourne, a certain amount can be deduced from blocks from the bridge reused elsewhere, principally in a structure by the north bank of the river downstream from the bridge (p 106). At the outset it can be stated that the ensuing discussion of construction techniques demonstrates an almost complete correspondence between Corbridge and bridge 2 at Chesters.

The most regular stonework is in the south abutment where the three rows of blocks which form the face consist of a row of headers between two rows of stretchers (the former shows some irregularities at the north end). As with bridge 2 at Chesters there is a tendency for the blocks to be roughly twice as long as they are wide and the range of sizes is again comparable with those of the blocks at Chesters.

In the remains of the bridge in the river clamps do not seem to occur; as at Chesters the blocks were bound together with lead tie-bars. These are described on p 130ff, and it need only be noted here that the technique is so far recorded nowhere else but at Chesters and Corbridge.

A further important resemblance is the distinction in techniques of construction demonstrated by the blocks from the base and the superstructure. In September 1984 a block with band anathyrosis was seen on the edge of the river at Corbridge just below the south abutment and fragments of others were seen downstream of the structure below the bridge by the north bank of the river (p 106). The blocks reused in this structure have crowbar slots, dowel holes and sockets for bar clamps. There are no architectural fragments on, or near, the site of the bridge but according to R Forster some of the blocks removed in about 1840

> 'were of great weight, many of them being fluted, grooved, and with fine mouldings.'
>
> Forster 1881, 12

The feathered tooling which occurs on the faces of the east abutment of bridge 2 at Chesters (Figure 82) has not been noted at Corbridge. At Hexham Abbey however, the crypt of St Wilfrid's Church, of *c* 675, is built of reused blocks many of which display feathered or basketwork tooling on their surfaces.

Amongst the reused inscriptions at Hexham there are some which certainly come from Corbridge (eg *RIB* 1151, 1172) and this was probably the source of most if not all of the reused stonework (cf p 32). The bridge is the only structure at Corbridge known to have been built in *opus quadratum* of this type (the masonry of the courtyard building on Site XI is of a quite different character) and was probably the source of much of the stonework in the crypt, and presumably in the vanished superstructure of the church above.

This nearly complete correspondence in techniques of stoneworking and construction at Corbridge and in bridge 2 at Chesters, including the otherwise unattested use of lead tie-bars, suggests very strongly that the two bridges were built at about the same time, perhaps by the same team of masons or under the direction of the same architect (cf Table 10) for the construction techniques of bridges with stone piers in northern Britain. We might therefore expect the bridge at Corbridge to have had stone arches and the same degree of architectural ornamentation as at Chesters. The date which is indicated for bridge 2 at Chesters is Severan and this means that the stone bridge at Corbridge will have had a predecessor, presumably of timber, for it is scarcely conceivable that Dere Street, the main route into Scotland, would have crossed the Tyne merely by a ford until the early third century. The location of this earlier bridge is quite uncertain. It was perhaps very close to the site of the later bridge but there are other possibilities. The original crossing of the Tyne might have been closer to the large Agricolan base at Red House, which preceded the main Corbridge site; a timber bridge forming part of the original construction of Dere Street might well have remained in use until the early third century.

Table 10   Construction techniques of stone bridges in northern Britain

Bridge	Date	1	2	3	4	5	6	7
Chesters 1	Hadrianic	-	-	*	-	*	-	-
Willowford 1	Hadrianic	*	-	*	-	-	-	-
Willowford 1A	Hadrianic-Antonine	-	-	-	*	-	-	-
Summerston 1	early Antonine	-	-	*	-	-	-	?
Willowford 2	Antonine	*	-	-	*	*	-	-
Willowford 3	Severan	-	-	-	-	*	-	-
Chesters 2	Severan	*	*	-	*	*	*	*
Corbridge	Severan	*	*	-	*	*	*	*
Stanwix	Hadrianic-Severan	*	*	*	*	-	-	-
Piercebridge	Severan?	*	-	-	*	*	-	-
Risingham	uncertain	-	-	*	-	*	-	-

KEY: * = present; - = absent; ? = uncertain.
1 = Lewis holes; 2 = Band anathyrosis; 3 = Dovetail clamps; 4 = Bar clamps; 5 = Dowels; 6 = Tie-bars; 7 = Feathered tooling

The structure on the north bank east of the Roman bridge at Corbridge

In September 1984 when the level of the river was low, R Selkirk drew the writers' attention to a structure downstream from the site of the Roman bridge on the north side of the river. At the time it seemed to be a new discovery and it was described as a possible Roman quay; in fact it had been described by R H Forster in 1907 and the late J P Gillam informed the writers that it was well known to him and to other residents of Corbridge. The structure has suffered much damage since 1907 and before describing its present state R H Forster's account must be given:

> 'About eighty yards [73m] below the line of the Roman bridge are the remains of what appears to be a medieval quay or ferry-landing: they consist of a platform with a river face of thirty-seven feet [11.28m] composed of large stones, evidently of Roman origin, with four massive timbers, about a foot [0.3m] square in section, one at either end of the platform, and two running at approximately equal intervals through the centre; between the first and second timbers at the west end there is a cross tie of the same thickness at the back of the stones. These timbers, which project from fifteen [0.46m] to twenty-four inches [0.61m] beyond the river front of the stones, and extend some feet behind them, have evidently been taken from some previously existing structure, being pierced with large slots, measuring twelve inches [0.3m] by three inches [0.08m]. The platform is nearly in a line with the present north bank: the south-western corner is forty-one feet [12.5m] from the water's edge, and the average breadth of the stonework is ten feet [3.05m].'

Forster 1907, 180

(The position of this structure is noted in Knowles 1907, 168 (fig) as a 'medieval ford').

In 1984 only what was apparently the west part of the structure survived; to the east were scattered and displaced blocks representing the remainder of the structure. Along the west side were two timbers running from north to south. One, represented by two fragments, had a length of at least 6.45m and a width of 0.4m (Figure 75, timber 1), the other with a surviving length of 5.2m and a width of 0.3m (Figure 75, timber 2). To the east were two more timbers (Figure 75, timbers 3 and 4) lying 2.4m apart. In the surfaces of all the timbers sockets had been cut to accommodate uprights, and those at either end of timber 2 preserved pairs of wooden dowels, to pin the bases of the uprights into the horizontal timbers. Several of the sockets were in line from east to west, but in spite of this R H Forster thought they were associated with the use of the timbers in some earlier structure. If the dimensions he gave for the platform

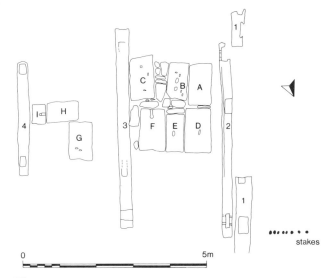

Figure 75   Structure east of the Roman bridge at Corbridge on the north side of the river.   Scale 1:100

are correct, some of the sockets recently exposed would originally have been covered by blocks, which would confirm his opinion. There is however, a discrepancy between the measurements given by R H Forster for the two timbers 'running at approximately equal intervals through the centre' of the platform, which should have been *c* 3.75m apart instead of 2.4m as recorded in 1984, if the overall length of the structure was 11.28m.

Between the timbers are a series of reused Roman blocks with cobbles and fragments of sandstone packed between them. They are principally of interest because comparison with blocks from bridge 2 at Chesters suggests that they originated from the superstructure of the Roman bridge at Corbridge (Figure 75). Blocks B, D and E have lewis holes, B and C have square dowel holes and F has an underside dowel hole; I has a slot for a bar clamp and on B, C and G there are crowbar slots. Further east amongst the scattered blocks there is one example with band anathyrosis.

The purpose of the structure is far from clear. It seems to have taken the form of a wall or platform 3.05m wide, supported on timbers perhaps forming a frame-work, if there had originally been more than one of the cross ties which R H Forster records. Unfortunately there is no mention of the height of the remains surviving in 1906, nor of whether there was any sign that they had orignally extended further to the east or west. R H Forster's suggestion that they represented a medieval quay or ferry landing has little to commend it. There is no mention in the various accounts of medieval Corbridge of either, or indeed of a road leading to the opposite point on the south bank. The medieval bridge, less than a kilometre downstream, was begun in 1236 and succeeded a ford to its east, established earlier in the medieval period to judge from the hollow road which approached it (Craster 1914, 64–5). There would certainly have been no need for a ferry after the construction of the bridge. As for the suggestion that the structure in question was a quay, there is no evidence for navigation on this part of the Tyne in the medieval period.

There are few indications of the date of the structure. R H Forster's suggestion that it was a medieval structure presumably means that local residents could not account for it as of recent date. The reuse of blocks which can be shown to have originated from the superstructure of the Roman bridge suggests that the structure was built at the end of the Roman period or later. If the testimony of R H Forster's workman is accepted, a coin of Constantine II was found beneath the upper metalling of the road leading to the north end of the bridge showing that it was still in use in the mid-fourth century (p 103).

Other information which might possibly have a bearing on the structure in question is contained in R Forster's *History of Corbridge* (1881) but unfortunately it is as vague as his account of the Roman bridge. To his description of how an area of land called the Green, extending from Corbridge Burn eastwards to within a short distance of the present town, was eroded by the river in the course of the hundred years before 1881, he appends the following note

'As the station had bordered close to the river, the Romans, with their usual foresight, had taken the precaution for the safety of their town and adjacent ground, to erect a strong wall which would appear to have extended from their bridge eastward for near 500 yards [457m]; as far as can be ascertained this protection not only existed during the Roman occupation, but for centuries afterwards, in fact it would appear to have existed, portions at least, until the close of the last century. 50 or 60 [years] ago the foundations and lower portions of this wall for a considerable distance were still there, and particularly noticed by youths while bathing there. Some now living recollect well seeing those remains and described them as being of considerable length, in some parts only the foundations were seen, in other places as if the wall had been thrown down; the thickness of the wall would appear to have been upwards of three feet [0.9m]. About the time referred to a quantity of the stones were removed and used for penning that portion of the field bounding on the river to protect it from the destructive inroads which the floods were making year after year; but this attempt was of short duration, even although assisted by Roman stones, for the impetuous Tyne soon swept piles of stone and mason work before it. In the summer of 1880 portions of the foundations were distinctly seen from the road side.'

Forster 1881, 13

The absence of detail in this account makes it impossible to be certain whether the structure which still exists was part of the wall described above. R

Forster's wall was 'upwards of three feet' (0.9m) in width, a great deal less than the width of ten feet (3.05m) recorded by R H Forster; but the qualification 'upwards' might mean that R Forster was unable to establish the overall width of the wall. It is nevertheless worth considering whether these remains might represent a defensive riverside wall. P Salway (1967, 56–9) has summarised present knowledge of the defences of Corbridge, which depends on work carried out before the First World War, apart from an unpublished excavation by R Birley in 1959. Salway argued that the defences consisted of a wall with a clay bank behind it which can be traced on the north and east sides of the town; some evidence for the existence of a possible gate on the north side has been recovered and his suggestion that a gate existed at the northern bridgehead has already been discussed p 103. The position of the defences on the south side has not been determined, but the remains on the Tyne bank may have some relevance: they cannot be easily tied in with any known Roman river crossing or other structure.

Stanwix

Stanwix is a natural bridging point of the Eden, as it is the first place above the Solway where the flood plain is relatively narrow and bordered by firm higher ground on either side. The first bridge was built to carry the main Agricolan road into south-west Scotland, and was guarded by a fort. The location and date of this bridge are discussed by Caruana and Coulston (1987), who consider that it is not necessarily as early as the Agricolan period and also argue that a sculptured block recovered from the Eden may have come from the shoulder of one of its piers. When Hadrian's Wall was built, a more westerly crossing of the Eden, below its confluence with the Caldew, was chosen so as to avoid the need to bridge the latter river as well (Figure 76). The northern bluff above the Eden has been eroded at this point (noted by Pennant in 1776; cited in Hutchinson 1794, vol 2, 579), presumably as a result of the flow of the Caldew into the Eden deflecting the current northwards, and the northern abutments of the bridge will thus have probably been destroyed. The southern abutments, and curtain immediately to the west, have also been destroyed by the north-westward movement of the Caldew in the post-Roman period, which has resulted in the confluence with the Eden now lying to the west of the bridge site. Following this downstream shift of the confluence, an alluvial terrace formed at the base of the river bluffs on the northern bank of the Eden. The earliest reference to the Wall bridge is made by Camden who, in his northern tour of 1599, noted that

[the Picts' Wall] 'neere unto a little village called Stanwicke...went over the very river just against the castle, where within the channel of the river, mighty stones, the remains thereof, are yet extant'

trans Holland 1637, 778–9

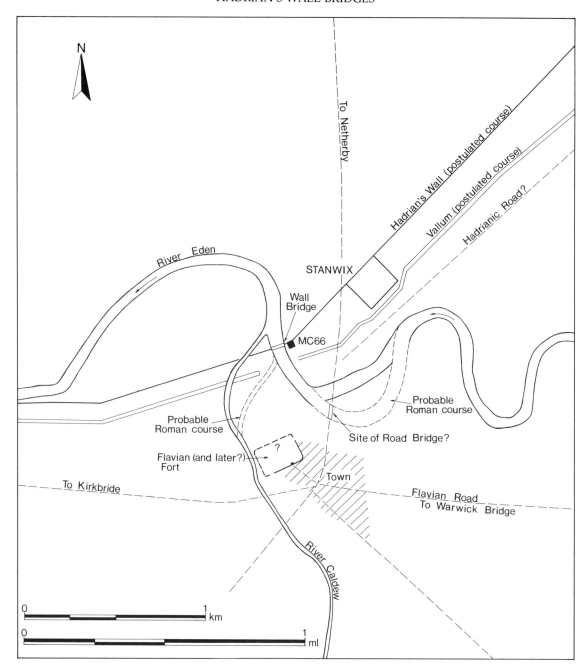

Figure 76   The Roman bridges at Stanwix.   Scale 1:20,000

Subsequently Pennant (cited in Hutchinson 1794, vol 2, 579) recorded the presence of a milecastle (Milecastle 66) on the edge of the bluffs to the north of the river but made no mention of any stones, and neither did Hutchinson (ibid), although he did record that large oak stakes were frequently pulled up in fishermen's nets. These stakes are more likely to have come from the Priestbeck bridge of *c* 1597–1601, which is known to have been constructed upon timber piling, than from the Wall bridge (Hogg 1952, 137).

In 1951 the bottom of the Eden was dredged to a depth of up to 1.83m, which resulted in the discovery of 80–90 blocks of St Bees sandstone,

some of which are now displayed in a public park adjacent to the bridge site (ibid, 150). Two main concentrations of blocks were recorded, 4.6m and 25.3m from the southern bank of the river.

Some of the blocks recovered from the river have been used on more than one occasion. Figure 77, block 6 for example, has sockets for dovetail and bar clamps on the same faces. At Chesters and Willowford only dovetail clamps were used in the original Hadrianic bridges; at Stanwix they are probably to be associated with the original use of the blocks, while the bar clamp sockets probably have been cut during reuse. None of the dovetail clamp sockets show traces of lead or extraction

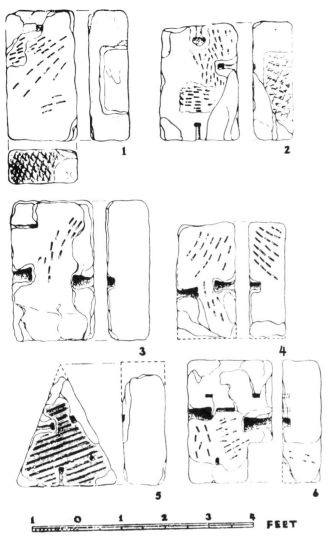

Figure 77   Blocks from the Wall-bridge at Stanwix, after Hogg 1952, fig 6.   Scale 1:25

scars so the clamps may have been of wood. The bar clamps however, were made wholly of lead and one block still retains the remains of two such clamps. The bar clamp sockets are characterised by shallow, and in places scarcely perceptible, chases.

Some blocks have lewis holes (Figure 77, block no 6) which may have been used in both periods of construction. One feature which is only associated with bar clamps however, is band anathyrosis which occurs in the long sides of some blocks (Figure 77, blocks nos 1 and 2). The areas within the margins are recessed by *c* 10–20mm and show coarser tooling (sometimes in a chevron pattern) than on the more finely worked margins, which are up to 170mm wide. Hogg (1952) considered that the recessed areas were filled with cement but the presence of clamps makes this very unlikely and the use of band anathyrosis can be paralleled in the bridges at Chesters and at Corbridge (p 118). Other blocks (Figure 77, no 6) have recesses cut from one corner, for the joggling of joints between blocks within a course. The recesses occur in blocks both with and without clamps. One block (Figure 78, no 8) has had a recess cut through its full width which is 0.11m wide and 0.16m deep. In the

base of the recess there are two bar clamp sockets. The recess was probably cut to a depth level with the top of an adjacent block within the course so as to allow a block in the course above to be laid across their joint. Both of these devices are encountered in bridge 1 at Willowford (p 69).

Another block (Figure 78, no 9) was originally pentagonal with one face 0.16m long and at an angle of 120 degrees to an adjacent face. At this corner the face is vertical but a chamfer commences along the face, which at the opposite corner, is at an angle of 60 degrees to the horizontal, producing an offset of 0.1m. The block has two sockets for bar clamps. The block might have been positioned in the angle between the front and wing of an abutment, where a chamfered string course along the face of the abutment, beneath the arch springing for the bridge began. This would indicate that the abutment wing met the axis of the bridge at a very acute angle(*c* 19 degrees) and would exclude the existence, at Stanwix, of a sharply-splayed abutment comparable with that at bridge 2 at Chesters. The block (Figure 77, no 5) came from the cutwater of one of the piers, but not from the actual point, as the uppermost edge is deliberately worked flat and is not merely fractured as Hogg's drawing suggests. The presence of bar clamp sockets also indicates that there were originally other blocks on either side of the stone. The sides of the block are angled at 70 degrees, which indicates that the pier must have had an unusually elongated cutwater (cf Cüppers 1969, Abb 172). A column base (Figure 78, no 7) was also recovered from the Eden in 1951 and is now in the grounds of the Tullie House Museum, Carlisle (accession no 59–1984). R Hogg (the then museum curator) noted in his museum diary on 24.4.62 that the stone had been found in the Eden in 1951 to the west of the cricket pavilion (a short distance upstream from the bridge site). The base is fractured and heavily water worn and has a diameter of *c* 0.9m. It has a prominent torus moulding 0.16m high and in the top there is a plug of modern concrete, *c* 70mm in diameter, which may be filling a dowel hole. The column base differs from the columns at Chesters and Risingham, which have square bases so that they could be recessed into the bridge parapet (p 41; p 114), some caution must therefore be shown in assigning the column to the bridge.

One block recovered in 1951 has a centurial inscription denoting the 'century of Vesnius Viator

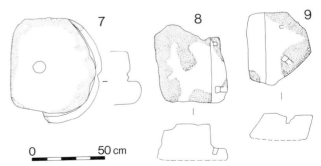

Figure 78   Blocks from the Wall-bridge at Stanwix, stippling denotes fractured surfaces.   Scale 1:25

(dressed this)' (*RIB* 2031). Birley (1951, 179) has argued, from the crudeness of the inscription, that it indicated a check on work done in the building yard, and that it would probably not have been visible when in position on the bridge. The block is heavily fractured and its original dimensions cannot now be determined. On the same surface as the inscription there are two bar clamp sockets (incorrectly called dowel holes in *RIB*). The clamp holes might have been secondary to the inscription however, so this cannot be used as evidence for its date. Birley favoured a Hadrianic date for the inscription on prosopographical grounds. Another block has the letters 'XIV' inscribed 40mm high upon one of its faces and these might also have been associated with a system of tallying during construction.

No voussoirs have been recovered from Stanwix although, as at Chesters, this does not necessarily mean that the bridge did not have stone arches (p 36). Rather, the lack of voussoirs may be a product of the extensive robbing of the bridge which occurred in the post-Roman period. The whole bridge super-structure would have been demolished, leaving only those portions of the piers and abutments which were below water level *in situ*, because of the difficulty of removing the stonework.

The two concentrations of blocks recorded by Hogg (1952, 150), 4.6m and 25.3m from the southern bank, probably indicate the site of two water piers of the latest Roman bridge. If the measured distance was from the approximate centre of the piers, and assuming that the present width of the Eden on the line of the Wall (*c* 60m) has remained more or less constant and that the bridge had equally-spaced waterways, then the Eden could have been spanned by a bridge of two piers and three arches.

There is therefore evidence for at least two bridges at Stanwix. The first is characterised by the use of dovetail clamps and was presumably the Hadrianic Wall bridge. The second bridge utilised bar clamps and band anathyrosis, both paralleled in bridge 2 at Chesters and Corbridge, and was probably associated with a restructuring of the road system in the Severan period (p 138).

Bridges south of Hadrian's Wall

Piercebridge

The fort at Piercebridge was built at the point where Dere Street crossed the Tees (Figure 71). The precise crossing point can be determined as the road has been found in excavation, immediately to the north of the river (Scott 1982, 77, fig 1). The remains of a bridge on this alignment have been seen at various times in the Tees. During a drought in 1933 a number of oak piles became visible in the bed of the river: one concentration lay 6m from the southern bank and was joined together by cross members, while another group of eight piles lay 9.1m from the bank (Richardson and Keeney 1934–6, 240; Scott 1982, fig 2). These piles were probably part of the timber structures first recorded by Hutchinson (1785–94, vol

3, 214). In 1915 a wedge-shaped stone with clamp sockets was recovered amongst the masonry from the river, and in 1933 blocks with lewis holes were also recognised (Wooler 1917, 88; Richardson and Keeney 1934–6, 240). One of the clamped stones was described as having a medieval mason's mark.

Scott (1982, 80) considered that these piles were part of a Roman timber bridge and that the stonework came from the extant sixteenth-century bridge a short distance to the west. A Roman date for the piles would now seem to be confirmed by the work of Mr R Selkirk (personal comment) who has recently found Roman pottery, glass and coins (ranging in date from the first to the fourth century) associated with a concentration of piles. The arrangement of the piles suggests that they originally formed a timber piling underlying stone piers and abutments rather than the supports of a completely timber structure (which were usually more widely spaced; cf the timber bridge at Aldwincle, Jackson and Ambrose 1976, fig 3). The blocks with clamp sockets and lewis holes therefore most probably came from this bridge. The date of construction of the bridge is uncertain: it is unlikely to have continued in use after the construction of a second bridge, 200m to the east in the later second century, (Figure 79, discussed below) and it is also improbable that a stone structure will have been associated with the original construction of the road. Excavation of Dere Street on the north bank of the Tees showed that the first metalled surface was constructed after *c* 90 (Scott 1982, 77). A date in the Hadrianic–Antonine period is perhaps likely, the stone bridge probably replacing a timber structure which was constructed during the initial period of campaigning.

At first sight the third and fourth century coins and pottery recovered by Mr Selkirk appear to contradict this suggestion. However it is difficult to accept that they relate to the period of use of the bridge for there is no evidence that the length of Dere Street immediately north of the river served as a major route in the late Roman period. Excavations by Scott in the 1970s have shown that the latest (fairly crude) road surface in this area is no later than the late second century (ibid) and also that the course of the road was encroached upon by the *vicus* buildings associated with the third and fourth century fort (*Britannia* 7 (1976), 313). It is therefore unlikely that Mr Selkirk's bridge dates to after the second century, and the late finds recovered from the river could be explained as material that had washed down the river as rubbish from occupation elsewhere, and accumulated between the piles.

The later second century Roman bridge, constructed *c* 200m downstream from the original site, was discovered during gravel quarrying in 1972, The remains are now in the care of English Heritage. The bridge can be associated with a branch road detected to the south of the Tees, which ran from Dere Street to the new crossing. Scott (1982, 77) has argued that the bridging point was moved because the river is wider at the new site, and so less pressure would have been created upon the structure during flooding. Indeed the most likely reason for the construction of the bridge is that the earlier second-

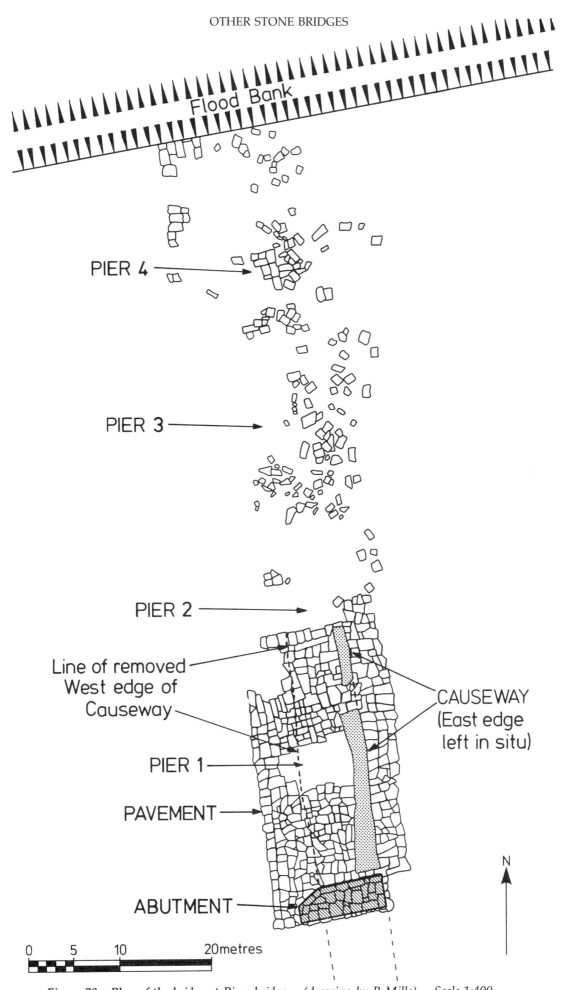

Flood Bank

PIER 4

PIER 3

PIER 2

Line of removed
West edge of
Causeway

CAUSEWAY
(East edge
left in situ)

PIER 1

PAVEMENT

ABUTMENT

N

0   5   10   20 metres

Figure 79   Plan of the bridge at Piercebridge.   (drawing by R Mills).   Scale 1:400

century bridge had collapsed as a result of flooding, which may have even been part of the same episode which caused the destruction of bridge 1A at Willowford (p 76). On the evidence of pottery, Scott (forthcoming) suggests a date of *c* 180 for the construction of the bridge and branch road.

The bridge consisted of stone abutments and piers set upon large sandstone paving slabs which covered the whole width of the river bed beneath the bridge (Figure 79, *Current Archaeol* **4** (1973–4), 136–9). The southern abutment, which survives to a height of two courses, was discovered 100m to the south of the present course of the river and so a considerable length of the Tees flood plain must have been bridged (even allowing for the northward movement of the river in the post-Roman period).

The abutment is 8.05m long and 3.1m wide, with an upstream cutwater the front four blocks of which are bound together by iron bar clamps set in lead. The carriageway would have been 6.1m wide. The dimensions of the piers can be determined because at one point, where the pavement survives intact (marked pier 4 on Figure 79), the base of a now destroyed pier has been recessed slightly into the top of the slabs, to provide a level platform for the blocks. The recessed area shows that the pier was 4.53m wide, with a cutwater upstream and a squared side downstream. Beneath the site of this pier the slabs are bound together with iron bar clamps, and dowel holes were used to fix the pier blocks to the pavement. A number of pier blocks which have dowel holes cut in their undersides were found strewn on the river bed in this area. The number and spacing of the piers are uncertain. The first two piers to the north of the southern abutment have been robbed, and their robber trenches were recognised in the excavation. If it is assumed that both piers were also 4.53m wide then the spacing between pier 1 and the abutment would have been *c* 10.5m and between pier 1 and pier 2 *c* 11.6m. It is thus apparent that the piers were not uniformly spaced across the river.

In the uppermost surviving course of the abutment five slots (two of which were unfinished) had been cut into the face of the blocks at about 1m intervals. The completed slots were 250mm–290mm wide, 115mm–140mm deep, and cut at an angle above the horizontal of 57–59 degrees. Slots may also have existed in the piers, as a loose block found near the site of pier 4 possessed a similar feature. Scott (forthcoming) thought that the slots were designed to hold wooden beams, but as two were unfinished they may never have been used, possibly because they were too low and were affected by flood water. They may have been recut on a higher course of the abutment which has since been removed. There are two suggested functions for the slots: either they were constructional features, perhaps part of the centering for stone arches, or they were structural and served as diagonal supporting struts for longitudinal timbers of the superstructure. Although the slots are not particularly substantial the latter explanation is perhaps the more likely and they can be compared with the slots in the sides of the piers at the Römerbrücke in Trier (Cüppers 1969, 65–70, Abb 151) (p 85). A timber superstructure resting upon

stone piers and abutments is therefore probable at Piercebridge.

Following the construction of the bridge the Tees shifted its course northward and by the later third or fourth century the water channels between at least the first three piers had silted up. At this date the southern end of the bridge was extensively re-modelled: the first two piers were completely robbed out (along with the underlying areas of sandstone pavement); the abutment was demolished down to its second course, and a causeway was constructed above the alluvium. The causeway was 6.1m wide and consisted of a revetment of dressed blocks, intact on its eastern side, with a core of cobbles. It was traced in excavation to 4.35m north of the site of pier 2 (see Figure 79), beyond which point it had been washed away. Presumably either pier 3, of which there is no trace, or pier 4 now acted as the southern abutment with the causeway forming the base of a ramp to carry Dere Street onto the bridge.

The bridge was eventually destroyed by a major flood. The causeway was cut through by the river, and the piers were scoured away. Many of the pier blocks now lie strewn around the river bed and much of the sandstone paving is also displaced. When the flood waters receded the whole area was engulfed in river gravel which had accumulated to a depth of 3–4m when the bridge was re-discovered in 1972.

Scott (1982, 80–1) has discussed the antiquarian literature on Piercebridge and concluded that the comments of Leland in 1542 'Persbrigg...sumtime of 5 arches but a late made new of 3 arches'), and Gough in 1806 'The Roman road comes immediately to the river a little lower than the present bridge, broad, strait and hard, the great original stone bridge not yet worn out' refer to the second Roman stone bridge. There is no reason, however, why Leland cannot have been referring to the remodelling of the medieval bridge in the sixteenth century. Gough's comments are more problematical but it is very unlikely that a stone bridge would have escaped the notice of Hutchinson (1785–94, **3**, 214) (who merely records timber piles on the line of Dere Street), or other earlier antiquaries. The best solution is there-fore to disregard Gough's testimony, it is perhaps a garbled conflation of the accounts of Hutchinson and previous editions of Camden. Consequently there is no reason to believe that the bridge discovered in 1972 was known to antiquaries.

Binchester

Dymond (1961, 138–9) identified four rusticated blocks (one with a splayed side) at the point where Dere Street crossed the river Wear (Figure 71). None of the blocks had clamps or lewis holes so the identification of the masonry as Roman must be treated with caution.

Hylton

On 25 April, 1883 the discovery of a supposed Roman bridge at Hylton, on the river Wear near Sunderland

(Figure 71), was discussed at a meeting of the Society of Antiquaries of Newcastle upon Tyne. It appears that in 1865 Mr J G Lister who owned a nearby shipyard saw 'hundreds of tons of stone' being taken out of the river by the River Wear Commissioners (*Proc Soc Antiq Newcastle upon Tyne* 1 ser, **1** (1882–4), 19–20). The local name for the place was 'Brigstuns' or 'Brigstanes' and the presence of a stone structure which continued across the whole width of the river had been an obstacle for keels carrying coal from collieries higher up the Wear (*Proc Soc Antiq Newcastle upon Tyne* 1 ser, **4** (1889–90), 230). The stones were 'clamped together and run with lead'. At the time of their removal Lister recorded in a notebook that they were built over an oak frame and that they included 'a circular stone with part of a vine leaf, another carved with a honeysuckle pattern and moulded and wedge-like stones.' In addition, a white metal plate bearing the letters IM..D..AVG was also recovered. Lister handed over his notebook to R E Hooppell, prominent in the excavation of the forts of South Shields and Binchester, but by that time the 'white metal' plate had been lost. It was published in *Ephemeris Epigraphica*, **7** (1892), no 987, by Haverfield, but was later doubted by him, and in *The Roman Inscriptions of Britain* (*RIB*, concordance Tables, 765) was rejected as not antique.

In 1968 Miss Pamela V Clarke wrote to the River Wear Commissioners to enquire if their records contained any account of the discoveries at Hylton. The General Manager and Clerk to the Commissioners, Mr E Lonsdale, replied that

> 'the Commissioners carried out a river improvement scheme, involving the dredging of stone, at Hylton between 1870 and 1881, although there is no record of a Roman bridge being encountered.'

At the time that the discoveries at Hylton were first discussed there were several local antiquarians who expressed scepticism, including T W U Robinson, C C Hodges, W H D Longstaffe and the Rev Canon Greenwell, and we may share their doubts. In this country not every ancient structure of squared stone clamped with iron is of Roman date, and the sculptured fragments might have been medieval rather than Roman. In 1984 the first named writer saw remains of old quays or revetting walls on both banks of the Wear at Hylton consisting of squared blocks joined with iron clamps, which seemed of no great age. The area was recently landscaped. There is no Roman route which is known to cross the Wear at Hylton, although for a time a Roman milestone from Lanchester stored at Greenwell Ford was mistakenly attributed to the village of Ford, now part of South Hylton (*RIB* 2295).

Ebchester

Hutchinson (1785–94, vol 2, 432) reported the remains of two piers 'supposed by some to be part of a Roman bridge' in the Derwent. Nothing has been subsequently attested.

Alston

The Roman fort of Whitley Castle is situated on the western slopes of the valley of the South Tyne. North-east of the fort, at a point some 2.2km north-west of Alston, are the remains of an old bridge consisting of a retaining wall of unmortared, roughly-coursed slabs with split faces, apparently part of the western abutment of the bridge. They have been claimed as the remains of a Roman bridge by R C Bosanquet

> '[who] pointed out that there is no evidence for a bridge having stood there in medieval times, let alone later, and the surviving masonry would accord well with Roman origin; and if the bridge was Roman, it must surely have been built to carry a road into Allendale. As one stands beside the abutment and looks at the steep eastern slope, across the river, one's eye is taken by the prominent double zig-zag of an ancient road climbing the hill...'
>
> Birley 1950, 150

There is also a very prominent terrace cutting obliquely across the slope down to the valley bottom behind the abutment but this is probably of recent origin.

There is nothing distinctively Roman about the masonry and in spite of Bosanquet's comments it probably belongs to a bridge of comparatively recent date. This reach of the South Tyne is of no great width and is crossed by a number of small bridges. Sopwith records that on 29 July, 1829

> 'these parts were visited by a dreadful storm of thunder and rain, which continued the whole of the afternoon and evening [water from the mountain-sides] rolled down with resistless violence, in many places tearing up the surface, and in great measure destroying the bridges over Gilderdale, Lort and Thornhope Burns.'
>
> Sopwith 1833, 72

The remains in question lie on the stretch of the river between the mouths of the Gilderdale and Thornhope Burns and perhaps belong to a small post-medieval bridge devastated by this or some other flood in recent times.

Bridges north of Hadrian's Wall

Risingham

John Hodgson visited Risingham (Figure 71) in 1824 and made some notes on the Roman bridge over the Rede (preserved in his notebook now held in the Northumberland Record Office).

> 'The foundations [of the bridge] laid bare two years since [are] laid bare now. The many stones of the buttresses at the ends of the Bridge thair [sic] had a hole in the centre of the upper surface, I think of the

lower bed too for the purpose of putting a
strong square oak pin in to prevent their
being moved off their beds singly. Riddle
[William Ridley: Birley 1961, 236] says they
were dowelled together with oak. When
the Reed a few years since tore away a part
of the meadow on its north side it exposed
two tall upright stones standing at 12 feet
[3.66m] distance [from the bank?]... They
were about 8 yards [7.3m] apart.'

ref no ZAN M15/A37, 153

Hodgson's accompanying sketch shows that the
structure visible in the bed of the Rede at the
confluence with the Chesterhope Burn was six blocks
long and three blocks wide. The blocks were square
to rectangular in shape, and had sockets for dovetail
clamps in adjacent faces.

The blocks most probably formed part of the
southern abutment of the bridge, since the river has
changed its course substantially since Roman times
(Figure 80). Today the Rede, in a pronounced
meander, cuts back across the line of Dere Street for
a second time a short distance to the north. Originally
the river flowed much closer to the north wall of the
fort, and at some date even scoured away a portion
of the defences. Only a single crossing of the Rede
by Dere Street would thus have been necessary in the
Roman period. Little can be said of the form of the
abutment although Hodgson's observation of oak
dowels is notable.

The two columns presumably stood on either side
of the carriageway on the north abutment of the
bridge. The fact that they were found upright and
apparently *in situ* is remarkable and suggests that
much of the abutment remained intact at that time.
Hodgson (ibid) records that the columns were
removed from the site in 1809 when it took three
horses to drag them out. One column was subsequently used as a garden gatepost in West
Woodburn while the other supported the roof of a
cart shed at High Leam Farm (W Davison 1933–4,
350). The West Woodburn stone (Figure 81) has since
been moved to the garden of the Grey Horse Inn in
the same village. The sandstone column is 1.96m
high, and its top is heavily weathered. Its diameter
immediately above the base is 0.39m which decreases
to 0.31m at the top. The base of the column has been
squared off probably so that it could be recessed into
the parapet of the bridge. The shaft is not strictly
circular but has one flattened side, in which, 0.96m
above the top of the base, is a rectangular socket
70mm wide and 90mm deep; it probably held a dowel
for an adjacent parapet slab. Both these features
occur on the columns found at Chesters. The High
Leam column has not been examined, but Davison
(ibid) records that it was in excess of 1.91m high and
its diameter varied from 0.48m to 0.50m. He was
unable to determine whether it had a squared base.

The present width of the Rede at Risingham is
c 20m and this may have been bridged by a single
span as no trace of a water pier has been recorded.
There is no evidence for the nature of the superstructure of the bridge. The Rede frequently floods in
winter and so to the south of the river, Dere Street

was carried across the flood plain upon a raised
embankment (Swinburne *et al* 1844, plate II, reproduced here as Figure 80). A similar embankment
probably existed to the north of the bridge as well,
but would have been destroyed by the movement of
the river channel.

In front of the probable site of the north gate at
Risingham a large 'wear' (D on plan, Figure 80) was
constructed which extended 82.3m from the fort wall,
and was composed largely of reused masonry, which
included some inscribed material (ibid, 157). It
appears to have been a particularly massive quadrilateral structure which prevented the Rede cutting
into its southern bank and threatening the safety of
the fort defences. Its construction is undated but it is
probably to be placed quite late in the history of the
fort.

Elishaw

(Figure 71)
Wallis records that Dere Street crossed the Rede by a
'bridge of arches, some of the stones still to be seen,
with iron cramps and melted lead.' Wallis 1769, 59.

The mention of arches clearly only refers to the
presence of stone piers, for Wallis used the same term
to describe the piers in the North Tyne at Chesters.
MacLauchlan further noted:

' in the south bank, however, there are
rotten small trees [laid horizontally] and
large stones evidently placed on them, so
exactly in line, that we are disposed to
think them the remains of the road,
though now four feet [1.22m] below the
surface. Very nearly in the same line, in
the bed of the river, and four feet [1.22m]
below the lowest water in dry seasons, is
to be seen a piece of timber fastened down
seemingly by piles driven on each side of
it.'

Maclauchlan 1852, 32

MacLauchlan appears to describe a timber pilework
with horizontal cross members which served as a
solid base for the clamped blocks of a pier, and
perhaps also the remains of the southern abutment.
Such construction is quite common in Roman
bridges, as for example in the Rhine bridge at Mainz,
(Cüppers 1969; 185–7 although timber pileworks are
notably absent at the bridges examined on Hadrian's
Wall). In June 1988, during a dry spell, the river was
thoroughly examined at the point where it intersects
the line of Dere Street; no traces of a Roman bridge
could be seen.

Newstead

Adam Milne noted

'at this place [Newstead, Figure 71]
likewise there has been a famous Bridge
over the Tweed; the entrance to it on the
south side is very evident and a great deal
of fine Stones are dug out of the Arches of
the Bridge when the water is low.'

Milne 1769, 7

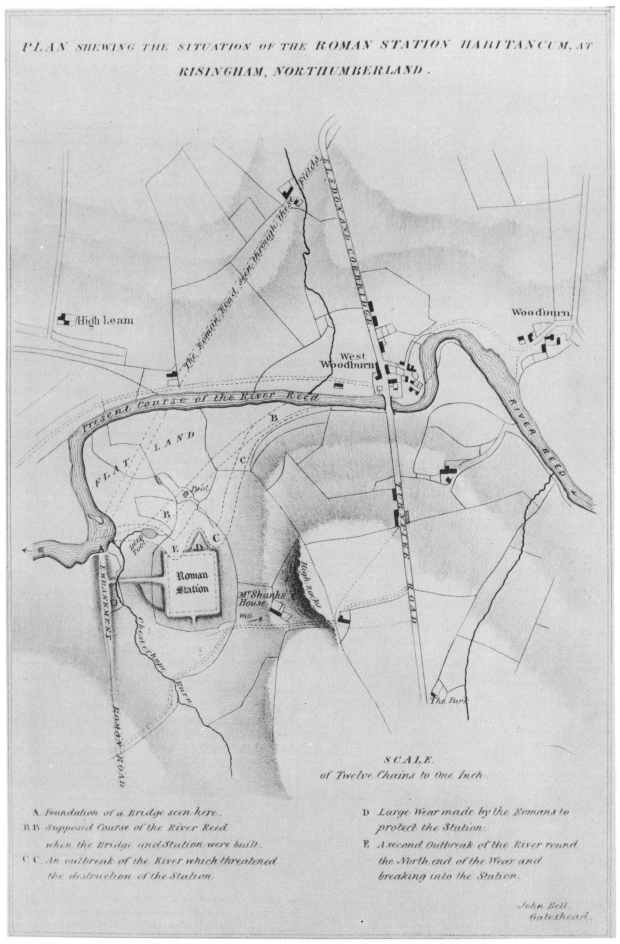

Figure 80   John Bell's plan of Risingham showing the line of Dere Street and marking the position of the bridge (after Swinburne et al 1844, pl 2)

*Figure 81   Stone column from the bridge at Risingham,
now in the garden of the Grey Horse Inn, West Woodburn.
Scale 1:25*

It would thus appear that at the time of Milne's visit
both the southern abutment and at least one pier
were visible in the Tweed. The site of the bridge is
not now accurately known although it has been
stated that it must have lain close to the existing ford
at the Eddy Pool (RCAM(S) 1956, 469). The proximity
of the bridge to the fort at Newstead makes it very
probable that the remains were Roman.

Summerston

In 1941 dredging of the river Kelvin to the north of
the fort at Balmuildy, on the Antonine Wall, led to
the discovery of a considerable number of sandstone
blocks and some fragments of timber (Davidson 1952,
88–94). Further blocks were recovered in 1982
(*Discovery Excav Scot* 1982, 29). While the blocks
undoubtedly derive from a Roman bridge, one piece
of timber has produced a dendrochronological date
of 1360 (*Discovery Excav Scot* 1979, 40) and so the
timbers are best excluded from an account of the
Roman structure.

In his description of the blocks Davidson (1952)
noted several features. A number of them displayed
decorative tooling, in diamond shaped, double
herringbone, and fern leaf patterns. Many of the
blocks also had dovetail clamp sockets; the clamps
were presumably of wood as no iron staining could
be detected. One block had a moulding, and another
recovered in 1982 had a recess cut from one corner
for the joggling of joints. A few blocks had one side
angled at 30 degrees to their bases. No recognisable
voussoirs were recovered. Davidson also noted that

two blocks showed evidence of reuse as they had
dovetail clamp sockets on both their top and bottom
faces. One of these blocks had also been fractured,
damaging the socket. This observation suggests that
the block may have been broken during the construction of the bridge, probably after it had been laid
in position and had its clamp sockets cut, and that it
was reused by simply being turned upside down.
Consequently the two reused blocks do not necessarily indicate that the bridge underwent major repair
or modification.

Few details of the form of the bridge can be
deduced. Davidson considered that the angled blocks
came from the shoulder of a pier or piers although
the angle of 30 degrees is extremely shallow for a
cutwater (cf Cüppers 1969, Abb 172) and perhaps the
angle between the front and wing of an abutment
may be a more likely location. The width of the river
Kelvin at this point (c 22m), however, makes the
presence of at least one pier likely.

The bridge at Summerston was constructed to carry
the Military Way, the lateral road which usually ran
c 36–46m behind the Antonine Wall. However, the
distribution of the blocks recovered in dredging
indicates that the bridge lay only c 9m behind the
Wall and so the Military Way must have been
brought up closer to the Wall as it approached the
bridge. This fact led S N Miller to state

> 'by this arrangement the bridge, with the
> Military Way behind its protecting parapet
> (and perhaps with an obstacle to bar
> passage through the openings under the
> platform), would take the place of the Wall
> and its rampart-walk at the crossing of the
> river and make the patrolled barrier
> continuous.'
>
>   Miller 1952, 213

There is no evidence for a physical connection
between the Antonine Wall and the bridge abutments
however, and for that matter it is by no means certain
that the Antonine Wall possessed a rampart-walk, as
a recent survey has stressed (Hanson and Maxwell
1983, 83). Miller also suggested that the bridge may
have had a more important function than merely to
carry the Military Way across the Kelvin. It perhaps
also served a north–south route; to the south the
road, running up the Clyde valley via Castledykes
and Bothwellhaugh, may have met the Antonine
Wall at Balmuildy, and to the north native traffic
which passed down the Blane valley may have been
allowed through the Wall at the fortlet at Summerston which lay c 600m to the north of the bridge.

1   The earlier Forster was a watchmaker who was prominent in
the foundation of the Free Methodist Church and his obituary
in the Hexham Courant (15 August 1885) describes his
'antiquarian tastes, which we fancy he caught from his relative,
the late Mr Joseph Fairless of Hexham' whose letter describing
a visit to the excavation of the bridge at Chesters in 1860 is
reproduced on p 5. Robert Henry Forster (1867–1923), although
trained as a barrister, appears to have been a man of
independent means; he wrote a number of historical novels,
now largely forgotten, and was mainly responsible for the
direction of the excavations at Corbridge in 1907–14 (Knowles
1923–4).

8 Techniques of construction

Introduction

One of the most important aspects of Bridge 2 at Chesters is that it represents the largest surviving example of the technique of construction known as *opus quadratum* available for study in Britain. *Opus quadratum* can be defined as

> 'construction with rectangular blocks laid in horizontal courses without mortar and sometimes joined together with clamps and dowels'
>
> Lugli 1957, 48

and was a technique already many centuries old when Britain became a Roman province. It had been brought to its highest stage of development by the Greeks in the fifth and fourth centuries BC by which time the use of the various types of clamps employed in the bridges at Chesters, Willowford and elsewhere in northern Britain was already established. Indeed by the first century AD in many large Roman buildings the use of mortared rubble, faced with stone or brick had superseded *opus quadratum*; in Britain mortared rubble was used to form the *podium* of the Temple of Claudius at Colchester and the foundation of the *podium* of the Flavian monument at Richborough. The use of *opus quadratum* however, continued, particularly in bridges, but the Severan bridges at Chesters and Corbridge can be numbered amongst the latest examples of the use of the technique in the western parts of the Empire.

The term *opus quadratum*, although attested in a few inscriptions, does not seem to have been in general use in classical times, When the technique is described by Vitruvius (II, VIII, 5–7) he uses Greek words to refer to the various forms of coursing found in *Graecorum structura* : *isodunum*, *pseudisodunum* and *enplecton*. Blake (1947, 2, no 2), following van Deman, preferred the term 'squared-stone construction', and 'high quality block-in-course work' is the classification of the Chesters masonry employed by Hill (1981, 18). In what follows the term '*opus quadratum*' is employed because it is in general usage and reflects differences between ancient and more recent techniques of construction.

In the discussion below it might seem that undue emphasis has been placed on parallels occurring in Greek buildings erected half a millennium earlier than the bridges in northern Britain. Unfortunately this cannot be avoided because the many detailed descriptions of Greek buildings with illustrations of many individual blocks and careful considerations of techniques of construction are not generally matched by similarly detailed descriptions of Roman buildings. The technique of *opus quadratum* was fully developed when it was introduced into Roman architecture but the evidence from Chesters and elsewhere shows that it is still worthy of detailed study. The lead tie-bars and bar clamps, and an unusual type of dowel hole, find few published parallels elsewhere and suggest that there still remains much to be discovered about what might have been provincial variations in the use of *opus quadratum* in the Roman period.

A notable feature of bridge 2 at Chesters, and also apparently of the bridge at Corbridge, was the use of different construction techniques in the base of the abutments and piers and in the superstructure. In the former, lead tie-bars, rather than clamps were used to hold the blocks together, but in the superstructures, in addition to tie-bars, bar clamps and dowels were employed for greater strength. Band anathyrosis also seems to have been confined to the superstructures; it was undoubtedly used to form the tightest possible joints in the most visible parts of the bridges. There is no reason to consider that the differences in construction techniques denote work of two seperate periods.

The dressing and finishing of stone

The dressing of the ordinary facing stones in the Wall and towers at Chesters and Willowford was carried out with an axe or adze, or possibly a chisel, and with a punch (point); Blagg (1976) and Hill (1981) have discussed these tools and how tool marks remaining on the stones can be used to distinguish which type was employed. The reader is referred to the descriptions of the various structures for comments on the tooling.

The dressing of the blocks is of considerable interest. It has already been established from the varying depths of the lewis holes that the upper surfaces of the blocks of the east abutment of bridge 2 at Chesters were dressed flat after they were set in position (p 120). The use of what appear to be quarry roughouts in the primary drain (context 132, Figure 15: p 27) suggests that the other surfaces were also worked on the site of the bridge. As on the ordinary facing stones, points and tools with cutting edges were used. The use of the point seems to have been more common but tool marks left by both types of implement often occur on the same block.

The most distinctive type of tooling, which is usually termed 'feathering', occurs on the external faces of the blocks of the east abutment of bridge 2 at Chesters (Figure 17) and also on a number of blocks from the superstructure (block no 25, which has it on the zone above a moulding of Type 2; blocks nos 50; 68; and 73, Figure 89, no 4, where it occurs on their angled faces; and blocks nos 8; and 60; which are ordinary facing blocks). The feathering consists of closely-set elliptical lines, cut with a fine point which curve in opposite directions, from the centre of the face at the top, towards the lower corners of the block. The upper edges of these blocks are often cut back to a flat surface by a depth of up to 40mm. Bruce (1867, 146) judged this work to be typical of Severan work 'in the stations on the northern section of Watling Street' but to illustrate this technique he chose a block tooled in a basketwork pattern, which occurs on only three loose blocks from the site, and on none of the blocks in position in the east abutment; blocks nos 27; and 118 are ordinary facing blocks and block no 41 is a cornice block with a moulding of Type 2, and

Figure 82   Block no 113 from Chesters, showing tooling in a chevron pattern and a probable dowel hole, scale 0.5m.   (Photo: P T Bidwell)

Figure 83   Block no 87 from Chesters, showing band anathyrosis.   Scale 0.50m

basketwork tooling on the zone above the moulding. None of these resembles the block which Bruce illustrates. Tooling, in a basketwork pattern, occurs on blocks reused in the crypt of Hexham Abbey (ibid, 343, fig, which, it is argued elsewhere (p 105), perhaps came principally from the bridge at Corbridge), and at the south gate of Risingham, supposedly of Severan date (Richmond 1936, fig 4). The only other examples of feathered tooling in the area of the Wall also occur in the crypt at Hexham Abbey (Bruce 1867, 344) and again probably came from the bridge at Corbridge. Blocks from the Antonine bridge at Summerston near Balmuildy have been described as having 'fern-leaf' tooling, by which might be meant feathered tooling.

A block (no 394, Figure 50, no 14, and Figure 53) reused in the foundations of the tower at Willowford has a carefully worked surface below a small moulding. A tool with a cutting edge 16mm wide, has been used to form vertical lines of diagonal tool marks giving a herringbone effect; the lines are so regularly cut that they must have been produced by a chisel and mallet. Herringbone tooling also occurs on a block reused in the sluices at Willowford. Both of these blocks will have originated from bridge 1 or 1A. A further example from Chesters (block no 113, Figure 82) has herringbone tooling on its unworn upper surface and a dowel hole with a groove leading to it on its lower surface; once the block was in position the elaborate tooling would have been concealed by overlying courses.

Tooling of the type described above is fairly commonly encountered in *opus quadratum* of the Roman period. Durm (1905, fig 211) illustrates examples from the Tomb of Caecilia Metella at Rome and from a tomb at Albano.

Another important aspect of the finishing of the blocks is the means by which the edges were worked to achieve the tightest possible joints. Crowbars were used to make the final adjustments to the position of blocks (p 119) but in addition a number of blocks in the superstructure of bridge 2 at Chesters were specially prepared. Twelve loose blocks display band

anathyrosis on one or more of their surfaces (block nos 3; 37; 76; 87, Figure 83; 99; and 118, which are rectangular blocks; Blocks nos 25; 43, Figure 30, no 4; 83, Figure 30, no 5; 87; and 120, Figure 30, no 6; which have mouldings of Type 2, and block no 35 which is a cornice block with the moulding missing). Four other blocks have edge anathyrosis (blocks nos 65; 74, Figure 89, no 1; and 84 which are rectangular blocks; block no 59, Figure 30, no 8, which has a moulding of Type 1) and one rectangular block (no 46) which has band anathyrosis on one side and edge anathyrosis on the other. These two techniques of finishing the sides of blocks were a labour-saving means of producing nearly plane surfaces along the edges of the blocks; the mason roughly dressed the centre of the side leaving the edges raised and subsequently to be worked with precision to a smooth surface. In edge anathyrosis 'the vertical joint faces met only at the edges, with the rest of the face roughly concave' (Coulton 1977, 47), who points out that any dressing which it was necessary to carry out after the blocks were set in position would have exposed the wider jointing behind the point of contact) the walls of the building on Site XI at Corbridge provide an excellent example of this technique.

Band anathyrosis consists of raised zones usually along the top and sides of the surface, the remainder of which has been cut back. On the blocks at Chesters the bands are usually at least 100mm in width and the recessed area they enclose is often neatly worked with diagonal lines cut with a punch or point. Band anathyrosis also occurs on blocks near the site of the Roman bridge at Corbridge (p 106), and on blocks from the bridge on the line of Hadrian's Wall dredged from the Eden below Stanwix (Figure 77, no 1, and 2, p 110). It is otherwise very rare in Britain: no examples are recorded from the other bridges in northern Britain, and the only structure in the south where it has been noted on rectangular blocks is the early second-century wall of the *colonia* at Gloucester (Hurst 1986, pl 20 b and c). Band anathyrosis is perhaps to be found more commonly on blocks which formed part of the architectural ornamentation of

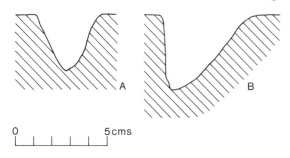

Figure 84   Typical cross-section of crowbar slots in blocks of bridge 2 at Chesters. Scale 1:2

structures: for example, the coping stones of the city wall of London (RCHM(E), 1928, pl 31) and blocks from various structures at Mainz (Büsing 1982, Taf 1, A3; 2, Bl; 4, B20; Taf 9, C32–3; Taf 21, G13).

Crowbar slots

Holmes observed that in the pier of bridge 1 at Chesters the surface of the blocks displayed

'at uncertain intervals wedge-shaped holes, the use of which is not clear [Figures 8, 9, 10]. They could not have been used for lifting, and are not holes for joggles to prevent the stones shifting on their beds. The likeliest use for them is to give point-hold to the crowbars used in forcing along the upper stones to their positions in the process of building.'

Holmes 1894, 330–1

Holes of identical form also occur in large numbers in the upper surfaces of the blocks in the later abutment. They are much smaller and less regularly formed than the lewis holes, their dimensions varying between 60 and 90mm in length and 30 and 50mm in width and depth. Most have a v-shaped profile (Figure 84, A) but in some cases one side of the slot is vertical and the other slopes at an angle of about 45 degrees (Figure 84, B). In many instances they lie only a centimetre or so from the faces of blocks, overlying those into the surfaces of which they were cut, for example, along the offsets on the face of the north wing, and at the point on the north wing where the sixth and seventh courses have been removed (Figure 15). The purpose of such slots was discussed in some detail by G Lugli (1957, 231–5) in his study of *opus quadratum*, confirming Holmes's conjecture that they were used as purchase points for crowbars when blocks of the overlying course were levered into position. Lugli suggested that a fulcrum was provided by a baulk of timber placed between the crowbar and the side of the block.

From the arrangement of the crowbar slots, the means by which the blocks on the abutment were placed in position can be deduced. Having been lowered by crane as close as possible to their intended position they were then dragged with ropes or hauled on rollers roughly into place. Crowbars were used to ensure a tight fit with adjacent blocks. The slots usually appear in groups of three at the sides of the blocks, the two outer slots in line, the central slot set back by about 50mm (in a few instances lewis holes served the purpose of crowbar slots). A crowbar was probably used first in the central slot to push the block roughly into position and then two crowbars on the outer slots to achieve the tightest possible joints with adjacent blocks. The position of the slots thus allows the direction in which the blocks were laid to be determined. For example, the blocks of the sixth course forming the face of the main abutment had been laid from the south end working north. The blocks of the same course forming the face of the south wing had been laid in the opposite direction, presumably because they were being moved into position after being set down by the crane in the centre of the south wing. Blocks of the seventh course on the north wing had been laid from the south working northwards. Crowbar slots also appear on the surface of the offsets on the north wing showing that the facing blocks were also levered back to form a tight joint with the blocks in the core of the wing.

Crowbar slots are generally confined to the front of the abutment and its wings and are entirely absent along the front of the surface of the fifth course at the south end of the south wing. Behind the face of the abutment and its wings they occur only occasionally and usually singly rather than in groups of three. It seems that very tight joints were required on the face of the abutment and its wings and indeed it is noticeable that the joints of blocks in this position are generally tighter than those between blocks behind the faces. This was probably not only for the sake of appearance but also because the front row of blocks was probably laid first to provide an accurately positioned border for the rest of the course (as T Blagg has suggested *in litt*). The general absence of crowbar slots behind the faces can be explained in some instances by the use of cranes to lower blocks directly into position; in many other instances lewis holes and joints between the course below probably offered sufficient purchase to allow the blocks to be levered into position.

Slots in the bottom of the grooves in the cornice blocks suggest that crowbars were also used to achieve tight joints between the parapet slabs (p 39).

Crowbar slots appear on numerous blocks from Willowford and are also to be seen on the blocks from the bridge over the Eden at Stanwix. At Corbridge their presence on the plinth courses of the east and west walls of Site XI shows that the blocks of one or more overlying courses have been robbed at some period from this supposedly unfinished building.

Lewis holes

In the centre of the upper surface of almost every block on the east abutment of bridge 2 at Chesters there is a lewis hole (Figure 15); a total of 145 can be seen and there are a further 18 examples in loose blocks on the site. The dimensions of the lewis holes vary between 22–30mm in width and 110–150mm in length. The majority are 50–110mm deep but some are represented by shallow depressions only a centimetre or so in depth. The reason for these variations in depth is that when the blocks were set in position with the lewis, their upper surfaces were still only roughly worked; once in position they were dressed flush with the upper surfaces of their neighbours, in some instances removing almost the full depth of the lewis hole.

Lewis holes are not present in the blocks of the pier of the first bridge incorporated in the later east abutment. However, there is one loose block (no 114) with a lewis hole which can certainly be attributed to the first bridge because it has sockets for dovetail clamps. Another less certain example is one of the possible voussoirs from the later bridge (Table 2, block no 52) which has a lewis hole near one edge, suggesting that it had been cut down from a larger block used in the first bridge. At Willowford there is rather more evidence for the use of the lewis in the construction of the first bridge. Two blocks (nos 373; and 395) reused in later structures have sockets for dovetail clamps and lewis holes and there is a lewis hole in the top of a voussoir (block no 172) attributable to bridge 1 or its repair. The lewis was certainly employed in the repair for one occurs in a block (no 553, Figure 57, no 22) with a socket for a bar clamp and a possible dowel hole, which came from the river deposits associated with the destruction of bridge 1A; there were also two blocks (nos 259; and 378) with lewis holes but no clamp sockets reused in bridge 2.

The infrequent occurrence of lewis holes in bridge 1 at Chesters is probably explained by the size of the blocks, which unlike those of the later bridge, were probably small enough to be manhandled into position. The lewis was perhaps only required to lift the blocks for the upper courses of the piers.

Although in the ancient world there were a number of different devices for fixing blocks with hooks for attachment to lifting devices, in Britain and the other north-western provinces of the Roman empire only the lewis seems to have been employed (Figure 88, a). Lewis irons have continued in use down to the present day and can take several forms. Heron's *Mechanica*, written in the first century AD, and surviving only as an Arabic translation apart from a few fragments, describes one particular type of lewis iron (cf Figure 88, a). After describing the hole that should be cut into the block to receive the lewis irons, Heron continues:

> 'Then we make two pegs of iron, whose ends are bent like the shape of the letter *gamma*, and let there be in their tops a ring or a hole. Then we fit those two together into the side of the hole and we put their bend into the slant of the cut; and we use also another, third peg of iron, and fit it in between these two pegs to hinder these two pegs from being moved. And let also the third peg be pierced in the top by a hole that comes into line with the two holes in the two other pegs.'
>
> translation in Drachmann 1963, 105–6 of the *Mechanica* III, 8

A bar or axle is then passed through the holes in the tops of the lewis irons which can then be attached to the crane.

Brewis (1925, 104–5) however, considered that lewis irons of this type could only have been used when the lewis holes were cut to dimensions with a variation of less than half an inch; a greater variation would mean that the lewis irons would either not fit into the hole or would not engage against the sloping sides of the hole when the block was lifted.

At Chesters and Rudchester Brewis noted that there was a considerable variation in the size of the lewis holes, either in structures which were likely to have been built at the same time or in one case within the same structure (the east gate at Chesters). The differences in the lengths of the lewis holes in bridge 2 at Chesters is also considerable (110–150mm) and can be compared with the variations in the length of lewis-hole openings (105–125mm) in a series of 62 blocks at South Shields from the piers of the forecourt colonnade of the *principia*, which were reused in various third-century structures within the fort (Bidwell and Speak forthcoming). Brewis believed that lewis holes which varied in length were suitable only for lewis irons consisting of

> 'two curved plugs of iron so arranged back to back that when the tackle is tightened their heads are drawn together with their feet spread out, accommodating themselves to varying sized holes and gripping the stone whether both bevels are alike or not'
>
> Brewis, 1925, 104-5

However, it seems doubtful whether variations in the length of lewis holes can be used to establish the use of lewis irons of the type which Brewis described. At Chesters these variations must have been largely the result of the dressing of the tops of the blocks after they had been set in position with a lewis (p 120); the length of the lewis hole of course, increases with its depth. Even when lewis holes were overcut it would have been possible to use the lewis irons described by Heron, by wedging pieces of wood or iron in any gaps.

Thus either of two types of lewis, the three pegged type described by Heron or the two curved plugs of iron could have been employed on bridge 2 at Chesters.

The use of the lewis does not always imply the use of a lifting device. In early Greek architecture blocks in some structures have U-shaped holes cut in their upper surfaces through which ropes were passed. Coulton (1974, 4) argued that these holes do not provide evidence for the use of cranes at such an early period and showed how, by slinging ropes from poles, blocks of a considerable weight could be lifted and carried manually. In 1986 during the reconstruction of the south-west gate of the Roman fort at South Shields the same method was used by masons to set into position some of the blocks of the gate piers, which weighed *c* 200kg each; in this instance chains slung from a scaffolding pole were attached to the blocks by a modern form of lewis iron (consisting of a split pin pivoted at the top, with two arms above which are brought together when the block is lifted, chipping large spalls of stone from the base of the parapet slab or from the sides of the groove in the cornice blocks. The voussoirs of the north gate at Milecastle 37 provide another example of blocks of fairly small size, with lewis holes, which could have been raised by hand without the use of a crane, by scaffolding around the arch, and then lowered into position by means of lewis irons slung by ropes or chains from poles.

The Crane

Halfway along the south wing of bridge 2 at Chesters and 2.15m from its face there is a regularly formed hole which passes through the edges of two adjacent blocks (Figure 15). The top of the hole was found to have been filled with modern soil to a depth of 0.2m, below which there was gravelly soil for another 0.6m. At a depth of 0.8m was the stump of an oak post 0.78m in length and with a maximum diameter of 0.26m (Figure 85). The lower end of the post had been cut to a point and it had been driven into the gravel underlying the masonry of the south wing. The top of the stump tapered, but this seems to have been the product of decay; the softer heartwood had rotted to a greater extent, forming a cavity in the top of the stump. A scaffolding frame was erected over the hole and after several attempts the timber was winched out intact. The hole in which the timber had been set passed through two courses, in each case through the joints of two adjacent blocks. The tooling on the sides of the blocks had been carried out with a point on a roughly horizontal plane and not at the nearly vertical angle which would have resulted from cutting the hole from the top of the blocks when they were in position. They had therefore been laid around the timber which would have already been driven into the gravel.

The hole was shown on the plan by Elliot and Wilson which accompanied Clayton's paper (1865, facing p 80; Figure 14) but was not described until Holmes published his reassessment of the bridge. There is no reason to depart from his interpretation of this feature:

> '[it] might have been for the insertion of a crane post during the erection of the work, as from this point a large area of the masonry could have been reached, and the employment of the lewis would almost certainly carry with it that of the crane.'
>
> Holmes 1894, 335

Only very rarely are emplacements for cranes or lifting machines encountered and this feature at Chesters is thus of considerable interest. The few other examples from Britain may be divided into two groups:

The first consists of single post-pits: at the Flavian forts of Oakwood and Fendoch in Scotland post-pits in front of the timber gates were thought to have held derricks used to hoist the gate timbers into position (Steer and Feachem 1951–2, 94–5, fig 6). The post-pit at the east gate of Oakwood measured roughly 2.0m by 0.8m by 0.9m deep and had a sloping channel

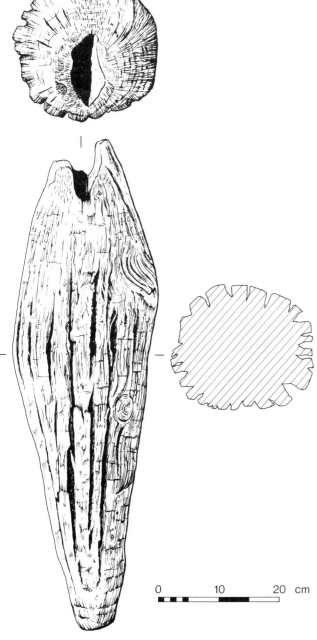

Figure 85   Base of crane post from bridge 2 at Chesters, scale 1:6. (Drawing: Ancient Monuments Drawing Office)

forcing the two halves of the pin outwards against the sides of the hole in which they have been inserted) and the blocks were raised and moved by men positioned at each end of the pole. Coulton (*ibid*, 7) believes that the lewis was introduced specifically for use with cranes, and at Chesters because of their large size there can be little doubt that most of the blocks were moved by mechanical means.

Lewis holes however, sometimes appear in stones of quite small size. An example at Chesters is the parapet slab block no 121 (Figure 30, no 9, Figure 32, and p 31) which could have been easily manhandled into position. The use of a lewis would have had the advantage of allowing the slab to be lowered vertically into the groove cut to receive it in the cornice blocks (p 39) thus reducing the risk of

leading into one end. At the base of the pit was a birch plank which might well have served as a bed plate for the derrick post.

The second consists of cross-shaped slots: the excavations of three public buildings in Britain have produced cross-shaped slots for bedding plates which probably supported vertical posts by means of four raking struts. The first to be discovered was in the theatre at *Verulamium*, at the centre of the *orchestra*:

> 'the purpose of this upright, whether a maypole, gibbet or post to which baited beasts could be chained, can only be a matter of surmise'

> Kenyon 1935, 281 and pls 60, 2 and 68

Its distance from the surrounding walls of the theatre seems to rule out an interpretation of it as a crane base. Another cross-shaped slot was found near the east corner of the forum at Exeter (Bidwell 1979, 88, fig 19). It lay about 9m from the nearest excavated structures, but it was bordered by one edge of the excavations, and might conceivably have been the base of a crane associated with a structure in the unexcavated part of the forum. The third example was situated in a recess at the north end of the basilica at Silchester and was interpreted by its excavator as a foundation intended to take a monumental statue (Fulford 1985, 51, fig 8). However, the wide opening of the recess, which replaced an unfinished apse, might well have been framed by large stone blocks requiring a crane to lift them into position.

Lifting machines must have been used on most major buildings and the infrequent occurrence of the features described above suggests that cranes more complex than the single fixed-post type were prevalent. Two types of cranes are described by Vitruvius (X, II, 1–10). The *trispastos* (or *pentaspaston* which has more pulleys) was a form of shear-legs; the *polyspaston* was a spar which could be moved by means of guide ropes in a vertical or horizontal plane. Cranes of this type, easy to reposition, would have been more serviceable on most types of building sites than the single fixed-post type. Their use might well leave no traces detectable or recognisable by excavation.

There are no detailed descriptions of the single fixed-post type of lifting machine from antiquity but this is what Vitruvius might well have been referring to when following his description of the *trispastos* and *polyspaston* he mentions cranes,

> 'some upright, others on the level, being fixed with revolving *carchesia*'
> (*aliae erectae, aliae planae in carchesîs versatilibus conlocatae*)

> X, II, 10

which among other purposes were used for loading and unloading ships. Two forms are possible for the single fixed-post type: a derrick with a jib fixed near to the base of the post which could have been raised or lowered and also turned on a horizontal plane, or a spar fixed to the top of the post by means of a universal joint so that it could be manoeuvred in any direction.

Derricks, although not described by ancient writers, are such simple devices that it is difficult to believe that they were not well known and widely employed in antiquity. An account by Athenaeus of a 'superfreighter' constructed for Hiero II, King of Syracuse in 269–215 BC, hints at their existence. Each of the three masts of this great ship were fitted with two booms for dropping chunks of lead or grappling hooks on enemy craft alongside and these booms could presumably be raised or lowered in the same way as the jib of a derrick (text and translation in Casson 1971, 179). Landels (1978, 94–8) has considered whether the *carchesium* mentioned by Vitruvius in the passage cited above might have been used in its sense as a main-top or crow's nest on a mast (cf Casson 1971, 233, n 36–7). Landels illustrates an upright post with a wooden collar resembling a miniature crow's nest near its base and forming a sort of flange which supports the end of a forked spar. The other end of the spar is connected by a rope to the top of the upright post (Landels, 1978, fig 31); the spar could thus revolve around the upright post and, if pulleys were employed, it would be possible to raise or lower it.

Landels also put forward a perhaps more plausible explanation of Vitruvius's use of the term *carchesium*. Describing the siege of Syracuse in 212 BC, Polybius (*Histories*, VIII, 5–6) refers to machines devised by Archimedes to disable the attacking Roman fleet by dropping stones on them, or by lifting them out of the water with grappling hooks and overturning them. These machines appear to have had swivelling arms and the term *carchesion* is used for the means by which they were swung around (ibid, 95–8). Landels argued that in this context the term could only mean 'a swivel mounting with bearings at each side', in effect a universal joint, the sense in which it is used in describing the mountings of catapults (by Heron; see Marsden 1971, 51 for a discussion of the universal joints used in catapult mountings). A reconstruction drawing by Landels (1978, fig 33) shows a spar, pivoted near its centre, at the top of a vertical post; the spar is raised and lowered by a tug-of-war team pulling on a pulley system running from one end of the beam to a collar near the base of the upright. This reconstruction is incorrect in one important detail for a description by Livy (XXIV, XXXIV, 11) of the same siege makes it clear that these machines were equipped with counterweights of lead. *Carchesia* also appear to be mentioned in connection with the two booms for dropping stones or grappling hooks, on Hiero II's 'superfreighter' (Marsden 1971, 52).

Of the two forms which single fixed-post lifting machines might have taken, the latter seems more likely to have been employed at Chesters. The blocks to be moved into position were roughly of the same weight (600kg) and the use of a counterweight would have saved much effort. This may have been the function of the barrel-shaped stone found in 1862–3 (Figure 87). It weights about 225kg and would have served to reduce the effort needed to lift a block of average size by about 30 per cent (assuming the horizontal spar to have been pivoted at its centre). In the reconstruction drawing (Figure 86) the machine

Figure 86   Reconstruction drawing of the crane on the south wing of bridge 2 at Chesters.   (Drawing:Irene Hagan)

is shown with an upright post 4.5m in height and a horizontal spar is attached to the top of the post by a universal joint or *carchesium* (Figure 86, inset). The counterweight is suspended from one end of the spar, which can be raised or lowered by a team pulling on a pulley system, attached to a revolving collar near the base of the upright post (for a large pulley from the Corbridge hoard of iron, see Daniels 1968, fig 3; Allason-Jones and Bishop 1988, 56 fig 77, no 97). From the other end of the spar the block with its lewis is suspended by a rope. Another rope attached to this end of the spar could have been used to swing it around.

The position of the crane would have allowed about 300 blocks with a total weight of over 200 tonnes to be lowered directly into position and an approximately equal number to have been brought close to their intended positions. It has been assumed that stone from the Black Pasture quarries (p 3) was brought to the site by a route which passed through the Wall at Milecastle 27 and joined the Military Way. As has already been seen (p 24), the construction of the tower was commenced before that of the abutment and, if at this stage the tower and ramp were built up to the intended level of the carriageway across the bridge, carts transporting the stone could have been brought up to the site of the abutment without negotiating the steep slope of the river bank. A crane placed on the tower could have lowered blocks to cranes at the level of the abutment to the north and south, thus greatly reducing the amount

of manhandling required for the blocks, estimated as numbering 13,512 with a total weight of 8115 tonnes (p 47).

The barrel-shaped stone (possible counterweight) from Chesters

Figure 87:   height 0.76m, maximum diameter 0.44. The surfaces have been roughly worked with an axe or a chisel; the top shows some wear, possibly the result of river action. Evenly placed around the girth of the stone are eight slots with profiles resembling those of lewis holes; the openings are on average 80mm in length, 25mm in width and 20mm deep. The stone was broken in 1966 but has since been repaired and is now displayed in Chesters Museum (Simpson 1976, 48-9).

The stone was found before 2 October 1861; a painting by H B Richardson displayed on that date to the Society of Antiquaries of Newcastle upon Tyne by Clayton shows it standing on the north wing of bridge 2 (p 5; Plate 5). In his lecture to the Society Clayton (1865, 85) mentioned conjectures that it had been used as 'part of the machinery for pounding mortar'; J C Bruce (1863, 77) added that it might have been 'part of the machinery of a *ballista*' although he later decided that its function was uncertain (1885a, 73). Holmes (1894, 334, pl XXVII, fig 28) noted the similarity of the stone, with its eight sockets presumably associated with the means for its suspension, to barrels used as counterweights for machinery in local collieries; he connected the stone with the existence of a drawbridge. Finally, the suggestion by Richmond (1947,79) that the stone was the hub of a water wheel has already been discounted (p 30–1).

It has been suggested in the preceding section that the stone might have served as the counterweight of a crane.

Clamps

Clamps were employed in all periods of construction at Chesters and Willowford, and in all the other bridges with stone piers discussed in Chapter 7. Two types occur: the dovetail clamp, either of iron run in with lead, or of wood (Figure 88, b–g), and the bar clamp, of iron run in with lead or entirely of lead (Figure 88, h–i). The tie-bars of lead which occur at

Chesters and Corbridge served the same purpose as clamps but are considered in a subsequent section.

When dovetail and bar clamps first appeared in Roman architecture in the first century BC (Blake 1947, 187), they were already of great antiquity: dovetail clamps were used in the Old Kingdom of Egypt and bar clamps, which originated as re-inforcing bars of bronze or iron in lead dovetail clamps, seem first to have appeared in the sixth or seventh century BC. (Nylander 1966, 132–4). In the Roman period the use of one type or the other is generally of no chronological significance, although in certain areas at certain periods one type might become more popular; for example in late Republican and Augustan Rome dovetail clamps of wood occurred much more commonly than iron clamps (Blake 1947, 187–8). There also seems to be no pattern in the use of the two types of clamp. Dovetail clamps are thicker than bar clamps and one might expect them to have been used in constructions with blocks of larger size than those in which bar clamps were employed but at Chesters the reverse is found.

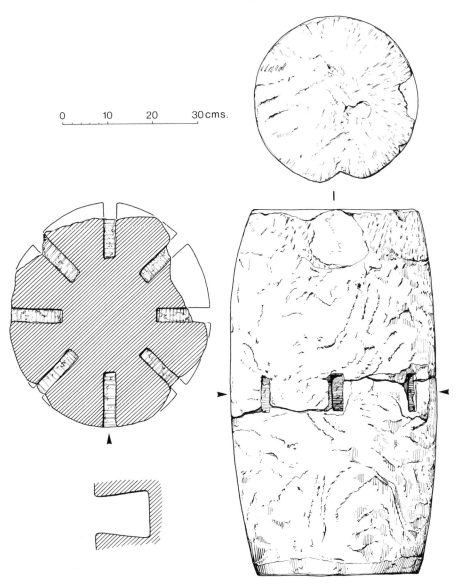

0   10   20   30 cms.

Figure 87   Stone from bridge 2 at Chesters, possibly a counterweight, scale 1:8. (Drawing: J Thorn)

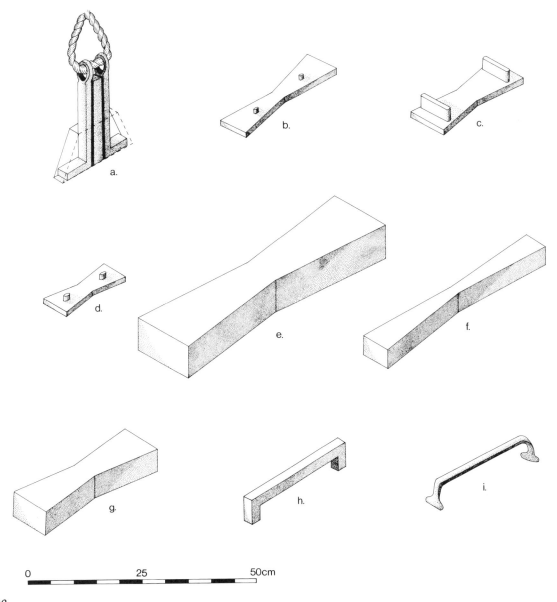

0   25   50cm

Figure 88
  a   *Lewis iron of the type described by Heron with the profile of the lewis hole outlined*
  b   *Dovetail clamp of iron from Delphi showing underside (after Durm 1910, Abb 137)*
  c   *Dovetail clamp of bronze from Baalbek showing the underside (after ibid, 137)*
  d   *Dovetail clamp of iron from bridge 1 at Chesters showing the underside; reconstructed from an impression
      of lead in a socket in the east pier*
  e   *Dovetail clamp of wood, of exceptionally large size, reconstructed from the dimensions of a socket in cutwater
      block no 520, from bridge 1, Willowford*
  f   *Dovetail clamp of wood reconstructed from the dimensions of a socket in a block from the fountain house at
      Corbridge (Knowles 1908, pl 6)*
  g   *Dovetail clamp of wood reconstructed from the dimensions of a socket in block 550 from Willowford (same
      context as 'e')*
  h   *Bar clamp of iron of the type employed in bridges 1A and 2 at Willowford*
  i   *Bar clamp of iron of the type employed in bridge 2 at Chesters.   Scale 1:8*

Dovetail clamps

These were first recorded at Chesters by Hodgson (1840, 181) although writers from Gordon (1726, 73) onwards had noted the presence of clamps without specifying their form. The only examples to survive in position are in the pier of the first bridge incorporated in the east abutment of bridge 2 where they are used to bind the facing blocks together and also to bind them to the blocks in the core of the pier (Figures 8, 9, 10). The dimensions of the sockets cut for the clamps are as follows: width 60–80mm tapering to a width of 30–50mm at the edge of the block; length 90–120mm; depth 40–75mm. The clamps are of iron run in with lead; when the east abutment of bridge 2 was robbed the majority were removed, leaving fractured surfaces around the clamp sockets where a chisel was employed to remove the lead and iron.

In some of the sockets are remains of the lead which had encased the iron clamps. In the sockets for the dovetail clamp which joined the central and northern blocks on the west side of the river pier the iron clamp has been removed and the impressions of small studs or bosses *c* 10mm in diameter are preserved in the lead at the centre of each socket (Figure 10, cf Figure 88, d). Studs or bosses of a similar type appear on dovetail clamps in Greek architecture at a very early date but these are accommodated in 'peg holes' cut in the base of the dovetail socket (Nylander 1966, 134, n 2, fig 3). At this period the clamps are entirely of bronze or lead but at a later date iron bars were introduced as reinforcements for the dovetail clamps, their down-turned ends fitting into holes cut in the base of the dovetail sockets, thus replacing the bosses found on early clamps (Martin 1965, 244–5, figs 113–4). From this it was a short step to omitting the dovetail clamps and joining the blocks solely with bar clamps (see below). The boss on the Chesters clamp might in some respects have been a survival of this early practice, but it does not appear to have fitted into a cavity in the base of the dovetail socket. Its purpose was probably to create a space between the body of the clamp and the base of the socket so that when lead was poured around the clamp it would have been completely encased. An iron dovetail clamp from Delphi, with cylindrical projections on the underside, illustrated by Durm (1910, Abb 137) seems to provide a parallel (Figure 88, b; cf Figure 88, c, a similar clamp of bronze from Baalbek).

A number of blocks with sockets for dovetail clamps were reused in the east abutment of bridge 2, mostly in the lowest courses of the north wing, but also in the rough packing behind it, and in the later extension of the south wing. A few of these preserve traces of lead, or show fractures around the clamp sockets, indicating the former presence of iron clamps. Others, however, display no such features and would have accommodated wooden clamps. These were perhaps employed in bridge 1 at a higher level than the surviving iron clamps. At Willowford none of the blocks with dovetail sockets attributable to the original bridge has produced evidence that the clamps had been of metal. Other notable examples of the use of wooden dovetail clamps occur at South Shields in the third-century strongroom of the *principia* (Richmond 1952, 6) and in the base of the fountain house at Corbridge (Knowles 1908, 272–81; cf Figure 88, f). Knowles and Forster (1909, 324) report that slight traces of 'cement' occurred in sockets underlying blocks found in their original position. This led Miller (1922, 17) to suggest that 'cement may have been used, or possibly an oaken dowel' in dovetail sockets cut in blocks forming the foundations of the towers of the north gate at Balmuildy. Blake (1947, 186–7, n 41) mentions a few instances of mortar found filling dovetail sockets in buildings at Rome and in its vicinity. In the past it had been suggested that the mortar filling signified that wooden clamps were only used to hold the

blocks in position when a course was being laid; once all the blocks were in position the clamps were removed for reuse and their sockets filled with mortar. Blake dismissed this hypothesis because the instances of mortar filled sockets were too few to be convincing, and it now seems to be generally agreed that the wooden clamps were intended to be permanent. At South Shields clamps of oak have been replaced in two of the sockets in the blocks of the third-century strongroom and their effectiveness in binding the masonry together will be assessed. At Corbridge the excavators perhaps mistook traces of lime for cement; in Rome 'a skin of lime was used regularly in all fine Augustan work' (Blake 1947, 187) not for its adhesive power, but to level the beds of each course, and at South Shields in the completed headquarters of the original stone fort lime was spread over the magnesian limestone slabs forming the base for the sandstone blocks of the forecourt colonnade (Bidwell and Speak forthcoming).

For strength and durability iron run in with lead was obviously better than wood for clamping blocks together. Nevertheless wooden clamps were sufficiently serviceable to have been widely employed; for example in late Republican and Augustan Rome they occurred much more commonly than clamps of iron (Blake 1947, 187–8).

Bar clamps

At Chesters nine blocks from bridge 2 have T-shaped sockets for iron clamps set in lead (blocks nos 25; 48, Figure 89, no 2; 53; 59, Figure 30, no 8; 62, Figure 89, no 3 ; 65; 74, Figure 89, no 1; 84; and 117). Three of these are cornice blocks (nos 25; 59; and 117); none has a channel to accommodate parapet slabs and the clamps would have been covered by overlying courses of masonry (p 47). Two other blocks have faces cut at an angle (blocks nos 62; and 84) with close-set curving lines of tooling as on the faces of the abutment and its wings. The dimensions of the sockets vary considerably, their lengths between 80 and 190mm, widths between 25 and 45mm, and depths between 15 and 60mm; the lengths of the cross-slots vary between 50 and 100mm and their depths between 40 and 70mm (Figures 88, i, and 90, no 2). Three of these blocks still preserve the remains of iron clamps set in lead: block no 74, Figure 89, no 1, has a bar with a section measuring 62 by 15mm and the sections of the bars in blocks nos 53 and 65 measure respectively 28 by 8mm and 31mm square.

Bar clamps appear at Willowford in bridge 1A, a repair of the original bridge. Five blocks with bar clamps, (nos 528, Figure 57, no 23; 544, Figures 48 and 57, no 20; 548; 553; and 555, Figure 57, no 22) were recovered from the area of scouring which had destroyed the east abutment and east river pier of this bridge (Figure 42). The clamps take a different form from those at Chesters: their sockets are between 120–150mm in length and 22–42mm in width with circular or square holes at the end 40–65mm across and 60–67mm deep (cf Figures 88, h, and 90, no 1). Twenty blocks reused in the water pier and abutment

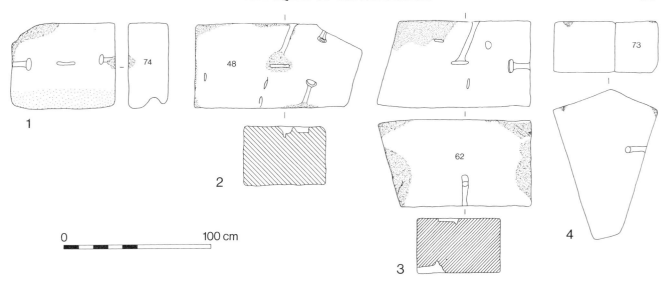

Figure 89   Blocks from bridge 2 at Chesters. Areas of light stippling denote worn surfaces; heavier stippling, fractured surfaces.   Scale 1:25

of bridge 3 have sockets of the same general dimensions and bar clamps were probably employed extensively in the fabric of bridge 2; only four of the reused blocks in these two structures have sockets for dovetail clamps, which suggests that they were reused for the second time in the bridge, and one (block no 7) also has bar clamps (but of lead rather than iron set in lead, see below). Fragments of the iron clamps were preserved in the holes at the end of the sockets in blocks nos 544, Figures 48, and 57, no 20; 548, Figure 57, no 21; and 555; they were approximately 20mm square in section which suggests that the clamps were of the same thickness throughout their length and that the holes at the ends of the sockets were wider than the channels leading to them solely to fix the down-turned ends of the clamps more securely in their encasing lead.

These two types of bar clamps are well known in Roman construction (Lugli 1957, figs 57c and 58) and they were in general use in Greek architecture from the fourth century BC (Martin 1965, 273–9); their

evolution from the iron strengthening bars set into dovetail clamps is described above.

As already briefly noted, one of the blocks reused in the water pier preserved the remains of a clamp entirely of lead rather than one of iron set in lead. Other examples of lead clamps occur in blocks from the Wall bridge at Carlisle (p 109 and Figure 78). They recall the earliest dovetail clamps of metal which were entirely of lead, copper or bronze (Nylander 1966, 133). A K Orlandos (1968, 103–4) has shown that these were made separately and then fitted into the sockets in the same way as wooden clamps. It is not possible to determine whether this was the case with the lead bar clamps from Willowford and Carlisle but if so it might explain the absence of extraction scars around some of the bar clamp sockets in blocks at Willowford. No direct parallels have been found for lead bar clamps but they can be compared to the lead tie-bars used in the second bridge at Chesters (p 130ff). At *Ostia* T-shaped holdfasts of lead are known (Becatti 1969, 28, tav XXXVI, no 2); such holdfasts are usually of iron.

Table 11   Dimensions of bar clamp sockets in bridge 2 at Chesters

Block no	Length	Channel Width	Depth	Length	Hole Width	Depth	Long Side	Short Side	Comments
25	190	30	37	58	30	70	*	-	On top of moulded block
48	-	45	29	65	23	55	*	-	On top with rust stains. Angled face
48b	-	32	28	70	30	55	*	-	As 48a but no rust
53a	-	35	15	55	25	45	*	-	
53b	-	38	15	55	32	-	*	-	Iron bar set in lead 28 × 8mm
53c	-	-	-	60	18	40	-	*	Iron bar set in lead 28 × 8mm
59a	80	-	-	70	18	50	-	*	Moulded, angled face. Dowel
59b	110	35	32	68	30	40	-	*	Rust stains. No channel
62	-	32	32	80	32	64	-	*	Angled block. Dowel
65	-	-	-	-	-	-	*	-	Iron clamp in lead 31 × 31mm
74a	110	-	-	-	-	-	*	-	
74b	40	40	-	-	-	-	*	-	Bar set in lead 62 × 15mm
84a	85	25	60	100	35	5	-	*	Side angled
84b	85	25	-	95	32	50	-	*	Side angled

Bar clamps from Chesters and Willowford

Figure 90, no 1:   length 303mm. Iron bar clamp of rectangular section encased in lead. The clamp is approximately 280mm in length and consists of a bar, with section measuring 11mm wide, and 21mm deep. One of the down-turned ends is 35mm in length; the other is completely encased in lead. The lead seems to have been poured into the clamp sockets after the bar clamp had been set in position. Willowford, found *in situ* in block 555, river gravel deposits associated with the destruction of bridge 1A (context 1092, Figure 45, section 6).

Figure 90, no 2:   length 93mm. Fragment of iron bar clamp with an expanded end. The section of the bar is 11mm in width and 9mm in depth. The down-turned end is 34mm in length and expands to a width of 33mm. Chesters, from the primary hearth (context 155) in the tower of bridge 2 (Figure 22).

Dowels

A few blocks from bridge 2 at Chesters have holes in their upper surfaces which appear to have been for wooden dowels (blocks nos 59, Figure 30, no 8; 60; 62, Figure 89, no 3; and 72). The holes tend to be circular in plan, with nearly vertical sides, and can easily be distinguished from crowbar slots; their diameters and depths approximate to about 50mm, except in the case of block no 72, where the hole is 81mm deep. Block no 59 has a moulding of Type 1 (p 39) but no groove and shows no sign of wear on its upper surface, which suggests that there had been courses of masonry above it (see further p 47); blocks nos 60; and 62 can be shown to have been facing blocks. Block no 72 is a cornice block, with its moulding missing but with a channel for parapet slabs; the presence of what appears to be a dowel hole in its upper surface cannot be explained. In none of the holes are there traces of iron corrosion or lead and the dowels will thus have been of wood.

The dowel holes from bridge 2 at Chesters resemble those in blocks which form the base of pier 4 at Piercebridge (p 112); the latter likewise show no traces of iron corrosion or lead and therefore also presumably accommodated wooden dowels. Not a single block from bridge 2 at Chesters however has a simple dowel hole in its underside corresponding to those described above. Instead, in the undersides of many cornice blocks, and certain other blocks, there are sockets which at first sight might be mistaken for bar clamp sockets. The sockets consist of grooves running at right angles to the edges of the blocks, between 100 and 210mm in length and 30 and 55mm in width and depth. At the ends of the grooves opposite the edges of the blocks there are deeper holes penetrating to depths of between 60 and 85mm below the surface of the undersides (Table 12). They occur in 18 stones where it is possible to determine which is the underside: of these 11 are cornice blocks (nos 25; 35; 43, Figure 30, no 4; 70, Figure 30 no 11; 71; 72; 79; 83, Figure 30, no 5; 87, Figure 83; 96, Figure

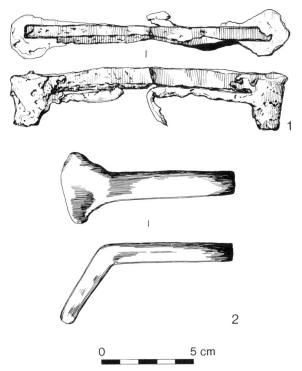

Figure 90   Iron bar clamps; no 1 from Willowford, and no 2 from Chesters.   Scale 1:2

31; and 98) and the remainder have T-shaped clamps, crowbar slots or lewis holes in various combinations on their upper surfaces (blocks nos 55; 62, Figure 89, no 11; 68; 73, Figure 89, no 4; 92; 105; and 113, Figure 82). There are six other blocks with sockets of the same type where it is not possible to determine which is the underside (blocks nos 55; 68; 73; 92; 105; and 113). None of the sockets preserves the remains of lead or shows any rust staining nor is there any fracturing of the surrounding surfaces to suggest the removal of iron clamps. At Chesters they can be easily distinguished from the sockets for bar clamps, which are T-shaped; they are also much more deeply cut than the sockets for simple bar clamps (cf Figure 88, h, i) occurring in blocks at Willowford, Carlisle and Piercebridge.

One block with a socket of the same type is still in position in the easternmost pier of bridge 1, forming the western angle at the base of the cutwater (Figure 8). Probing established that at the end of the groove there is a deeper hole and that it is directly above a hole cut in the surface of the block beneath; the groove measures 40mm by 60mm in height and is approximately 120mm in length. The coincidence in the position of the holes in the upper and lower blocks would seem to show that the holes had accommodated a wooden dowel.

There is another structure in Britain where blocks with sockets of this type survive in their original position: the recently excavated south portico, in the inner precinct of the Temple of Sulis Minerva at Bath, an addition of third-century date. On the north face of the north-east buttress, at the bases of two blocks, there are rectangular openings (Cunliffe and Davenport 1985, 58, figs, 36, 117, 133, elevations 4–5, pl XXIII). Probing showed that the openings are the ends of grooves (40mm wide and 75mm high). It was established that the groove in the central block terminates in a deeper hole, which coincides with a hole cut in the surface of the block below (Jane Bircher and Stephen Bird kindly arranged access to the structures). Several dowel holes are visible on the surface of blocks elsewhere in the buttress; they measure roughly 50mm square and 60mm in depth. There are similar sockets and dowel holes in the blocks forming the north-west buttress of the portico. Other instances of sockets of this type can be cited. At Piercebridge the presence of dowel holes in the base of pier 4 has already been noted (p 112); many of the loose blocks scattered nearby have sockets of the Chesters type cut in one surface and in some instances sockets for clamps in the opposite surface. At Willowford one block (no 39), which utilised bar clamps and is reused in the pier of bridge 3, has a socket occurring in its underside and a circular dowel hole on its upper surface. A Roman altar at Nether Denton Church also contains a similar socket of this type; it seems to have been fashioned from a block which once formed part of the bridge at Willowford (p 85). At Corbridge there is a reused block in the structure downstream from the Roman bridge with a similar socket (p 106).

Blocks from a monumental arch and other structures reused in the riverside defensive wall in London displayed sockets which were thought to have been for bar clamps. With two exceptions the sockets were in the undersides of the blocks, and this was seen as something of a problem (Hill, Millett, and Blagg 1980, 189 and fig 98). It was thought unlikely that the sockets were connected with the secondary use of the stones. If the sockets were primary it was admitted that, while it would have been possible to lower the blocks with prepared sockets onto upturned dowels, the practice of securing blocks with clamps on their upper and lower surfaces is not otherwise known in Roman building techniques. T Blagg *in litt* now considers it likely that these sockets were of the same type as those described in this section, and furthermore, that prye holes found in the blocks (ibid, 188 and fig 98), in this report termed crowbar slots, might indeed have been dowel holes.

Two blocks with mouldings illustrated by Büsing (1982, Taf 2, B1 and B4), which had been reused in the fourth-century town wall of Mainz, but which had originated from a gate of the fortress, have sockets on their undersides. The socket on block B1 was 140mm in length, its width 60mm, and depth 10mm, with a hole 160mm deep; the groove extended to a side treated with band anathyrosis. There were no signs that these blocks had been reused before being incorporated in the town wall. At Cologne some of the blocks of the rebuilt portion of a large Roman sewer next to the Römisch-Germanisches Museum also have sockets in their undersides. Three separate sites at Gloucester have also produced blocks from an architrave or cornice, which was probably associated with the city wall constructed of *opus quadratum* in the early second century (Hurst 1986, 126). Two of these blocks had sockets in their

undersides thought to have been for 'U-shaped clamps' (bar clamps). This would indicate that the blocks had been put to another use either before or after their incorporation in the architrave (Hassall and Rhodes 1975, 80; Hurst 1986, fig 34, no 4), but the example illustrated by Hurst is very similar to the sockets described above; the groove leading to the hole is 80mm deep, and the hole itself is 120mm deep. On the top of the block are the remains of a recess which can be tentatively identified as a dowel hole.

No exact parallels to these sockets are noted in the standard accounts of Greek and Roman architecture, but they were perhaps used as follows: a hole was cut in a block of the underlying course and a wooden dowel of the appropriate length inserted. Another hole was then cut in the underside of the block to be set above it, with a groove leading to it from one edge of the block. The block was then lowered carefully into position by a crane, the function of the groove cut from the dowel hole to the side of the block being to indicate the position of the dowel hole to those adjusting the position of the block as it was lowered. This operation would require the position of the dowel holes in the upper and lower blocks to be measured very accurately, but the same precision would also have been required when iron dowels run in with lead were used.

Sockets in the undersides of the blocks always occur singly and never in pairs, with examples on opposite sides as is the case with clamp sockets. This is presumably because when a block was added to a course under construction, only on the side opposite a block already in position, could the position of a dowel hole be made visible by a groove running out to the edge of the underside when the block was lowered into place.

By no means all the cornice blocks of bridge 2 at Chesters were secured in position with dowels; sufficient survived of nine blocks to show that they had not had sockets in their undersides (blocks nos 59, Figure 30, no 8; and 90; with mouldings of Type 1 and blocks nos 7; 28; 31; 82; 85; 88; and 91 with mouldings of Type 2). This raises the question of the purpose of the dowels. If they were intended primarily as ties between courses, it is curious that in the case of the twenty cornice blocks where the presence or absence of dowels can be established, in nine instances they were certainly omitted. Moreover, the sockets for dowels only occur singly. In Greek architecture dowels were usually employed in pairs and were often rectangular or T-shaped in plan to prevent the blocks skewing out of position (eg Martin 1965, figs 126, 130–2, 134; for metal dowels used in pairs in Roman construction see Lugli 1957, fig 58). In addition it seems normal for every block in every course to have been dowelled (Martin 1965, fig 129 shows the position of dowels in a wall of the Temple of Athena Nike on the Acropolis at Athens).

The purpose of the dowels at Chesters, given that only certain blocks were dowelled, was perhaps not to tie the courses together but rather to prevent blocks shifting their position when adjacent blocks were levered into position against them. The presence of a single dowel in any one face of the block, rather than the two required to prevent lateral skewing, is explained by the way in which crowbars were used (p 119). A single crowbar was used to manoeuvre the block roughly into position and then two crowbars were applied to the ends of the faces to achieve the final adjustment. Since the force applied to the face of the dowelled block when the adjacent block was being moved into position was uniform at every point, a single centrally-placed dowel would have been sufficient to prevent any skewing (see Figure 91) for the conjectural position of dowel holes in a length of the parapet of bridge 2 at Chesters). A possible parallel to this use of dowels is provided by the so-called 'preliminary dowels' found in Greek construction (Orlandos 1915), although their purpose has been disputed (cf Tschira 1941).

In Roman architecture iron dowels set in lead were perhaps in more common use than wooden dowels, particularly in joining sheets of marble wall-cladding; two examples from Britain are the marble slabs which cladded the exterior of the Flavian monument at Richborough (Strong in Cunliffe 1968, 63–4, pl XXII–XXV) and the sheets and mouldings of Purbeck marble used inside the Neronian legionary baths at Exeter (Bidwell 1979, 136–41, figs 45–6). When iron dowels run in with lead were employed in *opus quadratum*, in order to encase the upper part of the dowel, holes were drilled from the exterior of the block to the top of the dowel socket so that molten lead could be poured into the socket (Lugli 1957, fig 57). Wooden dowels are found in Greek construction as early as the seventh century BC and often took the form of cylindrical pegs of *c* 50mm diameter, which fitted into holes cut in blocks of wood, which in turn

were set in sockets in the surfaces of the blocks (Martin 1965, figs 135-7). At the same time wooden dowels that fitted directly into sockets cut in the blocks were in use (ibid, 292) and it is this simpler type of dowel which occurs at Chesters, and other bridges in north Britain (Table 10). Wooden dowels are not mentioned in the standard accounts of Roman construction techniques and it may be that at Rome itself and in Italy their use was infrequent.

Tie-bars

On the east abutment of bridge 2 at Chesters the surfaces of the fifth and sixth courses display continuous grooves 35–40mm in width and 25–30mm in depth, set back some 150mm from the edge of the facing blocks (Figure 15). The groove on the surface of the fifth course runs along the entire length of the abutment face and continues along the south wing for a distance of 8.45m, terminating with a transverse groove 200mm in length. Along the north wing the sixth course obscures the course of the groove, but the end of what appears to be a transverse groove, filled with lead, protrudes beyond the offset face of the sixth course at a distance of 9.3m from the south end of the wing. Behind the main abutment face there are four irregularly spaced extensions running eastwards from the main groove, and increasing in length from 1.5m to 2.8m from north to south. The three southern grooves are fully exposed and terminate in transverse grooves. The northern groove is largely concealed by blocks of the sixth course, but seems to have extended from the point where the main groove turned to run along the north wing; its transverse groove is filled with lead. The groove on

Table 12 Dimensions of dowel sockets in blocks from bridge 2 at Chesters

Block no	Length	Channel Width	Depth	Length	Hole Width	Depth	Long side	Short side	Comments
8	150	40	50	40	40	87	*	-	On underside – lewis and groove on top
12	140	35	45	45	35	80	*	-	On underside – lewis on top
25	100	25	27	-	-	-	*	-	On underside, unfinished?
35	?	?	?	?	?	?	*	-	Moulding, underside
43	180	35	40	30	30	72	*	-	Moulding, underside
48	150	40	40	40	40	60	-	*	On underside
55	170	40	48	32	40	82	-	*	Angled face, probably underside
68	175	40	55	30	30	86	*	-	Angled block, could be underside
70	135	40	45	40	29	60	-	-	Stepped moulding, underside
71	126	34	46	34	30	64	-	-	Stepped moulding, underside
72	126	34	46	34	30	64	-	-	Moulding, underside
73	145	45	41	32	45	75	*	-	Angled face, could be underside
76	150	30	45	50	50	75	*	-	Band anathyrosis. Underside
79	210	42	40	42	42	75	*	-	Moulding, underside
83	-	-	-	25	25	48	*	-	Moulding, underside
84	130	45	30	35	35	65	-	*	On underside
87	200	40	45	40	40	65	*	-	Moulding, underside
92	135	55	29	45	55	60	*	-	
96	190	40	35	30	30	60	*	-	Moulding, underside
98	130	50	28	30	30	50	*	-	Moulding, underside
105	140	50	40	40	40	70	-	*	Angled face
113	190	45	30	50	30	65	*	-	On face with herringbone tooling
118	210	40	45	45	40	62	-	*	Underside, facing block

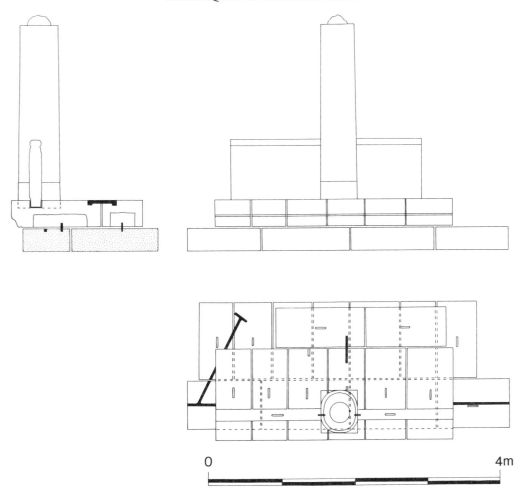

Figure 91   Reconstruction drawing of a length of parapet incorporating a column, showing system of clamps, dowels and tie-bars, bridge 2 at Chesters.   Scale 1:50

the surface of the sixth course of the north wing is 4.5m in length, less than half the length of the groove in the fifth course below.

A continuous groove is recorded just behind the face of the south wing of the west abutment and another still survives on three sides of the west pier (Figure 14, p 15). It is likely that what appear to have been two very large bar clamps at the north tip of this pier were in fact tie-bars. In the superstructure of the bridge, in addition to bar clamps and dowels, tie-bars were also employed, as the existence of grooves in three loose blocks demonstrates (blocks nos 8; 48, Figure 89, no 2; and 62).

The purpose of these grooves was readily apparent to Clayton and Bruce, although as will be shown below, their deductions were partly in error. In 1807 Lingard while visiting Chesters had been told by 'an old gentleman in the neighbourhood' that the blocks of the bridge

> 'were joined together by iron bars; some of which he broke and carried off as presents to the schoolteacher'
>
> Bosanquet 1929, 147

Before the excavations of 1860–3 this reference had puzzled Bruce because other sources had mentioned only clamps. Now its meaning seemed obvious and

Clayton was able to state with confidence that the blocks

> 'have been bound together by long rods of iron let into the stones and secured by molten lead.'
>
> Clayton 1865, 82, 85

However, an unstratified find from Victorian backfill in front of the main abutment face does not bear this out (Figure 92, no 1). It is a piece of solid lead with a cross section similar to that of the grooves; its depth (12mm) is somewhat shallower than that of the grooves (25–30mm) but in the two terminal grooves where the lead survives it leaves a gap of about a centimetre at the top. The grooves, it would seem, were filled with lead alone and this can be compared with the use of lead bars for clamps at Willowford and Carlisle (p 127). The 'iron bars' mentioned by Lingard were in fact quite possibly bar clamps and might have had nothing to do with the grooves.

Robert Forster's *History of Corbridge* describes the Roman bridge which carried Dere Street across the Tyne (p 104)and mentions a discovery which indicates that lead tie-bars were used in the piers at Corbridge. He noted the existence of 'iron cramps sunk into the stones and covered with lead' and added that

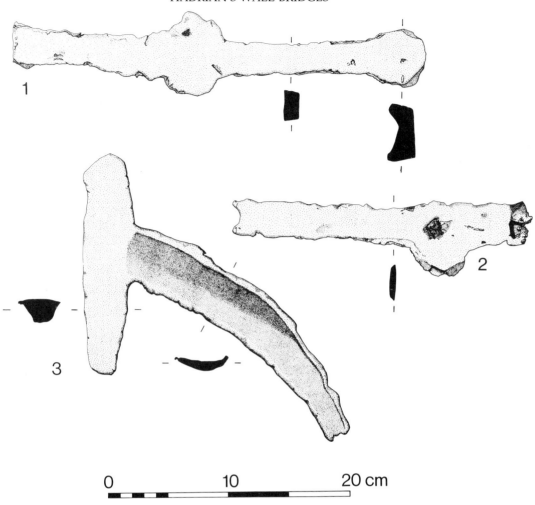

Figure 92   Lead tie-bars.   Scale 1:3

'the discovery and taking out of this lead upwards of fifty years ago, afforded a rich harvest for a number of youths who were bathing there, one of them finding the lead loose, undoubtedly caused by the rusting away of the iron cramps, at once proceeded to take it out, but not in detached pieces, for it was found to run from stone to stone at right angles, and when taken out in large squares looked something like window frames.'

Forster 1881, 11

During a survey of the remains undertaken in 1963–6 short lengths of lead bars were found in the south abutment and piers 1–3 (Bourne 1967, 22–3; Figure 74). A detached fragment was removed from the river from beside pier 4 and donated to the Museum of Antiquities in Newcastle upon Tyne (Figure 92, no 2 illustrates another fragment found at Corbridge in 1887).

The description by Forster given above thus seems to confuse two separate elements in the construction of the bridge: iron bar clamps and lead tie-bars. The latter were not used as at Chesters merely to bind the blocks of the abutment and pier faces together; in the light of Forster's mention of the lead running from stone to stone at right angles and of 'large

squares...like window frames' the tie-bars might have formed a grid extending through the whole fabric.

The same technique but employing wood rather than lead is found in Trajan's bridge over the Danube, built between AD 103 and 105 (Tudor 1974, 70–6). When in 1909 the remains of two piers, built of mortared rubble faced with stone, were removed because they were judged a hazard to shipping, their substructures were exposed. These consisted of several courses of stone blocks in the upper surfaces of which had been cut a series of intersecting channels 70–100mm in width and depth. They formed a grid covering the entire surface of each course so that the blocks could be knitted together with a network of oak beams, fragments of which survived in some of the channels (ibid, 105–111, figs 34–6)

The use of timbers to give additional strength to masonry structures was fairly common in ancient architecture. Vitruvius (I, V, 3) recommends beams of charred olive wood to tie the faces of a wall together, adding that the wood remains unimpaired when covered by earth or submerged in water. In the construction of the defensive walls of Saxon Shore Forts grids of timbers bound the foundations together (examples listed in Wilcox 1981, 21–7). In Greek architecture the use of iron bars to strengthen

6

architraves or stone ceilings is well documented (Dinsmoor 1922, 150–6). Moreover in the Theban Treasury at Delphi iron bars measuring 82mm in thickness, 100mm in width and up to 12.5m in length were set in continuous grooves cut into the upper surfaces of blocks in the foundation courses. This building was erected 'on a steep slope at a point swept by miniature rivers, which poured down the Sacred Way on rainy days' (ibid, 149–50)and the tie-bars were presumably inserted to prevent any lateral displacement of the blocks in each course. They provide a close parallel to the lead tie-bars at Chesters and Corbridge.

Fragments of lead tie-bars from Chesters and Corbridge

Figure 92, no 1: length 242mm, maximum width (excluding flange) 32mm, fractured at both ends. The underside preserves the impression of the groove into which the lead had been poured; a thin flange of lead on one side of the bar, clearly where the lead had spilt onto the surface of the block in which the groove had been cut, indicates that the depth of the groove was about 12mm. Found in modern topsoil in front of the main east abutment of bridge 2 at Chesters.

Figure 92, no 2: length 303mm, maximum width 50mm. The depth of the main groove seems to have been about 14mm to judge from the thickness of the tie-bar, that of the cross-slot about 20mm. The underside of the bar is rough and granular, a negative impression of the texture of the surfaces of the groove into which the lead had been poured. The label with the fragment reads: 'Lead from the cramp holes of the Roman bridge, Corstopitum. Found by W L S Charlton, July 1887' (cf Proc Soc Antiq Newcastle upon Tyne, 2 ser, **33** (1887), 169). The fragment originated from the terminal of a tie-bar with the same sort of cross-slot as can be seen on the abutment of bridge 2 at Chesters. Museum of Antiquities, Newcastle upon Tyne accession no 1956.73A.

The fragment of tie-bar recovered by Bourne (1967,23) is 525mm in length with a maximum width of 49mm; the width of the slot from which it originated was 35mm. One end is broken; the other is rounded, indicating that the slot had not terminated in a cross-slot. Museum of Antiquities, Newcastle upon Tyne accession no 1967.13.

Figure 92, no 3: length 337mm, width (excluding expansions) 33mm; to judge from the section of the bar the dimensions of the slot from which it came were 24mm in width by 12mm in depth. One end terminates in a circular expansion and there is another expansion in the middle of the bar; the other end is broken away. It is uncertain whether the fragment comes from a tie-bar or a large lead bar clamp. Found in modern topsoil in front of the main east abutment of bridge 2 at Chesters during the 1982–3 excavations.

9 The significance of the Wall bridges

Introduction

As constructed in the reign of Hadrian the bridges at Chesters and Willowford were designed merely to carry the mural barrier across the rivers North Tyne and Irthing. The bridges therefore provide an insight into the nature and purpose of Hadrian's Wall as originally conceived, and supply valuable evidence on the question of whether the Wall top was actively patrolled. The Wall bridges were subsequently converted to carry a road, probably in the reign of Severus, and this reconstruction can be associated with a restructuring of the road system across the isthmus. A study of the bridges cannot therefore be sensibly separated from a survey of the anatomy and development of the road system, and in particular the Military Way. Any discussion of this road, however, needs to take into account the nature and function of the existing road systems, and so in Appendix 1 the evidence for pre-Hadrianic and Hadrianic roads in the area between the river Tyne and the Solway estuary is discussed.

The function and significance of the Hadrianic Wall bridges

At Chesters and Willowford the Hadrianic bridges carried the Wall in some form across the rivers. They are exceptional because the purpose of bridges on other frontiers seems to have been merely to provide crossings for lateral roads. For example, at Summerston near the fort of Balmuildy on the Antonine Wall (p 116), the bridge over the Kelvin lay on the military way *c* 9m behind the wall. In general the frontier works terminated on the river banks, as at the crossing of the Altmühl at Gunzenhausen where the Raetian Wall ended in a dressed face on either bank leaving a gap of 50m (ORL, 14, 46, Taf 2). Only small streams and flood plains were traversed by the Raetian Wall, as at the crossing of the Altwasser where the excavators found a mass of timber piles (ORL, 13, Taf 4); these were interpreted as the remains of a footbridge but are far more likely to be the timber piling (Pfahlrost) which underlay the stone wall in marshy areas (cf an excavated example at Kreutweiher: Baatz 1975, 229, Abb 67).

One possible reason for the existence of bridges on the line of Hadrian's Wall is that they were intended to prevent intruders from using the rivers as ways through the Wall. Richmond (1966, 82) suggested that the columns of bridge 2 at Chesters were 'bollards ... to carry gratings, chains or hecks' and, although it has been demonstrated that the columns were purely decorative (p 43ff), the notion that the smaller arches of the Hadrianic Wall bridges were provided with obstructions against intruders is worth examining. Precedents for such obstructions can be found in Greek city defences where the mouths of drains and culverts were closed by iron railings

οβελίσκοι (*obeliskoi*) set in lead-packed sockets (Lawrence 1979, 270). The walled circuits of Messene and Samos included bridges, and although evidence is lacking, Lawrence (ibid) considered that the arches also would have been blocked with these railings. However, there is a great difference between the seasonal streams bridged by the Greek city defences and the major rivers of the North Tyne and Irthing where a build-up of debris against the railings could have seriously threatened the safety of the bridges. Such devices are therefore unlikely at Chesters and Stanwix although the possibility exists that some form of temporary barrier may have been used at Willowford in the summer months when it would have been possible to walk almost dry shod beneath the bridge.

A more effective way of preventing unauthorised passage through the Wall at river crossings would have been intensive patrolling of the river valleys north of the Wall. At Stanwix and Chesters there are cavalry forts very close to the bridges and near Willowford the fort at Birdoswald might conceivably at first have housed cavalry; the find of a tile stamp of *cohors I Tungrorum milliaria* at Hare Hill 4.5 km west of Birdoswald has suggested to some that this unit was perhaps the original garrison but the evidential value of a single stamped tile is weak (cf Roxan 1985, 97). More immediate surveillance could be carried out from the towers at the bridges; in addition at Chesters the fort overlooked the bridge, as did Milecastle 49 and Turret 48b at Willowford, and Milecastle 66 at Stanwix.

If the bridges were not intended, by means of grilles or other obstructions, to prevent intruders slipping through the Wall, some other reason must be sought for their existence. The most obvious is that their purpose was to carry a Wall walk across the rivers. However, it has sometimes been doubted whether the Wall top was patrolled, (Breeze and Dobson 1972, 187; *idem* 1987, 42; Dobson 1986, 9,) which would mean that there was no necessity for a Wall walk . The principal reason for such doubt seems to be the absence of parallels from other frontiers although there are other important components of the Hadrianic frontier, most notably the Vallum, which are without precedents elsewhere. Absence of 'direct evidence' has also been cited. There are in fact several pieces of structural evidence which suggest the existence of a Wall walk. Each is capable of more than one interpretation but their possible association with a Wall walk is a common denominator. They are set out below in what the writers believe to be their reverse order of importance:

The Rudge Cup and Amiens Skillet show crenellations on the towers below the horizontal bands bearing names of the forts on Hadrian's Wall. The Rudge Cup has been described as 'the only contemporary representation of the Roman Wall known to have survived to our times' (Cowen and Richmond 1935, 318).

This is perhaps an optimistic view because as the authors state (ibid, 328) crenellated walls, towers and gates appear in the decorative schemes of some mosaics and it may be added that they sometimes feature in the decoration of other objects, for example a water-heater from Pompeii (Mau 1902, fig 208). There can be no certainty that the decoration on these enamelled bowls is an actual representation of the Wall rather than a particularly appropriate borrowing from a standard decorative repertoire.

At Milecastle 48, Poltross Burn, stairs from the interior of the milecastle led up to the junction of the north and east walls (Gibson and Simpson 1911, 418–21). This establishes beyond reasonable doubt that there was a walkway around the walls of the milecastle but not perhaps that there was a walkway along the Wall itself.

In 1909 at Peel Crag, F G Simpson found a number of chamfered stones near the north face of the Wall; 169 are recorded from Peel Crag and a further 7 from Milecastle 38, Castle Nick (G Simpson 1976, 115–6). Many have also been recovered from this sector of the Wall during recent excavations (information from J Crow). In addition chamfered stones are known from Rudchester (Brewis 1925, 103; 1927, 115–8) and Bay's Leap, east of Turret 12b (Jobey 1958, 59–60, also mentioning further finds made during consolidation of the Wall west of Chesters, west of Housesteads and east of Birdoswald).

Chamfered stones of a very similar type were noted in collapsed sections of the fort wall at Worth where they appear to have formed a string course on the exterior of the fort wall immediately below the parapet (ORL, no 36, 6, Tafs 1–2). Two legionary fortresses in Britain furnish examples of surviving string courses in this position: at York at the east angle of the fortress the string course consisted of a single course of projecting stones with chamfered undersides (RCHM(E) 1962, 33, fig 24) but at Chester the string course was formed by blocks with elaborate mouldings (Strickland 1982, 1983). At South Shields chamfered stones were found with a window head, a merlon cap and quoin stones in the filling of a late Roman ditch in front of the south-west gate and were also reused in a number of late Roman structures, presumably having been salvaged from the original south-east wall of the fort which was probably demolished in *c* 208 (Bidwell and Speak forthcoming).

The chamfered stones from Hadrian's Wall have been recovered in sufficient quantities to suggest that they formed a continuous feature and the analogies provided by the defensive walls of forts and fortresses make it very probable that they came from a string course. As Jobey noted (1958, 59–60), the fact that many have been found at the base of the Wall, suggesting that they had been dislodged early in the decay of the fabric, lends support to the notion that they came from near the top of the Wall. The presence of a string course does not necessarily prove that there was a parapet but is entirely consistent with the existence of one. At this point it is necessary to note that there are no published stones from the Wall curtain which can be recognised as originating from merlons or crenellations (it is difficult to see why the three stones from Cawfields illustrated by Charlesworth (1968, figs 3 and 4) have been described as 'parapet stones'). Such stones are also known from the walls of only a few forts in Britain (eg South Shields, Housesteads, and Caernarvon); it seems most unlikely that the walls of forts were not crenellated and the reasons advanced elsewhere for the general absence of evidence for their existence (Bidwell *et al* 1989) applies equally to Hadrian's Wall. Some possible examples of merlon caps from turrets are known (listed in Charlesworth 1977, 14, with the addition of a stone from Tower 16a: Richmond 1956b, 65, fig 1) but this has no bearing on the question of whether the Wall itself was crenellated.

When large numbers of turrets were demolished, probably in the course of renovations made to the Wall on the orders of Severus (p 136), their recesses were walled up. This was not done because the removal of the turrets threatened the stability of the Wall; even where the turret recesses had been formed in the Narrow Wall a thickness of about a metre remained in front of the recesses. The most likely reason for the blockings is that the Wall walk had to be carried across the recesses (Bellhouse 1969, 86).

Bellhouse (ibid, 88–9) has noted that when the Stone Wall was brought up to some turrets originally set in the Turf Wall, the fronts of the turrets were left projecting about a metre beyond the Stone Wall. This he suggested was because the alignment of the Stone Wall was dictated by the position of the doors in either side of the turret at first floor level, which had originally given access to the top of the Turf Wall; the front of the Turf Wall was battered and the doors would necessarily have been set further back from the front of the turret than in the case of a turret which was of one build with the Stone Wall. The continuing use of these first floor doors in the turrets of the Turf Wall would indicate that the Stone Wall which replaced it also had a Wall walk.

To these various structural indications which supply evidence for a Wall walk can now be added the form of the Wall bridges. Since they were evidently not intended by means of grilles or other obstructions to prevent intruders, their purpose was probably to take some form of traffic across the rivers. The bridges are too narrow to have accommodated roads and in any event no traces have been found of ramps leading up to the bridges from ground level at the rear of the Wall. The only other possibility seems to be that they carried a Wall walk. The purpose of the towers was probably to facilitate surveillance of the area immediately in front of the bridges and to give access to the bridges for patrols at the rear of the Wall; they would have eventually been used by Vallum patrols.

In conclusion it may be stated that there are sufficient structural indications, not least amongst them the existence of the Wall bridges, to make it very probable that the Wall top was intended to be patrolled, and was thus presumably furnished with a parapet. The projection of the former Turf Wall turrets beyond the face of the later Stone Wall, parts of which may date to the Antonine period (Breeze and Dobson 1987, 128), suggests that the Wall walk remained an essential feature of the Wall. Indeed, if the significance of the blocking of the turret recesses has been rightly assessed by Bellhouse, the Wall walk was retained when the Wall was renovated by Severus.

The Wall bridges and the Military Way

In 1939 Richmond noted in a survey of advances in knowledge of the Wall that

'it might be expected that the enlargement of the bridges at North Tyne and Willowford also coincides with the coming of the Military Way, but the point is not yet proved'

Richmond 1939, 277

He did not suggest a date for these works, but in a later survey describing investigations of the Wall in the subsequent decade the relationship between the bridges and Military Way was expressed in much more emphatic terms: the creation of the Military Way

'coincides with immense alterations at the bridges on the North Tyne and the Irthing, and in further support of its altogether later date [ie later than the slighting of the Vallum and restoration to use of the milecastles], it should be recognised that the earliest dated milestone of the Military Way [RIB 2298] belongs to AD 213, though there is a series of fine uninscribed milestones to be taken into account.'

Richmond 1950, 56

Twenty years later Gillam and Mann took a different view:

'while there was no military way on Hadrian's Wall under Hadrian, there was a military way on the Antonine Wall early under Antoninus Pius. It is inconceivable that when Antoninus Pius took over Hadrian's Wall he should have failed to insist on as good a lateral communication as on his second frontier line.'

Gillam and Mann 1970, 16

The milestone of Caracalla from Welton Hall which Richmond mentions of course only supplies a *terminus ante quem* of AD 213 for the Military Way, and in support of an Antonine date Gillam and Mann drew attention to the significance of branch tracks leading from Turrets 29b and 37a to the Military Way. The pottery from Turret 29b was taken to show that it was one of those 'finally abandoned early in the third century' and therefore the Military Way with which the branch track connected will have been constructed at an earlier date. Breeze and Dobson (1987, 128) likewise attribute the Military Way perhaps to 'experience gained on the Antonine Wall'.

It is firmly established that the road bridge at Willowford is later than the Antonine period, and the weight of the evidence for the date of the road bridge at Chesters also suggest construction later than the Antonine period. If the Military Way is of Antonine date then Richmond was wrong to associate it with the construction of the road bridges, and the evidence of the branch tracks leading to the turrets

obviously assumes great importance. The clearest example is at Turret 37a where the track branching off the Military Way can be seen on an aerial photograph (St Joseph 1951, pl V). At Turret 29b Newbold (1913, 63–4) investigated a branch track where it met the Military Way at a point 12m from the turret. Another possible example occurs at Turret 34a where a path 'of small stones and amphora fragments' was found running southwards from its door (Charlesworth 1973, 100). Turrets 29b and 34a have been excavated, and most of the pottery recovered from them is of second-century date. They seem to conform to the pattern of an abandonment of many turrets in the central section, particularly on the crags, and a marked reduction in the number of turrets elsewhere on the Wall (Breeze and Dobson 1972, 203, n 121; idem 1987, 131–2). It has been suggested that in the 180s the turrets were no longer in use and their doors were blocked up; in the early third century they were demolished and their recesses were walled across flush with the rear face of the curtain. Most of the excavated turrets have produced pottery datable to after the mid-second century which shows that they were certainly reoccupied following the return to Hadrian's Wall.

The evidence of branch tracks, and pottery from the turrets to which they led, combines to make an Antonine date for the Military Way almost certain. The expected connection between the construction of it and the building of the road bridges at Chesters and Willowford is thus improbable.

What was the purpose of the Military Way? Recent assertions, noted above, that it was inspired by the Military Way on the Antonine Wall, imply that it was a major east–west route. There are two reasons for doubting this: firstly its relationship with the Vallum, and secondly the continuing importance of the Stanegate, the Flavian road which ran between Corbridge and Carlisle, and perhaps across the whole isthmus (Appendix 1).

Between Milecastles 30 and 33 there was no space for the Military Way to run between the Wall and the Vallum, and so it was laid along the Vallum north mound, except for the short lengths where it ran in front of milecastles (Simpson and Shaw 1922, 354, 417). Construction of the Military Way came after a series of breaches had been made at frequent intervals in the north and south Vallum mounds. This was apparently done to provide material for causeways across the Vallum ditch. This slighting of the Vallum is plausibly associated with the advance of the frontier into Scotland in *c* 140, and the cleaning out of the Vallum ditch with the return to Hadrian's Wall (Breeze and Dobson 1987, 88, 128; but cf Daniels 1978, 33). In this case construction of the Military Way will have taken place at the same time as the recommissioning of the Vallum ditch; no attempt seems to have been made to restore the south mound nor to fill in the gaps in the north mound where it was not overlain by the Military Way. The Vallum ditch might well have remained a boundary; where not immediately adjacent to the Military Way, the Vallum ditch was always within sight of it. Patrols on the Military Way would therefore have been able to deal with those who trespassed across the Vallum.

(For the question whether the Vallum was originally patrolled, see Heywood 1965, 89–90).

The Military Way provided direct communication between turrets, milecastles and forts, but there is no reason to suppose that it was intended to supersede the Stanegate which remained a perfectly serviceable 'military way'. Between the North Tyne and Irthing it often ran within sight of the Wall and never more than 3km to its south. It has been argued elsewhere (see Appendix 1) that with the construction of the Wall the Stanegate was extended eastwards to Newcastle north of the Tyne, and westwards to Carlisle and beyond, on the north side of the Irthing, although the exact lines of these extensions are yet to be discovered. The original intention seems to have been to station the forces controlling the Wall in forts on the Stanegate and it has been argued that Stone Fort 1 at *Vindolanda* was built in *c* 122–4 as part of that plan (Bidwell 1985, 9–10); Fort III at Corbridge might have been built at the same time although it was apparently left ungarrisoned when the Wall-Forts were built (Gillam 1977, 62), and a timber predecessor of the stone fort built at Carvoran in *c* 136–8 might also have been intended to house troops for the Wall. The continuing importance of the Stanegate after the construction of the Military Way is attested by milestones which show that it was maintained in repair until at least the early fourth century (*RIB* 2293, 2301–3) and by the addition of a small fort at Newbrough in the late Roman period.

The Military Way can thus be seen as a secondary route, its purpose being to link the various elements of the Wall together. It perhaps was also intended for patrols controlling a boundary represented by the Vallum ditch. At the points where it crossed the North Tyne and Irthing it is possible that there were bridges of timber or even perhaps of stone, yet to be discovered, but this need not necessarily have been so. Pedestrian traffic along the Vallum berms probably made use of the Wall bridges (p 136) and might have continued to do so when the Military Way was constructed, with wheeled traffic being diverted to the bridges or fords on the Stanegate.

The place of the bridges at Chesters and Willowford in the road system

In the preceding section the continuing importance of the Stanegate as an east–west route behind the Wall has been emphasised and the Military Way has been described as a secondary route giving direct communication between forts and milecastles and perhaps also playing a part in the supervision of a Vallum boundary. The provision of road bridges at Chesters and Willowford at a later stage might seem to suggest that the Military Way had come to be regarded as a major route, but this would have largely duplicated the function of the Stanegate, which continued in use into the fourth century. The monumental character of the bridge at Chesters seems out of all proportion to the modest function of the Military Way, and suggests that it was associated

with a more important route. An examination of the road system in the vicinity of Chesters shows how the bridge might have been connected with the Stanegate.

The exact course of the Military Way as it approached the fort at Chesters from the west has not been established but it presumably ran across the fort between the two *portae quintanae* and then directly onto the causeway on the west side of the bridge (Figure 2; p 15). The Stanegate lay 1.6km to the south and seems to have been connected with the fort by a branch road 2.5km in length (Figure 1; MacLauchlan 1858, 27–8). East of the branch road it ran to within a short distance of the west bank of the North Tyne, at which point it turned sharply southwards (Wright 1939; Sockett 1973). The remainder of its course eastwards to Corbridge is uncertain although it presumably crossed the North Tyne by means of a ford or bridge, at some point above the meeting of the waters at Warden.

East of the bridge the Military Way runs close to the Wall, often on the north mound of the Vallum, for a distance of 7.5km until it reaches Portgate where Dere Street passed through the Wall. Corbridge lies 4.5km south of Portgate. Less certain is the existence of other roads north of the Wall in the vicinity of Chesters. In the draft of a letter written by Christopher Hunter there is the following passage omitted from the version published in the *Philosophical Transactions* (Hunter 1702, 1131): after describing the Wall west of Chesters he states that

'lower down towards Walwick I saw two towers which stood so as the wall past as it were through the midst of them; whereas the rest were set on the inside.'

Rogan 1954, 123

E Birley (1961, 111) included Hunter's 'towers' in a list of possible gateways through the Wall. No Roman road north of the Wall in the vicinity of Chesters is mentioned by modern authorities, but Horsley (1732, 144, 158, nos 1 and 6 (maps)) considered that the Devil's Causeway continued westwards beyond its junction with Dere Street at Bewclay:

'there seems also a branch of a military way to have come from Watling Street [Dere Street], south of Risingham, to this station [Chesters], or to the bridge beside it; of which there are some visible remains, as well as of two or three tumuli, that are on the west side of it.'

If these old reports can be relied upon, the road and gateway might have been associated.

Sufficient is known about the road system on both sides of the North Tyne to suggest the purpose of the road bridge at Chesters. A pre-existing road linked Chesters with the Stanegate, which made it possible, at a date subsequent to the creation of the Military Way, to divert the river crossing to a point where it was overlooked by the fort to the west and by Milecastle 27 to the east. Traffic east of the North Tyne perhaps used the Military Way to reach Corbridge via Portgate and Dere Street. Another possibility is that a new road was constructed on the east side of the North Tyne connecting with the course of the Stanegate east of the original crossing. The present A6079 which passes through Wall and Acomb occupies a line suitable for such a road (the line of the A6079, which is of medieval origin, is marked on Figure 1).

The construction of a road bridge at Willowford was probably also associated with a modification of the road system. The presence of a stone bridge at Willowford, but not apparently at either Irthington or Warwick Bridge, indicates that the major lateral route was now diverted from the original Flavian course of the Stanegate to run via Willowford on the north side of the Irthing. To the west of Poltross Burn the Stanegate probably became correspondingly less important after the construction of the bridge (not a single milestone is known from this sector), and the abandonment of the *vicus* at Nether Denton may also date to this period. The recovery of pottery from the *vicus* area datable to the later second century, indicates its continued occupation after the abandonment of the fort, presumably in the Hadrianic period (Daniels 1978, 209–11). No later material has been found however, and perhaps the *vicus* continued as a roadside settlement on the Stanegate in the second century, the diversion of the main route to the north of the Irthing, in the Severan period, leading to its abandonment. To the east of Willowford it would have been a simple matter to provide a link from the Stanegate to the Military Way (which led to the bridge) for in Wall Mile 47 the two roads were only *c* 100m apart (although separated by the Vallum which was now perhaps no more than a boundary marker). To the west of the river the new route may have utilised the Hadrianic road to Carlisle (p 152ff), the Military Way performing the secondary function of linking the minor structures.

The remodelling of the original wall bridge at Stanwix may, like Chesters, be associated with a decision to place the major crossings on the line of the Wall, branch roads possibly connecting the bridge with the road to Kirkbride and the Cumbrian coast to the west, and the Hadrianic road to the east.

The date of the road bridges

It has been argued that the road bridges at Chesters and Willowford represent a replanning of the road system, which brought the river crossings of the Stanegate up to the line of the Wall, and placed them under closer military supervision. Unfortunately, at Willowford only the east abutment is known and not the bridge itself and it is impossible to establish any architectural similarities with Chesters; but to regard the two road bridges as of contemporaneous construction seems justified in view of their identical functions. At Stanwix there is evidence for a reconstruction of the Wall bridge in which blocks with band anathyrosis and bar clamps were employed (p 110) and this provides a link with Chesters; it is possible that at Stanwix also the main east–west route was brought up to the line of the Wall when the Wall bridge was rebuilt. Between Chesters and Corbridge (p 105) there are similarities of construction

technique so marked as to leave little doubt that they were built at the same time and even perhaps under the direction of the same architect. This establishes that improvements to the road system were not confined to the Stanegate and Military Way but were also made to Dere Street, the main route into Scotland from southern Britain. At Risingham, further north along Dere Street, no techniques of construction similar to those employed at Chesters and Corbridge have been noted and the bridge cannot be dated; the mere presence of columns is probably of no particular significance, for they were commonly to be found on bridges (p 43ff). Piercebridge (p 112) displays some techniques of construction also found at Chesters and Corbridge; it is dated to *c* 180 but the final report must be awaited before it is possible to see whether the evidence excludes the possibility that the bridge was built at the same time as Chesters and Corbridge.

Apart from those considered above, very few bridges with stone piers are known from Britain. The bridge at Summerston on the Antonine Wall has already been noted (p 116), as have the remains of the bridges at Elishaw and Newstead. In the civilian part of the province there seems to be firm evidence from Cirencester for a bridge with stone piers outside the *Verulamium* Gate of the town (Wacher 1961, 65); Dymond (1961, 155–60) lists other possible instances of Roman stone bridges, some extremely doubtful, and traces were recently noted of a stone bridge at Chester (*Britannia* **16** (1985), 281). However, most bridges in Britain seem to have been of timber. The Roman road system of the province was laid out in the immediate aftermath of its conquest and bridges constructed of timber, which was readily available in most areas, allowed speedier construction than the use of stone. These bridges might have lasted a century or two before substantial repairs or their replacement were required. In the third century there was perhaps neither Imperial benefaction nor local munificence to finance the more costly but durable substitution of stone bridges. In addition, the technology of stone bridge construction might not have been locally available or conveniently obtainable (T Blagg *in litt*)

The stone bridges associated with the east–west route behind Hadrian's Wall and on Dere Street are exceptional and thus there is reason to see them as the result of a single initiative directed towards a permanent improvement in communications. There are two possible historical contexts for this initiative, the first of which can be dealt with briefly. In 1972 an important study of samian ware by B R Hartley (Hartley 1972) established to the satisfaction of most students that there had been no lengthy re-occupation of the Antonine Wall after *c* 160. Reconstruction of Wall-forts in *c* 163 during the governorship of Calpurnius Agricola was associated with the recommissioning of Hadrian's Wall. References to an incursion by barbarians across the Wall in the early 180s, in which they killed a 'general' and massacred an army, thus bear on Hadrian's Wall and not the Antonine Wall. The governor Ulpius Marcellus is credited by some modern scholars with a restoration of the Wall in the aftermath of these events, which included the abandonment of many turrets, and changes in fort garrisons, including withdrawal from Newstead, and perhaps also Risingham (Breeze and Dobson 1987, 130–33). However, the case for the restoration of Hadrian's Wall in the early 180s has never been set out in full detail and cannot be accepted without reservation. Fortunately, it need not be discussed in detail here, for the road bridges at Chesters and Willowford are almost certainly later than the suggested restoration of the Wall in the early 180s.

The frontier policy of Septimius Severus in Britain provides another possible historical context for the construction of the road bridges, and one more in accordance with the dating evidence from Chesters and Willowford. In AD 193 following the defeat of Clodius Albinus at *Lugdunum*, Septimius Severus gained control of Britain. The following fifteen years saw intermittent if not continuous unrest in the frontier areas of Britain and at least one case of disaffection in the army of the province. Matters came to a head in AD 207 when the governor Alfenus Senecio wrote to Severus asking for reinforcements or an Imperial expedition. Severus resolved to come to Britain himself and over a period of three years conducted campaigns in Scotland which were brought to an end by his death at York in 211. The particular aspect of Severus' activities in Britain which might have a bearing on the construction of the road bridges is the building of a Wall with which late sources credit him (conveniently collected in Mann 1971, nos 141–6). Hadrian's Wall was long regarded as Severus' work by antiquarians. After it was established that the Tyne–Solway barrier in its original form was indeed the work of Hadrian, it was generally believed that the late sources referred in fact to the rebuilding of Hadrian's Wall by Severus rather than the construction of a Wall *de novo*. It has been said that his work on the Wall was 'sufficient in its reputation for Spartian writing in the fourth century to give Severus the credit for its inception.' (Frere 1978, 207).

Other views have been put forward. Jarrett and Mann (1970, 204) suggested that it was the Antonine Wall which Severus rebuilt but Hartley's work on samian from Scotland (1972) seems now to have ruled out any substantial re-occupation of the Antonine Wall after *c* 160. The restoration of Hadrian's Wall was thought likely to have been the responsibility of Caracalla rather than Severus by Gillam and Mann (1970, 43–4) because according to the various late sources the restoration was carried out after campaigning. But this would not exclude the possibility that the campaigning in question was that for which Alfenus Senecio was responsible and in any event it is questionable whether the sources are sufficiently reliable to justify such a narrow reading. Breeze and Dobson (1987, 133–41) do not discuss the sources which credit Severus with the restoration of the Wall; they argue that the disposition of garrisons in forts in the third century might have largely resulted from changes made in the 180s at which date 'major modifications to the Wall, which were to last through the rest of its history' were also made, perhaps following 'a thorough rethinking of the purpose and function of the Wall' (ibid, 144). They concede however, that the complete overhaul of the Wall was perhaps the responsibility of Severus' governors before his arrival in Britain.

The traditional view is that Severus' frontier policy in Britain fell into two parts. Until his arrival in AD 208 there was sporadic warfare, although this did not prevent rebuilding in forts and the restoration of the Wall in the governorship of Alfenus Senecio in *c* 205–7. Some have seen Severus' ensuing campaigns in Scotland as wars of devastation intended to remove the fighting capacity of tribes beyond the Wall (Collingwood and Myres 1937, 156–8; Frere 1978, 201). Others have argued that Severus' object was the conquest and permanent subjection of Scotland (Jarrett and Mann 1970, 204; A Birley 1971, 263) but this does not necessarily mean that he was not responsible for the earlier restoration of the Wall: the attempted conquest of Scotland might have merely represented a change of policy.

Severus' restoration of the Wall provides the historical context which accords best with the evidence for the construction date of the bridges at Chesters and Willowford and a larger programme of bridge construction for which there is some evidence. The reputation which Severus' work seems to have had in the fourth century might indeed have depended to a considerable extent on the building of bridges, if it is accepted that by reference to the building of the 'Wall', not only a restoration of Hadrian's Wall, but also a general renovation of the frontier system as a whole was understood. Repairs and modifications to the Wall itself which have been attributed to Severus are confined to the demolition of turrets and the rebuilding of some lengths of the curtain (Simpson *et al* 1934, 142–3). This work seems hardly calculated to have added much lustre to the name of Severus.

Bridge building was a different matter. Pliny suggesting to Caninius suitable topics for a poem to celebrate the first Dacian war wrote that:

> '*Dices immissa terris nova flumina, novos pontes fluminibus iniectos*'
> ('you will sing of rivers turned into new channels, and rivers bridged for the first time')
>
> Pliny Ep 8, 4

The building of bridges was commemorated on coins: issues of Augustus (*RIC* 315–8), mentioning the restoration of roads, have reverses showing bridges with arches on top of them. Coins of Antioch ad Maeandrum (*c* 253–68) and Mopsus in Cilicia (*c* 253–8) show bridges and were presumably issued to mark their construction or restoration (Price and Trell 1977, figs 82–3). A coin issued by Trajan (*RIC* 569 and pl X, 188) shows a bridge of a single span supporting what appears to be a two-storeyed portico with gates or arches surmounted by statues on either end. This reverse has long been claimed to represent Trajan's bridge over the Danube, although the authors of *RIC* rejected this identification, because of the lack of its resemblance to the bridge shown on the coin, and suggested that the bridge in question might have been the *Pons Sublicius*, in Rome. Tudor (1974, 58), however, considered that the coin was struck in AD 105 to mark the completion of the Danube bridge and the commencement of the war against Decebalus. The bridge portrayed on the reverse he considered to be a simplified representation, showing three concentric timber arcs connected by six vertical tie beams with portals at either end.

In AD 208 Septimius Severus struck coins with bridges on the reverses at the mint of Rome: an *aureus* (*RIC* 225) and an *as* (*RIC* 786); in addition a large bronze medallion is known which has a reverse identical to that of *RIC* 225 (Gnecchi 1912, vol 2, tav 94, no 2). The bridges are very similar to those shown on the Trajanic issue. Most of the occasional issues in 208 (eight out of eleven in gold and silver) seem to refer to planned events in Britain, and it is therefore only to be expected that scholars should have associated the issues showing bridges with Britain. In a recent paper (Robertson 1980, 137) it was suggested that the bridge shown on the coins, if in Britain at all, was 'permanent, monumental and long-established' and that a suitable location for it was York, which was Severus' base in Britain. But J C Bruce (1867, 147–8) believed, without stating his reasons, that the bridges at Chesters, Corbridge and Risingham were repaired or renewed at the same time and that the issues of Severus 'may have reference to all these works'. Contemporaneous construction of road bridges at Chesters, Corbridge and Willowford, and perhaps a larger programme of bridge building at the same time, would surely provide a substantial reason for a special issue. If the work was commenced on the instructions of Severus early in the governorship of Alfenus Senecio, the year 208 might have seen the successful completion of the programme. It might perhaps be objected that an undertaking of such importance would not have been overlooked by the historians of Severus' campaigns in Britain, Herodian and Cassius Dio, but Gillam and Mann (1970, 44) in explaining the absence of any reference by these historians to Severus' restoration of the Wall (and presumably the frontier system in general) noted that 'they were intent on describing aggressive campaigns, and wall-building would have little place in that kind of story.'

Herodian (III, 14, 4) and Cassius Dio (76, 13, 1) in fact mention engineering works in connection with Severus'campaigns, Herodian referring to the provision of causeways in marshy places, Dio specifically mentioning the bridging of rivers, but the context makes it plain that the rivers were those encountered during the advance into Caledonia. The *Via Traiana* built by Trajan at his own expense for a distance of about 200 miles between *Beneventum* and *Brundisium*, (Ashby and Gardner 1916) is an instance of a major engineering project ignored by ancient historians but of sufficient importance to the emperor to occasion special issues. The coins in question have a reverse with a reclining figure holding a wheel (*RIC* 266, 636–41 issued in 112–4) and the legend SPQR OPTIMO PRINCIPI and VIA TRAIANA in exergue.

The suggested programme of bridge building in northern Britain can be compared to a similar programme on the Euphrates frontier; both were carried out under the supervision of L Alfenus Senecio, successively governor of Syria and Britain. The bridge over the Cendere Çay (Figure 28) has already been mentioned (p 43ff); its dedicatory inscriptions can be dated to AD 200 (Leaning 1971). Bridges over the Marsyas (the modern Merzumen) at Rumkale and over the Singas (the modern Gök-su) have parapets with distinctive mouldings of octagonal section resembling those on the bridge over the Cendere Çay (Wagner 1972, 679 and Textabb 5). All three bridges are thought to have been built at the same time, and the bridge over the Kara-su, built by *legio IIII Sythica* which was based at Zeugma, is also thought to have been of contemporaneous construction (ibid, 681). Two further bridges, over the Afrin and the Sabin Souyou, display plans and techniques of construction nearly identical to those of the bridge over the Kara-su (Wagner 1977, 521, n 33). All these bridges lie along the road on the west side of the Euphrates or on roads in the hinterland; according to Hellenkemper (1977, 469), they were built as part of the extensive preparations for Severus's Parthian war.

As is so often the case, the marriage attempted in this section between imprecise archaeological evidence and a defective historical record is not an easy one. But it engenders a hypothesis which has the merit of showing why Severus' restoration of the Wall, and by implication, of the whole frontier system, was remarked upon by later writers, even if it was overlooked in his own times by those who lived through the aftermath of his death at York, and who were understandably more concerned to trace the dark undercurrent of omens, and to emphasise the rigours of campaigns perhaps never brought to a successful conclusion, that preceded his death.

It has already been noted that Severus' restoration of the Wall itself, apparently confined to the rebuilding of some stretches of the curtain and the demolition of turrets, does not seem a considerable achievement. The building of bridges linked to alterations in the road system would have added more substance to the reputation of Severus' work but perhaps as far as Hadrian's Wall was concerned it was Severus' assessment of its utility and its place in his policy of frontier defence that mattered, and not the amount of effort expended on its restoration. If the bridges at Corbridge and Willowford, and other bridges which might have been of contemporaneous construction, were as elaborate as Chesters, the inscriptions and sculptures which they would have accommodated probably served to proclaim the renewal of Hadrian's frontier works by the Severan dynasty.

10 The finds

Introduction

Very few finds were recovered from the excavations of 1982–5 at Chesters and Willowford. This was partly because much of the stratigraphy had been removed by previous excavators, but it is also true that bridges are a type of site unlikely to produce a great quantity of artefactual material. Where material survives from the previous excavations at the bridges it has been included in the following reports.

Stone artefacts

Inscriptions

There are three inscriptions from Chesters which were probably associated with the bridge.

Figure 93: stele 0.95m in height, 0.57m in width and 0.41m in depth, with an inscribed face enclosed by a narrow moulding which reads ...]cu|rante | Aelio | Longino praef(ecto) eq(uitum) (RIB 1470). In the left-hand side there is a small socket 40mm in width, 20mm high and 40mm deep, cut 100mm above the base of the stele and 200mm from its front; another socket of the same dimensions has been cut in the rear face at the centre 220mm above the base. The stele and the circumstances of its discovery were described in a letter to J C Bruce from John Clayton dated 12 January, 1863, bound into a copy of Bruce 1853, in Durham University Library:

> 'We have found amongst the Ruins of the bridge an inscribed tablet, the three last lines of which are perfect, the upper part being entirely worn away. The letters are well formed and apparently fresh: RANTE AELIO/LONGINO/PRAEFECT Q. The first five letters are, I doubt not, the concluding letters of the participle [illegible word](?). It is singular that all the preceding lines of the inscription are so entirely obliterated, which I think must be ascribed to the lower portion of the slab being buried in the river, whilst the upper part has been exposed to the constant flow of the current which has apparently worn away, what originally has been a long inscription. In a fortnight or three weeks the further exploration will be completed, when the bridge will be worth a visit.'

The inscription was first published in Bruce (1863)

Elsewhere it is argued that the stele was set in the parapet of bridge 2 (p 47, p 28, where its date is also discussed). Whether the stele represented the principal building inscription of the bridge is doubtful; third-century building inscriptions are often detailed and elaborate and the stele may have been a subsidiary dedication made by the prefect of the garrison of Chesters who might well not have been in charge of the construction.

Figure 93 Inscription dedicated by the prefect Aelius Longinus, attributable to bridge 2 at Chesters, scale 1:10. (Drawing by J Thorn)

Fragment inscribed [Nymp]his | [vexi]llatio | [leg(ionis) VI] Vic(tricis) and measuring 0.177m by 0.202m by 0.279m (RIB 1547). It can probably be identified as the fragment which is sketched in the same letter as Figure 93 above in a copy of Bruce 1853 in Durham University Library; it is labelled 'stone found in excavating the bridge' and the inscription is transcribed as follows: '...elis ...latio ...I Vic'.

R P Wright and R S O Tomlin explain in Britannia 16 (1985), 331, n 73, how this stone, as RIB 1547, was given the probably mistaken provenance 'found near Coventina's Well, west of Carrawburgh fort' and suggest that it might well be 'the unsatisfactory fragment of an inscription' noted by Clayton from the excavation of the east abutment at Chesters in Archaeol Aeliana 2 ser, 5 (1861), 143.

The Sixth Legion was apparently responsible for the construction of bridge 1 (p 13), but this inscription might actually be associated with bridge 2; the possibility that there was a shrine to the nymphs over one of the cutwaters of the piers has been noted on p 47.

Fragment, now lost, measuring 0.6m by 0.9m, which had apparently fallen from the cliff above the east bank of the river south of the bridge. The lettering, roughly executed with a pick, reads *SENC[... | CINA · VOTO | NE · QI · LICIAT | NE* (*RIB* 1486). The first line presumably gave the name of a centurion or century and *CINA* might have been part of *OFFICINA* (cf *RIB* 1009, an inscription from the Gelt quarries). The inscription may indicate the site of a quarry for stone used in the bridge (p 3).

Sculptures

by J C Coulston

Three small-scale sculptures have been found in association with the bridges at Chesters and Willowford.

No 1: (Figure 18) from Chesters. A large phallus points to the left at an ovoid, featureless object which appears to be incompletely sculpted. Both are executed in high relief on the face of the north wing of the eastern abutment of bridge 2 (p 19). The work is rough with heavy chisel marks similar to those dressing the abutment's ashlars. One posibility is that the ovoid object may be a stylised vulva, but in view of the extreme rarity of depictions of this in Roman art (Johns 1982, 74–5) perhaps it is more likely to be an Evil Eye being 'attacked' by the phallus. A comparable scene is visible on a block from Chesters fort where a phallus in relief points towards an elliptical object (Coulston and Phillips 1988, no 407). Dimensions: height 0.43m; width 1.32m. Coulston and Phillips 1988, No 404. Severan.

No 2: from Willowford (Figure 51). The upper part of a phallus survives in relief on a block, now at the south end of the abutment of bridge 3. the remainder having run across a lost second stone. Only the glans and part of the shaft are present. Roughly chiselled marks are visible on the sides of the shaft. The block was probably reused from bridge 1 (p 69). Dimensions: height 0.33m; width 0.12m. Coulston and Phillips 1988, No 457. Hadrianic.

No 3: from Willowford (Figure 63). A horned human figure with one raised arm is incised on a block found near the northern wing-wall of bridge 2 in 1924 (p 83). The size of the block and the longitudinal alignment of the figure make association with the bridge structure plausible, but not assured. The Willowford figure is paralleled by a relief of a horned god with spear and shield from Burgh-by-Sands (ibid, no 373). Horned heads sculpted in the round have been found at Chesters and Netherby (ibid, no 329, 337). Figures of gods without horns, but with warlike attributes, also occur at Great Chesters and in a rural shrine at Yardhope (ibid, no 360; Charlton and Micheson 1983, 144–6, see also Brewer 1986, no 15). All of these represent recognisably Celtic forms of deities (Ross 1967, 115–7, 201–15). If the Willowford block is indeed from the bridge it

is an interesting example of a Celtic deity relief found in association with a structure.
Dimensions: height 0.625m; width 0.175m.
Coulston and Phillips 1988, No 365.

The coins

Chesters

The following coins were found during the excavations of 1982–3:

No 1: illegible sestertius of first- or second-century date. Context 153, floor of tower, Severan.
No 2: corroded, plated copy of a denarius of Septimius Severus of AD 198–202. Obverse legend: **L SEPT SEV AVG I[MP XI P]AR[T] MA[X]**.
Context 154, occupation on floor of tower, Severan or later.
No 3: illegible copy, probably mid-fourth century. Unstratified in trench 5.

Clayton (1865, 84) records the following coins from the excavations of 1860–3:
Republican denarius of 57 BC;
bronze coin of Hadrian;
denarius of Julia Augusta (identifiable as *RIC* 559, of 196–211, from his description);
a coin of Tetricus,
a follis of Diocletian (of 294–305);
a coin of the family of Constantine.

Willowford

The following coins have been kindly identified by Norman Shiel; nos 5–7, from Shaw's excavations, are lost and identifications are based on the published descriptions:

No 4: denarius of Nero (*RIC* 60, of AD 56–8). Bridge 1A construction, context 1006.
No 5: denarius of Titus (*RIC* 22a, of AD 80). Bridge 2, occupation on primary floor in tower (Shaw 1926, 484–5).
No 6: denarius of Trajan (*RIC* 125, of AD 106–11). Context as no 5.
No 7: sestertius of Commodus (*RIC* 585, of AD 190–1).
Bridge 2A construction, cobbles to the north of the curtain wall (Shaw 1926, 499–500).

Metal and other finds (excluding structural metalwork)

Figure 94
No 1: belt plate, copper alloy, length 36mm. The main part of the belt plate has simple open work decoration, while the surviving end has two confronted *peltae* and a rivet hole. There are many general parallels, the closest on Hadrian's Wall being two unpublished examples from the fort at Great Chesters with open work decoration and pelta-

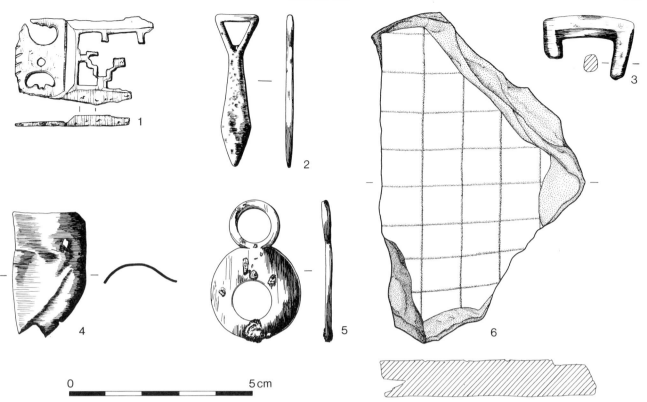

Figure 94 Small finds from Chesters and Willowford, no 1 from Willowford, nos 2–6 from Chesters. Scale 1:1

shaped terminals (information from Lindsay Allason-Jones; Museum of Antiquities, Newcastle upon Tyne accession no 1956.150.22A).
Willowford, context 1021, construction of bridge 2, Antonine.
No 2: pendant, copper alloy, length 40mm. A common type, cf Allason-Jones and Miket 1984, 3.597–607.
Chesters, Trench 1, context 51, probable Roman ground surface,
not closely datable.
No 3: part of buckle(?), copper alloy, width 250mm, not necessarily of Roman date.
Chesters, trench 1, topsoil
No 4: fragment of copper alloy sheeting, length 330mm.
Chesters, context 153, floor of tower,
Severan.
No 5: object of unknown purpose, possibly a pendant, copper alloy, length 37mm.
Context as no 4.
No 6: fragment of gaming board in a fine-grained, laminated and highly micaceous sandstone, length 177mm.
Chesters, context 154, occupation on floor of tower, Severan or later.
No 7: (not illustrated) melon bead, turquoise glass, diameter 11mm.
Chesters, context as no 6.
No 8: (not illustrated) gaming piece or unfinished spindlewhorl, maximum diameter 38mm. Cut from a grey ware sherd, probably a cooking-pot as Figure 95, no 3. Holes have been drilled in either face of the sherd; neither penetrates the full thickness of the sherd nor do their positions coincide.

Chesters, context as no 2
No 9: (Not illustrated) two featureless fragments from a Niedermendig lava quernstone.
Willowford, possibly representing the 'millstone' found by Shaw (1926, 485) 'in the open sluice'; these two fragments were found unstratified in excavation fill.

The Roman pottery

with contributions by J N Dore (samian) and K F Hartley (mortaria)

Chesters

Very little pottery was recovered during the excavations of 1982–3 and none is known to have survived from the earlier work on the site.
Figure 95
Nos 1 and 2: hard light grey ware with occasional dark soft inclusions. Both represent cooking pots of Gillam (1970), Type 115–7 (Hadrianic to early Antonine).
   No 1 was from the primary occupation in the tower (context 154). Sherds of grey ware and of Black Burnished Ware Category 1 with acute-angled lattice also came from the primary occupation deposit (context 154) and the hearth (contexts 156–7).
   No 2 came from the levelling in the interior of the tower (context 160), which also produced a sherd from a Dressel 20 amphora and a few sherds from another grey ware cooking pot.
No 3: grey ware cooking pot comparable in form

and fabric to vessels of the second quarter of the third century from *Vindolanda* (Bidwell 1985, fig 69, nos 85–90).

No 4: Black Burnished Ware Category 1 cooking pot.

Nos 3 and 4 came from a disturbed deposit in the tower probably containing material derived from the primary occupation.

No 5: cornice-rim beaker in orange fabric with small brown inclusions and some mica; much abraded with no traces remaining of a colour-coat.

From the fill of the cut behind the north wing of bridge 2 which also produced part of the neck of a flagon with sharply moulded rings, in an orange-buff fabric with numerous brown inclusions.

Both vessels from this context are perhaps to be dated as early as the Hadrianic period.

Unstratified

Not illustrated: a weathered fragment with an incomplete rim-section from a slightly burnt mortarium in cream fabric with tiny quartz and red-brown and black inclusions; no trituration grit survives. It would fit manufacture in the workshop of Bellicus at Corbridge, AD 160–200 (KFH). Three near-parallel cuts were made across the flange before the vessel was fired.

No 6: Jar or cooking pot in hard slightly gritty white fabric with red inclusions.

None of the few sherds of samian from the site, all apparently central Gaulish, came from usefully stratified contexts.

Willowford

Only a very small amount of pottery was recovered from the 1984–5 excavations compared with the fragments of at least 54 vessels found by Shaw in 1924 and reported on by D. Atkinson (Shaw 1926, 501–5). As the 1924 pottery is crucial to the reinterpretation of the site, and as some pieces are now redated, the pottery is re-published here (Figures 95–6). A number, prefixed by the letter A, in square brackets at the end of an entry provides a concordance with Atkinson's publication. In some cases more than one number may be given, as separate rim sherds from the same vessel were published. Where sherds from the same vessel were found in more than one level the vessel has been entered in its earliest stratigraphic context (eg sherds from vessel no 9 came from the original level of the tower while the rim was found in the deposit to the north of the Wall).

Few general comments are possible about the pottery although the complete absence of Black Burnished Ware Category 2 from the site is notable.

Construction of bridge 1A

From the core of the southern abutment wing-wall (context 1006, Figure 45, section 4)
Figure 95
No 7: mortarium of Gillam (1970), Form 255, in friable, soft, brown-cream fabric with no visible inclusions at ×10 magnification, or any surviving trituration grit. Imported, from either the Rhineland or *Gallia Belgica* and current in the period AD 150–200 on Hadrian's Wall although manufacture may well have continued into the third century. (KFH)
Not illustrated: sherds from two grey ware jars.

Destruction of bridge 1A

From river gravel deposits (context 1004, Figure 45, sections 4 and 5)
Figure 95
No 8: bodysherd from a jar in soft smooth light grey fabric with abundant frequency of small grit inclusions; cf Gillam (1970), Type 29, *c* 140–200.
Not illustrated:
sherds from two grey ware jars;
a vessel in a soft smooth light red fabric;
a minute fragment of black colour coated ware, probably rhenish ware (Moselkeramik) (Greene 1978, 19), this sherd cannot be used as dating evidence, as it is so small it could easily have been washed into the deposit subsequent to its formation.
Samian: Dr 18/31?, east Gaulish; first half of second century. (JND)

Construction of bridge 2

From the foundation level behind the southern abutment wing-wall
Samian: Dr 18/31, central Gaulish, first half of second century (JND). [A49]

Occupation of bridge 2 tower

'From original level of Tower'
It is not clear from Shaw's (1926, 484) description whether this pottery lay within the clay floor (ie dates to the construction of the tower) or was trampled into its surface (occupation of the tower). The latter explanation is the more likely however as sherds from vessel no 9 were also found on the ground surface to the north of the Wall, a rubbish deposit which accumulated during the occupation of the tower.
No 9: Severn Valley ware, cf Webster 1976, fig 1, no 4, second to fourth century. For a discussion of the distribution and dating of Severn Valley ware on Hadrian's Wall see Webster 1972, Bidwell 1985, 172–4. [A44]
No 10: Black Burnished Ware Category 1, another sherd (not joining) with acute angled lattice. [A5, A6, A7?]
No 11: Black Burnished Ware Category 1, cf Gillam 1976, fig 3, no 31, mid-second century.
Gillam (ibid, 67) has commented that nine out of ten published specimens of the bead rim cooking pot in northern England and Scotland are from Hadrianic or Antonine deposits and that importation of the class into the area ceased before the end of the second century. [A9]
No 12: Black Burnished Ware Category 1. [A8 and A10]

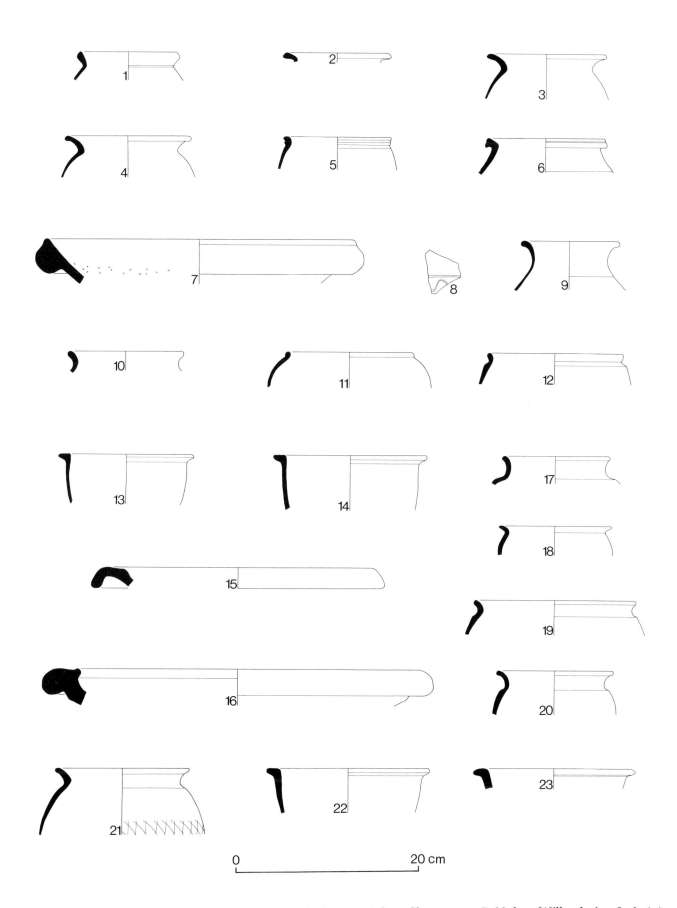

Figure 95   Coarse pottery from Chesters and Willowford, nos 1–6 from Chesters, nos 7–23 from Willowford.   Scale 1:4

No 13: soft smooth light pink fabric with sparse
frequency of small rounded grit inclusions. [A1]
Figure 96
No 14: soft smooth light red fabric with sparse
frequency of small–medium rounded grit inclusions;
another sherd (not joining) displays a carination, cf
Gillam (1970), Form 218, AD 125–40. [A2]
No 15: mortarium. Generally similar in form and
fabric to no 25 but from a different vessel. The
potter's stamp is too faint for identification, AD
140–80 (KFH). [A3]
No 16: mortarium. Fine textured cream fabric with
very tiny quartz and perhaps some flint inclusions;
the trituration grit included quartz. An import,
perhaps from *Gallia Belgica*; probably made AD
100–50. The rather uncommon profile can be closely
matched in a mortarium from Dover (Philp 1981, fig
53, no 377) (KFH). [A4]
Not illustrated:
Sherds from a grey ware jar;
mortarium fragment with incomplete rim-section in
fine-textured, deep orange-brown fabric with some
fine quartz inclusions, and a cream slip. A clearly
impressed but fragmentary potter's stamp survives.
This cannot be identified and may be from an
unknown die. (KFH)
Amphora: wall sherd of Dressel 20, cf rim and
handle, [A46, A55] found in a deposit to the north of
the Wall.
Samian: two wall sherds of a Dr 37 showing double
bordered ovolo with ring (?)tip, bead row below. The
sherds are abraded but the ovolo is likely to be Rogers
(1974) B105, used by a number of potters including
Albucius, Censorinus, Laxtucissa and Paternus II.
The date range which should include all these is AD
150–90 (JND). [A11 and A12]
One small sherd possibly from the base of a Dr 37,
probably central Gaulish.
Date: this group is Hadrianic–Antonine in character, with two pieces (no 15 and the samian Dr 37)
which are specifically Antonine. There is nothing
however in the group which need necessarily date to
the late second century.

'Found on the upper floor in the tower'
No 17: Black Burnished Ware Category 1. [A23]
No 18: soft coarse grey fabric with abundant
frequency of small rounded grit inclusions, cf Gillam
(1970), Form 116, AD 125–50. [A25]
No 19: Black Burnished Ware Category 1. [A24]
No 20: Black Burnished Ware Category 1. [A22]
No 21: Black Burnished Ware Category 1, cf Gillam
1976, fig 1, no 4, late second century. [A21]
No 22: soft smooth light buff fabric with moderate
frequency of small–medium angular grit inclusions cf
Gillam (1970), Form 218, AD 125–40. [A20]
No 23: Black Burnished Ware Category 1, cf Gillam
1976, fig 3, no 34, early to mid-second century. [A26]
No 24: mortarium. Hard orangy-brown fabric with
powdery surface; occasional quartz and blackish
inclusions; no trituration grit survives. Northern
England c 120–60 (KFH). [A18]
No 25: mortarium. Fine textured, white fabric with
pink core and some pink quartz and opaque,

red-brown inclusions; the trituration grit consists of
red-brown and dark brown material with rare quartz
grits. The fabric indicates origin in the Mancetter-
Hartshill potteries in Warwickshire and the profile, a
date c 130/140–80. The corner of a potter's stamp
survives but is too fragmentary for identification
(KFH). [A17]
Not illustrated:
Sherds from three oxidised jars in soft smooth pink
fabrics.
Base, (diameter 15mm), in a soft roughish light grey
fabric with smooth black burnish on both interior and
exterior.

From the ground surface to the north of Hadrian's Wall
No 26: soft roughish light grey fabric with moderate
frequency of small to medium grits. [A39]
No 27: soft fairly smooth light pink fabric. [A38]
No 28: hard light grey fabric with abundant
frequency of rounded grit inclusions, cf Gillam
(1970), Form 116, AD 125–50. [A37]
No 29: Black Burnished Ware Category 1, cf Gillam
(1970), Form 122, AD 125–60. [A41]
No 30: Black Burnished Ware Category 1. [A42]
No 31: Black Burnished Ware Category 1, cf Gillam
1976, fig 1, no 1, early to mid-second century. [A43]
No 32: soft smooth grey fabric with moderate
frequency of small rounded grit inclusions, another
sherd (not joining) displays acute angled lattice
decoration. [A35]
No 33: Black Burnished Ware Category 1, cf Gillam
1976, fig 1, no 4, late second century. [A34]
No 34: Black Burnished Ware Category 1. [A36 and
A40]
No 35: soft rough buff fabric with abundant
frequency of small sub-angular grit inclusions. [A32]
No 36: Black Burnished Ware Category 1, cf Gillam
1976, fig 3, no 34, early to mid-second century. [A31]
No 37: mortarium in soft, fine textured, yellowish-
cream fabric with fairly high sand content, some
ill-sorted quartz, and rare red-brown and black
inclusions. Two circular rivet-holes survive. The
fabric and form are typical of products of the
Colchester potteries. AD 130–80. (see Hull 1963, fig
8, no 1 for a close parallel) (KFH). [A33]
Not illustrated: neck of Dressel 20 amphora. [A46]
Samian: one wall sherd Dr 37 showing double
bordered ovolo with tongue with slightly enlarged
tip. The fabric suggests an east Gaulish origin. Ovolo
is possibly Ricken and Fischer (1963) E44 (Rheinzabern). Late second century–third century (JND).
[A45]
Date: the pottery found to the north of Hadrian's
Wall was probably discarded as rubbish from the
tower and so it can be used in conjunction with the
pottery from the second floor level to determine the
period of use of the tower.
The sherd of east Gaulish samian, and cooking pots
nos 21 and 33 indicate that the group was still open
in the late second century, although the absence of
Black Burnished Ware Category 1 cooking pots with
obtuse-angled lattice decoration demonstrates that
occupation had ceased within the tower by the
second quarter of the third century (Bidwell 1985,
174–6)

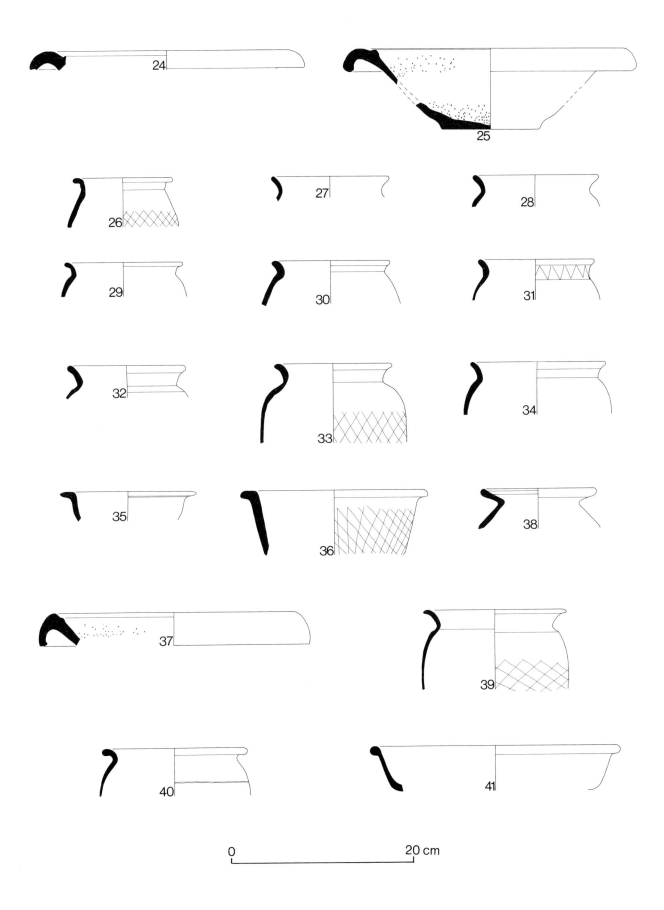

Figure 96   Coarse pottery from Willowford.   Scale 1:4

Miscellaneous deposits

From 'Debris above second floor'
Possibly deliberate infilling of levelled tower during the construction of the ramp of bridge 3 (p 93).
Not illustrated:
Two sherds from a colour-coated beaker in a fine soft pink fabric, with dark red slip, barbotine decoration shows the rear legs of a dog or stag. Possibly a Colchester product. Such vessels first appear in the north on the Antonine Wall, probably after *c* 150 (Gillam 1973, 56). [A51, 52]
Flange fragment from a mortarium in similar fabric to 37; generally similar to Hull (1963) Type 499, AD 140–80. (KFH)
Samian: one rim sherd, one base sherd Dr 31, east Gaulish
one rim sherd, three base sherds Dr 31R, central Gaulish. Both second half of second century. (JND)

Bridge 3 Modifications

From 'Gravel filling of sluice'
Not illustrated: base of a beaker in Nene Valley ware, white fabric, light brown slip. Nene Valley ware is not particularly common in northern Britain until the third century (Bidwell 1985, 180–2). [A48]

From 'Above gravel filling of sluice'
No 38: calcite gritted ware cf Gillam (1970), Type 158, *c* 290–350. [A47]

From 'Mixed soil east of tower'
Not illustrated:
Two body sherds from a cooking pot in calcite gritted ware (possibly part of no 38 above).
Mortarium fragment with incomplete rim-section. Mancetter-Hartshill potteries, AD 110–80. (KFH)
Samian: One rim sherd Dr 37 showing double bordered ovolo with tongue with ring tip. The sherd is worn but the ovolo could well be Rogers (1974) B103 used by Advocisus and Divixtus among others, *c* 140–90. [A54]
One rim sherd Dr 37 showing double bordered ovolo with straight tongue, bead row below. Ovolo is close to Rogers (ibid) B164, Stanfield and Simpson (1958), fig 36, no 1 used by Iullinus though the fabric and the execution of the decoration raises the possibility that the piece is east Gaulish. Second half of the second century (JND). [A55]

From 'Mixed debris above northern abutment wing-wall of bridge 2'
Samian: most of an applique spout in the shape of a lion's head from a Dr 45 mortarium. The fabric, and the fact that the motif is still recognisably lion-like, suggest a central Gaulish origin. The vessel form in general is unlikely to have reached the area before *c* 180 (JND). [A50]

From silting of the Wall ditch associated with a primary rubble spread (context 1009, Figure 45, section 7)
No 39: Black Burnished Ware Category 1, cf Gillam

1976, fig 1, no 8, mid-third century. The earliest deposits containing obtuse angled lattice decoration are the demolition levels of Stone Fort 1 and the construction levels of Stone Fort 2 at *Vindolanda* dated *c* 223–5 (Bidwell 1985, 174–6).
No 40: light grey fabric with abundant frequency of medium sub-angular grit inclusions.
No 41: mid-grey fabric with abundant frequency of small angular grit inclusions. Copy of Black Burnished Ware Category 2 dish, cf Gillam (1970), Form 313, *c* 190–240.

Unstratified

Samian:
Two rim sherds Dr 31R, central Gaulish, second half of the second century.
One small rim sherd Dr 37, heavily abraded. Fabric suggests east Gaulish origin though this is not certain.
One rim sherd Dr 37, heavily abraded, probably central Gaulish (JND).

Willowford Medieval Pottery

by L Bown

Pottery from both the 1924 and 1984–5 excavations was examined. No details of the find spots of the 1924 material exist although the majority was probably associated with the industrial activity in the tower (p 97). The twenty-two sherds divide broadly into five fabric types:

From the Backfill of Shaw's excavations in the tower (Shaw 1926, 484)
Not illustrated:
Fabric 1: one sherd, reminiscent of the Northern Gritty Ware tradition and therefore possibly Saxo-Norman, mid-11th to late 12th–early 13th century.
Fabric: very hard, smooth textured laminar clay with fine dense matrix giving a smooth slurried texture to the sherd which is broken by the larger quartz possibly added as temper.
Colour: redish/yellow throughout (5YR 6/6) (Munsell 1975)
Form: jar/cooking pot/pan. Possibly hand built, wheel or hand turned finish.

Context 1008, Figure 45, section 5, and 1924 finds
Fabric 2: three sherds, possibly 12th to 13th century
Fabric: Fairly soft, abundantly packed fine matrix with barely visible quartz sand, red iron oxide and mica. Larger matrix of subangular quartz sand 0.2mm to 0.3mm and occasional rounded quartz sand 0.5mm.
Colour: Very pale brown throughout (10 YR 8/4) (Munsell 1975) with reduced external greyish brown surface (10 YR 5/2) (Munsell 1975).
Form: Three vessels, two bases, sooted externally, cooking pots. One sherd with splash green lead glazing. Wheel thrown.

From context 1009, Figure 45, section 7
Fabric 3: two sherds, possibly 12th to 13th/early 14th century.
Fabric: hard gritty highly fired fabric. Moderate very angular fine, medium and coarse quartz. Occasional quartz sandstone. Distinctive siltstone pellets. Moderate black burnt out iron oxides?
Colour: varying between very pale brown (10 YR 7/4) (Munsell 1975) throughout and light grey (10 YR 7/0) (Munsell 1975) throughout.
Form: one vessel, a jar? Wheel thrown.

Context 1008, Figure 45, section 5, and topsoil
Eight sherds all of indeterminate fairly soft gritty fabrics are probably 13th–14th century date. They are a group of typically nebulous medieval fabrics with abundant fine quartz sand matrix and coarser moderate quartz tempered matrix up to 0.5mm size. All are oxidised sherds with grey core and splash lead glazing.

Topsoil
Fabric 4: one sherd, probably 13th to 14th century.
Fabric: hard gritty fabric with well sorted fine matrix of quartz sand approximately 0.1mm in size. Less frequent are coarser quartz 0.3mm–0.5mm. Also red iron oxide 0.1mm and occasionally 0.3mm. A number of black cinder-like inclusions are also present which produce black flecks under the glaze. And also burnt out rootlet impressions.

Colour: grey (2.5 YR 6/0) (Munsell 1975) with light grey external margin (2.5 YR 7/2) (Munsell 1975).
Form: unknown. Wheel thrown, continuous green/brown lead glaze on exterior.

1924 finds
Fabric 5: seven sherds, possibly mid 14th to 16th century Reminiscent of Reduced Greenware Tradition form 4 at Newcastle upon Tyne (Ellison 1981).
Fabric: very hard, fine dense fabric with quartz sand matrix less than 0.125mm. Occasionally larger quartz sand 0.2mm–0.3mm and 0.6mm size.
Colour: grey throughout (2.5 YR 5/0) (Munsell 1975).
Form: one vessel, a jug or cistern? Wheel thrown. Continuous green lead glaze on the exterior.

With such a small assemblage of sherds there are great limitations in identifying and dating the fabric types present. Great caution must therefore be used in consulting the dates suggested here. They are based, very generally, on visual comparisons made with similar types of fabrics in the North East.
The medieval sherds from Willowford Bridge do not form a particularly homogeneous group, but more of a variety of odd sherds ranging in date from one sherd (Fabric 1) which could be very early, 11th or 12th century, to the majority which are very indistinctive gritty medieval fabrics with green lead glazing spanning the 13th to the 15th centuries.

Appendix 1

The pre-Hadrianic and Hadrianic road systems between Tyne and Solway

The earliest military activity on the Tyne-Solway isthmus is generally dated to *c* AD 78–9 on the basis of Tacitus's narrative of events in the career of Agricola. Where the arterial roads from the south crossed the Tyne and Solway forts were built, at Red House, Corbridge (Hanson *et al* 1979, 42), and Annetwell Street, Carlisle (McCarthy 1984, 65), (Figure 97) and were followed by the construction of a road across the isthmus (now known as the Stanegate, the name of the medieval road that ran between Corbridge and Carlisle). Within a matter of years a number of other forts had been constructed between Tyne and Solway, some of which, such as *Vindolanda* and South Shields, may also have been originally Agricolan foundations (Hird 1977, 5; *Britannia*, **17** (1986), 374). The latter site raises the possibility that the Flavian system continued as far as the east coast, and a similar arrangement may also have occurred in the west: a fort is known at Kirkbride, and is said to have been a Trajanic foundation, although further excavation is required before the possibility of Flavian occupation can be firmly discounted (Bellhouse and Richardson 1982, 48–9).

The course of the Stanegate is known with most certainty in the central sector between Corbridge and Old Church, Brampton. At Corbridge the Stanegate formed the *via principalis* of successive forts and has been traced westwards to the Cor Burn, where the eastern abutment of a fourth-century bridge has been found (Wright 1941, 198). West of the burn the road probably passed along the margins of the Tyne floodplain to the North Tyne. The precise crossing-point of the North Tyne is unknown but it must have lain above the confluence with the South Tyne at Warden and yet to the south of Walwick Grange, as the road swung sharply south-east as it approached the river on its western side (p 137). From the North Tyne to Poltross Burn the course of the Stanegate has been clearly mapped by MacLauchlan (1858). In 1910 the Poltross Burn crossing was examined but no trace of a bridge was found (Simpson 1913, 382). West of Poltross Burn the road turned south-west and passed over the higher broken ground to the south of the Irthing valley, navigating deeply incised streams by cuttings and embankments (Simpson *et al* 1936a, 188). West of Nether Denton the road is lost and it may have ran either directly to the postulated crossing at Irthington or, perhaps more likely, turned south-west along the foot of Brampton Ridge towards the fort at Old Church, Brampton, which is probably Trajanic. This alignment would pass close to the pottery and tile kilns discovered in 1963 (Hogg 1965), and as it is now known that the kilns were exploiting a generally available source of clay, a roadside location appears highly likely (Bellhouse 1971, 43).

It has been claimed (Simpson *et al* 1936a, 186) that the Stanegate approached the crossing of the Irthing at Irthington by means of a causeway, now occupied by a farm track, which appears to be heading for a point about 73m south of the medieval bridge. No trace of a bridge has been found on this alignment, however, and this does not seem to substantiate the Roman date of the causeway. To the north of the river lengths of a Roman road have been claimed (ibid 182) as part of the original course of the Stanegate, although Daniels (1978, 243) has proposed that this stretch is a later addition to the road system and that the Stanegate originally followed a course to the south of the Irthing, crossing the Eden near Warwick Bridge, and then heading for Carlisle. This would explain why the fort at Carlisle was built to the south of the Eden rather than on the northern bank at Stanwix. No trace of a road has yet been found on the suggested alignment, although a lead coffin has been discovered at Botcherby, due east of Carlisle, which could have come from a roadside cemetery (Ferguson 1880, 325). Recent excavations in Carlisle have discovered an east-west road which ran towards the eastern end of the present cathedral before turning north-west to enter the Annetwell Street fort (McCarthy 1984, 72). West of Carlisle a road has been found in aerial survey, almost certainly heading for Kirkbride (Jones 1982, 285, fig 1; Bellhouse and Richardson 1982, 47–8).

It has long been considered that the Flavian road across the isthmus terminated at Corbridge, since there is no sign of it further east. The discovery of a new fort at Whickham and the possibility of earlier occupation at South Shields now suggests that a road did exist and that its course to the east of Corbridge probably lay south of the Tyne. The road could have utilised the stretch of Dere Street between the crossings of the Tyne at Corbridge and the Derwent at Ebchester before branching off north-eastwards to Whickham and ultimately to South Shields. A road between Ebchester and Whickham is not known although its line might be represented by a westward continuation of the Wrekendike, which is conceivably of Flavian origin (Wright 1940).

The possibility therefore exists that in the Flavian period a road ran from coast to coast across the isthmus, keeping to the south of the major rivers as far as was practicable. No remains of any bridge which dates to the initial construction of the road has yet been found, almost certainly because any such structures would have been built entirely of timber.

The Hadrianic road system

Although further forts were added to the Stanegate in the period after *c* AD 105 no changes are apparent in the road system (unless the stretch from Carlisle to Kirkbride dates from this period). Hadrian's Wall was constructed on a course north of the Tyne and Irthing, with the result that both east and west of the central sector the Wall was separated from the presumed course of the existing roads by rivers. In the central sector, after the decision to place the forts upon the Wall, the Stanegate clearly became the main

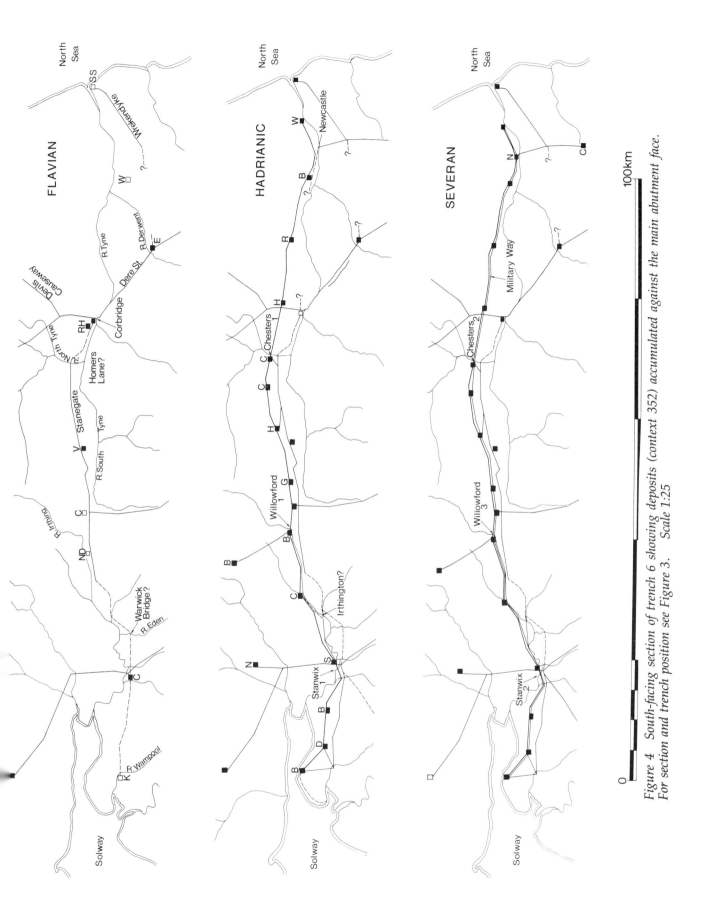

Figure 4 South-facing section of trench 6 showing deposits (context 352) accumulated against the main abutment face. For section and trench position see Figure 3. Scale 1:25

route of supply and communication between the garrisons. Branch roads ran from the Stanegate to the forts at Chesters, Housesteads and Great Chesters, with only Carrawburgh (which was not a primary fort) not so provided (p 153). A similar arrangement also existed to the west of Carlisle with a branch road running from the road terminus at Kirkbride to Drumburgh (Bellhouse 1952). Another road is visible on an aerial photograph heading north from Kirkbride, most probably towards Bowness, where a road heading south from the fort is known (Bellhouse and Richardson 1982, pl 1; Daniels 1978, 257).

It is argued above that the original course of the Stanegate lay completely south of the Irthing and crossed the Eden at Warwick Bridge. A road is known to the north of the Irthing, however, and, as its course closely mirrors the line of Hadrian's Wall, a Hadrianic date seems likely. It is also significant that no forts are known along this length, as would be expected if it were Flavian or Trajanic in date (the existence of a fort at High Crosby has now been firmly disproved; *Britannia*, **17** (1986), 383). MacLauchlan (1858, 70) traced the course of the road from Buckjumping to Crosby and this line has been verified by excavation (Simpson *et al* 1936a, 182). West of Crosby, MacLauchlan's course has the Roman road lying to the south of the Military Road, beyond which its route is lost. In 1975 G Richardson discovered two ditches, 30m apart, to the north of the Military Road which he considered to be the Stanegate (*Britannia*, **7** (1976), 310). It is unlikely that these are roadside ditches, however, as no trace of metalling was found and their spacing was too wide (the roadside ditches at Crosby were 6.4m apart). Further west at Tarraby a road has been found to the south of the Vallum which consisted of close-set cobbling with a single drainage ditch on its northern side (Smith 1978, 34). Sealed beneath the metalling, wheel ruts were visible in the underlying subsoil. West of Tarraby the road is lost, although it presumably headed for the road bridge over the Eden at Stanwix, and the discovery of various cremation urns has led Hogg (1952, 154) to postulate a roadside cemetery beneath Croft Road, Stanwix. Access to Hadrian's Wall could therefore have been provided by this road in the sector to the east of Stanwix although it is not known how far the road continued in this direction. MacLauchlan thought it ran to Castlesteads although he could see no definite trace, considering it to underlie the modern road. It is also likely that a branch route from this Hadrianic road crossed the Irthing in the vicinity of Irthington to connect with the Stanegate.

To the east of Castlesteads some evidence can be proposed for the road continuing as far as Birdoswald. The *praetentura* of the fort at Birdoswald projected north of the Turf Wall, the *portae principales* lying above the infilled Wall ditch; only the *porta decumana* and the posterns on the *via quintana* lay south of the Wall. Both of the latter gates were excavated in 1850 (although wrongly identified as the *portae principales* in the report; Potter 1855, 65–71) when ruts up to 0.1m deep were found worn into the threshold blocks. The excavator also recorded that a road could be traced for a short distance to the

south-east of the eastern postern and this was confirmed in 1896 by a trench dug 15.2m east of the gate (Haverfield 1897, pl 1). MacLauchlan (1858, 53) had also noticed the road and proposed a course down Harrow's Scar by Underheugh Farm, although Haverfield (1899, 185) dismissed the terrace as the result of a landslip and is to be preferred. This road is clearly not the Military Way as that was aligned upon the *via principalis*, as excavation to the west of the fort has shown (Haverfield 1897, pl 1). In fact the road is almost certainly contemporary with the construction of the fort, as the *portae quintanae* were the only gates a lateral road could have utilised in the period between the building of the fort on the Turf Wall and the construction of the Vallum. A substantially later date for the road can probably be excluded as both gates displayed two phases of blocking, the earlier perhaps contemporary with either the construction of the Vallum (see below), or the replacement of the Turf Wall by a stone curtain wall which abutted the north wall of the fort. The latter operation, which is believed to have occurred within the Hadrianic period, resulted in the *via principalis* lying to the south of the Wall and it was utilised by the Military Way in the Antonine period (p 95).

If the road was contemporary with the construction of Birdoswald, it must pre-date the Vallum (which is later than the primary forts on Hadrian's Wall). To the west of Birdoswald the Vallum was constructed so close behind the Turf Wall that there was insufficient room for the north mound, and the ditch had to make a diversion to avoid Milecastle 50 TW. This has led E Birley (1961, 122–3) to suggest that its course was dictated by a pre-existing route, the service track as he termed it, and that following the construction of the Vallum the service track ran along the south berm. While there might well have been a service track preceding the Vallum, the use of the south Vallum berm as a routeway linking milecastles and forts cannot be accepted. The principal objection is that it has now been shown that primary causeways across the Vallum ditch were not the norm, only one certain example, Milecastle 50 TW (Simpson *et al* 1936b, 158–64, Simpson and Richmond 1937, 166–70) and one possible example, Milecastle 51 (Wall Bowers, ibid, 158–66), having been discovered along the whole length of the Wall. Nor does the evidence for light metalling on the south berm in any way compare with the evidence found further west at Crosby and Tarraby. Metalling has been found at the following places: Milecastle 50 TW (although the 'heavy road bottoming' in High House paddock proved to be a post-Roman kiln: Swinbank 1952, 50); Carvoran; High Shield (Wall Mile 38); Mosskennels (Wall Mile 35); near Milecastle 34; west of Limestone Corner (Wall Mile 30) and Down Hill (Wall Mile 20; Swinbank 1954, 257–9). Metalling has also been found on the north Vallum berm at Appletree (Wall Mile 50; Daniels 1978, 217). This sporadic metalling is much more likely to have been associated with the needs of routine patrolling or perhaps even construction than a road: it is notable that near Milecastle 34 a turf layer had developed over the metalling prior to the construction of the marginal mound, which

Daniels (ibid, 33) has suggested may date as early as the Hadrianic period (Swinbank 1954, 257).

A better solution may be that to the west of Birdoswald the Vallum was constructed between the Turf Wall and a pre-existing road aligned upon the *via quintana* of the fort. If so, there is a problem at Milecastle 50 TW concerning the relationship between the milecastle, road and Vallum. Excavation produced evidence of a primary causeway across the Vallum ditch and as it was considered that the south mound was continuous at this point, access would have only been possible from the milecastle to the south berm. However, it is by no means certain that the sequence at the crossing has been correctly understood. In the south mound opposite the causeway there was an unusual feature which was not adequately explained: it consisted of two parallel turf kerbs, 6.4m apart, which passed through the width of the mound, boulder clay apparently filling the space between them. (Simpson *et al* 1936b, 159, Simpson and Richmond 1937, 167). No explanation of this feature was proposed in the report and E Birley subsequently suggested, once the unusualness of this crossing had become apparent, that it may represent the blocking of a primary gap through the mound (Breeze and Dobson 1972, 191). If this were so, access would thus have been available from a road to the south of the Vallum to the milecastle and beyond (there was also a causeway across the Turf Wall ditch), and Birley has suggested that this may have formed a branch road to the Maiden Way which ran from Birdoswald to Bewcastle. The south Vallum mound at Milecastle 50 TW appears to have been subsequently breached at some date after the original gap had been blocked, and a new wider roadway constructed, only to be blocked once more by embankments. Richmond (1966, 175) associated the destruction of the primary causeway with the general breaching of the Vallum upon the abandonment of Hadrian's Wall in favour of the Antonine Wall, and the construction of the embankments with the restoration of the barrier upon the return to Hadrian's Wall. If the road aligned upon the *via quintana* of Birdoswald did run to the south of the Vallum in this sector its line would have been cut through by the Vallum ditch as it passed southwards around the fort. The road may therefore have been realigned immediately to the west of the fort when the Vallum was constructed, probably so that it utilised the Vallum crossing to the south of the *porta decumana*; it was possibly at this date that the *portae quintanae* were blocked.

To the east of Corbridge the Wall was separated by the Tyne from the postulated Flavian road. A road may therefore have been constructed to follow the Wall line in this sector, possibly branching off Dere Street to the south of the Portgate. No trace of the road has yet been found (MacLauchlan's route from Dere Street to Down Hill is most probably a farm track; Swinbank 1954, 255) although the Vallum crossing at Benwell and the bridge at Newcastle (which is discussed on p 99ff) may suggest its existence. Excavation at Benwell revealed a Hadrianic causeway and monumental gate across the Vallum ditch to the south of the fort (Birley *et al* 1934). A road

led south from the causeway and the identification of *vicus* buildings on this alignment suggests that it may have extended some distance down the hill, possibly towards the junction with a lateral road. It is unlikely that the road merely served the *vicus*, as Hadrianic material is absent from this area and Salway (1967, 76) has considered the *vicus* to be a Severan foundation (although subsequent re-dating of certain pottery types may push this back into the second half of the second century).

Thus some evidence exists for a Hadrianic road serving the forts on Hadrian's Wall in those sectors cut off from the existing road system. It was not a direct route like the later Military Way, branch roads from the Stanegate and its extensions serving the forts in the sectors between North Tyne and Irthing and to the west of Carlisle. Nor is there any evidence that the road crossed the Irthing to provide access from the east to Birdoswald and beyond, although the existence of a timber road bridge downstream from the Wall bridge at Willowford cannot be entirely excluded.

The later Hadrianic road systems

Carrawburgh is not a primary Wall fort (it was built over the infilled Vallum ditch) and was probably constructed in the later Hadrianic period (Daniels 1978, 127). Warburton claimed that a branch road ran from the Stanegate to Carrawburgh but Horsley rejected this and is to be preferred (Birley 1961, 133). Carrawburgh is therefore the only fort in the central sector not provided with a branch road although it is significant that on either side of the fort the so-called 'Lesser Military Way' has been recorded. This term has been used by Birley (ibid, 115) to describe a track which was observed by Gordon and Horsley. Gordon (1726, 74) specifically distinguished a small track nearer the Wall from the Military Way in Wall Mile 28 and Horsley (1732, 118, 146) did likewise in Wall Miles 32 and 33 where the width of the track varied from 2.1m to 4.3m. These are the only two references to the track; it has never been traced by excavation. The absence of the track elsewhere on Hadrian's Wall indicates that it cannot have run continuously behind the curtain wall but may rather have only been built in this particular sector to provide access to the newly constructed fort at Carrawburgh.

Appendix 2

A note on Roman river transport in north-east England

In 1983 Mr Raymond Selkirk published *The Piercebridge Formula*, subtitled *A dramatic new view of Roman history*. The central thesis of the book was that the Roman army made extensive use of rivers in north-east England and elsewhere for the transport of supplies, and that many of the major rivers in the region were dammed or canalised to provide a sufficient depth of water for barges. Physical evidence for this engineering is claimed to survive at a number of sites, including some of those discussed in this volume. The present writers, while not denying that the Roman army, and indeed civilian traders, would have made the fullest use of any navigable rivers, nevertheless believe that Selkirk is wholly mistaken in his association with Roman river transport of the sites discussed in his book.

Certain features in the vicinity of the fort at Chester-le-Street with which he had long been familiar suggested to Selkirk the possibility that the Wear had been adapted by the Romans for river transport (ibid, 72–3). He had already doubted whether many Roman roads were suitable for more than 'fast, light communications' and the use of rivers for the transport of heavy goods would explain why steep gradients were not avoided by Roman road builders. Apparent proof of his hypothesis was supplied by a reconsideration of the bridge at Piercebridge discussed above (p 110ff). Relying on a very general guide to the newly discovered remains, Selkirk rejected the interpretation of them as a bridge and claimed instead that they represented the pavement, retaining wall, and abutment of a dam (Selkirk 1983, 98–111). He rightly questioned the reconstruction drawing published in Scott's guide, but then attempted to show why the remains could not have belonged to a bridge. It is unnecessary to refute the arguments advanced for the dam. The final Piercebridge report, on which the description in this volume is based, was not available to Selkirk. This makes clear beyond any reasonable doubt the true nature of the remains: the unambiguous evidence for the position and extent of pier 4, the base of which was recessed into the pavement, is alone fatal to Selkirk's hypothesis.

Believing that the Tees at Piercebridge had been dammed to give it sufficient depth for navigation by barges, Selkirk then extended his search to other rivers, where he found many features which suggested to him that these rivers, likewise, had been adapted for river transport. At Willowford for example he conjectured that the gap between the abutment and river pier was the spillway of a dam, only reserving judgement on account of the reported discovery of piers to the west (ibid, 123–5). He suggested that at Chesters a weir just downstream of the present bridge at Chollerford was of Roman origin and that the leat associated with the weir which serves the mill at Waterside was once a Roman by-pass canal (ibid, 127)

At Bywell, about 7km further down the Tyne from Corbridge, Selkirk has identified what he interprets as the remains of a Roman dam, pound lock, barge harbour and bridge, together with other remains which suggested to him the existence in the vicinity of a hitherto unknown Roman fort (ibid, 135–46). Leaving aside the question of the undated bridge, the remaining piers of which were demolished in 1836, there appears to be no substance to his other claims. What remains of the dam or weir is clearly of fairly recent date: Portland cement appears to have been used in its construction, and the so-called pound lock once held a timber framework secured to chases in its side by iron bolts with nuts threaded on to them, many of which still remain in position. The 'large V-shaped channels' on the north bank of the river, claimed as a barge harbour, are of uncertain date, and other more recent functions suggest themselves. There are undoubtedly large Roman blocks with lewis holes reused in the tower of St Andrew's church at Bywell; it seems likely that they came originally from the Roman bridge at Corbridge, rather than from an unknown site nearby.

None of the other sites described by Selkirk has produced evidence of Roman river engineering any more convincing than those discussed above. The 'Piercebridge Formula' remains an unproved hypothesis. Selkirk's real achievement is the discovery of a large number of sites, more or less incidentally to his search for the remains of Roman river engineering. These include forts, fortlets, marching camps, aqueducts and lengths of Roman roads, as well as prehistoric and native sites: some can be accepted without reserve, others require investigation and a few seem doubtful. Rarely have so many new sites been identified in north-east England in such a short space of time. When Selkirk's work has been fully published and the sites investigated in detail, the implications might well be as far-reaching as those claimed for the unproven and probably unprovable 'Piercebridge Formula'.

Summary

This survey has its origins in a study of the standing remains of Roman bridges at Chesters and Willowford in the care of English Heritage which was part of a programme of maintenance and consolidation. As well as giving a detailed record of the results of excavation and survey a wide range of related topics are covered. These include: a re-examination of the structural evidence provided by the stonework and loose blocks associated with both sites, a reassessment of the antiquarian sources and other previous work, a look at evidence for other Roman bridges in the areas north and south of Hadrian's Wall, and a discussion of the developing communications system of which these bridges formed a part.

The evidence which the work recovered suggests that both bridges were originally built to take the Wall walk across the Rivers North Tyne and Irthing on stone arches. At Willowford a tower by the east abutment gave access to the bridge from ground level behind the Wall; there was perhaps another tower at the west end of the bridge and similar towers might have existed at Chesters.

In the second half of the second century the bridge at Willowford was damaged by flooding on two occasions, after the second of which it was probably completely reconstructed and a new tower built. The easternmost arch at Chesters was also probably damaged by a flood and replaced by a solid causeway. In the early third century the Wall bridges were replaced by road bridges. Little is known of the bridge at Willowford but at Chesters sufficient survives to give an impression of the overall appearance of the bridge. The carriageway, which was carried across the river on four great arches, was lined on either side by stone parapets above moulded string courses, interrupted at intervals by columns and steles. Above one or more of the cutwaters there were perhaps raised platforms to accommodate shrines. From the east the road approached the bridge along a ramp behind the Wall, and then passed through an arch or more probably a gatehouse. The road bridge at Chesters was built entirely in *opus quadratum* (large blocks laid in horizontal courses and often secured with clamps, dowels, and tie-bars) employing techniques of stoneworking and clamping, all of which also appear in the almost certainly contemporaneous bridge at Corbridge. The bridges at Chesters, Willowford, and Corbridge, and perhaps also those at Stanwix and Piercebridge, seem to belong to a re-ordering and improvement of the road system in north Britain and would seem to have been an important part of Severus's restoration of the frontier. Coins issued in AD 208, a year when most of the special issues seem to refer to Britain, show bridges on their reverses and may have a connection with this programme of bridge building.

Little is known of the subsequent history of the bridges, although there are signs that at Chesters the destruction of the fabric took place in a number of stages. It seems however that by the later medieval period little remained of either of the two bridges.

Résumé

Cette enquête a son origine dans un étude des restes des ponts Romains à Chesters et Willowford qui a été un parti d'une programme d'entretien et consolidation en l'attention de `English Heritage'. Aussi qu'on donnait un rapport déaillé avec les résultats des fouilles et des arpentages une grande rangée des sujets sont discutés, y inclus un réexamen de l'evidence structural fourni par la maçonnerie et les blocs séparés en association avec les deux sites; un re-évaluation des sources anciennes et des autres travaux précédents, des recherches sur l'évidence pour d'autres ponts Romains au nord et sud du muraille d'Hadrien, et un discussion du système des communications duquel ces ponts ont été une partie.

L'évidence que ce travail a retrouvé suggère que les deux ponts étaient construits originalement pour continuer le promenade du muraille d'Hadrien à travers les rivières North Tyne et Irthing sur les arches construites de pierre. À Willowford un tour près de la butée a donné l'accès au pont au ras de sol en arrière de la muraille; il y avait peut-être un autre tour au bout ouest du pont et des tours semblables peuvent être exigérés à Chesters.

Pendant la dernière moitié du deuxième siècle le pont à Willowford a été dommagé deux fois par les inondations, et après la deuxième il a été reconstruit à nouveau et un tour a été ajouté. L'arche plus a l'est à Chesters était dommagé – peut-être au même temps – par une inondation et était remplacé par une chauseé solide. Au début du troisième siècle les ponts du muraille d'Hadrien ont été remplacés par les ponts qui ont porté des rues. Peu est établi du pont à Willowford mais à Chesters il y a assez qui survivait pour donner l'impression du l'apparence total du pont. La route carrossable qui a traversé la rivière sur quatre grandes arches a été ligné à chaque côté par les parapets de pierre sur les courses de cordes moulés qui sont interrompus par intervalles par des colonnes et stèles. En haut d'une ou plusieurs des piles du pont il y'avait peut-être des plate-formes elevés pour accommoder des lieux-saints. La rue approchait le pont de l'est par un rempart derrière la muraille et a passé sous un arc ou plus probablement par un corps-de-garde. Le pont routier à Chesters était construit entièrement en *Opus quadratum* (des gros blocs placés en courses horizontales et souvent bien attachés avec des agrafes, des goujons et des barres-liens) et on y a employé les techniques de maçonnerie et attachements qu'on peut voir dans le pont certainement contemporaire à Corbridge. Les ponts à Chesters, Willowford et Corbridge, et peut-être aussi ceux à Stanwix et Piercebridge, semblent appartenir à un réorganisation et amélioration du système des routes au nord de *Britannia* et semblent être une partie importante de la restauration de la frontière entreprise par Severus. Des monnaies émises en 208 après Jésus-Christ, une année dans laquelle la plupart des émissions spéciales semblent parler de *Britannia*, montrent les ponts sur leurs revers et peuvent faire rapport avec cette programme de construction des ponts.

On sait peu de l'histoire dernière des ponts, bien qu'il y a des signes que la déstruction de la structure à Chesters s'est passée par quelques phases. C'est semblable qu'au moyen âge il n'y avait que peu de vestiges de chacun des deux ponts.

Zusammenfassung

Diese Übersicht basiert auf einer Untersuchung des noch aufgehenden Mauerwerkes der sich in der Pflege der English Heritage befindlichen römischen Brücken in Chesters und Willowford und war ein Teil eines Instandhaltungs- und Konsolidierungsprogrammes. Neben einer eingehenden Darstellung der Ausgrabungs- und Vermessungsergebnisse bietet der Bericht auch eine weitreichende Gruppierung damit in Beziehung stehender Themen. Unter diesen Themen befinden sich: eine Neuuntersuchung des baulichen Befundes, der durch die zu beiden Fundstellen gehörigen Bauerreste und losen Bauteile gestellt wird; eine Neueinschätzung des überlieferten Quellenmaterials und früherer Studien; eine Überprüfung des Befundes im Bezug auf andere römische Brücken in den Gebieten nördlich und südlich des Hadrianswalles und eine Diskussion des sich entwickelnden Verkehrssystems, in dem diese Brücken eine Rolle spielen.

Der Befund, der durch die Untersuchungen sichergestellt wurde, deutet an, daß beide Brücken ursprünglich so angelegt waren, daß sie den Wehrgang auf steinernen Brückenbögen über die Flüsse North Tyne und Irthing trugen. Im Falle von Willowford erlaubte ein Turm auf dem östlichen Widerlager den Zugang zu der Brücke vom Erdboden hinter dem Wall; möglicherweise stand ein entsprechender Turm am westlichen Ende der Brücke und ähnliche Türme mögen auch in Chesters vorhanden gewesen sein.

In der zweiten Hälfte des zweiten Jahrhunderts n. Chr. wurde die Brücke in Willowford zweimal durch Flutwässer beschädigt. Nach der zweiten Zerstörung wurde sie wahrscheinlich von Grund auf neugebaut

und ein neuer Turm errichtet. Der östliche Brückenbogen in Chesters war wahrscheinlich ebenfalls durch Flutwasser beschädigt und danach durch einen Damm ersetzt worden. Im frühen dritten Jahrhundert wurden die Mauerbrücken durch Straßenbrücken ersetzt. Über die Brücke in Willowford ist wenig bekannt; in Chesters ist jedoch genügend erhalten, um einen Eindruck des Gesamtbildes der Brücke zu vermitteln. Der Fahrdamm, der auf vier gewaltigen Brückenbögen über den Fluß führte, war auf beiden Seiten durch steinerne Brückengeländer eingefaßt, die über einem profilierten Gesims verliefen und in bestimmten Abständen durch Säulen und Stelen unterbrochen wurden. Über einem oder über mehreren der Brückenpfeilerköpfe bestanden vielleicht erhöhte Absätze, die für die Errichtung von Schreinen gedacht waren. Von Osten her verlief die Straße auf einer Rampe hinter der Mauer, um dann durch einen Torbogen oder wahrscheinlicher durch einen Torturm zu führen. Die Straßenbrücke in Chesters war ausschließlich in *opus quadratum* ausgeführt (große Blöcke in horizontalen Lagen und oft durch Krampen, Dübel und Mauerspangen verbunden), wobei Techniken der Steinverarbeitung und Verklammerung verwendet wurden, die alle bei der höchstwahrscheinlich gleichzeitigen Brücke in Corbridge ebenfalls festzustellen sind. Die Brücken in Chesters, Willowford und Corbridge sowie vielleicht auch jene in Stanwix und Piercebridge scheinen Teil der Neuordnung und Verbesserung des Straßennetzes im Norden Britanniens gewesen zu sein und mögen daher ein wichtiges Glied in der Wiederherstellung der Grenze durch Severus dargestellt haben. Münzen aus dem Jahr 208 n. Chr., ein Jahr, in dem die meisten Sonderausgaben sich auf Britannien zu beziehen scheinen, zeigen Brücken auf ihrer Reverseite und mögen deshalb mit diesem Brückenbauprogramm in Verbindung stehen.

Wenig ist über die weitere Geschichte der Brücken bekannt, obwohl Anhaltspunkte dafür bestehen, daß das Mauerwerk der Brücke in Chesters in mehreren Stadien abgetragen worden ist. Es scheint jedoch, daß zu Beginn des Spätmittelalters nur noch wenige Reste von beiden Brücken erhalten waren.

Bibilography

Allason-Jones, L and Bishop, M C, 1988 *Excavatons at Corbridge: the Hoard* Historic Buildings and Monuments Commission for England Archaeol Rep 7

——, and McKay, B, 1985 *Coventina's Well*, Chesters

——, and Miket, R, 1984 *The catalogue of small finds from South Shields Roman fort*, Soc Antiq Newcastle upon Tyne Monog 2, Newcastle upon Tyne

Ashby, T, and Gardner, R, 1916 The via Traiana, *Pap Brit Sch Rome*, **5**, 104–171

Austen, P S, and Breeze, D J, 1979 A new inscription from Chesters on Hadrian's Wall, *Archaeol Aeliana*, 5 ser, **7**, 115–26

Baatz,D, 1975 *Der Römische Limes*, 2 edn, Berlin

——, 1976 *Die Wachttürme am Limes*, Stuttgart

Baker, I A, 1909 *A treatise on masonry construction*, 10 edn, London

Ballance, M H, 1951 The Roman bridges on the via Flaminia, *Pap Brit Sch Rome*, **19**, 78–117

Becatti, G, 1961 *Mosaici e pavimenti marmorei: Scavi di Ostia*, **4**, Rome

——, 1969 *Edificio con opus sectile Fuori Porta Marina: Scavi di Ostia*, **6**, Rome

Bede Colgrave, C, and Mynors, R A B (eds), 1969 *Ecclesiastical history of the English people*, Oxford

Bellhouse, R L, 1952 A newly-discovered Roman road from Drumburgh to Kirkbride, *Trans Cumberland Westmorland Antiq Archaeol Soc*, n ser, **52**, 41–5

——, 1969 Roman sites on the Cumberland coast 1966–67, *Trans Cumberland Westmorland Antiq Archaeol Soc*, n ser, **69**, 54–101

——, 1971 The Roman tileries at Scalesceugh and Brampton, *Trans Cumberland Westmorland Antiq Archaeol Soc*, n ser, **71**, 35–44

——, and Richardson, G G S, 1982 The Trajanic fort at Kirkbride; the terminus of the Stanegate frontier, *Trans Cumberland Westmorland Antiq Archaeol Soc*, n ser, **82**, 35–50

Bennett, J, 1983 The examination of Turret 10a and the Wall and Vallum at Throckley, Tyne and Wear, 1980, *Archaeol Aeliana*, 5 ser, **11**, 27–60

Bidwell, P T, 1979 *The legionary bath-house and basilica and forum at Exeter*, Exeter Archaeol Rep, 1, Exeter

——, 1985 *The Roman fort of Vindolanda at Chesterholm, Northumberland*, Historic Buildings and Monuments Commission for England, Archaeol Rep, 1, London

——,Miket, R, and Ford, W J, 1989 Evidence for the reconstruction of the south-west gate of the stone fort at South Shields in *Portae cum turribus: studies of Roman stone-built fort gates* (eds Bidwell, P T, Miket, R, and Ford, W J,), Oxford

——, and Speak forthcoming *The Roman fort at South Shields: the excavation of the headquarters and south-west gate*

Birley, A, 1971 *Septimius Severus, the African Emperor*, London

Birley, E, 1939 Roman inscriptions from Chesters (*Cilurnum*), a note on *ala II Asturum* and two milestones, *Archaeol Aeliana*, 4 ser, **16**, 237–59

——, 1950 A Roman altar from Staward Pele, and Roman remains in Allendale, *Archaeol Aeliana*, 4 ser, **28**, 132–51

——, 1951 A centurial inscription from Carlisle, *Trans Cumberland Westmorland Antiq Archaeol Soc*, n ser, **51**, 179–80

——, 1960 Hadrian's Wall: some structural problems, *Archaeol Aeliana*, 4 ser, **38**, 39–60

——, 1961 *Research on Hadrian's Wall*, Kendal

——, Brewis, P, and Charlton, J, 1934 Report for 1933 of the North of England Excavation Committee, *Archaeol Aeliana*, 4 ser, **11**, 176–84

——, ——, and Simpson, F G, 1932 Excavations on Hadrian's Wall between Heddon-on-the-Wall and North Tyne in 1931, *Archaeol Aeliana*, 4 ser, **9**, 255–9

Birley, R, 1977 *Vindolanda, a Roman frontier post on Hadrian's Wall*, London

Blagg, T F C, 1976 Tools and techniques of the Roman stonemason in Britain, *Britannia*, **7**, 152–72

——, 1980–1,Roman civil and military architecture in the province of Britian: aspects of patronage, influence and craft organisation, *World Archaeology*, **12**, no 1, 27–42

Blake, M E, 1947 *Ancient Roman Construction in Italy from the Prehistoric Period to Augustus*, Washington

Boon, G C, 1974 *Silchester, the Roman town of* Calleva, revised edn Newton Abbot

Bosanquet, R C, 1929 Dr John Lingard's notes on the Roman Wall, *Archaeol Aeliana*, 4 ser, **6**, 130–62

——, 1930 The Roman Bridge, in *A history of Northumberland*, (ed M H Dodds),**13** 507–14, Newcastle upon Tyne

Bourne, D, 1967 The Roman bridge at Corbridge, *Archaeol Aeliana*, 4 ser, **45**, 17–26

Brand, J, 1789 *The history and antiquities of Newcastle-upon-Tyne*, London

Breeze, D J, and Dobson, B, 1972 Hadrian's Wall: some problems, *Britannia*, **3**, 182–208

——, and ——, 1987 *Hadrian's Wall*, 3 edn, London

Brewer, R, 1986 *Corpus Signorum Imperii Romani*, Great Britain **I** (5), *Wales*, Oxford

Brewis, P, 1925 Roman Rudchester, report on excavations, 1924, *Archaeol Aeliana*, 4 ser, **1**, 93–120

——, 1927 The Roman Wall at Denton Bank, Great Hill and Heddon on the Wall, *Archaeol Aeliana*, 4 ser, **4**, 109–21

Briegleb, J, 1971, *Die vorrömischen Steinbrücken des Altertums*, Tübingen

Bruce, G B, 1905 *The Life and Letters of John Collingwood Bruce LLD, DCL, FSA, of Newcastle-upon-Tyne*, Edinburgh and London

Bruce, J C, 1851 *The Roman Wall*, 1 edn, Newcastle upon Tyne

——, 1853 *The Roman Wall*, 2 edn, Newcastle upon Tyne

——, 1863 *The Wallet-Book of the Roman Wall*, London and Newcastle upon Tyne

——, 1867 *The Roman Wall*, 3 edn, Newcastle upon Tyne

——, 1885a *Handbook to the Roman Wall*, 3 edn, Newcastle upon Tyne

——, 1885b The three bridges over the Tyne at Newcastle, *Archaeol Aeliana*, 2 ser, **10**, 1–11

Brusin, G, 1949-50 Sul percorso della via Annia tra il piave e la livenza e presso torviscosoa nuovi appunti, *Atti dell Istituto Veneto di Scienze, Lettere ed Arti, Parte Seconda classe di Scienze Morali e Lettere*, **108**, 115–28

Burford, A, 1960 Heavy transport in classical antiquity, *Econ Hist Rev*, 2 ser, **13**, 1–18

——, 1969 *The Greek temple builders at Epidauros*, Liverpool

Büsing, H H, 1982 *Römische Militärarchitektur in Mainz*, Römisch-germanisch Forschungen, **40**, Mainz

Butler, H C, 1919 *Princeton University Archaeological Expedition, Division II: Ancient Architecture in Syria, Section A, South Syria, Part 5*, Leiden

Camden, W, 1637 *Britannia*, trans P Holland, London

Caruana, I, and Coulston, J C, 1987 A Roman bridge stone from the River Eden, Carlisle, *Trans Cumberland Westmorland Antiq Archaeol Soc*, n ser, **87**, 43–51

Casson, L, 1971 *Ships and Seamanship in the Ancient World*, Princeton

Charlesworth, D, 1968 Recent work on Hadrian's Wall, Cawfields, *Archaeol Aeliana*, 4 ser, **46**, 69–74

——, 1973 A re-examination of two turrets on Hadrian's Wall, *Archaeol Aeliana*, 5 ser, **1**, 97–109

——, 1977 The turrets on Hadrian's Wall, in *Ancient monuments and their intepretation: essays presented to A J Taylor* (eds M R Apted, R Gilyard-Beer and A D Saunders), 13–23, London

Charlton, D B, and Micheson, M M, 1983 Yardhope, a shrine to Cocidius?, *Britannia*, **14**, 143–53

Choisy, A, 1873 *L'art de bâtir chez les Romains*, Paris

Clayton, J, 1865 The Roman bridge of *Cilurnum*, *Archaeol Aeliana*, 2 ser, **6**, 80–6

——, 1876 Notes on an excavation at *Cilurnum*, *Archaeol Aeliana*, 2 ser, **7**, 171–6

Collingwood, R G, 1933 J.C. Bruce, *Handbook to the Roman Wall*, 9 edn, Newcastle upon Tyne

——, and Myres, J N L, 1937 *Roman Britain and the English Settlements*, 2 edn, Oxford

Coulston, J C, and Phillips, E J, 1988 *Corpus Signorum Imperii Romani*, Great Britain **1** (6) *Hadrian's Wall west of the river North Tyne and Carlisle*, Oxford

Coulton, J J, 1974 Lifting in early Greek architecture, *J Hellenic Stud*, **94**, 1–19

——, 1977 *Greek Architects at work: problems of structure and design*, London

Cowen, J D, and Richmond, I A, 1935 The Rudge Cup, *Archaeol Aeliana*, 4 ser, **12**, 310–42

Craster, H H E, 1914 *A history of Northumberland, vol 10: the parish of Corbridge*, Newcastle upon Tyne

Cunliffe, B, and Davenport, P, 1985 *The temple of Sulis Minerva at Bath*: 1, The site, Oxford

Cüppers, H, 1969 *Die Trierer Römerbrücken, Trierer Grabungen und Forschungen, 5,* Mainz

Daniels, C M, 1968 A hoard of iron and other materials from Corbridge, *Archaeol Aeliana,* 4 ser, **46,** 115–26

——, 1978 J C Bruce, *Handbook to the Roman Wall,* 13 edn, Newcastle upon Tyne

——, and Harbottle, B, 1980 A new inscription of Julia Domna from Newcastle, *Archaeol Aeliana,* 5 ser, **8,** 65–73

Davidson, J M, 1952 The bridge over the Kelvin at Summerston, in *The Roman occupation of south-western Scotland* (ed S N Miller), 88–94, Glasgow

Davidson, W B, 1933–4 Two stone columns in the neighbourhood of *Habitancum, Proc Soc Antiq Newcastle,* 4 ser, **6,** 350

Davies, H, 1974 *A walk along the Wall,* London

Denham, M A, 1816 *An account of the great flood in the river Tyne on Saturday morning, December 30, 1815,* Newcastle upon Tyne

Dinsmoor, W B, 1922 Structural iron in Greek architecture, *American J Archaeol,* 2 ser, **26,** 148–58

Dixon, P, 1979 Towerhouses, pelehouses and Border society, *Archaeol J,* **136,** 240–52

Durm, J, 1905 *Die Baukunst der Römer, Handbuches der Architektur,* **2 (2),** Stuttgart

——, 1910 *Die Baukunst der Griechen, Handbuches der Architektur,* **2 (1),** 3 edn, Leipzig

Drachmann, A G, 1963 *The mechanical technology of Greek and Roman antiquity,* Copenhagen and Wisconsin

Dymond, D P, 1961 Roman bridges on Dere Street, with a general appendix on the evidence for bridges in Roman Britain, *Archaeol J,* **118,** 136–64

Ellison, M, 1981 The pottery, in B Harbottle and M Ellison, An excavation in the Castle Ditch, Newcastle, 1974–1976, *Archaeol Aeliana,* 5 ser, **9,** 95–164

Everett, A, 1981 *Materials (Mitchell's Building Series),* London

Ferguson, R S, 1880 An attempt at a survey of Roman Cumberland and Westmorland, continued Part IV. The camps and Mowbray and Whitbarrow. Also, some recent Roman finds, *Trans Cumberland Westmorland Antiq Archaeol Soc,* o ser, **4,** 318–28

Forster, R, 1881 *History of Corbridge and its antiquities,* Newcastle upon Tyne

Forster, R H, 1907 The bridge, 177–80, in Woolley, C L, *Corstopitum:* provisional report on the excavations in 1906, *Archaeol Aeliana,* 3 ser, **3,** 161–86

——, 1908 *Corstopitum:* Report on the excavations in 1907, *Archaeol Aeliana,* 3 ser, **4,** 205–303

Frere, S S, 1978 *Britannia, a history of Roman Britain,* rev edn, London

——, 1986 RIB 1322, *Britannia,* **17,** 329

Fulford, M, 1985 Excavations on the sites of the amphitheatre and forum-basilica at Silchester, Hampshire: an interim report, *Antiq J,* **65,** 39–81

Gazzola, P, 1963 *Ponti Romani,* Florence

Gibson, E, 1695 W Camden, *Britannia,* London

Gibson, J P, 1934 The Parish Church of Warden, Northumberland, *Trans Architect Archaeol Soc Durham Northumberland,* **7,** 216–22,

——, and Simpson, F G, 1911 The milecastle on the Wall of Hadrian at the Poltross Burn, *Trans Cumberland Westmorland Antiq Archaeol Soc,* n ser, **11,** 390–461

Gillam, J P, 1970 *Types of Roman coarse pottery in northern Britain,* 3 edn, Newcastle upon Tyne

——, 1973 Sources of pottery found on northern military sites, in *Current research in Romano-British coarse pottery* (ed Detsicas, A P), 53–65, London

——, 1976 Coarse fumed ware in north Britain and beyond, *Glasgow Archaeol J,* **4,** 57–80

——, 1977 The Roman forts at Corbridge, *Archaeol Aeliana,* 5 ser, **5,** 47–74

——, and Mann, J C, 1970 The Northern Frontier from Antoninus Pius to Caracalla, *Archaeol Aeliana,* 4 ser, **48,** 1–44

——, and Tait, J, 1968 The Roman fort at Chester-le-Street, *Archaeol Aeliana,* 4 ser, **46,** 75–96

Gnecchi, F, 1912 *I Medaglioni Romani,* 3 vols, Milan

Gordon, A, 1726 *Itinerarium Septentrionale,* London

Greene, K, 1978 Imported fine wares in Britain to AD 250: a guide to identification, in *Early fine wares in Roman Britain,* (eds Arthur P, and Marsh G,), 15–30, Oxford

Hafemann, D, 1956 *Beiträge zur Siedlungsgeographie des römischen Britannien, I: Die militärischen Siedlungen,* Wiesbaden

von Hagen, V W, 1967 *The roads that led to Rome,* London

Hammo Yassi, N, 1983 *Archaeomagnetic work in Britain and Iraq,* unpubl PhD thesis, Univ Newcastle upon Tyne

Hanson, W S, and Maxwell, G, 1983 *Rome's North West Frontier, The Antonine Wall,* Edinburgh

——, Daniels, C M, Dore, J N, and Gillam, J P, 1979 The Agricolan supply base at Red House, Corbridge, *Archaeol Aeliana,* 5 ser, **7,** 1–97

Hartley, B R, 1972 The Roman occupation of Scotland: the evidence of samian ware, *Britannia,* **3,** 1–55

Hassall, M, and Rhodes, J, 1975 Excavations at the new Market Hall, Gloucester, 1966–7, *Trans Bristol Gloucestershire Archaeol Soc,* **93,** 15–100

Haverfield, F, 1897 Report of the Cumberland Excavation Committee, 1896, *Trans Cumberland Westmorland Antiq Archaeol Soc,* o ser, **14,** 413–33

——, 1899 Report of the Cumberland Excavation Committee, 1897, *Trans Cumberland Westmorland Antiq Archaeol Soc,* o ser, **15,** 172–90

——, 1904 An inscribed slab mentioning the Second, Sixth and Twentieth Legions from the River Tyne, *Archaeol Aeliana,* 2 ser, **25,** 142–7

Hellenkemper, H, 1977 Der Limes am nordsyrischen Euphrat: Berichtzueiner archäologischen Landesaufnahme, *Studien zu den Militärgrerzen Roms II: Vorträge des 10. Internationalen Limeskongresses inder Germania Inferior,* 461-71, Cologne

Heslop, R O, 1904 A Roman altar to *Oceanus* and altar base from the Tyne Bridge, *Archaeol Aeliana,* 2 ser, **25,** 133–9

Heywood, B, 1965 The Vallum: its problems restated, in *Britain and Rome* (eds Jarrett M G, and Dobson B,), 85–94, Kendal

Hill, C, Millett, M, and Blagg, T, 1980 *The Roman riverside wall and monumental arch in London* Special paper no 3, London Middlesex Archaeol Soc, London

Hill, P R, 1981 Stonework and the Archaeologist including a stonemason's view of Hadrian's Wall, *Archaeol Aeliana,* 5 ser, **9,** 1–22

Hird, L, 1977 *Vindolanda V: the pre-Hadrianic pottery,* Bardon Mill

Hobley, B, 1972 Excavations at 'The Lunt' Roman military site, Baginton, Warwickshire, 1968–71, second interim report, *Trans Birmingham Warwickshire Archaeol Soc,* **85,** 7–92

Hodgson, J, 1840 *History of Northumberland,* vol 2, 3, Newcastle upon Tyne

Hogg, R, 1952 The historic crossings of the river Eden at Stanwix, and their associated road systems, *Trans Cumberland Westmorland Antiq Archaeol Soc,* n ser, **52,** 131–59

——, 1965 Excavation of the Roman auxiliary tilery, Brampton, *Trans Cumberland Westmorland Antiq Archaeol Soc* n ser, **65,** 133–68

Holmes, S, 1885-6 Roman bridge at Chollerford, *Proc Soc Antiq Newcastle-upon-Tyne,* 2 ser, **2,** 178–81

——S, 1894 The Roman bridges across the North Tyne river near Chollerford, *Archaeol Aeliana,* 2 ser, **16,** 328–38

Hornsby, W, and Laverick, J, 1932 The Roman signal station at Goldsborough, near Whitby, *Archaeol J,* **89,** 203–19

Horsley, J, 1732 *Britannia Romana,* London

Hull, M R, 1963 *The Roman potters' kilns at Colchester, Res Rep Comm Soc Antiq London,* **21,** Oxford

Hülsen, C, 1896 Di una pittura antica ritrovata sull'Esquelino nel 1668, *Mitteilungen des Kaiserlich Deutschen Archaeologischen Instituts, Römisch Abb* **11,** 213–26

Humann, K, and Puchstein, O, 1890 *Reisen in Kleinasien und Nord Syrien,* Berlin

Hunter, C, 1702 Part of some letters from Mr Christopher Hunter to Dr Martin Lister, FRS, concerning several Roman inscriptions and other antiquities in Roman Yorkshire, *Phil Trans Royal Soc London AB,* **23,** 1129–32

Hurst, H R, 1986 *Gloucester, the Roman and later defences,* Gloucester

Hutchinson, W, 1785-94 *History and antiquities of the County Palatine of Durham,* 3 vols, Newcastle upon Tyne

——, 1794 *History of the county of Cumberland and some places adjacent,* 2 vols, Carlisle

Jackson, D A, and Ambrose, T M, 1976 A Roman timber bridge at Aldwincle, Northants, *Britannia,* **7,** 39–72

Jarrett, M G, and Mann, J C, 1970 Britain from Agricola to Gallienus, *Bonner Jahrbüch,* **170,** 178–210

Jenkinson, H I, 1875 *Jenkinson's Practical Guide to Carlisle, Gilsland, Roman Wall and Neighbourhood,* London

Jobey, G, 1958   The Wall Ditch, Bay's Leap, Heddon on the Wall, *Archaeol Aeliana*, 4 ser, **36**, 55–60

Johns, C, 1982   *Sex or symbol. Erotic images of Greece and Rome*, London

Jones, G B D, 1982   The Solway Frontier: interim report 1976-81, *Britannia*, **13**, 283–97

Kenyon, K M, 1935   The Roman theatre at Verulamium, St Albans, *Archaeologia*, **84**, 213–81

Kewley, J, 1973   Inscribed capitals on Roman altars from northern Britain, *Archaeol Aeliana*, 5 ser, **1**, 129–31

Knowles, W H, 1908   Site VIII: the fountain and architectural details, in R H Forster 1908, 272–7

——, 1923–4   Robert Henry Forster, *Proc Soc Antiq Newcastle-upon-Tyne*, 4 ser, **1**, 122–4

——, and Forster, R H, 1909   *Corstopitum*: report on the excavations in 1908, *Archaeol Aeliana*, 3 ser, **5** 305–424

Landels, J G, 1978   *Engineering in the Ancient World*, London

Laursen, E M, 1960   Scour at bridge crossings, *Amer Soc Civil Engineers Proc*, **86**, HY2, 39–53

Lawrence, A W, 1979   *Greek aims in fortification*, Oxford

Lawson, W, 1966   The origin of the military road from Newcastle to Carlisle, *Archaeol Aeliana*, 4 ser, **44**, 185–207

Leaning, J B, 1971   The date of the repair of the bridge over the river Chabinas: L Alfenus Senecio and L Marius Perpetuus in Syria Coele, *Latomus*, **30**, 386–9

Leland   Smith, L T (ed), 1964, *The Itinerary of John Leland*, London

Lugli, G, 1957   *La Tecnica Edilizia Romana*, Rome

McCarthy, M R, 1984   Roman Carlisle, in *Settlement and society in the Roman North*(eds Wilson,P R, Jones, R F J, and Evans, D M,), 65–74, Bradford

MacLauchlan, H, 1852   *Memoir written during a survey of the Watling Street from the Tees to the Scotch Border in the years 1850 and 1851*, London

——, 1858   *Memoir written during a survey of the Roman Wall, through the Counties of Northumberland and Cumberland in the years 1852–1854*, London

MacKenzie, E, 1825   *An Historical, Topographical, and Descriptive view of the county of Northumberland, etc*, Newcastle upon Tyne

Mann, J C, 1971   *The Northern Frontier in Britain from Hadrian to Honorius: literary and epigraphic sources*, Newcastle upon Tyne

Marsden, E W, 1971   *Greek and Roman Artillery. Technical Treatises*, Oxford

Martin, R, 1965   *Manuel d'Architecture Grecque 1, Matériaux et techniques*, Paris

Mau, A, 1902   *Pompeii, Its life and art* (trans F W Kelsey), rev edn, London

Miller, S N, 1922   *The Roman Fort at Balmuildy*, Glasgow

——, 1952   An historical survey, in *The Roman occupation of south-western Scotland* (ed Miller, S N,), 195–239, Glasgow

Milne, A, 1769   *A description of the Parish of Melrose*, Melrose

Molyneux, L, 1971   A complete result magnetometer for measuring the remanent magnetization of rocks, *Geophys J Royal Astr Soc*, **24**, 429–33

Moritz, L A, 1958   *Grain-mills and flour in classical antiquity*, Oxford

Munsell, 1975   *Munsell soil colour charts*, Baltimore

Mylne, R, 1772   *Mr Mylne's report respecting Tyne Bridge*, Newcastle upon Tyne

NCH iv Hodgson, J C, 1897   *A history of Northumberland, vol 4: Hexhamshire, pt II, and Chollerton, Kirkheaton and Thockrington*, Newcastle upon Tyne

Newbold, O, 1913   Excavations on the Roman Wall at Limestone Bank, *Archaeol Aeliana*, 3 ser, **9**, 54–74

Nylander, C, 1966   Clamps and chronology (Achaemenian Problems II), *Iranica Antiqua*, **6**, 130–46

ORL, Der Obergermanisch-Raetische Limes des Römerreiches, 1894–1937

Orlandos, A C, 1915   Preliminary dowels, *American J Archaeol*, 2 ser, **19**, 175–8

Orlandos, A K, 1968   *Les matériaux de construction et la technique architecturale des anciens Grecs: seconde partie, École Française d'Athènes: Travaux et Mémoires, Fasc* **16b**, Paris

Painter, K S, 1975   Roman Flasks with scenes of Baiae and Puteoli, *J Glass Stud*, **17**, 54–67

Platner, S B, and Ashby, T, 1929   *A topographical dictionary of ancient Rome*, Oxford

Philp, B, 1981   *The excavation of the Roman forts of the Classis Britannica at Dover 1970–77*, Dover

Potter, H G, 1855   Amboglanna, *Archaeol Aeliana*, 1 ser, **4**, 63–75 and 141–9

Price, M J, and Trell, B L, 1977   *Coins and their Cities: Architecture on the ancient Coins of Greece, Rome and Palestine*, London

RCAM(S), 1956   *An inventory of the ancient and historical monuments of Roxburghshire*, 2 vols, Royal Commission on the Ancient Monuments of Scotland, Edinburgh

RCHM(E), 1928   *Roman London*, Royal Commission on Historical Monuments for England, London

RCHM(E), 1962   *Eburacum: Roman York*, Royal Commission on Historical Monuments for England, London

RIB, Collingwood, R G, and Wright, R P, 1965   *The Roman Inscriptions of Britain: 1,Inscriptions on Stone*, Oxford

RIC, Mattingly, H, and Sydenham, E A, 1923–82   *The Roman Imperial Coinage*, London

Richardson, G H, and Keeney, G S, 1934–6   Excavations at the Roman fort of Piercebridge 1933–4, *Trans Architect Archaeol Soc Durham Northumberland*, **7**, 235–66

Richmond, I A, 1929   Excavations on Hadrian's Wall in the Gilsland-Birdoswald-Pike Hill sector, 1928, *Trans Cumberland Westmorland Antiq Archaeol Soc*, n ser, **29**, 303–15

——, 1935   Trajan's Army on Trajan's Column, *Pap British Sch Rome*, **13**, 1–40

——, I A, 1936   Excavations at High Rochester and Risingham, 1935, *Archaeol Aeliana*, 4 ser, **13**, 170–98

——, 1939   Hadrian's Wall, 1938, *Archaeol Aeliana*, 4 ser, **16**, 264–77

——, 1947   J C Bruce, *Handbook to the Roman Wall*, 10 edn, Newcastle upon Tyre

——, 1950   Hadrian's Wall, 1939–49, *J Roman Stud*, **40**, 43–56

——, 1952   *The Roman Fort at South Shields, A Guide*, South Shields

——, 1956a   Excavations at Milecastle 49 (Harrow's Scar), 1953, *Trans Cumberland Westmorland Antiq Archaeol Soc*, n ser, **56**, 18–27

——, 1956b   Cote How Tower (16a) on the Cumberland coast, *Trans Cumberland Westmorland Antiq Archaeol Soc*, n ser, **56**, 62–6

——, 1957   J C Bruce, *Handbook to the Roman Wall*, 11 edn, Newcastle upon Tyne

——, 1966   J C Bruce, *Handbook to the Roman Wall*, 12 edn, Newcastle upon Tyne

——, and Child, F A, 1942   Gateways of forts on Hadrian's Wall, *Archaeol Aeliana*, 4 ser, **20**, 134–54

Ricken, H, and Fischer, C, 1963   *Die Bilderschüsseln der römischen Töpfer von Rheinzabern*, Bonn

Robertson, A S, 1980   The bridges on Severan coins of AD 208 and 209, in *Roman Frontier Studies 1979*, **1** (eds Hanson, W S, and Keppie, L J F,), BAR International Ser, **71**, 131–9, Oxford

Robinson, J R, 1964   *Piers, abutments and formwork for bridges*, London

Rogan, J, 1954   Christopher Hunter: Antiquary, *Archaeol Aeliana*, 4 ser, **32**, 116–25

Rogers, G B, 1974   *Poteries sigillées de la Gaule Centrale, tome 1: les motifs non figurés (27ᵉ Supplément à Gallia)*, Paris

Ross, A, 1967   *Pagan Celtic Britain*,London

Roxan M M, 1985   The Roman military diploma, in Bidwell P T, 1985,95–102

Rye, H A, 1911   Roman bridge at Chollerford, *Proc Soc Antiq Newcastle-upon-Tyne*, 3 ser, **5**, 166–7

St Joseph, J K, 1951   Air reconnaissance of North Britain, *J Roman Stud*, **41**, 52–65

Salway, P, 1959   Excavation at Longbyre, Haltwhistle, *Archaeol Aeliana*, 4 ser, **37**, 211–15

——, 1967   *The Frontier People of Roman Britain*, Cambridge

Scott, P R, 1982   The bridges at Piercebridge, Co Durham; a reassessment, *Trans Architect Archaeol Soc Durham Northumberland*, n ser, **6**, 77–82

——, forthcoming   *Excavations at Roman Piercebridge* (ed Fitz-patrick, A,)

Selkirk, R, 1983   *The Piercebridge Formula: A dramatic new view of Roman History*,Cambridge

Shaw, R C, 1926   Excavations at Willowford, *Trans Cumberland Westmorland Antiq Archaeol Soc*, n ser, **26**, 429–506

Simpson, F G, 1913   Excavations on the line of the Roman Wall in Cumberland during the years 1909–12, *Trans Cumberland Westmorland Antiq Archaeol Soc*, n ser, **13**, 297–397

——, 1928   Excavations on Hadrian's Wall in the Gilsland – Birdoswald – Pike Hill sector, 1927, *Trans Cumberland Westmorland Antiq Archaeol Soc*, n ser, **28**, 377–88

——, 1941   Proceedings, *Trans Cumberland Westmorland Antiq Archaeol Soc*, n ser, **41**, 214

——, and Richmond, I A, 1933 Excavations on Hadrian's Wall, 1, Birdoswald, *Trans Cumberland Westmorland Antiq Archaeol Soc*, n ser, **33**, 246–62

——, and ——, 1937 Report of the Cumberland Excavation Committee for 1936, *Trans Cumberland Westmorland Antiq Archaeol Soc*, n ser, **37**, 157–77

——, and ——, 1941 The Roman Fort on Hadrian's Wall at Benwell, *Archaeol Aeliana*, 4 ser, **19**, 1–43

——, ——, and McIntyre, J, 1934 Garthside Turret 54a, *Trans Cumberland Westmorland Antiq Archaeol Soc*, n ser, **34**, 138–44

——, et al 1936a Simpson, F G, Richmond, I A, Hodgson K S, and St Joseph, K, The Stanegate; Report of the Cumberland Excavation Committee for 1935, *Trans Cumberland Westmorland Antiq Archaeol Soc*, n ser, **36**, 182–91

——, et al 1936b Simpson, F G, Richmond, I A, and St Joseph, K, The Vallum at High House Turf–Wall Milecastle 50 TW; Report of the Cumberland Excavation Committee for 1935, *Trans Cumberland Westmorland Antiq Archaeol Soc*, n ser, **36**, 158–70

——, and Shaw, R C, 1922 The purpose and date of the Vallum and its crossings, *Trans Cumberland Westmorland Antiq Archaeol Soc*, n ser, **22**, 353–433

Simpson, G, 1976 *Watermills and Military Works on Hadrian's Wall: Excavations in Northumberland 1907–1913 by F Gerald Simpson* (ed Simpson, G,), Kendal

Smeaton, J, and Wooler, J, 1772 *A report relative to Tyne Bridge*, Newcastle upon Tyne

Smith, G H, 1978 Excavations near Hadrian's Wall at Tarraby Lane 1976, *Britannia*, **9**, 19–56

Sockett, E W, 1973 The Stanegate at Homer's Lane, *Archaeol Aeliana*, 5 ser, **1**, 241–3

Sopwith, T, 1833 *An account of the mining districts of Alston Moor, Weardale and Teesdale in Cumberland and Durham*, Alnwick

Spain, G R B, and Simpson, F G, 1930 The frontier works in *A history of Northumberland*, vol 13: *Heddon on the Wall*, etc (ed Dodds, M H,), 484–540, Newcastle upon Tyne

Spain, R J, 1984 Romano-British Watermills, *Archaeol Cantiana*, **100**, 101–28

Stanfield, G A, and Simpson, G, 1958 *Central Gaulish Potters*, London

Steer, K A, and Feachem, R W, 1951–2 The Roman fort and temporary camp at Oakwood, Selkirkshire, *Proc Soc Antiq Scotland*, **86**, 81–105

Stevens, C E, 1966 *The Building of Hadrian's Wall*, Cumberland Westmorland Antiq Archaeol Soc Extra ser, **20**, Kendal

Strickland, T J, 1982 The defences of Roman Chester: A note on discoveries made on the North Wall, 1982, *J Chester Archaeol Soc*, **65**, 25–35

——, 1983 The defences of Roman Chester: discoveries made on the East Wall, 1983, *J Chester Archaeol Soc*, **66**, 5–11

Strong in Cunliffe, B, 1968 *Fifth report on the excavations of the Roman fort at Richborough, Kent, Res Rep Comm Soc Antiq London*, **23**, London

Swinbank, B, 1952 Excavations in High House paddock, Cumberland, *Trans Cumberland Westmorland Antiq Archaeol Soc*, n ser, **52**, 46–54

——, 1954 *The Vallum reconsidered*, unpubl PhD thesis, Univ Durham

——, and Gillam, J P, 1950 Pottery from the Vallum Filling at Birdoswald, *Trans Cumberland Westmorland Antiq Archaeol Soc*, n ser, **50**, 54–62

Swinburne, J, Trevelyan, A, Bell, J, and Shanks, R, 1844 Notices respecting the Roman Station of *Habitancum* (now Risingham), *Archaeol Aeliana*, 1 ser, **3**, 156–60

Tarling, D H, and Symons, D T A, 1967 A stability index of remanence in palaeo-magnetism, *Geophys J Royal Astr Soc*, **12**, 443–8

Terzaghi, K, and Peck, R B, 1967 *Soil mechanics in engineering practice*, 2 edn, New York

Tschira, A, 1941 Keildübel, *Mitt des Deutsch Arch Inst: Ath Abt*, **66**, 166–9

Tudor, D, 1974 *Les ponts romains du Bas-Danube, Bibliotheca Historica Romaniae Études*, **51**, Bucharest

Tylecote, R F, 1965 Medieval bloomeries in the north of England, in *Vita Pro Ferro, feschrift for Robert Durrer* (ed Guyan, W U,), 115–34, Schaffhausen

——, 1981 The medieval smith and his methods, in *Medieval Industry* (ed Crossley, D W,), 42–50, London

Wacher, J S, 1961 Cirencester, 1960, first interim report, *Antiq J*, **41**, 65–71

Wagner, J, 1972 Vorarbeiten zur Karte 'Ostgrenze des römischen Reiches im Tübinger Atlas des Vorderen Orients, in *Actes du IXe Congrès International d'études sur les frontièrs romaines* (ed Fitz, J,), 669–703, Mamaia

——, 1977 Legio IIII Scythica in Zeugma am Euphrat, *Studien zuden Militärgrenzen Roms II: Vorträge des 10. Internationalen Limesknogresses in der Germania inferior*, 517–39, Cologne

Wallis, J, 1769 *The Natural History and Antiquities of Northumberland*, Newcastle upon Tyne

Webster, P V, 1972 Severn Valley ware on Hadrian's Wall, *Archaeol Aeliana*, 4 ser, **50**, 191–203

——, 1976 Severn Valley ware: a preliminary study, *Trans Bristol Gloucestershire Archaeol Soc*, **94**, 18–45

Welford, R, 1907 Art and Archaeology: the three Richardsons, *Archaeol Aeliana*, 3 ser, **3**, 135–51

Welsby, D A, 1985 The pottery from the two turrets at Garthside on Hadrian's Wall, *Trans Cumberland Westmorland Antiq Archaeol Soc*, n ser, **85**, 71–6

Whitby, L M, 1985 Justinian's bridge over the Sangarius and the date of Procopius *de Aedificiis, J Hellenic Stud*, **105**, 129–48

Wilcox, R P, 1981 *Timber and iron reinforcement in early buildings, Soc Antiq London Occasional pap* n ser, **2**, London

Wilkes, J J, 1985 *RIB* 1322: a note, *Zeitschrift für Papyrologie und Epigraphik*, **59**, 291–5

Wooler, E, 1917 *The Roman fort at Piercebridge*, Frome and London

Wright, R P, 1939 The Stanegate at Walwick Grange, *Archaeol Aeliana*, 4 ser, **16**, 140–7

——, 1940 The Wrekendike and Roman road-junction on Gateshead Fell, *Archaeol Aeliana*, 4 ser, **17**, 54–64

——, 1941 The Stanegate at Corbridge, *Archaeol Aeliana*, 4 ser, **19**, 194–209

——, and Phillips E J, 1975 *Catalogue of the Roman inscribed and sculpted stones in Carlisle Museum, Tullie House*, Carlisle

Index

Compiled by Lyn Greenwood

Page references in italic are to Figures

161